AIDS TO REFLECTION

BY

SAMUEL TAYLOR COLERIDGE

D1188345

Prophets of Sensibility:
Precursors of Modern Cultural Thought

GENERAL EDITOR
PROFESSOR HAROLD BLOOM
YALE UNIVERSITY

CHELSEA HOUSE
NEW YORK 1983

**This edition is an edited reprint of the 1884 edition
by George Bell and Sons**
Copyright © 1983 by Chelsea House Publishers
All rights reserved
Printed and bound in the United States of America

ISBN: 0-87754-335-6

PROPHETS OF SENSIBILITY: PRECURSORS OF MODERN CULTURAL THOUGHT

by Harold Bloom
Professor of the Humanities
Yale University

It was one of the peculiarities of literary Modernism, in the Age of Pound, Joyce and Eliot, and of their New Critical followers, to argue that the imaginative literature of the twentieth century had its true origins in seventeenth-century sensibility. In this polemical contention, Eliot could insist that his poetic and critical stance, or more simply his personal culture, had its sources in Lancelot Andrewes and John Donne, rather, say, than in Walter Pater and Matthew Arnold. Assertions of a remote ancestry have the special charm of escaping the immediate squalors of the family romance. We need not smile too ironically at the personal mythologies of an Eliot or a Pound when we reflect upon the even more formidable Sigmund Freud, who in *Beyond the Pleasure Principle* cheerfully proclaims his descent from Empedocles, safely distant at two millennia, while stubbornly denying his palpable precursor, Arthur Schopenhauer.

But the wry humor of these necessary stratagems of the spirit cannot be allowed to obscure the truth of intellectual and aesthetic genealogy. Wallace Stevens once remarked that genealogy is the art of correcting other genealogists' mistakes. One broad way of characterizing the Prophets of Sensibility series is to observe that it intends to correct Eliot's persuasive misreading of the family relationship between nineteenth- and twentieth-century thought and literature. A book like Walter Pater's early masterpiece, *The Renaissance,* reverberates endlessly in such characteristic modern creators as Yeats, Eliot, Joyce, Pound, Stevens, Woolf, Hart Crane, and even in a vitalistic heretic like D. H. Lawrence. None of them (except for Yeats) would have granted Pater's authority and fatherhood, yet he haunts them all (and many others) both in cadence and in concept. Pater, like Arnold, Ruskin, Carlyle, Butler, Hazlitt, De Quincey, and Coleridge is simply too close for the comfort of autonomy to assert itself.

Certainly the anxiety of influence is a crucial sorrow in the vexed story of the true heritage of Modernism. But, as an anxiety, it may conceal deeper continuities between Romantic and Victorian forerunners and their belated heirs. Prophecy, an ancient Hebraic mode of literature, became in the nineteenth century a new kind of vitalistic mode, one that erased the always wavering boundaries between criticism and creation. What, after all, is the literary genre of Pater's *The Renaissance?* The prose *Imaginary Conversa-tions* of Landor and the verse monologues of Browning are no more radical as experiments than are these reveries of Walter Pater. Pater blends moral reflection, prose poetry, psychological portraiture, art and literary criticism, cultural history and a curious kind of mythopoeic fiction into an amalgam that defies conventional description, but that has the ultimate purpose of subverting Christian evaluations of the *agon* between the desires of this world and the work of the spirit. As a prophet, Pater restores to art the epiphanies appropriated by orthodox dualisms, whether of religion or of philosophy.

Pater's *The Renaissance* dramatizes the authentic burden of the Prophet of Sensibility. This burden is not so much secularization as it is the problematic transferences and descents of authority from earlier times, when it could be recognized and accepted, to the threshold of our age, where authority can be recognized precisely as what has vanished, and what could not be accepted if somehow it reappeared. Freud, who devised the clinical transference of the model of the taboo, attempted to make of psycho-analysis a modernist *praxis* that would reestablish the images of authority upon a supposedly scientific basis. Ruskin, Carlyle, Pater and the other Victorian prophets assumed, rather, that authority could be established again only upon an aesthetic basis. Had Freud (and Nietzsche) written in English, we would group them now with the Prophets of Sensibility. Science and philosophy, like religion, have yielded to the literary culture, and the pragmatic consequences of that yielding are at the center of Romantic and Victorian prophecy.

Prophecy, in the Hebraic sense, was moral truth-telling of the most violent kind, always following the formula of "The Word of God came to me . . ." The God Word that came to the nineteenth-century prophets mixed percep-tion and sensation into a new kind of sensibility, one that is still with us today. Difficult to describe, this sensibility emphasizes a continuum haunted by in-timations of mortality punctuated by brief bursts of radiance–privileged moments in which a peculiar vividness gives the illusion of redeeming life. It may be the stigma of the nineteenth-century Prophets of Sensibility that (except for Pater) they sought to combat this climate of the spirit but oddly fostered it implicitly (even as Pater did so overtly). The increasing internaliza-tion of the self depended upon an augmentation of estrangement from the object world, and what was intended as prophetic warning and lament as to this estrangement became instead a subtle suggestion of an inevitable move-ment in elite sensibility.

Today we have the strange anomaly that Nietzsche, the Continental version of the Prophets of Sensibility, is credited with fathering the future, while the

Prophets are neglected. But time's revenges work themselves out, and these writers will father the future again, even as they prophesied our current sensibility. They could not save or even preserve the post-Christian spirituality they sought to imbue in society, but they fostered in its place a pragmatic triumph of literary culture, beyond religion and beyond speculative philosophy. Psychoanalysis, despite its scientism, is only another form of that literary culture. So, in another way, are the textualist literary criticism and language-oriented "human sciences" that are vivid parts of Structuralist and post-Structuralist formulations. There are true and false prophets of sensibility, even as there were true and false prophets among the ancient Hebrews. The test for prophecy finally is canonization; the books that return from the dead certify themselves as inescapable, and so as a vital part of the truth. We can say of each of us in relation to the books in this Prophets of Sensibility series what Pater said of his hero in *Marius the Epicurean*. The experience of reading them

    . . . gave him a definitely ascertained measure of his moral or intellectual need, of the demand his soul must make upon the powers, whatsoever they might be, which had brought him, as he was, into the world at all. . . .

AIDS TO REFLECTION

AND

THE CONFESSIONS OF AN INQUIRING SPIRIT.

BY

SAMUEL TAYLOR COLERIDGE.

TO WHICH ARE ADDED

HIS ESSAYS ON FAITH AND THE BOOK OF
COMMON PRAYER, ETC.

NEW EDITION, REVISED.

LONDON: GEORGE BELL AND SONS, YORK STREET,
COVENT GARDEN.
1884.

THE AUTHOR'S ADDRESS TO THE READER.

FELLOW-CHRISTIAN! the wish to be admired as a fine writer held a very subordinate place in my thoughts and feelings in the composition of this volume. Let then its comparative merits and demerits, in respect of style and stimulancy, possess a proportional weight, and no more, in determining your judgment for or against its contents. Read it *through*: then compare the state of your mind, with the state in which your mind was, when you first opened the book. Has it led you to reflect? Has it supplied or suggested fresh subjects for reflection? Has it given you any new information? Has it removed any obstacle to a lively conviction of your responsibility as a moral agent? Has it solved any difficulties, which had impeded your faith as a Christian? Lastly, has it increased your power of thinking connectedly? Especially on the Scheme and purpose of the Redemption by Christ? If it have done none of these things, condemn it aloud as worthless: and strive to compensate for your own loss of time, by preventing others from wasting theirs. But if your conscience dictates an affirmative answer to all or any of the preceding questions, declare this too aloud, and endeavour to extend my utility.[1]

[1] In the place of this Address the first edition, 1825, had the Advertisement which we now print at the end of the Author's Preface, p. xix. —ED.

ADVERTISEMENT TO THE FOURTH EDITION.

[BY HENRY NELSON COLERIDGE.]

THIS corrected Edition of the Aids to Reflection is commended to Christian readers, in the hope and the trust that the power which the book has already exercised over hundreds, it may, by God's furtherance, hereafter exercise over thousands. No age, since Christianity had a name, has more pointedly needed the mental discipline taught in this work than that in which we now live; when, in the Author's own words, all the great ideas or verities of religion seem in danger of being condensed into idols, or evaporated into metaphors. Between the encroachments, on the one hand, of those who so magnify means that they practically impeach the supremacy of the ends which those means were meant to subserve; and of those, on the other hand, who, engrossed in the contemplation of the great Redemptive Act, rashly disregard or depreciate the appointed ordinances of grace;—between those who, confounding the sensuous Understanding, varying in every individual, with the universal Reason, the image of God, the same in all men, inculcate a so-called faith, having no demonstrated harmony with the attributes of God, or the essential laws of humanity, and being sometimes inconsistent with both; and those again who requiring a logical proof of that which, though not contradicting, does in its very kind, transcend, our reason, virtually deny the existence of true faith altogether;—between these almost equal enemies of the truth, Coleridge, —in all his works, but pre-eminently in this—has kindled an inextinguishable beacon of warning and of guidance. In so doing, he has taken his stand on the sure word of

Scripture, and is supported by the authority of almost every one of our great divines, before the prevalence of that system of philosophy, (Locke's,) which no consistent reasoner can possibly reconcile with the undoubted meaning of the Articles and Formularies of the English Church :—

In causaque valet, causamque juvantibus armis.

The Editor had intended to offer to the reader a few words by way of introduction to some of the leading points of philosophy contained in this Volume. But he has been delighted to find the work already done to his hand, in a manner superior to anything he could have hoped to accomplish himself, by an affectionate disciple of Coleridge on the other side of the Atlantic. The following Essay was written by the Rev. James Marsh, President of the University of Vermont, United States of America, and prefixed by him to his Edition of the Aids to Reflection, published at Burlington in 1829. The Editor has printed this Essay entire ; [1]—as well out of respect for its author, as believing that the few paragraphs in it having a more special reference to the state of opinion in America, will not be altogether without an interest of their own to the attentive observers of the progress of Truth in this or any other country.

Lincoln's Inn, 25th April, 1839.

[1] See pp. xxiii-lxxvi. Mr. H. N. Coleridge gave the first edition of Dr. Marsh's Essay. The reader has in the present volume the essay as it appeared in its second and revised edition, 1840.—ED.

Οὕτως πάντα πρὸς ἑαυτὴν ἐπάγουσα, καὶ συνηθροισμένη ψυχῇ,
αὐτὴ εἰς αὑτὴν, ῥᾷστα καὶ μάλα βεβαίως μακαρίζεται.

MARINUS.

Omnis divinæ atque humanæ eruditionis elementa tria, Nosse, Velle,
Posse; quorum principium unum Mens; cujus oculus Ratio; cui lumen
* * præbet Deus.

VICO.

———

Naturam hominis hanc Deus ipse voluit, ut duarum rerum cupidus et
appetens esset, religionis et sapientiæ. Sed homines ideo falluntur, quod
aut religionem suscipiunt omissa sapientia; aut sapientiæ soli student
omissa religione; cum alterum sine altero esse non possit verum.

LACTANTIUS.

THE AUTHOR'S PREFACE.

A^N Author has three points to settle: to what sort his work belongs, for what description of readers it is intended, and the specific end, or object, which it is to answer. There is indeed a preliminary question respecting the end which the writer himself has in view, whether the number of purchasers, or the benefit of the readers. But this may be safely passed by; since where the book itself or the known principles of the writer do not supersede the question, there will seldom be sufficient strength of character for good or for evil, to afford much chance of its being either distinctly put or fairly answered.

I shall proceed therefore to state as briefly as possible the intentions of the present volume in reference to the three first-mentioned points, viz. *What?* For *Whom?* and *For* what?

I. WHAT? The answer is contained in the title-page.[1] It belongs to the class of *didactic* works. Consequently, those who neither wish instruction for themselves, nor assistance in instructing others, have no interest in its contents. *Sis sus, sis Divus: sum caltha, et non tibi spiro.*

II. FOR WHOM? *Generally*, for as many in all classes as wish for aid in disciplining their minds to habits of reflection—for all who, desirous of building up a manly character in the light of distinct consciousness, are content to study the principles of moral architecture on the several grounds of prudence, morality, and religion. And lastly,

---

[1] Coleridge's original title-page, viz., that to the 1825 edition, is given at p. ix. That edition bore the imprint of Taylor and Hessey, 93, Fleet Street, and 13, Waterloo Place, Pall Mall.—ED.

for all who feel an interest in the Position, I have undertaken to defend—this, namely, that the CHRISTIAN FAITH
⟨*in which I include every article of belief and doctrine professed by the first Reformers in common*⟩ [1] IS THE PERFECTION
OF HUMAN INTELLIGENCE,—an interest sufficiently strong to
insure a patient attention to the arguments brought in its
support.

But if I am to mention any particular class or description of readers, that were prominent in my thought during
the composition of the volume, my reply must be ; that it
was *especially* designed for the studious Young at the close
of their education or on their first entrance into the duties
of manhood and the rights of self-government.   And of
these, again, in thought and wish I destined the work (the
latter and larger portion, at least) yet more particularly to
Students intended for the Ministry ; *first*, as in duty bound,
to the members of our two Universities : *secondly*, (but
only in respect of this mental precedency *second*) to all
alike of whatever name, who have dedicated their future
lives to the cultivation of their race, as Pastors, Preachers,
Missionaries, or Instructors of Youth.

III. FOR WHAT ?   The worth of an author is estimated
by the ends, the attainment of which he proposed to himself
by the particular work; while the value of the work
depends on its fitness, as the Means.   The objects of the
present volume are the following, arranged in the order of
their comparative importance.

1. To direct the reader's attention to the value of the
Science of Words, their use and abuse (see *Note, p.* 5) and
the incalculable advantages attached to the habit of using
them appropriately, and with a distinct knowledge of their
primary, derivative, and metaphorical senses.   And in
furtherance of this Object I have neglected no occasion of

---

[1] This parenthesis was in editions one to three, but was dropped out
of the fourth.—ED.

enforcing the maxim, that to expose a sophism and to detect the equivocal or double meaning of a word is, in the great majority of cases, one and the same thing.   Horne Tooke entitled his celebrated work, Ἔπεα πτεόεντα, Winged Words : or Language, not only the *Vehicle* of Thought but the *Wheels*.   With my convictions and views, for ἔπεα I should substitute λόγοι, that is, Words *select* and *determinate*, and for πτερόεντα ζῶοντες, that is, *living* Words.   The *Wheels* of the Intellect I admit them to be ; but such as Ezekiel beheld in *the visions of God* as he sate among the captives by the river of Chebar.   *Whithersoever the Spirit was to go, the wheels went, and thither was their Spirit to go : for the Spirit of the living creature was in the wheels also.*

2. To establish the *distinct* characters of Prudence, Morality, and Religion : and to impress the conviction, that though the second requires the first, and the third contains and supposes both the former ; yet still Moral Goodness is other and more than Prudence, or the Principle of Expediency ; and Religion more and higher than Morality.   For this distinction the better schools even of Pagan Philosophy contended.   (*See pp.* 20, 21.)

3. To substantiate and set forth at large the momentous distinction between Reason and Understanding.   Whatever is achievable by the Understanding for the purposes of worldly interest, private or public, has in the present age been pursued with an activity and a success beyond all former experience, and to an extent which equally demands my admiration and excites my wonder.   But likewise it is, and long has been, my conviction, that in no age since the first dawning of Science and Philosophy in this island have the truths, interests, and studies that especially belong to the Reason, contemplative or practical, sunk into such utter neglect, not to say contempt, as during the last century.   It is therefore one main object of this volume to establish the position, that whoever transfers to the

Understanding the primacy due to the Reason, loses the one and spoils the other.

4. To exhibit a full and consistent Scheme of the Christian Dispensation, and more largely of all the *peculiar* doctrines of the Christian Faith ; and to answer all the objections to the same, which do not originate in a corrupt Will rather than an erring Judgment ; and to do this in a manner intelligible for all who, possessing the ordinary advantages of education, do in good earnest desire to form their religious creed in the light of their own convictions, and to have a reason for the faith which they profess. There are indeed Mysteries, in evidence of which no reasons can be brought. But it has been my endeavour to show, that the true solution of this problem is, that these Mysteries *are* Reason, Reason in its highest form of Self-affirmation.

Such are the special Objects of these " Aids to Reflection." Concerning the general character of the work, let me be permitted to add the few following sentences. St. Augustine, in one of his Sermons, discoursing on a high point of theology, tells his auditors—*Sic accipite, ut mereamini intelligere. Fides enim debet præcedere intellectum, ut sit intellectus fidei præmium.* Now without a certain portion of gratuitous and (as it were) *experimentative* faith in the writer, a reader will scarcely give that degree of continued attention, without which no *didactic* work worth reading can be read to any wise or profitable purpose. In *this* sense, therefore, and to *this* extent, *every* author, who is competent to the office he has undertaken, may without arrogance repeat St. Augustine's words in his own right, and advance a similar claim on similar grounds. But I venture no further than to imitate the sentiment at a humble distance, by avowing my belief that he who seeks *instruction* in the following pages, will not fail to find *entertainment* likewise ; but that whoever seeks entertainment only will find neither.

READER!—You have been bred in a land abounding with men, able in arts, learning, and knowledges manifold, this man in one, this in another, few in many, none in all. But there is one art, of which every man should be master, the art of REFLECTION. If you are not a *thinking* man, to what purpose are you a *man* at all? In like manner, there is one knowledge, which it is every man's interest and duty to acquire, namely, SELF-KNOWLEDGE: or to what end was man alone, of all animals, endued by the Creator with the faculty of *self-consciousness?* Truly said the Pagan moralist, *e cælo descendit*, Γνῶθι σέαυτον.

But you are likewise born in a CHRISTIAN land: and Revelation has provided for you new subjects for reflection, and new treasures of knowledge, never to be unlocked by him who remains self-ignorant. Self-knowledge is the key to this casket; and by reflection alone can it be obtained. Reflect on your own thoughts, actions, circumstances, and —which will be of especial aid to you in forming a *habit* of reflection,—accustom yourself to reflect on the words you use, hear, or read, their birth, derivation and history. For if words are not THINGS, they are LIVING POWERS, by which the things of most importance to mankind are actuated, combined, and humanized. Finally, by reflection you may draw from the fleeting facts of your worldly trade, art, or profession, a science permanent as your immortal soul; and make even these subsidiary and preparative to the reception of spiritual truth, " doing as the dyers do, who having first dipt their silks in colours of less value, then give them the last tincture of crimson in grain."

[ADVERTISEMENT.[1]—In the bodies of several species of animals there are found certain parts of which neither the office, the functions, nor the relations could be ascertained by the Com-

---

[1] Coleridge's advertisement to the first edition, 1825. It has been omitted since, until now.—ED.

parative Anatomist till he had become acquainted with the
state of the animal before birth. Something sufficiently like
this (for the purpose of an illustration at least) applies to the
work here offered to the public. In the introductory portion
there occur several passages, which the reader will be puzzled to
decipher, without some information respecting the ·original
design of the volume, and the changes it has undergone during
its immature and embryonic state. On this account only, I
think myself bound to make it known, that the work was
begun as a mere selection from the Writings of Archbishop
Leighton, under the usual title of " The Beauties of Archbishop
Leighton," with a few notes and a biographical preface by the
Selector. Hence the term *Editor*, subscribed to the notes, and
prefixed, alone or conjointly to the Aphorisms, according as the
passage was written entirely by myself, or only modified and
(*avowedly*) interpolated.[1] I continued the use of the word on
the plea of uniformity; though, like most other deviations from
propriety of language, it would, probably, have been a wiser
choice to have omitted or exchanged it. The various Reflections,
however, that pressed on me while I was considering the motives
for selecting this or that passage ; the desire for enforcing, and
as it were entegrating, the truths contained in the original
author, by adding those which the words suggested or recalled
to my own mind ; the conversations with men of eminence in
the literary and religious circles, occasioned by the objects which
I had in view ; and, lastly, the increasing disproportion of the
Commentary to the Text, and the too marked difference in the
frame, character, and colours of the two styles ; soon induced
me to recognize and adopt a revolution in my plan and object,
which had in fact actually taken place without my intention,
and almost unawares. It would indeed be more correct to say,
that the present volume owed its accidental origin to the intention of compiling one of a different description than to speak of
it as the same work. It is not a change in the child, but a
changeling.

Still, however, the selections from Leighton, which will be
found in the Prudential and Moral sections of this work, and
which I could retain consistently with its present form and
matter, will both from the intrinsic excellence and from the
characteristic beauty of the passages, suffice to answer two
prominent purposes of the original plan, that of placing in a clear

---

[1] In the first edition the Aphorisms were superscribed "Leighton,"
&c., when selected, and " Editor " when by Coleridge himself. Some
later editions excluded these useful headings. We revert to the author's
first plan, substituting the name Coleridge for " Editor."—ED.

light the principle which pervades all Leighton's writings —his sublime view, I mean, of Religion and Morality as the means of reforming the human Soul in the Divine Image (*Idea*); and that of exciting an interest in the works, and an affectionate reverence for the name and memory of this severely tried and truly primitive Churchman.

S. T. C.]

PRELIMINARY ESSAY.

BY THE REV. JAMES MARSH.[1]

WHETHER the present state of religious feeling, and the prevailing topics of theological inquiry among us, are particularly favourable to the success of the Work herewith offered to the Public can be determined only by the result. The question, however, has not been left unconsidered; and however that may be, it is not a work, the value of which depends essentially upon its relation to the passing controversies of the day. Unless I distrust my own feelings and convictions altogether, I must suppose, that for some, I hope for many, minds, it will have a deep and enduring interest. Of those classes, for whose use it is more especially designated in the Author's Preface, I trust there are many also in this country, who will justly appreciate the objects at which it aims, and avail themselves of its instruction and assistance. I could wish it might be received, by all who concern themselves in religious inquiries and instruction especially, in the spirit which seems to me to have animated its great and admirable author; and I hesitate not to say, that to all of every class, who shall so receive it, and peruse

[1] President of the University of Vermont, United States, where this Essay was first published with Dr. Marsh's edition of the 'Aids,' 1829. See Mr. H. N. Coleridge's Advertisement to the Fourth Edition, *ante*, p. xii.—ED.

it with the attention and thoughtfulness, which it demands and deserves, it will be found by experience to furnish, what its title imports, "AIDS TO REFLECTION" on subjects, upon which every man is bound to reflect deeply and in earnest.

What the specific objects of the Work are, and for whom it is written, may be learned in a few words from the Preface of the Author. From this, too, it will be seen to be professedly didactic. It is designed to aid those who wish for instruction, or assistance in the instruction of others. The plan and composition of the Work will to most readers probably appear somewhat anomalous; but reflection upon the nature of the objects aimed at, and some little experience of its results, may convince them that the method adopted is not without its advantages. It is important to observe, that it is designed, as its general characteristic, to aid REFLECTION, and for the most part upon subjects which can be learned and understood only by the exercise of reflection in the strict and proper sense of that term. It was not so much to teach a speculative system of doctrines built upon established premises, for which a different method would have been obviously preferable, as to turn the mind continually back upon the premises themselves—upon the inherent grounds of truth and error in its own being. The only way in which it is possible for any one to learn the science of words, which is one of the objects to be sought in the present Work, and the true import of those words especially, which most concern us as rational and accountable beings, is by reflecting upon and bringing forth into distinct consciousness, those mental acts which the words are intended to designate. We must discover and distinctly apprehend different meanings, before we can appropriate to each a several word, or understand the words so appropriated by others. Now it is not too much to say, that most men, and even a large proportion of educated men, do not reflect sufficiently upon their own inward being, upon the constituent laws of their own understanding, upon the mysterious powers and agencies of reason, and conscience, and will, to apprehend with much distinctness the objects to be named, or of course to refer the names with correctness to their several objects. Hence the necessity of associating the study of words with the study of morals and religion; and that is the most effectual method of instruction, which enables the teacher most successfully to fix the attention upon a definite meaning, that is, in these studies, upon a particular act, or process, or law of the mind—to call it into distinct consciousness, and assign to it its proper name, so that the name shall thenceforth have for the learner a distinct, definite, and intelligible sense. To impress upon the reader the importance of this, and to exemplify it in the particular subjects taken up in the Work, is a leading aim of the Author throughout; and it is obviously the only possible way by which we can arrive at any satisfactory and conclusive results on subjects of philosophy, morals, and religion. The first principles, the ultimate grounds, of these, so far as they are possible objects of knowledge for us, must be sought and found in the laws of our being, or they are not found at all. The knowledge of these, terminates in the knowledge of ourselves, of our rational and personal being, of our proper and distinctive humanity, and of that Divine Being, in whose image we are created. "We must retire inward," says St. Bernard, "if we would ascend upward." It is by self-inspection, by reflecting upon the mysterious grounds of our own being, that we can alone arrive at any rational knowledge of the central and absolute ground of all being. It is by this only, that we can discover that principle of unity and consistency, which reason instinctively seeks after, which shall reduce to an harmonious system all our views of truth and of being, and destitute of which all the knowledge that comes to us from without is fragmentary, and in its relation to our highest interests as rational beings but the patch-work of vanity.

Now, of necessity, the only method, by which another can aid our efforts in the work of reflection, is by first reflecting himself, and so pointing out the process and marking the result by words, that we can repeat it, and try the conclusions by our own consciousness. If he have reflected aright, if he have excluded all causes of self-deception, and directed his thoughts by those principles of truth and reason, and by those laws of the understanding, which belong in common to all men, his conclusions must be true for all. We have only to repeat the process, impartially to reflect ourselves, unbiassed by received opinions, and undeceived by the idols of our own understandings, and we shall find the same truths in the depths of our own self-consciousness. I am persuaded that such, for the most part, will be found to be the case with regard to the principles developed in the present Work, and that those who, with serious reflection and an unbiassed love of truth, will refer them to the laws of thought in their own minds, to the requirements of their own reason, will find there a witness to their truth.

Viewing the Work in this manner, therefore, as an instructive and safe guide to the knowledge of what it concerns all men to know, I cannot but consider it in itself as a work of great and permanent value to any Christian community. Whatever indeed tends to awaken and cherish the power, and to form the habit, of reflection upon the great constituent principles of our own permanent being and proper humanity, and upon the abiding laws of truth and duty, as revealed in our reason and conscience, cannot but promote our highest interests as moral and rational beings. Even if the particular conclusions, to which the Author has arrived, should prove erroneous, the evil is comparatively of little importance, if he have at the same time communicated to our minds such powers of thought, as will enable us to detect his errors, and attain by our own efforts to a more perfect knowledge of the truth. That some of his views may not be erroneous, or that they are to be received on his authority, the Author, I presume, would be the last to affirm ; and although in the nature of the case it was impossible for him to aid reflection without anticipating, and in some measure influencing, the results, yet the primary tendency and design of the Work is, not to establish this or that system, but to cultivate in every mind the power and the will to seek earnestly and steadfastly for the truth in the only direction, in which it can ever be found. The work is no further controversial, than every work must be, " that is writ with freedom and reason " upon subjects of the same kind ; and if it be found at variance with existing opinions and modes of philosophizing, it is not necessarily to be considered the fault of the writer.

In republishing the Work in this country, I could wish that it might be received by all, for whose instruction it was designed, simply as a didactic work, on its own merits, and without controversy. I must not, however, be supposed ignorant of its bearing upon those questions, which have so often been, and still are, the prevailing topics of theological controversy among us. It was indeed incumbent on me, before inviting the attention of the religious community to the Work, to consider its relation to existing opinions, and its probable influence on the progress of truth. This I have done with as severe thought as I am capable of bestowing upon any subject, and I trust too with no want of deference and conscientious regard to the feelings and opinions of others. I have not attempted to disguise from myself, nor do I wish to disguise from the readers of the Work, the inconsistency of some of its leading principles with much that is taught and received in our theological circles. Should it gain much of the public attention in any way, it will become, as it ought to do, an object of special and deep interest to all, who would contend for the truth, and labour to establish it upon a permanent basis. I venture to assure such, even those of them who are most capable of comprehending the philosophical grounds of truth in our speculative systems of theology, that in its relation to this whole subject they will find it to be a Work of great depth and power, and, whether right or wrong, eminently deserving their attention. It is not to be supposed that all who read, or even all who comprehend it, will be convinced of the soundness of its views, or be prepared to abandon those which they have long considered essential to the truth. To those, whose understandings by long habit have become limited in their powers of apprehension, and as it were identified with certain schemes of doctrine, certain modes of contemplating all that pertains to religious truth, it may appear novel, strange, and unintelligible, or even dangerous in its tendency, and be to them an occasion of offence. But I have no fear that any earnest and single-hearted lover of the truth as it is in Jesus, who will free his mind from the idols of preconceived opinion, and give himself time and opportunity to understand the Work by such reflection as the nature of the subject renders unavoidable, will find in it any cause of offence, or any source of alarm. If the Work become the occasion of controversy at all, I should expect it from those, who, instead of reflecting deeply upon the first principles of truth in their own reason and conscience and in the word of God, are more accustomed to speculate—that is, from premises given or assumed, but considered unquestionable, as the constituted point of observation, to look abroad upon the whole field of their intellectual vision, and thence to decide upon the true form and dimensions of all which meets their view. To such I would say with deference, that the merits of this Work cannot be determined by the merely relative aspect

of its doctrines, as seen from the high ground of any prevailing metaphysical or theological system.   Those on the
contrary who will seek to comprehend it by reflection, to
learn the true meaning of the whole and of all its parts, by
retiring into their own minds and finding there the true
point of observation for each, will not be in haste to question the truth or the tendency of its principles.   I make
these remarks because I am anxious, as far as may be, to
anticipate the causeless fears of all, who earnestly pray and
labour for the promotion of the truth, and to preclude that
unprofitable controversy, which might arise from hasty or
prejudiced views of a Work like this.   At the same time I
should be far from deprecating any discussion which might
tend to unfold more fully the principles which it teaches,
or to exhibit more distinctly its true bearing upon the
interests of theological science and of spiritual religion.   It
is to promote this object, indeed, that I am induced in the
remarks which follow to offer some of my own thoughts on
these subjects, imperfect I am well aware, and such as, for
that reason, as well as others, worldly prudence might
require me to suppress.   If, however, I may induce reflecting men, and those who are engaged in theological inquiries
especially, to indulge a suspicion that all truth, which it is
important for them to know, is not contained in the systems
of doctrine usually taught, and that this Work may be
worthy of their serious and reflecting perusal, my chief
object will be accomplished.   I shall of course not need to
anticipate in detail the contents of the Work itself, but
shall aim simply to point out what I consider its distinguishing and essential character and tendency, and then
direct the attention of my readers to some of those general
feelings and views on the subjects of religious truth, and
of those particulars in the prevailing philosophy of the age,
which seem to me to be exerting an injurious influence on
the cause of theological science and of spiritual religion,

and not only to furnish a fit occasion, but to create an imperious demand, for a Work like that which is here offered to the public.

In regard then to the distinguishing character and tendency of the Work itself, it has already been stated to be didactic, and designed to aid reflection on the principles and grounds of truth in our own being; but in another point of view, and with reference to my present object, it might rather be denominated A PHILOSOPHICAL STATEMENT AND VINDICATION OF THE DISTINCTIVELY SPIRITUAL AND PECULIAR DOCTRINES OF THE CHRISTIAN SYSTEM. In order to understand more clearly the import of this statement, and the relation of the Author's views to those exhibited in other systems, the reader is requested to examine in the first place, what he considers the *peculiar doctrines of Christianity*, and what he means by the terms *spirit* and *spiritual*. A synoptical view of what he considers peculiar to Christianity as a revelation is given in Aphorism VII., on Spiritual Religion, and, if I mistake not, will be found essentially to coincide, though not perhaps in the language employed, with what among us are termed the Evangelical doctrines of religion. Those who are anxious to examine further into the orthodoxy of the Work in connection with this statement, may consult the articles on ORIGINAL SIN and REDEMPTION,[1] though I must forewarn them that it will require much study in connection with the other parts of the Work, before one unaccustomed to the Author's language, and unacquainted with his views, can fully appreciate the merit of what may be peculiar in his mode of treating those subjects. With regard to the term *spiritual*, it may be sufficient to remark here, that he regards it as having a specific import, and maintains that in the sense of the New Testament, *spiritual* and *natural* are contradistinguished, so that what is spiritual is different

---

[1] See pp. 172, 208, 223, &c.—ED.

in kind from that which is natural, and is in fact *super-natural*. So, too, while morality is something more than prudence, religion, the spiritual life, is something more than morality.

In vindicating the peculiar doctrines of the Christian system so stated, and a faith in the reality of agencies and modes of being essentially spiritual or supernatural, he aims to show their consistency with reason and with the true principles of philosophy, and that indeed, so far from being irrational, CHRISTIAN FAITH IS THE PERFECTION OF HUMAN REASON. By reflection upon the subjective grounds of knowledge and faith in the human mind itself, and by an analysis of its faculties, he developes the distinguishing characteristics and necessary relations of the natural and the spiritual in our modes of being and knowing, and the all-important fact, that although the former does not comprehend the latter, yet neither does it preclude its existence. He proves, that " the scheme of Christianity, * * * though not discoverable by human reason, is yet in accordance with it; that link follows link by necessary consequence; that Religion passes out of the ken of Reason only where the eye of Reason has reached its own horizon—and that Faith is then but its continuation." [1]   Instead of adopting, like the popular metaphysicians of the day, a system of philosophy at war with religion, and which tends inevitably to undermine our belief in the reality of any thing spiritual in the only proper sense of that word, and then coldly and ambiguously referring us for the support of our faith to the authority of Revelation, he boldly asserts the reality of something distinctively spiritual in man, and the futility of all those modes of philosophizing, in which this is not recognized, or which are incompatible with it. He considers it the highest and most rational purpose of any

[1] Coleridge's 'Biographia Literaria,' p. 301, Bohn's edition.—ED.

system of philosophy, at least of one professiug to be
Christian, to investigate those higher and peculiar attributes, which distinguish us from the brutes that perish—
which are the image of God in us, and constitute our
proper humanity. It is in his view the proper business and
the duty of the Christian philosopher to remove all appearance of contradiction between the several manifestations of
the one Divine Word, to reconcile reason with revelation, and
thus to justify the ways of God to man. The methods by
which he accomplishes this, either in regard to the terms in
which he enunciates the great doctrines of the Gospel, or
the peculiar views of philosophy by which he reconciles
them with the subjective grounds of faith in the universal
reason of man, need not be stated here. I will merely
observe, that the key to his system will be found in the
distinctions, which he makes and illustrates between *nature*
and *free-will*, and between the *understanding* and *reason.*
It may meet the prejudices of some to remark farther, that
in philosophizing on the grounds of our faith he does not
profess or aim to solve all mysteries, and to bring all truth
within the comprehension of the understanding. A truth
may be mysterious, and the primary ground of all truth
and reality must be so. But though we may believe what
passeth all understanding, we *cannot* believe what is *absurd*,
or contradictory to *reason.*

Whether the Work be well executed, according to the
idea of it, as now given, or whether the Author have accomplished his purpose, must be determined by those who
are capable of judging, when they shall have examined and
reflected upon the whole as it deserves. The inquiry which I
have now to propose to my readers is, whether the idea itself
be a rational one, and whether the purpose of the Author be
one which a wise man and a Christian ought to aim at, or
which in the present state of our religious interests, and of
our theological science, specially needs to be accomplished.

No one, who has had occasion to observe the general feelings and views of our religious community for a few years past, can be ignorant, that a strong prejudice exists against the introduction of philosophy, in any form, in the discussion of theological subjects. The terms *philosophy* and *metaphysics*, even *reason* and *rational*, seem, in the minds of those most devoted to the support of religious truth, to have forfeited their original, and to have acquired a new import, especially in their relation to matters of faith. By a philosophical view of religious truth would generally be understood a view, not only varying from the religion of the Bible in the form and manner of presenting it, but at war with it; and a rational religion is supposed to be of course something diverse from revealed religion. A philosophical and rational system of religious truth would by most readers among us, if I mistake not, be supposed a system deriving its doctrines not from revelation, but from the speculative reason of men, or at least relying on that only for their credibility. That these terms have been used to designate such systems, and that the prejudice against reason and philosophy so employed is not, therefore, without cause, I need not deny; nor would any friend of revealed truth be less disposed to give credence to such systems, than the Author of the Work before us.

But, on the other hand, a moment's reflection only can be necessary to convince any man, attentive to the use of language, that we do at the same time employ these terms in relation to truth generally in a better and much higher sense. *Rational*, as contradistinguished from *irrational* and *absurd*, certainly denotes a quality, which every man would be disposed to claim, not only for himself, but for his religious opinions. Now, the adjective *reasonable* having acquired a different use and signification, the word *rational* is the adjective corresponding in sense to the substantive *reason*, and signifies what is conformed to reason. In one sense, then, all men would appeal to reason in behalf of their religious faith ; they would deny that it was irrational or absurd. If we do not in this sense adhere to reason, we forfeit our prerogative as rational beings, and our faith is no better than the bewildered dream of a man who has lost his reason. Nay, I maintain that when we use the term in this higher sense, it is impossible for us to believe on any authority what is directly contradictory to reason and seen to be so. No evidence from another source, and no authority could convince us, that a proposition in geometry, for example, is false, which our reason intuitively discovers to be true. Now if we suppose (and we may at least suppose this,) that reason has the same power of intuitive insight in relation to certain moral and spiritual truths, as in relation to the truths of geometry, then it would be equally impossible to divest us of our belief of those truths.

Furthermore, we are not only unable to believe the same proposition to be false, which our reason sees to be true, but we cannot believe another proposition, which by the exercise of the same rational faculty we see to be incompatible with the former, or to contradict it. We may, and probably often do, receive with a certain kind and degree of credence opinions, which reflection would show to be incompatible. But when we have reflected, and discovered the inconsistency, we cannot retain both. We cannot believe two contradictory propositions knowing them to be such. It would be irrational to do so.

Again, we cannot conceive it possible, that what by the same power of intuition we see to be universally and necessarily true should appear otherwise to any other rational being. We cannot, for example, but consider the propositions of geometry as necessarily true for all rational beings. So, too, a little reflection, I think, will convince any one, that we attribute the same necessity of reason to the principles of moral rectitude. What in the clear day-light of our reason, and after mature reflection, we see to be right, we cannot believe to be wrong in the view of other rational beings in the distinct exercise of their reason. Nay, in regard to those truths, which are clearly submitted to the view of our reason, and which we behold with distinct and steadfast intuitions, we necessarily attribute to the Supreme Reason, to the Divine Mind, views the same, or coincident, with those of our own reason. We cannot, (I say it with reverence and I trust with some apprehension of the importance of the assertion,) we *cannot* believe that to be right in the view of the Supreme Reason, which is clearly and decidedly wrong in the view of our own. It would be contradictory to reason, it would be irrational, to believe it, and therefore we cannot do so, till we lose our reason, or cease to exercise it.

I would ask, now, whether this be not an authorized use of the words reason and rational, and whether so used they do not mean something. If it be so—and I appeal to the mind of every man capable of reflection, and of under-standing the use of language, if it be not—then there is meaning in the terms *universal reason*, and *unity of reason*, as used in this Work. There is, and can be, in this highest sense of the word but one reason, and whatever contradicts that reason, being seen to do so, cannot be received as matter either of knowledge or faith. To reconcile religion with reason used in this sense, therefore, and to justify the ways of God to man, or in the view of reason, is so far from being irrational that reason imperatively demands it of us. We cannot, as rational beings, believe a proposition on the grounds of reason, and deny it on the authority of revelation. We cannot believe a proposition in philosophy, and deny the same proposition in theology; nor can we believe two incompatible propositions on the different grounds of reason and revelation. So far as we compare our thoughts, the objects of our knowledge and faith, and by reflection refer them to their common measure in the universal laws of reason, so far the instinct of reason impels us to reject whatever is contradictory and absurd, and to bring unity and consistency into all our views of truth. Thus, in the language of the Author of this Work, though "the word *rational* has been strangely abused of late times, this must not disincline us to the weighty consideration, that thoughtfulness, and a desire to rest all our convictions on grounds of right reason, are inseparable from the character of a Christian." [1]

But I beg the reader to observe, that in relation to the doctrines of spiritual religion—to all that he considers the peculiar doctrines of the Christian revelation, the Author assigns to reason only a negative validity. It does not teach us what those doctrines are, or what they are not, except that they are not, and cannot be, such as contradict the clear convictions of right reason. But his views on this point are fully stated in the Work. [2]

If then it be our prerogative, as rational beings, and our duty as Christians, to think, as well as to act, *rationally,*— to see that our convictions of truth rest on the grounds of right reason; and if it be one of the clearest dictates of reason, that we should endeavour to shun, and on discovery should reject, whatever is contradictory to the universal laws of thought, or to doctrines already established, I know not by what means we are to avoid the application of philosophy, at least to some extent, in the study of theology. For to determine what *are* the grounds of right reason, what are those ultimate truths, and those universal laws of thought, which we cannot rationally contradict, and by reflection to compare with these whatever is proposed for

[1] Introductory Aphorisms, XVI., p. 8.—ED.

[2] Also in Appendix B of the 'Statesman's Manual, Bohn's edition, p. 337.—ED.

our belief, is in fact to philosophize; and whoever does this to a greater or less extent, is so far a philosopher in the best and highest sense of the word. To this extent we are bound to philosophize in theology, as well as in every other science. For what is not rational in theology, is, of course, irrational, and cannot be of the household of faith; and to determine whether it be rational in the sense already explained or not, is the province of philosophy. It is in this sense that the Work before us is to be considered a philosophical work, namely, that it proves the doctrines of the Christian Faith to be rational, and exhibits philosophical grounds for the *possibility* of a truly spiritual religion. The *reality* of those experiences, or states of being, which constitute experimental or spiritual religion, rests on other grounds. It is incumbent on the philosopher to free them from the contradictions of reason, and nothing more; and who will deny, that to do this is a purpose worthy of the ablest philosopher and the most devoted Christian? Is it not desirable to convince all men that the doctrines, which we affirm to be revealed in the Gospel, are not contradictory to the requirements of reason and conscience? Is it not, on the other hand, vastly important to the cause of religious truth, and even to the practical influence of religion on our own minds, and the minds of the community at large, that we should attain and exhibit views of philosophy and doctrines in metaphysics, which are at least compatible with, if they do not specially favour, those views of religion, which, on other grounds, we find it our duty to believe and maintain? For, I beg it may be observed, as a point of great moment, that it is not the method of the genuine philosopher to separate his philosophy and religion, and adopting his principles independently in each, to leave them to be reconciled or not, as the case may be. He has, and can have, rationally but one system, in which his philosophy becomes religious, and his religion philosophical.

Nor am I disposed in compliance with public opinion to limit the application of this remark, as is usually done, to the mere external evidences of revelation.   The philosophy which we adopt will and must influence not only our decision of the question, whether a book be of divine authority, but our views also of its meaning.

But this is a subject, on which, if possible, I would avoid being misunderstood, and must, therefore, exhibit it more fully, even at the risk of repeating what was said before, or is elsewhere found in the Work.   It has been already, I believe, distinctly enough stated, that reason and philosophy ought to prevent our reception of doctrines claiming the authority of revelation only so far as the very necessities of our rational being require.   However mysterious the thing affirmed may be, though *it passeth all understanding,* if it cannot be shown to contradict the unchangeable principles of right reason, its being incomprehensible to our understandings is not an obstacle to our faith.   If it contradict reason, we cannot believe it, but must conclude, either that the writing is not of divine authority, or that the language has been misinterpreted.   So far it seems to me, that our philosophy ought to modify our views of theological doctrines, and our mode of interpreting the language of an inspired writer.   But then we must be cautious, that we philosophize rightly, and "do not call *that* reason which is not so."   Otherwise we may be led by the supposed requirements of reason to interpret metaphorically, what ought to be received literally, and evacuate the Scriptures of their most important doctrines.   But what I mean to say here is, that we cannot avoid the application of our philosophy in the interpretation of the language of Scripture, and in the explanation of the doctrines of religion generally. We cannot avoid incurring the danger just alluded to of philosophizing erroneously, even to the extent of rejecting as irrational that which tends to the perfection of reason

itself. And hence I maintain, that instead of pretending
to exclude philosophy from our religious inquiries, it is
very important that we philosophize in earnest—that we
should endeavour by profound reflection to learn the real
requirements of reason, and attain a true knowledge of
ourselves.

If any dispute the necessity of thus combining the study
of philosophy with that of religion, I would beg them to
point out the age since that of the Apostles, in which the
prevailing metaphysical opinions have not distinctly manifested themselves in the prevailing views of religion; and
if, as I fully believe will be the case, they fail to discover a
single system of theology, a single volume on the subject
of the Christian religion, in which the author's views are
not modified by the metaphysical opinions of the age or of
the individual, it would be desirable to ascertain, whether
this influence be accidental or necessary. The metaphysician
analyzes the faculties and operations of the human mind,
and teaches us to arrange, to classify, and to name them,
according to his views of their various distinctions.   The
language of the Scriptures, at least to a great extent,
speaks of subjects that can be understood only by a reference
to those same powers and processes of thought and feeling,
which we have learned to think of, and to name, according
to our particular system of metaphysics. How is it possible
then to avoid interpreting the one by the other ?   Let us
suppose, for example, that a man has studied and adopted
the philosophy of Brown, is it possible for him to interpret
the 8th chapter of Romans, without having his views of its
meaning influenced by his philosophy ? Would he not unavoidably interpret the language and explain the doctrines,
which it contains, differently from one, who should have
adopted such views of the human mind as are taught in
this Work ? I know it is customary to disclaim the influence
of philosophy in the business of interpretation, and every

writer now-a-days on such subjects will assure us, that he
has nothing to do with metaphysics, but is guided only by
common sense and the laws of interpretation. But I should
like to know how a man comes by any common sense in
relation to the movements and laws of his intellectual and
moral being without metaphysics. What is the common
sense of a Hottentot on subjects of this sort? I have no
hesitation in saying, that from the very nature of the case,
it is nearly, if not quite, impossible for any man entirely
to separate his philosophical views of the human mind
from his reflections on religious subjects. Probably no
man has endeavoured more faithfully to do this, perhaps no
one has succeeded better in giving the truth of Scripture
free from the glosses of metaphysics, than Professor Stuart.
Yet, I should risk little in saying that a reader deeply
versed in the language of metaphysics, extensively acquainted with the philosophy of different ages, and the
peculiar phraseology of different schools, might ascertain
his metaphysical system from many a passage of his Commentary on the Epistle to the Hebrews. What then, let
me ask, is the possible use to the cause of truth and of
religion, from thus perpetually decrying philosophy in
theological inquiries, when we cannot avoid it if we would?
Every man, who has reflected at all, has his metaphysics;
and if he reads on religious subjects, he interprets and
understands the language which he employs, by the help
of his metaphysics. He cannot do otherwise.—And the
proper inquiry is, not whether we admit our philosophy
into our theological and religious investigations, but whether
our philosophy be right and true. For myself, I am fully
convinced that we can have no right views of theology, till
we have right views of the human mind; and that these
are to be acquired only by laborious and persevering
reflection. My belief is, that the distinctions unfolded in
this Work will place us in the way to truth, and relieve us

from numerous perplexities, in which we are involved by
the philosophy which we have so long taken for our guide.
For we are greatly deceived, if we suppose for a moment
that the systems of theology which have been received
among us, or even the theoretical views which are now
most popular, are free from the entanglements of worldly
wisdom.   The readers of this Work will be able to see, I
think, more clearly the import of this remark, and the
true bearing of the received views of philosophy on our
theological inquiries.   Those who study the Work without
prejudice, and adopt its principles to any considerable
extent, will understand too how deeply an age may be
ensnared in the metaphysical webs of its own weaving, or
entangled in the net which the speculations of a former
generation have thrown over it, and yet suppose itself
blessed with a perfect immunity from the dreaded evils of
metaphysics.

But before I proceed to remark on those particulars, in
which our prevailing philosophy seems to be dangerous in
its tendency, and unfriendly to the cause of spiritual
religion, I must beg leave to guard myself and the Work
from misapprehension on another point of great importance
in its relation to the whole subject. While it is maintained
that reason and philosophy, in their true character, *ought*
to have a certain degree and extent of influence in the formation of our religious system, and that our metaphysical
opinions, whatever they may be, *will* almost unavoidably,
modify more or less our theoretical views of religious truth
generally, it is yet a special object of the Author of the
Work to show that the spiritual life, or what among us is
termed experimental religion, is, in itself, and in its own
proper growth and development, essentially distinct from
the forms and processes of the understanding; and that,
although a true faith cannot contradict any universal
principle of speculative reason, it is yet in a certain sense

independent of the discursions of philosophy, and in its proper nature beyond the reach " of positive science and theoretical *insight*." " Christianity is not a *theory* or a *speculation;* but a *life.* Not a *philosophy* of life, but a life and a living process." It is not, therefore, so properly a species of knowledge, as a form of being. And although the theoretical views of the understanding, and the motives of prudence which it presents, may be, to a certain extent, connected with the development of the spiritual principle of religious life in the Christian, yet a true and living faith is not incompatible with at least some degree of speculative error. As the acquisition of merely speculative knowledge cannot of itself communicate the principle of spiritual life, so neither does that principle, and the living process of its growth, depend wholly, at least, upon the degree of speculative knowledge with which it co-exists. That religion, of which our blessed Saviour is himself the essential Form and the living Word, and to which he imparts the actuating Spirit, has a principle of unity and consistency in itself distinct from the unity and consistency of our theoretical views. Of this we have evidence in every day's observation of Christian character; for how often do we see and acknowledge the power of religion, and the growth of a spiritual life in minds but little gifted with speculative knowledge, and little versed in the forms of logic or philosophy! How obviously, too, does the living principle of religion manifest the same specific character, the same essential form, amidst all the diversities of condition, of talents, of education, and natural disposition, with which it is associated; every where rising above nature, and the powers of the natural man, and unlimited in its goings on by the forms in which the understanding seeks to comprehend and confine its spiritual energies. *There are diversities of gifts, but the same Spirit:* and it is no less true now than in the age of the Apostles, that in all lands, and in every variety of circumstances, the manifestations of spiritual life are essentially the same ; and all who truly believe in heart, however diverse in natural condition, in the character of their understandings, and even in their theoretical views of truth, are *one* in *Christ Jesus.* The essential faith is not to be found in the understanding or the speculative theory, but " the *life*, the *substance*, the *hope*, the *love*—in one word, the *faith*—these are derivatives from the practical, moral, and spiritual nature and being of man." Speculative systems of theology indeed have often had little connection with the essential spirit of religion, and are usually little more than schemes resulting from the strivings of the finite understanding to comprehend and exhibit under its own forms and conditions a mode of being and spiritual truths essentially diverse from their proper objects, and with which they are incommensurate.

This I am aware is an imperfect, and I fear may be an unintelligible, view of a subject exceedingly difficult of apprehension at the best. If so, I must beg the reader's indulgence, and request him to suspend his judgment, as to the absolute intelligibility of it, till he becomes acquainted with the language and sentiments of the Work itself. It will, however, I hope, be so far understood, at least, as to answer the purpose for which it was introduced—of precluding the supposition that, in the remarks which preceded, or in those which follow, any suspicion was intended to be expressed, with regard to the religious principles or the essential faith of those who hold the opinions in question. According to this view of the inherent and essential nature of Spiritual Religion, as existing in the *practical reason* of man, we may not only admit, but can better understand the possibility of what every charitable Christian will acknowledge to be a fact, so far as human observation can determine facts of this sort—that a man may be truly religious, and essentially a believer at heart, while his

understanding is sadly bewildered with the attempt to
comprehend and express philosophically, what yet he feels
and knows spiritually. It is indeed impossible for us to
tell, how far the understanding may impose upon itself by
partial views and false disguises, without perverting the
will, or estranging it from the laws and the authority of
reason and the divine word. We cannot say to what extent
a false system of philosophy and metaphysical opinions,
which in their natural and uncounteracted tendency would
go to destroy all religion, may be received in a Christian
community, and yet the power of spiritual religion retain
its hold and its efficacy in the hearts of the people. We
may perhaps believe that in opposition to all the might of
false philosophy, so long as the great body of the people
have the Bible in their hands, and are taught to reverence
and receive its heavenly instructions, though the Church
may suffer injury from unwise and unfruitful speculations,
it will yet be preserved; and that the spiritual seed of the
divine word, though mingled with many tares of worldly
wisdom and philosophy falsely so called, will yet spring up,
and bear fruit unto everlasting life.

But though we may hope and believe this, we cannot
avoid believing, at the same time, that injury must result
from an unsuspecting confidence in metaphysical opinions,
which are essentially at variance with the doctrines of
Revelation. Especially must the effect be injurious, where
those opinions lead gradually to alter our views of religion
itself and of all that is peculiar in the Christian system.
The great mass of the community, who know little of
metaphysics, and whose faith in Revelation is not so readily
influenced by speculations not immediately connected with
it, may, indeed, for a time, escape the evil, and continue to
receive with meekness the ingrafted word. But in the minds
of the better educated, especially those who think and
follow out their conclusions with resolute independence of

thought, the result must be either a loss of confidence in the opinions themselves, or a rejection of all those parts of the Christian system which are at variance with them. Under particular circumstances, indeed, where both the metaphysical errors, and the great doctrines of the Christian Faith, have a strong hold upon the minds of a community, a protracted struggle may take place, and earnest and long-continued efforts may be made to reconcile opinions which we are resolved to maintain, with a faith which our consciences will not permit us to abandon. But so long as the effort continues and such opinions retain their hold upon our confidence, it must be by some diminution of the fulness and simplicity of our faith. To a greater or less degree, according to the education and habits of thought in different individuals, the word of God is received with doubt, or with such glozing modifications as enervate its power. Thus the light from heaven is intercepted, and we are left to a shadow-fight of metaphysical schemes and metaphorical interpretations. While one party, with conscientious and earnest endeavours, and at great expense of talent and ingenuity, contends for the Faith, and among the possible shapings of the received metaphysical system, seeks that which will best comport with the simplicity of the Gospel,—another more boldly interprets the language of the Gospel itself in conformity with those views of religion to which their philosophy seems obviously to conduct them. The substantial being and the living energy of the WORD, which is not only the light but the life of men, is either misapprehended or denied by all parties : and even those who contend for what they conceive the literal import of the Gospel, do it—as they must, to avoid too glaring absurdity—with such explanations of its import as make it to become, in no small degree, the *words of man's wisdom*, rather than a simple *demonstration of the Spirit, and of power*. Hence, although such as have ex-

perienced the spiritual and life-giving power of the Divine
Word, may be able, through the promised aids of the Spirit,
to overcome the natural tendency of speculative error, and,
by *the law of the Spirit of life* which is in them, may at
length be made *free from the law of sin and death*, yet who
can tell how much they may lose of the blessings of the
Gospel, and be retarded in their spiritual growth when
they are but too often fed with the lifeless and starveling
products of the human understanding, instead of that
living bread which came down from heaven? Who can tell,
moreover, how many, through the prevalence of such
philosophical errors as lead to misconceptions of the truth
or create a prejudice against it, and thus tend to intercept
the light from heaven, may continue in their ignorance,
alienated from the life of God, and groping in the darkness
of their own understandings?

But however that may be, enlightened Christians, and
especially Christian instructors, know it to be their duty,
as far as possible, to prepare the way for the full and
unobstructed influence of the Gospel, to do all in their
power to remove those natural prejudices, and those errors
of the understanding, which are obstacles to the truth,
that the word of God may find access to the heart, and
conscience, and reason of every man, that it may have *free
course, and run, and be glorified.* My own belief, that such
obstacles to the influence of truth exist in the speculative
and metaphysicaal opinions generally adopted in this
country, and that the present Work is in some measure at
least calculated to remove them, is pretty clearly indicated
by the remarks which I have already made. But, to be
perfectly explicit on the subject I do not hesitate to express
my conviction, that the natural tendency of some of the
leading principles of our prevailing system of metaphysics,
and those which must unavoidably have more or less
influence on our theoretical views of religion, are of an

injurious and dangerous tendency, and that so long as we retain them, however we may profess to exclude their influence from our theological inquiries, and from the interpretation of Scripture, we can maintain no consistent system of Scriptural theology, nor clearly and distinctly apprehend the spiritual import of the Scripture language. The grounds of this conviction I shall proceed to exhibit, though only in a partial manner, as I could not do more without anticipating the contents of the Work itself, instead of merely preparing the reader to peruse them with attention. I am aware, too, that some of the language, which I have already employed, and shall be obliged to employ, will not convey its full import to the reader, till he becomes acquainted with some of the leading principles and distinctions unfolded in the Work. But this also is an evil which I saw no means of avoiding without incurring a greater, and writing a book instead of a brief essay.

Let it be understood, then, without further preface, that by the prevailing system of metaphysics, I mean the system, of which in modern times Locke is the reputed author, and the leading principles of which, with various modifications, more or less important, but not altering its essential character, have been almost universally received in this country. It should be observed, too, that the causes enumerated by the Author, as having elevated it to its " pride of place " in Europe, have been aided by other favouring circumstances here. In the minds of our religious community, especially, some of its most important doctrines have become associated with names justly loved and revered among ourselves, and so connected with all our theoretical views of religion, that a man can hardly hope to question their validity without hazarding his reputation, not only for orthodoxy, but even for common sense. To controvert, for example, the prevailing doctrines with regard to the freedom of the will, the sources of our knowledge, the nature of the understanding as containing the controlling principles of our whole being, and the universality of the law of cause and effect, even in connection with the argument and the authority of the most powerful intellect of the age, may even now be worse than in vain. Yet I have reasons for believing there are some among us, and that their number is fast increasing, who are willing to revise their opinions on these subjects, and who will contemplate the views presented in this Work with a liberal, and something of a prepared feeling, of curiosity. The difficulties in which men find themselves involved by the received doctrines on these subjects, in their most anxious efforts to explain and defend the peculiar doctrines of spiritual religion, have led many to suspect that there must be some lurking error in the premises. It is not that these principles lead us to mysteries which we cannot comprehend; they are found, or believed at least by many, to involve us in absurdities which we can comprehend. It is necessary indeed only to form some notion of the distinctive and appropriate import of the term spiritual, as opposed to natural in the New Testament, and then to look at the writings, or hear the discussions, in which the doctrines of the Spirit and of spiritual influences are taught and defended, to see the insurmountable nature of the obstacles, which these metaphysical dogmas throw in the way of the most powerful minds. To those who shall read this Work with any degree of reflection, it must, I think, be obvious, that something more is implied in the continual opposition of these terms in the New Testament, than can be explained consistently with the prevailing opinions on the subjects above enumerated; and that through their influence our highest notions of that distinction have been rendered confused, contradictory, and inadequate. I have already directed the attention of the reader to those parts of the Work, where this distinction is unfolded; and had I no other grounds than the arguments and views there exhibited, I should be convinced that so long as we hold the doctrines of Locke and the Scotch metaphysicians respecting power, cause and effect, motives, and the freedom of the will, we not only can make and defend no essential distinction between that which is *natural*, and that which is *spiritual*, but we cannot even find rational grounds for the feeling of *moral obligation*, and the distinction between *regret* and *remorse*.

According to the system of these authors, as nearly and distinctly as my limits will permit me to state it, the same law of cause and effect is the law of the universe. It extends to the moral and spiritual—if in courtesy these terms may still be used—no less than to the properly natural powers and agencies of our being. The acts of the free-will are pre-determined by a cause *out of the will*, according to the same law of cause and effect which controls the changes in the physical world. We have no notion of power but uniformity of antecedent and consequent. The notion of a power in the will to act freely is therefore nothing more than an inherent capacity of being acted upon, agreeably to its nature, and according to a fixed law, by the motives which are present in the understanding. I feel authorized to take this statement partly from Brown's Philosophy, because that work has been decidedly approved by our highest theological authorities; and indeed it would not be essentially varied, if expressed in the precise terms used by any of the writers most usually quoted in reference to these subjects.

I am aware that variations may be found in the mode of stating these doctrines, but I think every candid reader, who is acquainted with the metaphysics and theology of this country, will admit the above to be a fair representation of the form in which they are generally received. I am aware, too, that much has been said and written to make out, consistently with these general principles, a distinction between natural and moral causes, natural and moral ability, and inability, and the like. But I beg all lovers of sound and rational philosophy to look carefully at the general principles, and see whether there be, in fact, ground left for any such distinctions of this kind as are worth contending for. My first step in arguing with a defender of these principles, and of the distinctions in question, as connected with them, would be to ask for his definition of nature and *natural*. And when he had arrived at a distinctive general notion of the import of these, it would appear, if I mistake not, that he had first subjected our whole being to the law of nature, and then contended for the existence of something which is not nature. For in their relation to the law of moral rectitude, and to the feeling of moral responsibility, what difference is there, and what difference can there be, between what are called natural and those which are called moral powers and affections, if they are all under the control of the same universal *law* of cause and effect? If it still be a mere nature, and the determinations of our will be controlled by causes out of the will, according to our nature, then I maintain that a moral nature has no more to do with the feeling of responsibility than any other nature.

Perhaps the difficulty may be made more obvious in this way. It will be admitted that brutes are possessed of various natures, some innocent or useful, otherwise noxious, but all alike irresponsible in a moral point of view. But why? Simply because they act in accordance with their natures. They possess, each according to its proper nature, certain appetites and susceptibilities which are stimulated and acted upon by their appropriate objects in the world of the senses; and the relation—the law of action and reaction—subsisting between these specific susceptibilities and their corresponding outward objects, constitutes their nature. They have a power of selecting and choosing in the world of sense the objects appropriate to the wants of their nature; but that nature is the sole law of their being. Their power of choice is but a part of it, instrumental in accomplishing its ends, but not capable of rising above it, of controlling its impulses, and of determining itself with reference to a purely ideal law, distinct from their nature. They act in accordance with the law of cause and effect, which constitutes their several natures, and cannot do otherwise. They are, therefore not responsible—not capable of guilt, or of remorse.

Now let us suppose another being, possessing, in addition to the susceptibilities of the brute, certain other specific susceptibilities with their correlative objects, either in the sensible world, or in a future world, but that these are subjected, like the other, to the same binding and inalienable law of cause and effect. What, I ask, is the amount of the difference thus supposed between this being and the brute? The supposed addition, it is to be understood, is merely an addition to its nature; and the only power of will belonging to it is, as in the case of the brute, only a capacity of choosing and acting uniformly in accordance with its nature. These additional susceptibilities still act but as they are acted upon; and the will is determined accordingly. What advantage is gained in this case by calling these supposed additions moral affections, and their correlative stimulants moral causes? Do we thereby find any rational ground for the feeling of moral responsibility, for conscience, for remorse? The being acts according to its nature, and why is it blameworthy more than the brute? If the moral law existing out of the will be a power or cause which, in its relation to the specific susceptibility of the moral being, produces under the same circumstances uniformly the same result, according to the law of cause and effect; if the acts of the will be subject to the same law, as mere links in the chain of antecedents and consequents, and thus a part of our nature, what is gained, I ask again, by the distinction of a moral and a physical nature? It is still only a nature under the law of cause and effect, and the liberty of the moral being is under the same condition with the liberty of the brute. Both are free to follow and fulfil the law of their nature, and both are alike bound by that law, as by an adamantine chain. The very conditions of the law preclude the possibility of a power to act otherwise than according to their nature. They preclude the very idea of a free-will, and render the feeling of moral responsibility not an enigma merely, not a mystery, but a self-contradiction and an absurdity.

Turn the matter as we will—call these correlatives, namely, the inherent susceptibilities and the causes acting on them from without, natural, or moral, or spiritual—so long as their action and reaction, or the law of reciprocity, which constitutes their specific natures, is considered as the controlling law of our whole being, so long as we refuse to admit the existence in the will of a power capable of rising above this law, and controlling its operation by an act of absolute self-determination, so long we shall be involved in perplexities both in morals and religion. At all events, the only method of avoiding them will be to adopt the creed of the Necessitarians entire, to give man over to an irresponsible nature as a better sort of animal, and resolve the will of the Supreme Reason into a blind and irrational Fate.

I am well aware of the objections that will be made to this statement, and especially the demonstrated incomprehensibleness of a self-determining power. To this I may be permitted to answer, that, admitting the power to originate an act or state of mind may be beyond the capacity of our understandings to comprehend, it is still not contradictory to reason; and that I find it more easy to believe the existence of that which is simply incomprehensible to my understanding, than of that which involves an absurdity for my reason. I venture to affirm, moreover, that however we may bring our understandings into bondage to the more comprehensible doctrine, simply because it is comprehensible under the forms of the understanding, every man does, in fact, believe himself possessed of freedom in the higher sense of self-determination. Every man's conscience commands him to believe it, as the only rational ground of moral responsibility. Every man's conscience, too, betrays the fact that he does believe it, whenever for a moment he indulges the feeling either of moral self-approbation, or of remorse. Nor can we on any other grounds justify the ways of God to man upon the supposition that he inflicts or will inflict any other punishment than that which is simply remedial or disciplinary. But this subject will be found more fully explained in the course of the Work. My present object is merely to show the necessity of some system in relation to these subjects different from the received one.

It may perhaps be thought, that the language used above is too strong and too positive. But I venture to ask every candid man, at least every one who has not committed himself by writing and publishing on the subject, whether in considering the great questions connected with moral accountability and the doctrine of rewards and punishments, he has not felt himself pressed with such difficulties as those above stated; and whether he has ever been able fully to satisfy his reason, that there was not a lurking contradiction in the idea of a being created and placed under the law of its nature, and possessing at the same time a feeling of moral obligation to fulfil a law above its nature. That many have been in this state of mind I know. I know, too, that some whose moral and religious feelings had led them to a full belief in the doctrines of spiritual religion, but who at the same time had been taught to receive the prevailing opinions in metaphysics, have found

these opinions carrying them unavoidably, if they would be
consequent in their reasonings, and not do violence to their
reason, to adopt a system of religion which does not profess
to be spiritual, and thus have been compelled to choose
between their philosophy and their religion. In most cases
indeed, where men reflect at all, I am satisfied that it
requires all the force of authority, and all the influence of
education, to carry the mind over these difficulties; and
that then it is only by a vague belief that, though we
cannot see how, there must be some method of reconciling
what seems to be so contradictory.

If examples were wanting to prove that serious and
trying difficulties are felt to exist here, enough may be
found, as it has appeared to me, in the controversy respecting the nature and origin of sin, which is at this
moment interesting the public mind. Let any impartial
observer trace the progress of that discussion, and after
examining the distinctions which are made or attempted
to be made, decide whether the subject, as there presented,
be not involved in difficulties, which cannot be solved on
the principles to which, hitherto, both parties have adhered;
whether, holding as they do the same premises in regard to
the freedom of the will, they can avoid coming to the same
conclusion in regard to the nature and origin of sin; whether in fact the distinctions aimed at must not prove
merely verbal distinctions, and the controversy a fruitless
one. But in the September number of the "Christian
Spectator" for 1829,[1] the reader will find remarks on this
subject, to which I beg leave to refer him, and which I
could wish him attentively to consider in connection with

[1] The 'Quarterly Christian Spectator,' of New Haven, U.S. The
letter referred to is signed "Pacificus," and appeared in answer to a
review of "Taylor and Harvey" (American divines), "On Human
Depravity," which had appeared in the previous number of the
Q. C. S.—ED.

the remarks which I have made. I allude to the correspondence with the editors near the end of the number.
The letter there inserted is said to be, and obviously is,
from the pen of a very learned and able writer; and I
confess it has been no small gratification and encouragement to me, while labouring to bring this Work and this
subject before the public, to find such a state of feeling
expressed, concerning the great question at issue, by such a
writer. It will be seen by reference to p. 545 of the C. S.,
that he places the "*nucleus* of the dispute" just where
it is placed in this Work and in the above remarks.
It will be seen, too, that by throwing authorities aside,
and studying his own mind, he has "come seriously to
doubt," whether the received opinions with regard to
motives, the law of *cause and effect*, and the *freedom of the
will*, may not be erroneous. They appear to him "to be
bordering on fatalism, if not actually embracing it." He
doubts whether the mind may not have within itself the
adequate cause of its own acts; whether indeed it have
not a self-determining power, "for the power in question
involves the idea of originating volition. Less than this
it cannot be conceived to involve, and yet be *free* agency."
Now, this is just the view offered in the present Work;
and, as it seems to me, these are just the doubts and conclusions which every one will entertain, who lays aside
authority, and reflects upon the goings-on of his own mind,
and the dictates of his own reason and conscience.

But let us look for a moment at the remarks of the
editors in reply to the letter above quoted. They maintain,
in relation to original sin and the perversion of the will,
that from either the *original* or the *acquired* strength of
certain natural appetites, principles of self-love, &c., "left
to themselves," the corruption of the heart will certainly
follow. "In every instance the will does, in fact, yield to
the demands of these. But whenever it thus yielded, *there*

was power to the contrary ; otherwise there could be no freedom of moral action." Now I beg leave to place my finger on the phrase in italics, and ask the editors what they mean by it. If they hold the common doctrines with regard to the relation of cause and effect, and with regard to power as connected with that relation, and apply these to the acts of the will, I can see no more possibility of conceiving a *power to the contrary* in this case, than of conceiving such a power in the current of a river. But if they mean to assert the existence in the will of an *actual* power to rise above the demands of appetite, &c., above the law of nature and to decide *arbitrarily,* whether to yield or not to yield, then they admit that the will is not determined *absolutely* by the extraneous *cause,* but is in fact *self*-determined. They agree with the letter-writer ; and the question for them is at rest. Thus, whatever distinctions may be attempted here, there can be no real distinction but between an irresponsible nature and a will that is self-determined.

I cannot but be aware, that the views of the Will here exhibited will meet with strong prejudices in a large portion, at least, of our religious community. I could wish that all such would carefully distinguish between the Author's views of the doctrines of religion and the philosophical grounds on which he supposes those doctrines are to be defended. If no one disputes, and I trust no one will dispute, the substantial orthodoxy of the Work, without first carefully examining what has been the orthodoxy of the church in general, and of the great body of the Reformers, then I should hope it may be wisely considered, whether, as a question of philosophy, the metaphysical principles of this Work are not in themselves more in accordance with the doctrines of a spiritual religion, and better suited to their explanation and defence, than those above treated of. If on examination it cannot be disputed that they are, then, if not before, I trust the two systems may be compared without undue partiality, and the simple question of the truth of each may be determined by that calm and persevering reflection, which alone can determine questions of this sort.

If the system here taught be true, then it will follow, not, be it observed, that our religion is necessarily wrong, or our essential faith erroneous, but that the *philosophical grounds*, on which we are accustomed to defend our faith, are unsafe, and that their *natural tendency* is to error. If the spirit of the Gospel still exert its influence; if a truly spiritual religion be maintained, it is in *opposition* to our philosophy, and not at all by its aid. I know it will be said, that the practical results of our peculiar forms of doctrine are at variance with these remarks. But this I am not prepared to admit. True, religion and religious institutions have flourished; the Gospel, in many parts of our country, has been affectionately and faithfully preached by great and good men; the word and the Spirit of God have been communicated to us in rich abundance; and I rejoice with heartfelt joy and thanksgiving, in the belief, that thereby multitudes have been regenerated to a new and spiritual life. But so were equal or greater effects produced under the preaching of Baxter, and Howe, and other good and faithful men of the same age, with none of the peculiarities of our theological systems. Neither reason nor experience indeed furnish any ground for believing that the living and life-giving power of the Divine Word has ever derived any portion of its efficacy, in the conversion of the heart to God, from the forms of metaphysical theology, with which the human understanding has invested it. It requires, moreover, but little knowledge of the history of philosophy, and of the writings of the 16th and 17th centuries to know, that the opinions of the Reformers, and of all the great divines of that period, on subjects of this sort, were far different from those of

Mr. Locke and his followers, and were in fact essentially the same with those taught in this Work. This last remark applies not only to the views entertained by the eminent philosophers and divines of that period on the particular subject above discussed, but to the distinctions made, and the language employed, by them with reference to other points of no less importance in the constitution of our being.

It must have been observed by the reader of the foregoing pages, that I have used several words, especially *understanding* and *reason*, in a sense somewhat diverse from their present acceptation; and the occasion of this I suppose would be partly understood from my having already directed the attention of the reader to the distinction exhibited between these words in the Work, and from the remarks made on the ambiguity of the word "reason" in its common use. I now proceed to remark, that the ambiguity spoken of, and the consequent perplexity in regard to the use and authority of reason, have arisen from the habit of using, since the time of Locke, the terms understanding and reason indiscriminately, and thus confounding a distinction clearly marked in the philosophy and in the language of the older writers. Alas! had the *terms* only been confounded, or had we suffered only an inconvenient ambiguity of language, there would be comparatively little cause for earnestness upon the subject; or had our views of the things signified by these terms been only partially confused, and had we still retained correct notions of our prerogative, as rational and spiritual beings, the consequences might have been less deplorable. But the misfortune is, that the powers of understanding and reason have not merely been blended and confounded in the view of our philosophy, the higher and far more characteristic, as an essential constituent of our proper humanity, has been as it were obscured and hidden from our observation in the inferior power, which belongs to us in common with the brutes which perish. According to the old, the more spiritual, and genuine philosophy, the distinguishing attributes of our humanity—that *image of* God in which man alone was created of all the dwellers upon earth, and in virtue of which he was placed at the head of this lower world, was said to be found in the *reason* and *free-will*. But understanding these in their strict and proper sense, and according to the true *ideas* of them, as contemplated by the older metaphysicians, we have literally, if the system of Locke and the popular philosophy of the day be true, neither the one nor the other of these—neither reason nor free-will. What they esteemed the image of God in the soul, and considered as distinguishing us specifically, and so vastly too, above each and all of the irrational animals, is found, according to this system, to have in fact no real existence. The reality neither of the free-will, nor of any of those laws or ideas, which spring from, or rather constitute reason, can be authenticated by the sort of proof which is demanded, and we must therefore relinquish our prerogative, and take our place with becoming humility among our more unpretending companions. In the ascending series of powers, enumerated by Milton, with so much philosophical truth, as well as beauty of language, in the fifth book of Paradise Lost, he mentions

> *Fancy* and *understanding*, whence the soul
> REASON receives. And reason is her *being*,
> Discursive or intuitive.

But the highest power here, that which is the being of the soul, considered as any thing differing in kind from the understanding, has no place in our popular metaphysics. Thus we have only the *understanding*, "the faculty judging according to sense," a faculty of abstracting and generalizing, of contrivance and forecast, as the highest of our intellectual powers; and this, we are expressly taught, belongs to us in common with brutes. Nay, these views of our essential being, consequences and all, are adopted by men, whom one would suppose religion, if not philosophy, should have taught their utter inadequateness to. the true and essential constituents of our humanity. Dr. Paley tells us in his Natural Theology, that only " CONTRIVANCE," a power obviously and confessedly belonging to brutes, is necessary to constitute *personality*. His whole system both of theology and morals neither teaches, nor implies, the existence of any specific difference either between the understanding and reason, or between nature and the will. It does not imply the existence of any power in man, which does not obviously belong, in a greater or less degree, to irrational animals. Dr. Fleming, another reverend prelate in the English Church, in his " Philosophy of Zoology," maintains in express terms that we have no faculties differing in kind from those which belong to brutes. How many other learned; and reverend, and wise men adopt the same opinions, I know not: though these are obviously not the peculiar views of the individuals, but conclusions resulting from the essential principles of their system. If, then, there is no better *system*, if this be the genuine philosophy, and founded in the nature of things, there is no help for us, and we must believe it—*if we can*. But most certainly it will follow, that we ought, as fast as the pre-judices of education will permit, to rid ourselves of certain notions of prerogative, and certain feelings of our own superiority, which somehow have been strangely prevalent among our race. For though we have indeed, according to this system, a little *more* understanding than other animals —can abstract and generalize and forecast events, and the consequences of our actions, and compare motives *more* skilfully than they : though we have thus *more* knowledge and can circumvent them ; though we have *more* power and can subdue them ; yet, as to any *distinctive* and *peculiar* characteristic—as to any inherent and essential *worth*, we are after all but little better—though we may be better off—than our dogs and horses. There is no essential difference, and we may rationally doubt—at least we might do so, if by the supposition we were rational beings— whether our fellow animals of the kennel and the stall are not unjustly deprived of certain *personal rights*, and whether a dog charged with trespass may not *rationally* claim to be tried by a jury of his *peers*. Now however trifling and ridiculous this may appear, I would ask in truth and sober- ness, if it be not a fair and legitimate inference from the premises, and whether the *absurdity* of the one does not *demonstrate* the utter falsity of the other. And where, I would beg to know, shall we look, according to the popular system of philosophy, for that *image of God* in which we are created ? Is it a thing of *degrees ?* And is it simply because we have something *more* of the same faculties which belong to brutes, that we become the objects of God's special and fatherly care, the *distinguished* objects of his Providence, and the *sole* objects of his Grace ?—*Doth God take care for oxen ?* But why not ?

I assure my readers, that I have no desire to treat with disrespect and contumely the opinions of great or good men ; but the distinction in question, and the assertion and exhibition of the higher prerogatives of reason, as an essen- tial constituent of our being, are so vitally important, in my apprehension, to the formation and support of any rational system of philosophy, and—no less than the dis- tinction before treated of—so pregnant of consequences to the interests of truth, in morals, and religion, and indeed of all truth, that mere opinion and the authority of names may well be disregarded. The discussion, moreover, relates to facts, and to such facts, too, as are not to be learned from the instruction, or received on the authority, of any man. They must be ascertained by every man for himself, by

reflection upon the processes and laws of his own inward
being, or they are not learned at all to any valuable purpose.
We do indeed find in ourselves then, as no one will deny,
certain powers of intelligence, which we have abundant
reason to believe the brutes possess in common with us in a
greater or less degree. The functions of the understanding,
as treated of in the popular systems of metaphysics, its
faculties of attention, of abstraction, of generalization, the
power of forethought and contrivance, of adapting means
to ends, and the law of association, may be, so far as we can
judge, severally represented more or less adequately in the
instinctive intelligence of the higher orders of brutes. But,
not to anticipate too far a topic treated of in the Work, do
these, or any and all the faculties which we discover in
irrational animals, satisfactorily account to a reflecting
mind for all the *phenomena* which are presented to our
observation in our own consciousness ? Would any sup-
posable addition to the *degree* merely of those powers
which we ascribe to brutes, render them *rational* beings, and
remove the sacred distinction, which law and reason have
sanctioned, between things and persons ? Will any such
addition account for our having—what the brute is not
supposed to have—the pure *ideas* of the geometrician, the
power of ideal construction, the intuition of geometrical or
other necessary and universal truths ? Would it give rise,
in irrational animals, to a *law of moral rectitude* and *to
conscience* — to the feelings of moral *responsibility* and
remorse ? Would it awaken them to a reflective self-consciousness, and lead them to form and contemplate the
ideas of the *soul*, of *free-will*, of *immortality*, and of God.
It seems to me, that we have only to reflect for a serious
hour upon what we mean by these, and then to compare
them with our notion of what belongs to a brute, its
inherent powers and their correlative objects, to feel that
they are utterly incompatible—that in the possession of

these we enjoy a prerogative which we cannot disclaim without a violation of reason, and a voluntary abasement of ourselves—and that we must therefore be possessed of some *peculiar* powers—of some source of ideas *distinct* from the understanding, differing *in kind* from any and all of those which belong to us in common with inferior and irrational animals.

But what these powers are, or what is the precise nature of the distinction between the understanding and reason, it is not my province, nor have I undertaken, to show. My object is merely to illustrate its necessity, and the palpable obscurity, vagueness, and deficiency, in this respect, of the mode of philosophizing, which is held in so high honour among us. The distinction itself will be found illustrated with some of its important bearings in the Work, and in the notes attached to it ; and cannot be too carefully studied —in connection with that between nature and the will—by the student who would acquire distinct and intelligible notions of what constitutes the truly spiritual in our being, or find rational grounds for the possibility of a truly spiritual religion. Indeed, could I succeed in fixing the attention of the reader upon this distinction, in such a way as to secure his candid and reflecting perusal of the Work, I should consider any personal effort or sacrifice abundantly recompensed. Nor am I alone in this view of its importance. A literary friend, whose opinion on this subject would be valued by all who knew the soundness of his scholarship, says in a letter just now received,—" if you can once get the attention of thinking men fixed on his distinction between the reason and the understanding, you will have done enough to reward the labour of a life. As prominent a place as it holds in the writings of Coleridge, he seems to me far enough from making too much of it." No person of serious and philosophical mind, I am confident, can reflect upon the subject, enough to understand it in its various aspects, without arriving at the same views of the *importance* of the distinction, whatever may be his conviction with regard to its truth.

But, indeed, the only grounds which I find, to apprehend that the reality of the distinction and the importance of the consequence resulting from it, will be much longer denied and rejected among us, is in the overweening assurance which prevails with regard to the adequateness and perfection of the system of philosophy which is already received. It is taken for granted, as a fact undisputed and indisputable, that this is the most enlightened age of the world, not only with regard to the more general diffusion of certain points of practical knowledge; in which, probably, it may be so, but *in all respects;* that our whole system of the philosophy of mind as derived from Lord Bacon, especially, is the only one, which has any claims to common sense; and that all distinctions not recognized in that are consequently unworthy of our regard. What those Reformers, to whose transcendant powers of mind, and to whose characters as truly spiritual divines, we are accustomed to look with feelings of so much general regard, might find to say in favour of their philosophy, few take the pains to inquire. Neither they nor the great philosophers with whom they held communion on subjects of this sort can appear among us to speak in their own defence: and even the huge folios and quartos, in which, though dead, they yet speak—and ought to be heard—have seldom strayed to this side of the Atlantic. All our information respecting their philosophical opinions, and the grounds on which they defended them, has been received from writers, who were confessedly advocating a system of recent growth, at open war with every thing more ancient, and who, in the great abundance of their self-complacency, have represented their own discoveries as containing the sum and substance of all philosophy, and the accumulated

treasures of ancient wisdom as unworthy the attention of
"this enlightened age." Be it so—yet the *foolishness*
of antiquity, if it be *of God*, may prove *wiser than men*. It
may be found that the philosophy of the Reformers and
their religion are essentially connected, and must stand or
fall together. It may at length be discovered that a system
of religion essentially spiritual, and a system of philosophy
which excludes the very idea of all spiritual power and
agency, in their only distinctive and proper character,
cannot be consistently associated together.

It is our peculiar misfortune in this country that, while
the philosophy of Locke and the Scottish writers has been
received in full faith, as the only rational system, and its
leading principles especially passed off as unquestionable,
the strong attachment to religion, and the fondness for
speculation, by both of which we are strongly characterized,
have led us to combine and associate these principles, such
as they are, with our religious interests and opinions, so
variously and so intimately, that by most persons they are
considered as necessary parts of the same system; and
from being so long contemplated together, the rejection of
one seems impossible without doing violence to the other.
Yet how much evidence might not an impartial observer
find in examining the theological discussions which have
prevailed, the speculative systems which have been formed
and arrayed against each other, for the last seventy years,
to convince him that there must be some discordance in
the elements, some principle of secret but irreconcilable
hostility between a philosophy and a religion, which, under
every ingenious variety of form and shaping, still stand
aloof from each other and refuse to cohere. For is it not
a fact, that in regard to every speculative system which has
been formed on these philosophical principles,—to every
new shaping of theory which has been devised and has
gained adherents among us,—is it not a fact, I ask, that, to

all, except those adherents, the *system*—the philosophical *theory*—has seemed dangerous in its tendency, and at war with orthodox views of religion—perhaps even with the attributes of God ? Nay, to bring the matter still nearer and more plainly to view, I ask, whether at this moment the organs and particular friends of our leading theological seminaries in New England, both devotedly attached to an orthodox and spiritual system of religion, and expressing mutual confidence as to the *essentials* of their mutual faith, do not each consider the other as holding a philosophical *theory* subversive of orthodoxy ? If I am not misinformed, this is the simple fact.

Now, if these things be so, I would ask again with all earnestness, and out of regard to the interests of truth alone, whether serious and reflecting men may not be permitted, without the charge of heresy in RELIGION, to stand in doubt of this PHILOSOPHY *altogether;* whether these facts which will not be disputed, do not furnish just grounds for suspicion, that the principles of our philosophy may be erroneous, or at least induce us to look with candour and impartiality at the claims of another and a different system ?

What are the claims of the system, to which the attention of the public is invited in this Work, can be understood fully, only by a careful and reflecting examination of its principles in connection with the conscious wants of our own inward being—the requirements of our own reason and consciences. Its purpose and tendency, I have endeavoured in some measure to exhibit; and if the influence of authority, which the prevailing system furnishes against it, can and must be counteracted by anything of a like kind—(and whatever professions we may make, the influence of authority produces at least a predisposing effect upon our minds)—the remarks which I have made, will show, that the principles here taught are not wholly unauthorized by men, whom we have been taught to reverence among the great and good. I cannot but add, as a matter of simple justice to the question, that however our prevailing system of philosophizing may have appealed to the authority of Lord Bacon, it needs but a candid examination of his writings, especially the first part of his *Novum Organum*, to be convinced that such an appeal is without grounds; and that in fact the fundamental principles of his philosophy are the same with those taught in this work. The great distinction especially, between the understanding and the reason, is clearly and fully recognized; and as a philosopher he would be far more properly associated with Plato, or even Aristotle, than with the modern philosophers, who have miscalled their systems by his name. In our own times, moreover, there is abundant evidence, whatever may be thought of the principles of this Work here, that the same general views of philosophy are regaining their ascendancy elsewhere. In Great Britain there are not few, who begin to believe that the deeptoned and sublime eloquence of Coleridge on these great subjects may have something to claim their attention besides a few peculiarities of language. In Paris, the doctrines of a rational and spiritual system of philosophy are taught to listening and admiring thousands by one of the most learned and eloquent philosophers of the age; and in Germany, if I mistake not, the same general views are adopted by the serious friends of religious truth among her great and learned men.

Such—as I have no doubt—must be the case, wherever thinking men can be brought distinctly and impartially to examine their claims; and indeed to those who shall study and comprehend the general history of philosophy, it must always be matter of special wonder, that in a Christian community, anxiously striving to explain and defend the doctrines of Christianity in their spiritual sense, there

should have been a long-continued and tenacious adherence
to philosophical principles, so subversive of their faith in
everything distinctively spiritual; while those of an
opposite tendency, and claiming a near relationship and
correspondence with the truly spiritual in the Christian
system, and the mysteries of its sublime faith, were looked
upon with suspicion and jealousy, as unintelligible or
dangerous metaphysics.

And here I must be allowed to add a few remarks with
regard to the popular objections against the system of
philosophy, the claims of which I am urging, especially
against the writings of the Author, under whose name it
appears in the present Work. These are various and
often contradictory, but usually have reference either to
his peculiarities of language, or to the depth—whether
apparent or real,—and the unintelligibleness, of his
thoughts.

To the first of these it seems to me a sufficient answer,
for a mind that would deal honestly and frankly by itself,
to suggest that in the very nature of things it is impossible
for a writer to express by a single word any truth, or to
mark any distinction, not recognized in the language of
his day, unless he adopts a word entirely new, or gives to
one already in use a new and more peculiar sense. Now
in communicating truths, which the writer deems of great
and fundamental importance, shall he thus appropriate a
single word old or new, or trust to the vagueness of
perpetual circumlocution? Admitting for example, the
existence of the important distinction, for which this writer
contends, between the understanding and reason, and that
this distinction when recognized at all, is confounded in
the common use of language by employing the words
indiscriminately, shall he still use these words indiscriminately, and either invent a new word, or mark the distinction by descriptive circumlocutions, or shall he assign

a more distinctive and precise meaning to the words already used ? It seems to me obviously more in accordance with the laws and genius of language to take the course which he has adopted. But in this case and in many others, where his language seems peculiar, it cannot be denied that the words had already been employed in the same sense, and the same distinctions recognized, by the older and many of the most distinguished writers in the language.

With regard to the more important objection, that the *thoughts* of Coleridge are *unintelligible*, if it be intended to imply, that his language is not in itself expressive of an intelligible meaning, or that he affects the appearance of depth and mystery, while his thoughts are common-place, it is an objection, which no one who has read his Works attentively, and acquired a feeling of interest for them, will treat their Author with so much disrespect as to answer at all. Every such reader *knows* that he uses words uniformly with astonishing precision, and that language becomes, in his use of it—in a degree, of which few writers can give us a conception—a living power, " consubstantial " with the power of thought, that gave birth to it, and awakening and calling into action a corresponding energy in our own minds. There is little encouragement, moreover, to answer the objections of any man, who will permit himself to be incurably prejudiced against an Author by a few peculiarities of language, or an apparent difficulty of being understood, and without inquiring into the cause of that difficulty, where at the same time he cannot but see and acknowledge the presence of great intellectual and moral power.

But if it be intended by the objection to say simply, that the thoughts of the Author are often difficult to be apprehended—that he makes large demands not only upon the attention, but upon the reflecting and thinking powers, of his readers, the fact is not, and need not be, denied ; and

e 2

it will only remain to be decided, whether the instruction offered, as the reward, will repay us for the expenditure of thought required, or can be obtained for less. I know it is customary in this country, as well as in Great Britain— and that too among men from whom different language might be expected—to affect either contempt or modesty, in regard to all that is more than common-place in philosophy, and especially "Coleridge's Metaphysics," as "too deep for them." Now it may not be every man's duty, or in every man's power, to devote to such studies the time and thought necessary to understand the deep things of philosophy. But for one who professes to be a scholar, and to cherish a manly love of truth for the truth's sake, to object to a system of metaphysics because it is "too *deep* for him," must be either a disingenuous insinuation, that its depths are not worth exploring—which is more than the objector knows—or a confession, that—with all his professed love of truth and knowledge—he prefers to "sleep after dinner." The misfortune is, that men have been cheated into a belief, that all philosophy and metaphysics worth knowing are contained in a few volumes, which can be understood with little expense of thought; and that they may very well spare themselves the vexation of trying to comprehend the depths of "Coleridge's Metaphysics." According to the popular notions of the day, it is a very easy matter to understand the philosophy of mind. A new work on philosophy is as easy to read as the last new novel; and superficial, would-be scholars, who have a very sensible horror at the thought of studying Algebra, or the doctrine of fluxions, can yet go through a course of moral sciences, and know all about the philosophy of the mind.

Now why will not men of sense, and men who have any just pretensions to scholarship, see that there must of necessity be gross sophistry somewhere in any system of metaphysics, which pretends to give us an adequate and scientific self-knowledge—to render comprehensible to us the mysterious laws of our own inward being, with less manly and persevering effort of thought on our part, than is confessedly required to comprehend the simplest of those sciences, all of which are but some of the *phœnomena* from which the laws in question are to be inferred?—Why will they not see and acknowledge—what one would suppose a moment's reflection would teach them—that to attain true self-knowledge by reflection upon the objects of our inward consciousness—not merely to understand the motives of our conduct as conscientious Christians, but to know ourselves scientifically as philosophers—must, of necessity, be the most deep and difficult of all our attainments in knowledge? I trust that what I have already said will be sufficient to expose the absurdity of objections against metaphysics in general, and do something towards showing, that we are in actual and urgent need of a system somewhat deeper than those, the contradictions of which have not without reason made the name of philosophy a terror to the friends of truth and of religion. "False metaphysics can be effectually counteracted by true metaphysics alone; and if the reasoning be clear, solid, and pertinent, the truth deduced can never be the less valuable on account of the depth from which it may have been drawn." It is a fact, too, of great importance to be kept in mind, in relation to this subject, that in the study of ourselves—in attaining a knowledge of our own being,—there are truths of vast concernment, and lying at a great depth, which yet no man can draw for another. However the depth may have been fathomed, and the same truth brought up by others, for a light and a joy to their own minds, it must still remain, and be sought for by us, each for himself, at the bottom of the well.

The system of philosophy here taught does not profess to make men philosophers, or—which ought to mean the same thing—to guide them to the knowledge of themselves, without the labour both of attention and of severe thinking. If it did so, it would have, like the more popular works of philosophy, far less affinity than it now has, with the mysteries of religion, and those profound truths concerning our spiritual being and destiny, which are revealed in the *things hard to be understood* of St. Paul and of the *beloved disciple.* For I cannot but remind my readers again, that the Author does not undertake to teach us the philosophy of the human mind, with the exclusion of the truths and influences of religion. He would not undertake to philosophize respecting the being and character of man, and at the same time exclude from his view the very principle which constitutes his proper humanity: he would not, in teaching the doctrine of the solar system, omit to mention the sun, and the law of gravitation. He professes to investigate and unfold the being of man *as man*, in his higher, his peculiar, and distinguishing attributes. These it is, which are hard to be understood, and to apprehend which requires the exercise of deep reflection and exhausting thought. Nor in aiming at this object would he consider it very philosophical to reject the aid and instruction of eminent writers on the subject of religion, or even of the volume of Revelation itself. He would consider St. Augustine as none the less a philosopher, because he became a Christian. The Apostles John and Paul were, in the view of this system of philosophy, the most rational of all writers, and the New Testament the most philosophical of all books. They are so because they unfold more fully, than any other, the true and essential principles of our being; because they give us a clearer and deeper insight into those constituent laws of our humanity, which as men, and therefore as philosophers, we are most concerned to know. Not only to those, who seek the practical self-knowledge of the humble, spiritually-minded Christian, but to those also, who are impelled by the "heaven descended γνῶθι σεαυτόν" to study themselves as philosophers, and to make self-knowledge a science, the truths of Scripture are a light and a revelation. The more earnestly we reflect upon these and refer them, whether as Christians or as philosophers, to the movements of our inward being—to the laws which reveal themselves in our own consciousness, the more fully shall we understand, not only the language of Scripture, but all that most demands and excites the curiosity of the genuine philosopher in the mysterious character of man. It is by this guiding light, that we can best search into and apprehend the constitution of that "marvellous microcosm," which, the more it has been known, has awakened more deeply the wonder and admiration of the true philosopher in every age.

Nor would the Author of this Work, or those who have imbibed the spirit of his system, join with the philosophers of the day in throwing aside and treating with a contempt, as ignorant as it is arrogant, the treasures of ancient wisdom. *He*, says the son of Sirach, *that giveth his mind to the law of the Most High, and is occupied in the meditation thereof, will seek out the wisdom of all the ancient.* In the estimation of the true philosopher, the case should not be greatly altered in the present day ; and now that two thousand years have added such rich and manifold abundance to those ancient "sayings of the wise," he will still approach them with reverence, and receive their instruction with gladness of heart. In seeking to explore and unfold these deeper and more solemn mysteries of our being, which inspire us with awe, while they baffle our comprehension, he will especially beware of trusting to his own understanding, or of contradicting, in compliance with the self-flattering inventions of a single age, the universal faith and consciousness of the human race. On such subjects, though he would call no man master, yet neither would he willingly forego the aids to be derived, in the search after truth, from those great oracles of human wisdom—those giants in intellectual power who from generation to generation were admired and venerated by the great and good. Much less could he think it becoming, or consistent with his duty to hazard the publication of his own thoughts on subjects of the deepest concernment, and on which minds of greatest depth and power had been occupied in former ages, while confessedly ignorant alike of their doctrines and of the arguments by which they are sustained.

It is in this spirit, that the Author of the work here offered to the public has prepared himself to deserve the candid and even confiding attention of his readers, with reference to the great subject of which he treats.

And although the claims of the Work upon our attention, as of every other work, must depend more upon its inherent and essential character, than upon the worth and authority of its Author, it may yet be of service to the reader to know, that he is no hasty or unfurnished adventurer in the department of authorship to which the Work belongs. The discriminating reader of this Work cannot fail to discover his profound knowledge of the philosophy of language, the principles of its construction, and the laws of its interpretation. In others of his works, perhaps more fully than in this, there is evidence of an unrivalled mastery over all that pertains both to logic and philology. It has been already intimated, that he is no contemner of the great writers of antiquity and of their wise sentences; and probably few English scholars, even in those days when there were giants of learning in Great Britain, had minds more richly furnished with the treasures of ancient lore. But especially will the reader of this Work observe with admiration the profoundness of his philosophical attainments, and his thorough and intimate knowledge, not only of the works and systems of Plato and Aristotle, and of the celebrated philosophers of modern times, but of those too much neglected writings of the Greek and Roman Fathers, and of the great leaders of the Reformation, which more particularly qualified him for discussing the subjects of the present Work. If these qualifications, and—with all these, and above all—a disposition professed and made evident seriously to value them, chiefly as they enable him more fully and clearly to apprehend and illustrate the truths of the Christian system,—if these, I say, can give an Author a claim to serious and thoughtful attention, then may the Work here offered urge its claim upon the reader. My own regard for the cause of truth, for the interests of philosophy, of reason, and of religion, lead me to hope that they may not be urged in vain.

Of his general claims to our regard, whether from exalted personal and moral worth, or from the magnificence of his intellectual powers, and the vast extent and variety of his accumulated stores of knowledge, I shall not venture to speak. If it be true indeed that a really great mind can be worthily commended only by those who adequately both appreciate and *comprehend* its greatness, there are few who should undertake to estimate, and set forth in appropriate terms, the intellectual power and moral worth of Samuel Taylor Coleridge. Neither he, nor the public, would be benefited by such commendations as I could bestow. The few among us who have read his works with the attention which they deserve, are at no loss what rank to assign him among the writers of the present age; to those who have not, any language which I might use would appear hyperbolical and extravagant. The character and influence of his principles as a philosopher, a moralist, and a Christian, and of the writings by which he is enforcing them, do not ultimately depend upon the estimation in which they may now be held; and to posterity he may safely entrust those "productive ideas" and "living words"—those

—— truths that wake,
To perish never,

the possession of which will be for their benefit, and connected with which, in the language of the Son of Sirach,—
His own memorial shall not depart away, and his name shall live from generation to generation.

J. M.[1]

[1] Dr. Marsh's signature to the "Advertisement" published with the above essay in its revised American edition was dated "Burlington, Dec. 26, 1839."—ED.

AIDS TO REFLECTION.

INTRODUCTORY APHORISMS.

APHORISM I.

IN philosophy equally as in poetry, it is the highest and most useful prerogative of genius to produce the strongest impressions of novelty, while it rescues admitted truths from the neglect caused by the very circumstance of their universal admission. Extremes meet. Truths, of all others the most awful and interesting, are too often considered as *so* true, that they lose all the power of truth, and lie bed-ridden in the dormitory of the soul, side by side with the most despised and exploded errors.

APHORISM II.

There is one sure way of giving freshness and importance to the most *common-place* maxims—that of *reflecting* on them in direct reference to our own state and conduct, to our own past and future being.

APHORISM III.

To restore a common-place truth to its first *uncommon* lustre, you need only *translate* it into action. But to do this, you must have *reflected* on its truth.

APHORISM IV.

LEIGHTON AND COLERIDGE.

It is the advice of the wise man, 'Dwell at home,' or, with yourself; and though there are very few that do this, yet it is surprising that the greatest part of mankind cannot be prevailed upon, at least to visit themselves sometimes; but, according to the saying of the wise Solomon, *The eyes of the fool are in the ends of the earth.*

A reflecting mind, says an ancient writer, is the spring and source of every good thing. (*'Omnis boni principium intellectus cogitabundus.'*) It is at once the disgrace and the misery of men, that they live without fore-thought. Suppose yourself fronting a mirror. Now what the objects behind you are to their images at the same apparent distance before you, such is Reflection to Fore-thought. As a man without Fore-thought scarcely deserves the name of a man, so Fore-thought without Reflection is but a metaphorical phrase for the *instinct* of a beast.

APHORISM V.

As a fruit-tree is more valuable than any one of its fruits singly, or even than all its fruits of a single season, so the noblest object of reflection is the mind itself, by which we reflect:

And as the blossoms, the green, and the ripe, fruit, of an orange-tree are more beautiful to behold when on the tree and seen as one with it, than the same growth detached and seen successively, after their importation into another country and different clime; so is it with the manifold objects of reflection, when they are considered principally in reference to the reflective power, and as part and parcel of the same. No object, of whatever value our passions may represent it, but becomes *foreign* to us, as soon as it is altogether unconnected with our intellectual, moral, and spiritual life. To be *ours*, it must be referred to the mind either as motive, or consequence, or symptom.

APHORISM VI.

LEIGHTON.

He who teaches men the principles and precepts of
spiritual wisdom, before their minds are called off from
foreign objects, and turned inward upon themselves, might
as well write his instructions, as the Sibyl wrote her prophecies, on the loose leaves of trees, and commit them to
the mercy of the inconstant winds.

APHORISM VII.

In order to learn we must *attend*: in order to profit by
what we have learnt, we must *think*—*i. e.* reflect. He only
thinks who *reflects*.[1]

APHORISM VIII.

LEIGHTON AND COLERIDGE.

It is a matter of great difficulty, and requires no ordinary skill and address, to fix the attention of men on the
world within them, to induce them to study the processes
and superintend the works which they are themselves
carrying on in their own minds; in short, to awaken in
them both the faculty of thought[2] and the inclination to

---

[1] The indisposition, nay, the angry aversion to *think*, even in persons
who are most willing to *attend*, and on the subjects to which they are
giving studious *attention*—as Political Economy, Biblical Theology,
Classical Antiquities, and the like,—is the phenomenon that forces itself
on my notice afresh, every time I enter into the society of persons in
the higher ranks. To assign a *feeling* and a determination of *will*, as
a satisfactory reason for embracing or rejecting this or that opinion
or belief, is of ordinary occurrence, and sure to obtain the sympathy
and the suffrages of the company. And yet to me, this seems little less
irrational than to apply the nose to a picture, and to decide on its
genuineness by the sense of smell.

[2] *Distinction between Thought and Attention.*—By THOUGHT is here
meant the voluntary reproduction in our own minds of those states of
consciousness, or (to use a phrase more familiar to the religious reader)
of those inward experiences, to which, as to his best and most authentic
documents, the teacher of moral or religious truth refers us. In ATTEN-
TION, we keep the mind *passive*: in THOUGHT we rouse it into activity.

exercise it. For alas! the largest part of mankind are nowhere greater strangers than at home.

APHORISM IX.

Life is the one universal soul, which, by virtue of the enlivening BREATH, and the informing WORD, all organized bodies have in common, each *after its kind*. This, therefore, all animals possess, and man as an animal. But, in addition to this, God transfused into man a higher gift, and specially imbreathed:—even a living (that is, self-subsisting) soul, a soul having its life in itself. "And man became a living soul." He did not merely *possess* it, he *became* it. It was his proper *being*, his truest *self*, *the* man *in* the man. None then, not one of human kind, so poor and destitute, but there is provided for him, even in his present state, *a house not built with hands*. Aye, and spite of the philosophy (falsely so called) which mistakes the causes, the conditions, and the occasions of our becoming *conscious* of certain truths and realities for the truths and realities themselves—a house gloriously furnished. Nothing is wanted but the eye, which is the light of this house, the light which is the eye of this soul. This *seeing* light, this *enlightening* eye, is Reflection.[1] It is more, indeed, than is ordinarily meant by that word; but it is what a Christian ought to. mean by it, and to know too, whence it first came, and still continues to come—of what light even this light is *but* a reflection. This, too, is THOUGHT; and all thought is but unthinking that does not flow out of this, or tend towards it.

In the former, we submit to an impression—we keep the mind steady in order to *receive* the stamp. In the latter, we seek to *imitate* the artist, while we ourselves make a copy or duplicate of his work. We may learn arithmetic, or the elements of geometry, by continued attention alone; but *self*-knowledge, or an insight into the laws and constitutions of the human mind, and the *grounds* of religion and true morality, in addition to the effort of attention requires the energy of THOUGHT.

[1] The "*dianoia*" of St. John, I. Ep. v. 20, inaccurately rendered "understanding" in our translation. To exhibit the full force of the Greek word, we must say, *a power of discernment by Reason.*

APHORISM X.

Self-superintendence! that anything should overlook itself! Is not this a paradox, and hard to understand? It is, indeed, difficult, and to the imbruted sensualist a direct contradiction: and yet most truly does the poet exclaim,

> —— Unless *above* himself he can
> Erect himself, how mean a thing is man!

APHORISM XI.

An hour of solitude passed in sincere and earnest prayer, or the conflict with, and conquest over, a single passion or "subtle bosom sin," will teach us more of thought, will more effectually awaken the *faculty*, and form the *habit*, of reflection, than a year's study in the schools without them.

APHORISM XII.

In a world, the opinions of which are drawn from out-side shows, many things may be *paradoxical*, (that is, con-trary to the common notion) and nevertheless true: nay, *because* they are true. How should it be otherwise, as long as the imagination of the Worldling is wholly occupied by surfaces, while the Christian's thoughts are fixed on the substance, that which *is* and abides, and which, *because* it is the substance,[1] the outward senses cannot recognize. Tertullian had good reason for his assertion, that the simplest Christian (if indeed a Christian) knows more than the most accomplished irreligious philosopher.

[1] *Quod stat subtus*, that which stands *beneath*, and (as it were) sup-ports, the appearance. In a language like ours, where so many words are derived from other languages, there are few modes of instruction more useful or more amusing than that of accustoming young people to seek for the etymology, or primary meaning, of the words they use. There are cases, in which more knowledge of more value may be con-veyed by the history of a *word*, than by the history of a campaign.

COMMENT.

Let it not, however, be forgotten, that the powers of the understanding and the intellectual graces are precious gifts of God; and that every Christian, according to the opportunities vouchsafed to him, is bound to cultivate the one and to acquire the other. Indeed, he is scarcely a Christian who wilfully neglects so to do. What says the apostle? Add to your faith *knowledge*, and to knowledge *manly energy*: for this is the proper rendering of ἀρὲτην, and not *virtue*, at least in the present and ordinary acceptation of the word.[1]

APHORISM XIII.

Never yet did there exist a full faith in the Divine Word (by whom *light*, as well as immortality, was brought into the world), which did not expand the intellect, while it purified the heart;—which did not multiply the aims and objects of the understanding, while it fixed and simplified those of the desires and passions.[2]

---

[1] I am not ashamed to confess that I dislike the frequent use of the word virtue, instead of righteousness, in the pulpit: and that in prayer or preaching before a Christian community, it sounds too much like *Pagan* philosophy. The passage in St. Peter's epistle is the only scripture authority that can be pretended for its use, and I think it right, therefore, to notice that it rests either on an oversight of the translators, or on a change in the meaning of the word since their time.

[2] The effects of a zealous ministry on the intellects and acquirements of the labouring classes are not only attested by Baxter, and the Presbyterian divines, but admitted by Bishop Burnet, who, during his mission in the west of Scotland, was "amazed to find a poor commonalty so able to argue," &c. But we need not go to a sister church for proof or example. The diffusion of light and knowledge through this kingdom, by the exertions of the Bishops and clergy, by Episcopalians and Puritans, from Edward VI. to the Restoration, was as wonderful as it is praiseworthy, and may be justly placed among the most remarkable facts of history.

COMMENT.

If acquiescence without insight; if warmth without light; if an immunity from doubt, given and guaranteed by a resolute ignorance; if the habit of *taking for granted* the words of a catechism, remembered or forgotten; if a mere *sensation* of positiveness substituted—I will not say, for the *sense* of *certainty ;* but—for that calm assurance, the very means and conditions of which it supersedes; if a belief that seeks the darkness, and yet strikes no root, immovable as the limpet from the rock, and like the limpet, fixed there by mere force of adhesion; if these suffice to make men Christians, in what sense could the apostle affirm that believers receive, not indeed worldly wisdom, that comes to nought, but the wisdom of God, that we might *know and comprehend* the things that are freely given to us of God ? On what grounds could he denounce the sincerest *fervour* of spirit as *defective,* where it does not likewise bring forth fruits in the UNDERSTANDING ?

APHORISM XIV.

In our present state, it is little less than impossible that the affections should be kept constant to an object which gives no employment to the understanding, and yet cannot be made manifest to the senses. The exercise of the reasoning and reflecting powers, increasing insight, and enlarging views, are requisite to keep alive the substantial faith in the heart.

APHORISM XV.

In the state of perfection, perhaps, all other faculties may be swallowed up in love, or superseded by immediate vision; but it is on the wings of the CHERUBIM, that is, (according to the interpretation of the ancient Hebrew doctors) the *intellectual* powers and energies, that we must first be borne up to the "pure empyrean." It must be seraphs, and not the hearts of imperfect mortals, that can burn unfuelled and self-fed. *Give me understanding* (is the prayer of the Royal Psalmist), *and I shall observe thy law with my whole heart.*[1]—*Thy law is exceeding broad*—that is, comprehensive, pregnant, containing far more than the apparent import of the words on a first perusal. *It is my meditation all the day.*[2]

COMMENT.

It is worthy of especial observation, that the Scriptures are distinguished from all other writings pretending to inspiration, by the strong and frequent recommendations of knowledge, and a spirit of inquiry. Without reflection, it is evident that neither the one can be acquired nor the other exercised.

APHORISM XVI.

The word *rational* has been strangely abused of late times. This must not, however, disincline us to the weighty consideration, that thoughtfulness, and a desire to rest all our convictions on grounds of right reasoning, are inseparable from the character of a Christian.

APHORISM XVII.

A reflecting mind is not a flower that grows wild, or comes up of its own accord. The difficulty is indeed greater than many, who mistake quick recollection for thought, are disposed to admit; but how much less than it would be, had we not been born and bred in a Christian and Protestant land, few of us are sufficiently aware. Truly may we, and thankfully ought we to, exclaim with the Psalmist: *The entrance of thy words giveth light; it giveth understanding unto the simple.*[3]

[1] Ps. cxix. 34.—ED.   [2] Ps. cxix. 97.—ED.   [3] Ps. cxix. 130.—ED.

APHORISM XVIII.

Examine the journals of our zealous missionaries, I will not say among the Hottentots or Esquimaux, but in the highly *civilized*, though fearfully *uncultivated*, inhabitants of ancient India. How often, and how feelingly, do they describe the difficulty of rendering the simplest chain of thought intelligible to the ordinary natives, the rapid exhaustion of their whole power of attention, and with what distressful effort it is exerted while it lasts! Yet it is among these that the hideous practices of self-torture chiefly prevail. O, if folly were no *easier* than wisdom, it being often so very much more *grievous*, how certainly might these unhappy slaves of superstition be converted to Christianity! But, alas! to swing by hooks passed through the back, or to walk in shoes with nails of iron pointed upwards through the soles—all this is so much less *difficult*, demands so much less exertion of the will than to *reflect*, and by reflection to gain knowledge and tranquillity!

COMMENT.

It is not true, that ignorant persons have no notion of the *advantages* of truth and knowledge. They confess, they see and bear witness to these advantages in the conduct, the immunities, and the superior powers of the possessors. Were they attainable by pilgrimages the most toilsome, or penances the most painful, we should assuredly have as many pilgrims and self-tormentors in the service of true religion, as now exist under the tyranny of Papal or Brahman superstition.

APHORISM XIX.

In countries enlightened by the gospel, however, the most formidable and (it is to be feared) the most frequent impediment to men's turning the mind inward upon themselves, is that they are afraid of what they shall find there.

There is an aching hollowness in the bosom, a dark cold speck at the heart, an obscure and boding sense of somewhat, that must be kept *out of sight* of the conscience; some secret lodger, whom they can neither resolve to eject or retain.[1]

COMMENT.

Few are so obdurate, few have sufficient strength of character, to be able to draw forth an evil tendency or immoral practice into distinct *consciousness*, without bringing it in the same moment before an awaking *conscience*. But for this very reason it becomes a duty of conscience to form the mind to a habit of distinct consciousness. An unreflecting Christian walks in twilight among snares and pitfalls ! He entreats the heavenly Father not to lead him into temptation, and yet places himself on the very edge of it, because he will not kindle the torch which his Father had given into his hands, as a means of prevention, and lest he should pray too late.

[1] The following sonnet was extracted by me from Herbert's ' Temple,' in a work long since out of print, for the purity of the language and the fulness of the sense. But I shall be excused, I trust, in repeating it here for higher merits and with higher purposes, as a forcible comment on the words in the text.

Graces vouchsafed in a Christian land.

Lord ! with what care hast thou begirt us round !
Parents first season us. Then schoolmasters
Deliver us to laws. They send us bound
To rules of reason. Holy messengers ;
Pulpits and Sundays ; sorrow dogging sin ;
Afflictions *sorted ;* anguish of all sizes ;
Fine nets and stratagems to catch us in !
Bibles laid open ; millions of surprizes ;
Blessings beforehand ; ties of gratefulness ;
The sound of glory ringing in our ears :
Without, our shame ; within, our consciences ;
Angels and grace ; eternal hopes and fears !
Yet all these fences, and their whole array,
One cunning BOSOM-SIN blows quite away.

APHORISM XX.

Among the various undertakings of men, can there be mentioned one more important, can there be conceived one more sublime, than an intention to form the human mind anew after the DIVINE IMAGE? The very intention, if it be sincere, is a ray of its dawning.

The requisites for the execution of this high intent may be comprised under three heads; the prudential, the moral, and the spiritual.

APHORISM XXI.

First, RELIGIOUS PRUDENCE.—What this is, will be best explained by its effects and operations. PRUDENCE in the service of RELIGION consists in the prevention or abatement of hindrances and distractions; and consequently in avoiding, or removing, all such circumstances as, by diverting the attention of the workman, retard the progress and hazard the safety of the work. It is likewise (I deny not) a part of this unworldly prudence, to place ourselves as much and as often as it is in our power so to do, in circumstances directly favourable to our great design; and to avail ourselves of all the *positive* helps and furtherances which these circumstances afford. But neither dare we, as Christians, forget whose and under what dominion the things are, *quæ nos circumstant*, that is, which *stand around* us. We are to remember, that it is the *world* that constitutes our outward circumstances; that in the form of the world, which is evermore at variance with the Divine form (or idea) they are cast and moulded; and that of the means and measures which the same prudence requires in the forming anew of the Divine Image in the soul, the far greater number suppose the world at enmity with our design. We are to avoid its snares, to repel its attacks, to suspect its aids and succours, and even when compelled to receive them as allies within our trenches, we are to commit the outworks alone to their charge, and to keep them at a jealous distance from the citadel. The powers of the world are often *christened*, but seldom christianized. They are but *proselytes of the outer gate ;* or like the Saxons of old, enter the land as auxiliaries,. and remain in it as conquerors and lords.

APHORISM XXII.

The rules of prudence in general, like the laws of the stone tables, are for the most part prohibitive. *Thou shalt not* is their characteristic formula : and it is an especial part of Christian prudence that it should be so. Nor would it be difficult to bring under this head, all the social obligations that arise out of the relations of the present life, which the sensual understanding (τὸ φρόνημα τῆς Σαρκὸς, *Romans* viii. 6.) is of itself able to discover, and the performance of which, under favourable circumstances, the merest worldly self-interest, without love or faith, is sufficient to enforce; but which Christian Prudence enlivens by a higher principle, and renders symbolic and sacramental. (*Ephesians* v. 32.)

COMMENT.

This then, under the appellation of prudential requisites, comes first under consideration : and may be regarded as the shrine and frame-work for the Divine image, into which the worldly human is to be transformed. We are next to bring out the Divine Portrait itself, the distinct features of its countenance, as a sojourner among men; its benign aspect turned towards its fellow-pilgrims, the extended arm, and the hand that blesseth and healeth.

APHORISM XXIII.

The outward service (Θρησκἐια [1]) of ancient religion, the

[1] See the epistle of St. James, c. i. v. 26, 27, where, in the authorized version, the Greek word θρησκἐια is falsely rendered *religion ;* whether by mistake of the translator, or from the intended sense having become obsolete, I cannot decide. At all events, for the English reader of our times it has the effect of an erroneous translation. It not only obscures the connexion of the passage, and weakens the peculiar force and

rites, ceremonies and ceremonial vestments of the old law, had morality for their substance. They were the *letter*, of which morality was the *spirit;* the enigma, of which morality was the *meaning*. But morality itself is the service and ceremonial (cultus exterior, θρησκεία) of the Christian religion. The scheme of grace and truth that *became*[1] through Jesus Christ, the faith that *looks*[2] *down*

sublimity of the thought, rendering it comparatively flat and trivial, almost indeed tautological, but has occasioned this particular verse to be perverted into a support of a very dangerous error ; and the whole epistle to be considered as a *set-off* against the epistles and declarations of St. Paul, instead of (what in fact it is) a masterly comment and confirmation of the same. I need not inform the religious reader, that James, c. i. v. 27, is the favourite text and most boasted authority of those divines who represent the Redeemer of the world as little more than a moral reformer, and the Christian faith as a code of ethics, differing from the moral system of Moses and the prophets by an additional motive ; or rather, by the additional strength and clearness which the historical fact of the resurrection has given to the same motive.

[1] The Greek word ἐγένετο, unites in itself the two senses of *began to exist* and *was made to exist*. It exemplifies the force of the *middle voice*, in distinction from the verb reflex. In answer to a note on John i. 2., in the Unitarian version of the New Testament, I think it worth noticing, that the same word is used in the very same sense by Aristophanes in that famous parody on the cosmogonies of the Mythic poets, or the creation of the finite, as delivered, or supposed to be delivered, in the Cabiric or Samothracian mysteries, in the Comedy of the Birds.

—————— γένετ᾿ Οὐρανὸς, Ὠ᾿κεανός τε
Καὶ Γῆ.

[2] James c. i. v. 25. Ὁ δὲ παρακύψας εἰς νόμον τέλειον τὸν τῆς ἐλευθερίας. The Greek word, *parakupsas*, signifies the incurvation or bending of the body in the act of *looking down into;* as, for instance, in the endeavour to see the reflected image of a star in the water at the bottom of a well. A more happy or forcible word could not have been chosen to express the nature and ultimate object of reflection, and to enforce the necessity of it, in order to discover the living fountain and spring-head of the evidence of the Christian faith in the believer himself, and at the same time to point out the seat and region, where alone it is to be found. *Quantum sumus, scimus*. That which we find within ourselves, which is more than ourselves, and yet the ground of whatever is good and permanent therein, is the substance and life of all other knowledge.

N.B. The Familists of the sixteenth century, and similar enthusiasts of later date, overlooked the essential point, that it was a *law*, and a law that involved its own end (τέλος), a *perfect* law (τέλειος) or law that perfects or completes itself; and therefore, its obligations are called, in reference to human statutes, *imperfect* duties, i.e. incoercible from

into the perfect law of liberty, has *light for its garment: its very robe is righteousness.*

COMMENT.

Herein the apostle places the pre-eminence, the peculiar and distinguishing excellence, of the Christian religion. The ritual is of the same kind, (ὁμοούσιον) though not of the same order, with the religion itself—not arbitrary or conventional, as types and hieroglyphics are in relation to the things expressed by them ; but inseparable, consubstantiated (as it were), and partaking therefore of the same life, permanence, and intrinsic worth' with its spirit and principle.

APHORISM XXIV.

Morality is the body, of which the faith in Christ is the soul—so far indeed its earthly body, as it is adapted to its state of warfare on earth, and the appointed form and instrument of its communion with the present world ; yet not "terrestrial," nor of the world, but a celestial body, and capable of being transfigured from glory to glory, in accordance with the varying circumstances and outward relations of its moving and informing spirit.

APHORISM XXV.

Woe to the man, who will believe neither power, freedom, nor morality ; because he nowhere finds either entire, or unmixed with sin, thraldom and infirmity. In the natural and intellectual realms, we distinguish what we cannot separate ; and in the moral world, we must distinguish *in order to* separate. Yea, in the clear distinction of good from evil the process of separation commences.

without. They overlooked that it was a law that *portions out* (Νόμος *from* νέμω *to allot, or make division of*) to each man the sphere and limits within which it is to be exercised—which as St. Peter notices of certain profound passages in the writings of St. Paul, (2 Pet. c. iii. v. 16.)—οἱ ἀμαθεῖς καὶ ἀστήρικτοι στρεβλῶυσιν, ὡς καὶ τὰς λοίπας γραφὰς, πρὸς τὴν ἰδίαν αὐτῶν ἀπώλειαν.

Comment.

It was customary with religious men in former times, to make a rule of taking every morning some text, or aphorism,[1] for their occasional meditation during the day, and thus to fill up the intervals of their attention to business. I do not point it out for imitation, as knowing too well, how apt these self-imposed rules are to degenerate into superstition or hollowness; otherwise I would have recommended the following as the first exercise.

APHORISM XXVI.

It is a dull and obtuse mind, that must divide in order to distinguish; but it is a still worse, that distinguishes in order to divide. In the former, we may contemplate the source of superstition and idolatry;[2] in the latter, of schism, heresy,[3] and a seditious and sectarian spirit.[4]

[1] In accordance with a preceding remark, on the use of etymology in disciplining the youthful mind to thoughtful habits, and as consistent with the title of this work, ' Aids to Reflection,' I shall offer no apology for the following and similar notes:

Aphorism, determinate position, from the Greek, *ap*, from; and *horizein*, to bound or limit; whence our horizon.—In order to get the full sense of a word, we should first present to our minds the visual image that forms its primary meaning. Draw lines of different colours round the different counties of England, and then cut out each separately, as in the common play-maps that children take to pieces and put together—so that each district can be contemplated apart from the rest, as a whole in itself. This twofold act of circumscribing, and detaching, when it is exerted by the mind on subjects of reflection and reason, is to *aphorize*, and the result an *aphorism*.

[2] Τὸ Νόητον διῃρήκασιν εἰς πολλῶν Θεῶν Ἰδιοτήτας.—*Damasc. de Myst. Egypt;* that is, They *divided* the intelligible into many and several individualities.

[3] From αἵρεσις. Though well aware of its formal and apparent derivation from *haireo*, I am inclined to refer both words to *airo*, as the primitive term, containing the primary visual image, and therefore should explain *hæresis*, as a wilful raising into public notice, an uplifting (for display) of any particular opinion differing from the established belief of the church at large, and making it a ground of schism, that is, division.

[4] I mean these words in their large and philosophic sense in relation to the *spirit*, or originating temper and tendency, and not to any one

APHORISM XXVII.

Exclusive of the abstract sciences, the largest and worthiest portion of our knowledge consists of *aphorisms* : and the greatest and best of men is but an *aphorism*.

APHORISM XXVIII.

On the prudential influence which the fear or foresight of the *consequences* of his actions, in respect of his own loss or gain, may exert on a newly-converted Believer.

PRECAUTIONARY REMARK.—I meddle not with the dispute respecting *conversion*, whether, and in what sense, necessary in all Christians. It is sufficient for my purpose, that a very *large* number of men, even in Christian countries, *need* to be converted, and that not a few, I trust, have been. The tenet becomes fanatical and dangerous, only when rare and extraordinary exceptions are made to be the general rule;—when what was vouchsafed to the apostle of the Gentiles by especial grace, and for an especial purpose, namely, a conversion[1] begun and completed in the same moment, is demanded or expected of all men, as a necessary sign and pledge of their election. Late observations have shown, that under many circumstances the magnetic needle, even after the disturbing influence has been removed, will keep wavering, and require many days before it points aright, and remains steady to the pole. So is it ordinarily with the soul, after it has begun to free itself from the disturb-

mode under which, or to any one class, in or by which it may be displayed. A seditious spirit may (it is possible, though not probable) exist in the council-chamber of a palace as strongly as in a mob in Palace-Yard; and a sectarian spirit in a cathedral, no less than in a conventicle.

[1] Whereas Christ's other disciples had a breeding under him, St. Paul was *born* an apostle; not carved out, as the rest, by degrees and in course of time, but a *fusile* apostle, an apostle poured out and cast in a mould. As Adam was a perfect man in an instant, so was St. Paul a perfect Christian. The same spirit was the lightning that melted, and the mould that received and shaped him.—Donne's Sermons—*quoted from memory*.

ing forces of the flesh and the world, and to convert[1]
itself towards God.

APHORISM XXIX.

Awakened by the cock-crow, (a sermon, a calamity, a
sick bed, or a providential escape) the Christian pilgrim
sets out in the morning twilight, while yet the truth (the
νόμος τέλειος ὁ τῆς ἐλευθερίας) is below the horizon. Certain
necessary *consequences* of his past life and his present undertaking will be *seen* by the refraction of its light : more will
be apprehended and conjectured. The phantasms, that had
predominated during the hours of darkness, are still busy.
Though they no longer present themselves as distinct forms,
they yet remain as formative motions in the pilgrim's soul,
unconscious of its own activity and overmastered by its
own workmanship. Things take the signature of thought.
The shapes of the recent dream become a *mould* for the
objects in the distance ; and these again give an outward-
ness and a sensation of reality to the shapings of the
dream. The bodings inspired by the long habit of selfishness, and self-seeking cunning, though they are now commencing the process of their purification into that fear
which is the *beginning* of wisdom, and which, as such, is
ordained to be our guide and safeguard, till the sun of love,
the perfect law of liberty, is fully arisen—these bodings
will set the fancy at work, and haply, for a time, transform
the mists of dim and imperfect knowledge into determinate
superstitions. But in either case, whether seen clearly or
dimly, whether beholden or only imagined, the *consequences*,
contemplated in their bearings on the individual's inherent[2]

---

[1] From the Latin, *convertere*—that is, by an act of the WILL *to turn*
towards the true pole, *at the same time* (for this is the force of the pre-
positive *con*) that the understanding is convinced and made aware of its
existence and direction.

[2] The following extract from Leighton's 'Theological Lectures,' sect.
II. may serve as a comment on this sentence :

"The human mind, however stunned and weakened by the fall, still
retains some faint idea of the good it has lost ; a kind of languid sense
of its misery and indigence, with affections suitable to these obscure
notions. This at least is beyond all doubt and indisputable, that all

desire of happiness and dread of pain, become *motives:* and
(unless all distinction in the words be done away with, and
either prudence or virtue be reduced to a superfluous
synonyme, a redundancy in all the languages of the civilized
world), these motives, and the acts and forbearances directly
proceeding from them, fall under the head of PRUDENCE, as
belonging to one or other of its four very distinct species.

I. It may be a prudence, that stands in opposition to a
higher moral life, and tends to preclude it, and to prevent
the soul from ever arriving at the hatred of sin for its own
exceeding sinfulness (*Rom.* vii. 13) : and this is an EVIL
PRUDENCE.

II. Or it may be a *neutral* prudence, not incompatible
with spiritual growth : and to this we may, with especial
propriety, apply the words of our Lord, "What is not
against us is for us." It is therefore an innocent, and
(being such) a proper, and COMMENDABLE PRUDENCE.

III. Or it may lead and be subservient to a higher
principle than itself. The mind and conscience of the
individual may be reconciled to it, in the foreknowledge of
the higher principle, and with a yearning towards it that
implies a foretaste of future freedom. The enfeebled con-
valescent is reconciled to his crutches, and thankfully makes
use of them, not only because they are necessary for his
immediate support, but likewise, because they are the

men wish well to themselves; nor can the mind divest itself of this propensity, without divesting itself of its being. This is what the schoolmen
mean, when in their manner of expression they say, that 'the will
(voluntas, *not* arbitrium) is carried towards happiness not simply as *will*,
but as *nature*."

I venture to remark that this position, if not more *certainly* would be
more *evidently* true, if instead of *beatitudo,* the word *indolentia* (that is,
freedom from pain, negative happiness) had been used. But this depends
on the exact meaning attached to the term *self,* of which more in another
place. One conclusion, however, follows inevitably from the preceding
position, namely, that this propensity can never be legitimately made the
principle of morality, even because it is no part or appurtenance of the
moral will ; and because the proper object of the moral principle is to
limit and control this propensity, and to determine in what it *may* be,
and in what it *ought* to be gratified ; while it is the business of philosophy
to instruct the understanding, and the office of religion to convince the
whole man, that otherwise than as a *regulated,* and of course therefore a
subordinate, end, this propensity, innate and inalienable though it be,
can never be realized or fulfilled.

means and conditions of EXERCISE; and by exercise, of establishing, *gradatim paulatim*, that strength, flexibility, and almost spontaneous obedience of the muscles, which the idea and cheering presentiment of health hold out to him. He finds their *value* in their present necessity, and their *worth* as they are the instruments of finally superseding it. This is a faithful, a WISE PRUDENCE, having indeed, its birth-place in the world, and the *wisdom of this world* for its father; but naturalized in a better land, and having the wisdom from above for its sponsor and spiritual parent. To steal a dropt feather from the spicy nest of the Phœnix, (the fond humour, I mean, of the mystic divines and allegorizers of Holy Writ,) it is the *son of Terah from Ur of the Chaldees*, who gives a tithe of all to the King of Righteousness, without father, without mother, without descent, (Νόμος αὐτονόμος), and receives a blessing on the remainder.

IV. Lastly, there is a prudence that co-exists with morality, as morality co-exists with the spiritual life: a prudence that is the organ of both, as the understanding is to the reason and the will, or as the lungs are to the heart and brain. This is A HOLY PRUDENCE, the steward faithful and discreet, (οἰκονόμος πίστος και φρόνιμος, *Luke* xii. 42), the "eldest servant" in the family of faith, *born in the house*, and "made the ruler over his lord's household."

Let not, then, I entreat you, my purpose be misunderstood; as if, in *distinguishing* virtue from prudence, I wished to divide the one from the other. True morality is hostile to that prudence only, which is preclusive of true morality. The teacher, who *subordinates* prudence to virtue, cannot be supposed to *dispense* with it; and he who teaches the proper connexion of the one with the other, does not depreciate the lower in any sense; while by making it a link of the same chain with the higher, and receiving the same influence, he raises it.

In general, Morality may be compared to the consonant, Prudence to the vowel. The former cannot be *uttered* (reduced to practice) but by means of the latter.

APHORISM XXX.

What the duties of MORALITY are, the apostle instructs
the believer in full, comprising them under the two heads
of negative and positive; negative, to keep himself pure
from the world; and positive, beneficence from lovingkindness, that is, love of his fellow-men (his kind) as himself.

APHORISM XXXI.

Last and highest, come the *spiritual*, comprising all the
truths, acts, and duties that have an especial reference to the
Timeless, the Permanent, the Eternal: to the sincere love
of the True, *as* truth; of the Good, *as* good: and of God
as both in one. It comprehends the whole ascent from
uprightness (morality, virtue, inward rectitude) to *godlikeness*, with all the acts, exercises, and disciplines of mind,
will, and affection, that are requisite or conducive to the
great design of our Redemption from the form of the evil
one, and of our second creation or birth in the divine
image.[1]

---

[1] It is worthy of observation, and may furnish a fruitful subject for
future reflection, how nearly this scriptural division coincides with the
Platonic, which, *commencing* with the prudential, or the habit of act and
purpose proceeding from enlightened self-interest, [*qui animi imperio,
corporis servitio, rerum auxilio, in proprium sui commodum et sibi pro-
vidus utitur, hunc esse prudentem statuimus*] *ascends* to the moral, that is,
to the *purifying* and *remedial* virtues; and seeks its *summit* in the imitation
of the Divine nature. In this last division, answering to that which we
have called the Spiritual, Plato includes all those inward acts and aspirations, waitings, and watchings, which have a growth in godlikeness for
their immediate purpose, and the union of the human soul with the
Supreme Good as their ultimate object. Nor was it altogether without
grounds that several of the Fathers ventured to believe that Plato had
some dim conception of the necessity of a Divine Mediator, whether
through some indistinct echo of the patriarchal faith, or some rays of
light refracted from the Hebrew prophets through a Phœnician medium,
(to which he may possibly have referred in his phrase, θεοπαραδότος
σοφία, the wisdom delivered from God), or by his own sense of the mysterious contradiction in human nature between the will and the reason,
the natural appetences and the not less innate law of conscience (*Romans*

APHORISM XXXII.

It may be an additional aid to reflection, to distinguish the three kinds severally, according to the faculty to which each corresponds, the part of our human nature which is more particularly its organ. Thus: the prudential corresponds to the sense and the understanding; the moral to the heart and the conscience; the spiritual to the will and the reason, that is, to the finite will reduced to harmony with, and in subordination to, the reason, as a ray from that true light which is both reason and will, universal reason, and will absolute.

II. 14, 15), we shall in vain attempt to determine. It is not impossible that all three may have co-operated in partially unveiling these awful truths to this plank from the wreck of paradise thrown on the shores of idolatrous Greece, to this Divine Philosopher,

> Che 'n quella schiera andó più presso al segno
> Al qual aggiunge, a chi dal cielo è dato.
>
> *Petrarch: Del Trionfo della Fama, Cap. III. 5, 6.*

REFLECTIONS,

MORAL AND RELIGIOUS APHORISMS.

ON SENSIBILITY.

IF Prudence, though practically inseparable from Morality, is not to be confounded with the Moral Principle; still less may Sensibility, that is, a constitutional quickness of Sympathy with Pain and Pleasure, and a keen sense of the gratifications that accompany social intercourse, mutual endearments, and reciprocal preferences, be mistaken, or deemed a Substitute for either. Sensibility is not even a sure pledge of a GOOD HEART, though among the most common meanings of that many-meaning and too commonly misapplied expression.

So far from being either Morality, or one with the Moral Principle, it ought not even to be placed in the same rank with Prudence. For Prudence is at least an offspring of the Understanding; but Sensibility (the Sensibility, I mean, here spoken of), is for the greater part a quality of the nerves, and a result of individual bodily temperament.

Prudence is an *active* Principle, and implies a sacrifice of Self, though only to the same Self *projected*, as it were, to a distance. But the very term Sensibility, marks its *passive* nature; and in its mere self, apart from Choice and Reflection, it proves little more than the coincidence or contagion of pleasurable or painful Sensations in different persons.

Alas! how many are there in this over-stimulated age, in which the occurrence of excessive and unhealthy sensitiveness is so frequent, as even to have reversed the current meaning of the word, *nervous.* How many are[1] there whose sensibility prompts them to remove those evils alone, which by hideous spectacle or clamorous outcry are present to their senses and disturb their selfish enjoyments. Provided the dunghill is not before their parlour window, they are contented to know that it exists, and perhaps as the hotbed on which their own luxuries are reared. Sensibility is not necessarily Benevolence. Nay, by rendering us tremblingly alive to trifling misfortunes, it frequently prevents it, and induces an effeminate Selfishness instead,

> ────── pampering the coward heart,
> With feelings all too delicate for use.
> Sweet are the Tears, that from a Howard's eye
> Drop on the cheek of one, he lifts from earth:
> And he, who works me good with unmoved face,
> Does it but half. He chills me, while he aids,
> My Benefactor, not my Brother Man.
> But even this, this *cold* benevolence,
> Seems Worth, seems Manhood, when there rise before me,
> The sluggard Pity's vision-weaving tribe,
> Who sigh for wretchedness yet shun the wretched,
> Nursing in some delicious solitude,
> Their slothful Loves and dainty Sympathies.[2]

Lastly, where Virtue is, Sensibility is the ornament and becoming Attire of Virtue. On certain occasions it may almost be said to *become*[3] Virtue. But Sensibility and all

[1] This paragraph is abridged from the *Watchman*, No. IV. March 25, 1796; respecting which the inquisitive Reader may consult my 'Literary Life.'—*Author's note* in editions 1 (1825) and 1836, since suppressed.—Ed.

[2] Coleridge's 'Reflections On Having Left a Place of Retirement,' l. 48, &c. ('Sibylline Leaves,' 1797).—Ed.

[3] There sometimes occurs an apparent *play* on words, which not only to the Moralizer, but even to the philosophical Etymologist, appears more than a mere Play. Thus in the double sense of the word, *become.* I have known persons so anxious to have their dress *become* them, as to convert it at length into their proper self, and thus actually to *become*

the amiable qualities may likewise become, and too often *have* become, the panders of Vice and the instruments of Seduction.

So must it needs be with all qualities that have their rise only in *parts* and *fragments* of our nature.   A man of warm passions may sacrifice half his estate to rescue a friend from prison; for he is naturally sympathetic, and the more social *part* of his nature happened to be upper-most.   The same man shall afterwards exhibit the same disregard of money in an attempt to seduce that friend's wife or daughter.

All the evil achieved by Hobbes, and the whole School of Materialists will appear inconsiderable, if it be compared with the mischief effected and occasioned by the senti-mental Philosophy of STERNE, and his numerous imitators. The vilest appetites and the most remorseless inconstancy towards their objects, acquired the titles of *the Heart, the irresistible Feelings, the too tender Sensibility;* and if the Frosts of Prudence, the icy chains of Human Law thawed and vanished at the genial warmth of Human *Nature,* who *could help it ?*   It was an amiable Weakness !

About this time, too, the profanation of the word Love, rose to its height.   The French Naturalists, Buffon and others, borrowed it from the sentimental Novelists : the Swedish and English Philosophers took the contagion; and the Muse of Science condescended to seek admission into the Saloons of Fashion and Frivolity, *rouged* like a harlot, and with the harlot's wanton leer.   I know not how the Annals of Guilt could be better forced into the service of Virtue, than by such a Comment on the present paragraph, as would be afforded by a selection from the sentimental correspondence produced in Courts of Justice within the last thirty years, fairly translated into the true meaning of the words, and the actual Object and Purpose of the infa-mous writers.

Do you in good earnest aim at Dignity of Character ? By all the treasures of a peaceful mind, by all the charms of an open countenance, I conjure you, O youth ! turn

---

the dress.   Such a one, (safeliest spoken of by the *neuter* pronoun), I consider as but a suit of *live* finery.   It is indifferent whether we say— It *becomes* he, or, he *becomes* it.

away from those who live in the Twilight between Vice and Virtue. Are not Reason, Discrimination, Law, and deliberate Choice, the distinguishing Characters of Humanity ? Can aught, then, worthy of a human Being, proceed from a Habit of Soul, which would exclude all these and (to borrow a metaphor from Paganism) prefer the den of Trophonius to the Temple and Oracles of the God of Light ? Can any thing *manly*, I say, proceed from those, who for Law and Light would substitute shapeless feelings, sentiments, impulses, which as far as they differ from the vital workings in the brute animals, owe the difference to their former connexion with the proper Virtues of. Humanity ; as dendrites derive the outlines, that constitute their value above other clay-stones, from the casual neighbourhood and pressure of the plants, the names of which they assume ? Remember, that Love itself in its highest earthly Bearing, as the ground of the marriage union,[1] becomes Love by an inward FIAT of the Will, by a

---

[1] It might be a mean of preventing many unhappy marriages, if the youth of both sexes had it early impressed on their minds, that Marriage contracted between Christians is a true and perfect Symbol or Mystery ; that is, the actualizing Faith being supposed to exist in the Receivers, it is an outward Sign co-essential with that which it signifies, or a living Part of that, the whole of which it represents. Marriage, therefore, in the Christian sense (*Ephesians* v. 22—33), as symbolical of the union of the Soul with Christ the Mediator, and with God through Christ, is perfectly a *sacramental* ordinance, and not retained by the Reformed Churches as one of THE Sacraments, for two reasons ; first, that the Sign is not *distinctive* of the Church of Christ, and the Ordinance not peculiar nor owing its origin to the Gospel Dispensation ; secondly, it is not of universal obligation, not a means of Grace enjoined on all Christians. In other and plainer words, Marriage does not contain in itself an open Profession of Christ, and it is not a Sacrament of the *Church*, but only of certain Individual Members of the Church. It is evident, however, that neither of these reasons affect or diminish the *religious* nature and dedicative force of the marriage Vow, or detract from the solemnity in the Apostolic Declaration : THIS IS A GREAT MYSTERY.

The interest which the state has in the appropriation of one woman to one man, and the civil obligations therefrom resulting, form an altogether distinct consideration. When I meditate on the words of the Apostle, confirmed and illustrated as they are, by so many harmonies in the Spiritual Structure of our proper Humanity, (in the image of God, male and female created he the man), and then reflect how little claim so large a number of legal cohabitations have to the name of Christian marriages—I feel inclined to doubt whether the plan of celebrating

completing and sealing Act of Moral Election, and lays claim to permanence only under the form of DUTY.

marriages universally by the Civil Magistrate, in the first instance, and leaving the *religious* Covenant and sacramental Pledge to the election of the parties themselves, adopted during the Republic in England, and in our own times by the French Legislature, was not *in fact*, whatever it might be in intention, *reverential* to Christianity. At all events, it was their own act and choice, if the parties made bad worse by the profanation of a Gospel Mystery.

PRUDENTIAL APHORISMS.

APHORISM I.

LEIGHTON AND COLERIDGE.

WITH respect to any final aim or end, the greater part of mankind live at hazard. They have no certain harbour in view, nor direct their course by any fixed star. But to him that knoweth not the port to which he is bound, no wind can be favourable; neither can he who has not yet determined at what mark he is to shoot, direct his arrow aright.

It is not, however, the less true, that there is a proper object to aim it; and if this object be meant by the term happiness, (though I think that not the most appropriate term for a state, the perfection of which consists in the exclusion of all *hap* (that is, chance), I assert that there is such a thing as human happiness, as *summum bonum*, or ultimate good. What this is, the Bible alone shows clearly and certainly, and points out the way that leads to the attainment of it. This is that which prevailed with St. Augustine to study the Scriptures, and engaged his affection to them. "In Cicero, and Plato, and other such writers," says he, "I meet with many things acutely said, and things that excite a certain warmth of emotion, but in none of them do I find these words, *Come unto me, all ye that labour, and are heavy laden, and I will give you rest.*" [1]

---

[1] *Apud Ciceronem et Platonem, aliosque ejusmodi scriptores, multa sunt acute dicta, et leniter calentia, sed in iis omnibus hoc non invenio, Venite ad me*, &c. [Matt. xii. 28.]

COMMENT.

Felicity, *in its proper* sense, is but another word for fortunateness, or happiness; and I can see no advantage in the improper use of words, when proper terms are to be found, but, on the contrary, much mischief. For, by familiarizing the mind to *equivocal* expressions, that is, such as may be taken in two or more different meanings, we introduce confusion of thought, and furnish the sophist with his best and handiest tools. For the juggle of sophistry consists, for the greater part, in using a word in one sense in the premise, and in another sense in the conclusion. We should accustom ourselves to *think*, and *reason*, in precise and stedfast terms; even when custom, or the deficiency, or the corruption of the language will not permit the same strictness in speaking. The mathematician finds this so necessary to the truths which he is seeking, that his science begins with, and is founded on, the definition of his terms. The botanist, the chemist, the anatomist, &c., feel and submit to this necessity at all costs, even at the risk of exposing their several pursuits to the ridicule of the many, by technical terms, hard to be remembered, and alike quarrelsome to the ear and the tongue. In the business of moral and religious reflection, in the acquisition of clear and distinct conceptions of our duties, and of the relations in which we stand to God, our neighbour, and ourselves, no such difficulties occur. At the utmost we have only to rescue words, already existing and familiar, from the false or vague meanings imposed on them by carelessness, or by the clipping and debasing misusage of the market. And surely happiness, duty, faith, truth, and final blessedness, are matters of deeper and dearer interest for all men, than circles to the geometrician, or the characters of plants to the botanist, or the affinities and combining principle of the elements of bodies to the chemist, or even than the mechanism (fearful and wonderful though it be!) of the perishable Tabernacle of the Soul can be to the anatomist. Among the *aids to* reflection, place the following maxim prominent: let distinctness in expression advance side by side with distinction in thought.

For one useless subtlety in our elder divines and moralists, I will produce ten sophisms of equivocation in the writings of our modern preceptors: and for one error resulting from excess in *distinguishing* the indifferent, I would show ten mischievous delusions from the habit of *confounding* the diverse.   Whether you are reflecting for yourself, or reasoning with another, make it a rule to ask yourself the precise meaning of the word, on which the point in question appears to turn ; and if it may be (that is, by writers of authority *has been*) used in several senses, then ask which of these the word is at present intended to convey.   By this mean, and scarcely without it, you will at length acquire a facility in detecting the *quid pro quo*.   And believe me, in so doing you will enable yourself to disarm and expose four-fifths of the main arguments of our most renowned irreligious philosophers, ancient and modern. For the *quid pro quo* is at once the rock and quarry, on and with which the strong-holds of disbelief, materialism, and (more pernicious still) epicurean morality are built.

APHORISM II.

Leighton.

If we seriously consider what religion is, we shall find the saying of the wise king Solomon to be unexceptionably true : *Her ways are ways of pleasantness, and all her paths are peace.*[1]

Doth religion require anything of us more than that we live *soberly, righteously, and godly in this present world ?* Now what, I pray, can be more pleasant or peaceable than these ?   Temperance is always at leisure, luxury always in a hurry : the latter weakens the body and pollutes the soul; the former is the sanctity, purity, and sound state of both.   It is one of Epicurus's fixed maxims, " That life can never be pleasant without virtue."

---

[1] Proverbs iii. 17.—Ed.

COMMENT.

In the works of moralists, both Christian and Pagan, it is often asserted (indeed there are few common-places of more frequent recurrence) that the happiness even of this life consists solely, or principally, in virtue; that virtue is the only happiness of this life; that virtue is the truest *pleasure*, &c.

I doubt not that the meaning, which the writers intended to convey by these and the like expressions, was true and wise. But I deem it safer to say, that in all the outward relations of this life, in all our outward conduct and actions, both in what we should do, and in what we should abstain from, the dictates of virtue are the very same with those of self-interest, tending *to*, though they do not proceed *from*, the same point. For the outward object of virtue being the greatest producible sum of happiness of all men, it must needs include the object of an intelligent self-love, which is the greatest possible happiness of one individual; for what is true of all, must be true of each. Hence, you cannot become better (that is, more virtuous), but you will become happier: and you cannot become worse (that is, more vicious), without an increase of misery (or at the best a proportional loss of enjoyment) as the consequence. If the thing were not inconsistent with our well-being, and known to be so, it would not have been classed as a *vice*. Thus what in an enfeebled and disordered mind is called prudence, is the voice of nature in a healthful state: as is proved by the known fact, that the prudential duties, (that is, those actions which are commanded by virtue *because* they are prescribed by prudence), the animals fulfil by natural instinct.

The pleasure that accompanies or depends on a healthy and vigorous body will be the consequence and reward of a temperate life and habits of active industry, whether this pleasure were or were not the chief or only determining *motive* thereto. Virtue may, possibly, add to the pleasure a good of another kind, a higher good, perhaps, than the worldly mind is capable of understanding, a spiritual complacency, of which in your present sensualized state you can form no idea. It may *add*, I say, but it cannot detract from it. Thus the reflected rays of the sun that gave light, distinction, and endless multiformity to the mind, afford at the same time the pleasurable sensation of *warmth* to the body.

If then the time has not yet come for any thing higher, act on the maxim of seeking the most pleasure with the least pain : and, if only you do not seek where you yourself *know* it will not be found, this very pleasure and this freedom from the disquietude of pain may produce in you a state of being directly and indirectly favourable to the germination and up-spring of a nobler seed. If it be true, that men are miserable because they are wicked, it is likewise true, that many men are wicked because they are miserable. Health, cheerfulness, and easy circumstances, the ordinary consequence of Temperance and Industry, will at least leave the field clear and open, will tend to preserve the scales of the judgment even : while the consciousness of possessing the esteem, respect, and sympathy of your neighbours, and the sense of your own increasing power and influence, can scarcely fail to give a tone of dignity to your mind, and incline you to hope nobly of your own Being. And thus they may prepare and predispose you to the sense and acknowledgment of a principle, differing not merely in degree but in *kind* from the faculties and instincts of the higher and more intelligent species of animals, (the ant, the beaver, the elephant), and which principle is therefore your proper humanity. And on this account and with this view alone may certain modes of pleasurable or *agreeable* sensation, without confusion of terms, be honoured with the title of refined, intellectual, ennobling pleasures. For Pleasure (and happiness in its proper sense is but the continuity and sum-total of the pleasure which is allotted or happens to a man, and hence by the Greeks called εὐτυχία, that is, good-hap, or more religiously εὐδαιμονία, that is, favourable providence)—pleasure, I say, consists in the harmony between the specific excitability of a living creature, and the exciting causes correspondent thereto. Considered therefore exclusively in and for itself, the only question is, *quantum*, not *quale ?* *How much on the whole ?* the contrary, that is, the painful and disagreeable having been subtracted. The quality is a matter of *taste : et de gustibus non est disputandum* No man can judge for another.

This, I repeat, appears to me a safer language than the sentences quoted above, (that virtue alone is happiness; that happiness consists in virtue, &c.) sayings which I find it hard to reconcile with other positions of still more frequent occurrence in the same divines, or with the declaration of St. Paul : "If in this life only we have hope, we are of all men most miserable."

At all events, I should rely far more confidently on the converse, namely, that to be vicious is to be *miserable.* Few men are so utterly reprobate, so imbruted by their vices, as not to have some lucid, or at least quiet and sober, intervals; and in such a moment, *dum desæviunt iræ,* few can stand up unshaken against the appeal to their own experience—what have been the wages of sin ? what has the devil done for you ? What sort of master have you *found* him ? Then let us in befitting *detail,* and by a series of questions that ask no loud, and are secure against any *false,* answer, urge home the proof of the position, that to be vicious is to be wretched : adding the fearful corollary, that if even in the body, which as long as life is in it can never be *wholly* bereaved of pleasurable sensations, vice is found to be misery, what must it not be in the world to come? There, where even the *crime* is no longer possible, much less the gratifications that once attended it—where nothing of vice remains but its guilt and its misery—vice must be misery itself, all and utter misery.—So best, if I err not, may the motives of prudence be held forth, and the impulses of self-love be awakened, in alliance with truth, and free from the danger of confounding things (the Laws of Duty, I mean, and the Maxims of Interest) which it deeply concerns us to keep distinct, inasmuch as this distinction and the faith therein are essential to our moral nature, and this again the ground-work and pre-condition of the spiritual state, in which the Humanity strives after Godliness, and, in the name and power, and through the prevenient and assisting grace, of the Mediator, will not strive in vain.

The *advantages* of a life passed in conformity with the

precepts of virtue and religion, and in how many and various respects they recommend virtue and religion, even on grounds of prudence, form a delightful subject of meditation, and a source of refreshing thought to good and pious men. Nor is it strange if, transported with the view, such persons should sometimes discourse on the charms of forms and colours to men whose eyes are not yet *couched;* or that they occasionally seem to invert the relations of cause and effect, and forget that there are acts and determinations of the will and affections, the *consequences* of which may be plainly foreseen, and yet cannot be made our proper and primary *motives* for such acts and determinations, without destroying or entirely altering the distinct nature and character of the latter. Sophron is well informed that wealth and extensive patronage will be the consequence of his obtaining the love and esteem of Constantia. But if the foreknowledge of this consequence were, and were *found out* to be, Sophron's main and determining motive for seeking this love and esteem; and if Constantia were a woman that merited, or was capable of feeling, either the one or the other; would not Sophron find (and deservedly too) aversion and contempt in their stead? Wherein, if not in this, differs the friendship of worldlings from true friendship? Without kind offices and useful services, wherever the power and opportunity occur, love would be a hollow pretence. Yet what noble mind would not be offended, if he were thought to value the love for the sake of the services, and not rather the services for the sake of the love?

APHORISM III.

Though prudence in itself is neither virtue nor spiritual holiness, yet without prudence, or in opposition to it, neither virtue nor holiness can exist.

APHORISM IV.

Art thou under the tyranny of sin ? a slave to vicious habits ? at enmity with God, and a skulking fugitive from thy own conscience ? O, how idle the dispute, whether the listening to the dictates of *prudence* from prudential and self-interested motives be virtue or merit, when the *not* listening is guilt, misery, madness, and despair ! The best, the most *Christianlike* pity thou canst show, is to take pity on thy own soul. The best and most acceptable service thou canst render, is to do justice and show mercy to *thyself*.

MORAL AND RELIGIOUS APHORISMS.

APHORISM I.

LEIGHTON.

WHAT the Apostles were in an extraordinary way, befitting the first annunciation of a Religion for all Mankind, this all Teachers of Moral Truth, who aim to prepare for its reception by calling the attention of men to the Law in their own hearts, may, without presumption, consider themselves to be, under ordinary gifts and circumstances; namely, Ambassadors for the Greatest of Kings, and upon no mean employment, the great Treaty of Peace and Reconcilement betwixt him and Mankind.

APHORISM II.

On the Feelings Natural to Ingenuous Minds towards those who have first led them to Reflect.

LEIGHTON.

Though Divine Truths are to be received equally from every Minister alike, yet it must be acknowledged that there is something (we know not what to call it) of a more acceptable reception of those which at first were the means of bringing men to God, than of others ; like the opinion some have of physicians, whom they love.

APHORISM III.

LEIGHTON AND COLERIDGE.

The worth and value of Knowledge is in proportion to the worth and value of its object. What, then, is the best knowledge?

The exactest knowledge of things, is, to know them in their causes; it is then an excellent thing, and worthy of their endeavours who are most desirous of knowledge, to know the best things in their highest causes; and the happiest way of attaining to this knowledge, is, to possess those things, and to know them in experience.

APHORISM IV.

LEIGHTON.

It is one main point of happiness, that he that is happy doth know and judge himself to be so. This being the peculiar good of a reasonable creature, it is to be enjoyed in a reasonable way. It is not as the dull resting of a stone, or any other natural body in its natural place; but the knowledge and consideration of it is the fruition of it, the very relishing and tasting of its sweetness.

REMARK.

As in a Christian land we receive the lessons of Morality in connexion with the Doctrines of Revealed Religion, we cannot too early free the mind from prejudices widely spread, in part through the abuse, but far more from ignorance, of the true meaning of doctrinal Terms, which, however they may have been perverted to the purposes of Fanaticism, are not only scriptural, but of too frequent occurrence in Scripture to be overlooked or passed by in silence. The following extract, therefore, deserves attention, as clearing the doctrine of Salvation, in connexion with the divine Foreknowledge, from all objections on the score of Morality, by the just and impressive view which the Archbishop here gives of those occasional revolutionary moments, that *Turn of the Tide* in the mind and character of certain Individuals, which (taking a religious course, and referred immediately to the Author of all Good) were in his day, more generally than at present, entitled EFFECTUAL CALLING. The theological interpretation and the philosophic validity of this Apostolic Triad, Election, Salvation, and Effectual Calling, (the latter being the intermediate), will be found among the Comments on the Aphorisms of Spiritual Import. For our present purpose it will be sufficient if only I prove, that the Doctrines are in themselves *innocuous*, and may be both holden and taught without any practical ill-consequences, and without detriment to the moral frame.

APHORISM V.

LEIGHTON.

Two Links of the Chain (namely, Election and Salvation) are up in heaven in God's own hand ; but this middle one (that is, Effectual Calling) is let down to earth, into the hearts of his children, and they laying hold on it have sure hold on the other two : for no power can sever them. If, therefore, they can read the characters of God's image in their own souls, those are the counterpart of the golden characters of his love, in which their names are written in the book of life. Their believing writes their names under the promises of the revealed book of life (the Scriptures) and thus ascertains them, that the same names are in the secret book of life which God hath by himself from eternity. So that finding the stream of grace in their hearts, though they see not the fountain whence it flows, nor the ocean into which it returns, yet they know that it hath its source in their eternal election, and shall empty itself into the ocean of their eternal salvation.

If *election, effectual calling,* and *salvation* be inseparably linked together, then, by any one of them a man may lay hold upon all the rest, and may know that his hold is sure ; and this is the way wherein we may attain and ought to seek, the comfortable assurance of the love of God. Therefore *make your calling sure*, and by that your *election;* for that being done, this follows of itself. We are not to pry immediately into the decree, but to read it in the performance. Though the mariner sees not the *pole-star*, yet the needle of the compass which points to it, tells him which way he sails : thus the heart that is touched with the loadstone of divine love, trembling with godly fear, and yet still looking towards God by fixed believing, interprets the fear by the love *in* the fear, and tells the soul that its course is heavenward, towards the haven of eternal rest. He that loves may be sure he was loved first; and he that chooses God for his delight and portion, may conclude confidently, that God has chosen him to be one of those that shall enjoy him, and be happy in him for ever; for that our love and electing of him is but the return and repercussion of the beams of his love shining upon us.

Although from present unsanctification, a man cannot infer that he is not *elected;* for the decree may, for part of a man's life, run (as it were) underground ; yet this is sure, that that estate leads to death, and unless it be broken, will prove the black line of reprobation. A man hath no portion amongst the children of God, nor can read one word of comfort in all the promises that belong to them, while he remains unholy.

REMARK.

In addition to the preceding, I select the following paragraphs, as having nowhere seen the terms, Spirit, the Gifts of the Spirit, and the like, so effectually vindicated from the sneers of the Sciolist on the one hand, and protected from the perversions of the Fanatic on the other. In these paragraphs the Archbishop at once shatters and precipitates the only draw-bridge between the fanatical and the orthodox doctrine of Grace, and the Gifts of the Spirit. In Scripture the term Spirit, as a power or property seated in the human soul, never stands singly, but is always *specified* by a genitive case following ; this being a Hebraism instead of the adjective which the writer would have used if he had *thought*, as well as *written*, in Greek. It is "the Spirit of Meekness" (a meek Spirit), or "the Spirit of Chastity," and the like. The moral Result, the specific Form and Character in which the Spirit *manifests* its presence, is the only sure pledge and token of its presence; which is to be, and which safely may be, inferred from its practical effects, but of which an *immediate* knowledge or consciousness is impossible; and every pretence to such knowledge is either hypocrisy or fanatical delusion.

APHORISM VI.

LEIGHTON.

If any pretend that they have the Spirit, and so turn away from the straight rule of the Holy Scriptures, they have a spirit indeed, but it is a fanatical spirit, the spirit of delusion and giddiness; but the Spirit of God, that leads his children in the way of truth, and is for that purpose sent them from Heaven to guide them thither, squares their thoughts and ways to that rule whereof it is author, and that word which was inspired by it, and sanctifies them to obedience. *He that saith I know him, and keepeth not his commandments, is a liar, and the truth is not in him.* (1 *John* ii. 4.)

Now this Spirit which sanctifieth, and sanctifieth to obedience, is within us the evidence of our election, and the earnest of our salvation. And whoso are not sanctified and led by this Spirit, the Apostle tells us what is their condition: *If any man have not the Spirit of Christ, he is none of his.*[1] The stones which are appointed for that glorious temple above, are hewn, and polished, and prepared for it here; as the stones were wrought and prepared in the mountains, for building the temple at Jerusalem.

COMMENT.

There are many serious and sincere Christians who have not attained to a fulness of knowledge and insight, but are

[1] Romans viii. 9.—ED.

well and judiciously employed in preparing for it. Even
these may study the master-works of our elder Divines
with safety and advantage, if they will accustom themselves to translate the theological terms into their *moral*
equivalents; saying to themselves—This may not be *all*
that is meant, but this *is* meant, and it is that portion
of the meaning, which belongs to *me* in the present stage of
my progress. For example: render the words, sanctification
of the Spirit, or the sanctifying influences of the Spirit, by
Purity in Life and Action from a pure Principle.

We need only reflect on our own experience to be convinced, that the man makes the *motive*, and not the motive
the man. What is a strong motive to one man, is no motive
at all to another. If, then, the man determines the motive,
what determines the man—to a good and worthy act, we
will say, or a virtuous Course of Conduct ? The intelligent
Will, or the self-determining Power ? True, *in part* it is;
and therefore the Will is pre-eminently the *spiritual* Constituent in our Being. But will any reflecting man admit,
that his own Will is the only and sufficient determinant of
all he *is*, and all he does ? Is nothing to be attributed to
the harmony of the system to which he belongs, and to the
pre-established Fitness of the Objects and Agents, known
and unknown, that surround him, as acting *on* the will,
though, doubtless, *with* it likewise ? a process, which the
co-instantaneous yet reciprocal action of the air and the
vital energy of the lungs in breathing may help to render
intelligible.

Again : in the world we see every where evidences of a
Unity, which the component parts are so far from explaining, that they necessarily pre-suppose it as the cause and
condition of their existing *as* those parts ; or even of their
existing at all. This antecedent Unity, or Cause and
Principle of each Union, it has since the time of Bacon and
Kepler been customary to call a law. This crocus, for
instance : or any other flower the reader may have in
sight or choose to bring before his fancy. That the root,
stem, leaves, petals, &c. cohere to one plant, is owing to an
antecedent Power or Principle in the Seed, which existed
before a single particle of the matters that constitute the
size and visibility of the crocus, had been attracted from

the surrounding soil, air, and moisture. Shall we turn to
the seed ? Here too the same necessity meets us. An
antecedent Unity (I speak not of the parent plant, but of
an agency antecedent in the order of operance, yet remaining present as the conservative and reproductive Power)
must here too be supposed. Analyze the seed with the
finest tools, and let the Solar Microscope come in aid of
your senses, what do you find ? Means and instruments, a
wondrous Fairy-tale of Nature, magazines of food, stores
of various sorts, pipes, spiracles, defences—a house of
many chambers, and the owner and inhabitant invisible !
Reflect further on the countless millions of seeds of the
same name, each more than numerically differenced from
every other : and further yet, reflect on the requisite harmony of all surrounding things, each of which necessitates
the same process of thought, and the coherence of all of
which to a System, a World, demands its own adequate
Antecedent Unity, which must therefore of necessity be
present *to* all and *in* all, yet in no wise excluding or suspending the individual Law or Principle of Union in each.
Now will Reason, will common Sense, endure the assumption, that in the material and visible system, it is highly
reasonable to believe a Universal Power, as the cause and
pre-condition of the harmony of all particular Wholes, each
of which involves the working Principle of its own Union
—that it is reasonable, I say, to believe this respecting the
Aggregate of *Objects*, which without a *Subject* (that is, a sentient and intelligent Existence) would be purposeless ; and
yet unreasonable and even superstitious or enthusiastic
to entertain a similar Belief in relation to the System of
intelligent and self-conscious Beings, to the moral and
personal World ? But if in *this* too, in the great Community
of *Persons*, it is rational to infer a One universal Presence,
a One present to all and in all, is it not most irrational to
suppose that a finite Will can exclude it ?

Whenever, therefore, the man is determined (that is,
impelled and directed) to act in harmony of inter-communion, must not something be attributed to this all-present
power as acting *in* the Will ? and by what fitter names
can we call this than the LAW, as empowering; THE WORD,
as informing ; and THE SPIRIT, as actuating ?

What has'been here said amounts (I am aware) only to
a negative conception; but this is all that is required for
a mind at that period of its growth which we are now supposing, and as long as Religion is contemplated under the
form of Morality. A *positive* insight belongs to a more
advanced stage; for spiritual truths can only spiritually be
discerned. This we know from Revelation, and (the existence of spiritual truths being granted) Philosophy is compelled to draw the same conclusion. But though merely
negative, it is sufficient to render the union of Religion
and Morality *conceivable;* sufficient to satisfy an unprejudiced inquirer, that the spiritual Doctrines of the Christian
Religion are not at war with the reasoning Faculty, and
that if they do not run on the same Line (or Radius) with
the Understanding, yet neither do they cut or cross it. It
is sufficient, in short, to prove, that some distinct and consistent meaning may be attached to the assertion of the
learned and philosophic Apostle, that "the Spirit itself
beareth witness with our spirit"[1]—that is, with *the Will,*
as the supernatural in man and the Principle of our Personality—of that, I mean, by which we are responsible
Agents; *Persons,* and not merely living *Things.*[2]

It will suffice to satisfy a reflecting mind, that even at
the porch and threshold of Revealed Truth there is a great
and worthy sense in which we may believe the Apostle's
assurance, that not only doth "the Spirit aid our infirmities;"[3]
that is, *act on* the Will by a predisposing influence *from
without,* as it were, though in a spiritual manner, and
without suspending or destroying its freedom (the possibility of which is proved to us in the influences of education, of providential occurrences, and, above all, of example) but that in regenerate souls it may act *in* the will;

---

[1] Romans viii. 16.—ED.

[2] Whatever is comprised in the Chain and Mechanism of Cause and
Effect, of course *necessitated,* and having its necessity in some other
thing, antecedent or concurrent—this is said to be *Natural;* and the
Aggregate and System of all such things is NATURE. It is, therefore,
a contradiction in terms to include in this the Free-will, of which the
verbal definition is—that which *originates* an act or state of Being. In
this sense, therefore, which is the sense of St. Paul, and indeed of the
New Testament throughout, Spiritual and Supernatural are synonymous.

[3] Romans viii. 26.—ED.

that uniting and becoming one [1] with our will or spirit, it may make "intercession for us;"[2] nay, in this intimate union taking upon itself the form of our infirmities, may intercede for us "with groanings that cannot be uttered." Nor is there any danger of Fanaticism or Enthusiasm as the consequence of such a belief, if only the attention be carefully and earnestly drawn to the concluding words of the sentence (*Romans* viii. v. 26); if only the due force and *full* import be given to the term *unutterable* or *incommunicable*, in St. Paul's use of it. In this, the strictest and most proper use of the term, it signifies, that the subject, of which it is predicated, is something which I *cannot*, which from the nature of the thing it is impossible that I should, communicate to any human mind (even of a person under the same conditions with myself) so as to make it *in itself* the object of his direct and immediate consciousness. It cannot be the object of *my own* direct and immediate Consciousness; but must be *inferred*. Inferred it may be *from* its workings; it cannot be perceived *in* them. And, thanks to God! in all points in which the knowledge is of high and necessary concern to our moral and religious welfare, from the *Effects* it may safely be inferred by us, from the Workings it may be assuredly known; and the Scriptures furnish the clear and unfailing Rules for directing the inquiry, and for drawing the conclusion.

If any reflecting mind be surprised that the aids of the Divine Spirit should be deeper than our Consciousness can reach, it must arise from the not having attended sufficiently to the nature and necessary limits of human Consciousness. For the same impossibility exists as to the first acts and movements of our own will—the farthest distance our recollection can follow back the traces, never leads us to the first foot-mark—the lowest depth that the light of our Consciousness can visit even with a doubtful

---

[1] Some distant and faint *similitude* of this, that merely as a similitude may be innocently used to quiet the Fancy, provided it be not imposed on the understanding as an analogous fact or as identical in kind, is presented to us in the power of the Magnet to awaken and strengthen the magnetic power in a bar of Iron, and (in the instance of the compound Magnet) acting in and with the latter.

[2] Romans viii. 26.—Ed.

glimmering, is still at an unknown distance from the ground : and so, indeed, must it be with all Truths, and all modes of Being that can neither be counted, coloured, or delineated. Before and After, when applied to such Subjects, are but allegories, which the Sense or Imagination supplies to the Understanding. The Position of the Aristotelians, *nihil in intellectu quod non prius in sensu*, on which Mr. Locke's Essay is grounded, is irrefragable : Locke erred only in taking half the Truth for a whole Truth. Conception is consequent on Perception. What we cannot *imagine*, we cannot, in the proper sense of the word, conceive.

I have already given one definition of Nature. Another, and differing from the former in words only, is this : Whatever is representable in the forms of Time and Space, is Nature. But whatever is comprehended in Time and Space, is included in the Mechanism of Cause and Effect. And conversely, whatever, by whatever means, has its principle in itself, so far as to *originate* its actions, cannot be contemplated in any of the forms of Space and Time ; it must, therefore, be considered as *Spirit* or *Spiritual* by a mind in that stage of its developement which is here supposed, and which we have agreed to understand under the name of Morality, or the Moral State : for in this stage we are concerned only with the forming of *negative* conceptions, *negative* convictions ; and by *spiritual* I do not pretend to determine *what* the Will *is*, but what it is *not*—namely, that it is not Nature. And as no man who admits a Will at all, (for we may safely presume that no man not meaning to speak figuratively, would call the shifting current of a stream the WILL[1] of the river), will suppose it *below* Nature, we may safely add, that it is super-natural ; and

[1] " The river windeth * at his own sweet will."

Wordsworth's exquisite Sonnet on Westminster-bridge at Sun-rise.

But who does not see that here the poetic charm arises from the known and felt *impropriety* of the expression, in the technical sense of the word *impropriety*, among grammarians ?

* The latest editions of Wordsworth have " glideth " for " windeth." —ED.

this without the least pretence to any positive Notion or Insight.

Now Morality accompanied with Convictions like these, I have ventured to call *Religious* Morality. Of the importance I attach to the state of mind implied in these convictions, for its own sake, and as the natural preparation for a yet higher state and a more substantive knowledge, proof more than sufficient, perhaps, has been given in the length and minuteness of this introductory Discussion, and in the foreseen risk which I run of exposing the volume at large to the censure which every work, or rather which every writer, must be prepared to undergo, who, treating of subjects that cannot be seen, touched, or in any other way made matters of outward sense, is yet anxious both to attach to, and to convey a distinct meaning by, the words he makes use of—the censure of being dry, abstract, and (of all qualities most scaring and opprobrious to the ears of the present generation) *metaphysical;* though how it is possible that a work not *physical,* that is, employed on objects known or believed on the evidence of the senses, should be other than *meta*physical, that is, treating on Subjects, the evidence of which is not derived from the senses, is a problem which critics of this order find it convenient to leave unsolved.

The author of the present volume will, indeed, have reason to think himself fortunate, if this be all the charge! — How many smart quotations, which (duly cemented by personal allusions to the author's supposed pursuits, attachments, and infirmities), would of themselves make up "a review" of the volume, might be supplied from the works of Butler, Swift, and Warburton. For instance: "It may not be amiss to inform the Public, that the Compiler of the Aids to Reflection, and Commenter on a Scotch Bishop's Platonico-Calvinistic commentary on St. Peter, belongs to the sect of the *Æolists,* whose fruitful imaginations lead them into certain notions, which, although in appearance *very unaccountable, are not without their mysteries and their meanings;* furnishing plenty of matter for such, *whose converting Imaginations dispose them to reduce all things into* TYPES; *who can make* SHADOWS, *no thanks to the Sun; and then mould them into* SUBSTANCES, *no thanks to*

Philosophy: whose peculiar Talent lies in fixing TROPES *and*
ALLEGORIES *to the* LETTER, *and refining what is* LITERAL *into*
FIGURE *and* MYSTERY."—*Tale of the Tub,* Sect. xi.

And would it were my lot to meet with a Critic, who, in
the might of his own Convictions, and with arms of equal
point and efficiency from his own forge, would come forth
as my assailant; or who, as a friend to my purpose, would
set forth the objections to the matter and pervading Spirit
of these Aphorisms, and the accompanying Elucidations.
Were it my task to form the mind of a young man of talent,
desirous to establish his opinions and belief on solid principles, and in the light of distinct understanding,—I would
commence his theological studies, or, at least, that most
important part of them respecting the aids which Religion
promises in our attempts to realize the ideas of Morality, by
bringing together all the passages scattered throughout
the writings of Swift and Butler, that bear on Enthusiasm,
Spiritual Operations, and pretences to the Gifts of the Spirit,
with the whole train of New Lights, Raptures, Experiences,
and the like.   For all that the richest Wit, in intimate
union with profound Sense and steady Observation, can
supply on these topics, is to be found in the works of these
satirists; though unhappily alloyed with much that can
only tend to pollute the imagination.

Without stopping to estimate the degree of caricature in
the portraits sketched by these bold masters, and without
attempting to determine in how many of the Enthusiasts,
brought forward by them in proof of the influence of false
Doctrines, a constitutional Insanity that would probably
have shown itself in some other form, would be the truer
solution, I would direct my pupil's attention to one feature
common to the whole group—the pretence, namely, of
possessing, or a Belief and Expectation grounded on other
men's assurances of their possessing, an immediate Consciousness, a sensible Experience, of the Spirit in and
during its operation on the soul.   It is not enough that you
grant them a consciousness of the Gifts and Graces infused,
or an assurance of the Spiritual Origin of the same, grounded
on their correspondence to the Scripture *promises,* and
their conformity with the *idea* of the Divine Giver.   No!
they all alike, it will be found, lay claim (or at least look

forward), to an inward perception of the Spirit itself and of its operating.

Whatever must be misrepresented in order to be ridiculed, is in fact *not* ridiculed ; but the thing substituted for it. It is a satire on something else, coupled with a lie on the part of the satirist, who knowing, or having the means of knowing the truth, chose to call one thing by the name of another. The Pretensions to the Supernatural, *pilloried* by Butler, sent to Bedlam by Swift, and (on their re-appearance in public) *gibbetted* by Warburton, and *anatomized* by Bishop Lavington, one and all have *this* for their essential character, that the Spirit is made the immediate Object of Sense or Sensation. Whether the spiritual Presence and Agency are supposed congizable by indescribable Feeling or unimaginable Vision by some specific visual energy ; whether seen, or heard, or touched, smelt and tasted—for in those vast Store-houses of fanatical assertion, the volumes of Ecclesiastical History and religious Auto-biography, instances are not wanting even of the three latter extravagancies ;—this variety in the mode may render the several pretensions more or less offensive to the *taste ;* but with the same absurdity for the *reason,* this being derived from a contradiction in terms common and radical to them all alike,—the assumption of a something essentially supersensual, that is nevertheless the object of Sense, that is, *not* supersensual.

Well then !—for let me be allowed still to suppose the Reader present to me, and that I am addressing him in the character of Companion and Guide—the positions recommended for your examination not only do not involve, but they exclude, this inconsistency. And for aught that hitherto appears, we may see with complacency the arrows of satire feathered with Wit, weighted with Sense, and discharged by a strong arm, fly home to their mark. Our conceptions of a possible Spiritual Communion, though they are but negative and only preparatory to a faith in its actual existence, stand neither in the level or in the direction of the shafts.

If it be objected, that Swift and Warburton did not choose openly to set up the interpretations of later and more rational divines against the decisions of their own

Church, and from *prudential* considerations did not attack
the doctrine *in toto*: that is *their* concern (I would answer),
and it is more charitable to think otherwise. But we are
in the silent school of Reflection, in the secret confessional
of Thought. Should we *lie for God*, and that to our
own thoughts ? They, indeed, who dare do the one, will
soon be able to do the other.—So did the Comforters of
Job : and to the divines, who resemble Job's Comforters,
we will leave both attempts.

But, (it may be said), a possible Conception is not necessarily a true one ; nor even a probable one, where the
Facts can be otherwise explained. In the name of the
supposed pupil I would reply—That is the very question I
am preparing myself to examine ; and am now seeking the
Vantage-ground where I may best command the Facts. In
my own person, I would ask the Objector, whether he
counted the Declarations of Scripture among the Facts to be
explained. But both for myself and my pupil, and in
behalf of all rational inquiry, I would demand that the
decision should not be such, in itself or in its effects, as
would prevent our becoming acquainted with the most
important of these Facts ; nay, such as would, for the mind
of the decider, preclude their very existence.—*Unless ye
believe*, says the prophet, *ye cannot understand.* Suppose
(what is at least possible) that the facts should be consequent on the belief, it is clear that without the belief the
materials, on which the understanding is to exert itself,
would be wanting.

The reflections that naturally arise out of this last
remark, are those that best suit the stage at which we last
halted, and from which we now recommence our progress
—the state of a *Moral* Man, who has already welcomed
certain truths of Religion, and is inquiring after other and
more special doctrines : still however as a Moralist,
desirous indeed to receive them into combination with
Morality, but to receive them as its Aid, not as its Substitute.
Now, to such a man I say ; Before you reject the Opinions
and Doctrines asserted and enforced in the following
extract from Leighton, and before you give way to the
Emotions of Distaste or Ridicule, which the Prejudices of
the circle in which you move, or your own familiarity with

the mad perversions of the doctrine by fanatics in all ages, have connected with the very words, Spirit, Grace, Gifts, Operations, &c., re-examine the arguments advanced in the first pages of this Introductory Comment, and the simple and sober view of the doctrine, contemplated in the first instance as a mere idea of the reason, flowing naturally from the admission of an infinite omnipresent Mind as the Ground of the Universe. Reflect again and again, and be sure that you *understand* the doctrine before you determine on rejecting it. That no false judgments, no extravagant conceits, no practical ill-consequences need arise out of the Belief of the Spirit, and its possible communion with the Spiritual Principle in man, *can* arise out of the *right* Belief, or are compatible with the doctrine truly and scripturally explained, Leighton, and almost every single period in the passage here transcribed from him, will suffice to convince you.

On the other hand, reflect on the consequences of rejecting it. For surely it is not the act of a reflecting mind, nor the part of a man of sense to disown and cast out one tenet, and yet persevere in admitting and clinging to another that has neither sense nor purpose, that does not *suppose* and rest on the truth and reality of the former! If you have resolved that all belief of a divine Comforter present to our inmost Being and aiding our infirmities, is fond and fanatical—if the Scriptures promising and asserting such communion are to be explained away into the action of circumstances, and the necessary movements of the vast machine, in one of the circulating chains of which the human Will is a petty Link—in what better light can Prayer appear to you, than the groans of a wounded lion in his solitary den, or the howl of a dog with his eyes on the moon? At the best, you can regard it only as a transient bewilderment of the Social Instinct, as a social Habit misapplied! Unless indeed you should adopt the theory which I remember to have read in the writings of the late Dr. Jebb, and for some supposed beneficial re-action of praying on the prayer's own mind, should practise it as a species of *Animal-Magnetism* to be brought about by a wilful eclipse of the reason, and a temporary *make-believe* on the part of the self-magnetizer!

E

At all events, do not pre-judge a Doctrine, the utter rejection of which must oppose a formidable obstacle to your acceptance of Christianity itself, when the books, from which alone we can learn what Christianity is and what it teaches, are so strangely written, that in a series of the most concerning points, including (historical facts excepted) all the *peculiar* Tenets of the Religion, the plain and obvious meaning of the words, that in which they were understood by learned and simple, for at least sixteen centuries, during the far larger part of which the language was a living language, is no sufficient guide to their actual sense or to the writer's own meaning! And this, too, where the literal and received Sense involves nothing impossible, or immoral, or contrary to reason. With such a persuasion, Deism would be a more consistent creed. But, alas! even this will fail you. The utter rejection of all present and living communion with the Universal Spirit impoverishes Deism itself, and renders it as cheerless as Atheism, from which indeed it would differ only by an obscure impersonation of what the Atheist receives unpersonified, under the name of Fate or Nature.

APHORISM VII.

Leighton and Coleridge.

The proper and natural Effect, and in the absence of all disturbing or intercepting forces, the certain and sensible accompaniment of Peace, (or Reconcilement) with God, is our own inward Peace, a calm and quiet temper of mind. And where there is a consciousness of earnestly desiring, and of having sincerely striven after the former, the latter may be considered as a *Sense* of its presence. In this case, I say, and for a soul watchful, and under the discipline of the Gospel, the Peace with a man's self may be the medium or organ through which the assurance of his Peace with God is conveyed. We will not therefore condemn this mode of speaking, though we dare not greatly recommend it. Be it, that there is, truly and in sobriety of speech, enough of just analogy in the subjects meant, to make

this use of the words, if less than proper, yet something
more than metaphorical; still we must be cautious not to
transfer to the Object the defects or the deficiency of the
Organ, which must needs partake of the imperfections of
the imperfect beings to whom it belongs. Not without
the co-assurance of other senses and of the same sense in
other men, dare we affirm that what our eye beholds, is
verily there to be beholden. Much less may we conclude
negatively, and from the inadequacy, or the suspension, or
from any other affection of sight infer the non-existence,
or departure, or changes of the thing itself. The chame-
leon darkens in the shade of him who bends over it to
ascertain its colours. In like manner, but with yet greater
caution, ought we to think respecting a tranquil habit of
inward life, considered as a spiritual *sense*, as the medial
Organ in and by which our Peace with God, and the lively
Working of his Grace on our Spirit, are perceived by us.
This Peace which we have with God in Christ, is invio-
lable; but because the sense and persuasion of it may be
interrupted, the soul that is truly at peace with God may
for a time be disquieted in itself, through weakness of
faith, or the strength of temptation, or the darkness of
desertion, losing sight of that grace, that love and light of
God's countenance, on which its tranquillity and joy depend.
Thou didst hide thy face, saith David, *and I was troubled.*[1]
But when these eclipses are over, the soul is revived with
new consolation, as the face of the earth is renewed and
made to smile with the return of the sun in the spring;
and this ought always to uphold Christians in the saddest
times, namely, that the grace and love of God towards
them depend not on their sense, nor upon anything in
them, but is still in itself, incapable of the smallest alteration.

A holy heart that gladly entertains grace, shall find that
it and peace cannot dwell asunder; while an ungodly man
may sleep to death in the lethargy of carnal presumption
and impenitency; but a true, lively, solid peace, he cannot
have. *There is no peace to the wicked, saith my God.* Isa.
lvii. 21.

---

[1] Psalm xxx. 7.—ED.

APHORISM VIII.

Worldly Hopes.

LEIGHTON.

Worldly hopes are not living, but lying hopes; they die often before us, and we live to bury them, and see our own folly and infelicity in trusting to them; but at the utmost, they die with us when we die, and can accompany us no further. But the lively Hope, which is the Christian's Portion, answers expectation to the full, and much beyond it, and deceives no way but in that happy way of far exceeding it.

A living hope, living in death itself! The world dares say no more for its device, than *Dum spiro spero:* but the children of God can add, by virtue of this living hope, *Dum exspiro spero.*

APHORISM IX.

The Worldling's Fear.

LEIGHTON.

It is a fearful thing when a man and all his hopes die together. Thus saith Solomon of the wicked, Prov. xi. 7.— When he dieth, then die his hopes; (many of them *before,* but at the utmost *then,* all of them;) but *the righteous hath hope in his death,* Prov. xiv. 32.[1]

APHORISM X.

Worldly Mirth.

LEIGHTON AND COLERIDGE.

As he that taketh away a garment in cold weather, and as vinegar upon nitre, so is he that singeth songs to a heavy heart,

[1] One of the numerous proofs against those who with a strange inconsistency hold the Old Testament to have been inspired throughout, and yet deny that the doctrine of a future state is taught therein.

Prov. xxv. 20.   Worldly mirth is so far from curing spiritual grief, that even worldly grief, where it is great and takes deep root, is not allayed but increased by it.   A man who is full of inward heaviness, the more he is encompassed about with mirth, it exasperates and enrages his grief ths more; like ineffectual weak physic, which removes not the humour, but stirs it and makes it more unquiet.   But spiritual joy is seasonable for all estates: in prosperity, it is pertinent to crown and sanctify all other enjoyments, with this which so far surpasses them; and in distress, it is the only *Nepenthe*, the cordial of fainting spirits: so, Psal. iv. 7.   *He hath put joy into my heart.* This mirth makes way for itself, which other mirth cannot do. These songs are sweetest in the night of distress.

There is something exquisitely beautiful and touching in the first of these similes: and the second, though less pleasing to the imagination, has the charm of propriety, and expresses the transition with equal force and liveliness. A grief of recent birth is a sick infant that must have its medicine administered in its milk, and sad thoughts are the sorrowful heart's natural food.   This is a complaint that is not to be cured by opposites, which for the most part only reverse the symptoms while they exasperate the disease—or like a rock in the mid-channel of a river swoln by a sudden rain-flush from the mountains, which only detains the excess of waters from their proper outlet, and makes them foam, roar, and eddy.   The soul in her desolation hugs the sorrow close to her, as her sole remaining garment: and this must be drawn off so gradually, and the garment to be put in its stead so gradually slipt on and feel so like the former, that the sufferer shall be sensible of the change only by the refreshment.—The true Spirit of Consolation is well content to detain the tear in the eye, and finds a surer pledge of its success, in the smile of Resignation that dawns through that, than in the liveliest shows of a forced and alien exhilaration.

APHORISM XI.

Plotinus thanked God, that his soul was not tied to an immortal body.

APHORISM XII.

LEIGHTON AND COLERIDGE.

What a full Confession do we make of our dissatisfaction with the Objects of our bodily senses, that in our attempts to express what we conceive the Best of Beings, and the Greatest of Felicities to be, we describe by the exact Contraries of all, that we experience here—the one as *In*finite, *In*comprehensible, *Im*mutable, &c., the other as *in*corruptible, *un*defiled, and that passeth *not* away. At all events, this Coincidence, say rather, Identity of Attributes, is sufficient to apprize us, that to be inheritors of bliss we must become the children of God.

This remark of Leighton's is ingenious and startling. Another, and more fruitful, perhaps more solid inference from the fact would be, that there is something in the human mind which makes it know (as soon as it is sufficiently awakened to reflect on its own thoughts and notices), that in all finite Quantity there is an Infinite, in all measures of Time an Eternal; that the latter are the basis, the substance, the true and abiding *reality* of the former; and that as we truly *are*, only as far as God is with us, so neither can we truly *possess* (that is, enjoy) our Being or any other real Good, but by living in the sense of his holy presence.

A life of wickedness is a life of lies; and an evil being, or the being of evil, the last and darkest mystery.

APHORISM XIII.

The Wisest Use of the Imagination.

LEIGHTON.

It is not altogether unprofitable; yea, it is great wisdom in Christians to be arming themselves against such temptations as may befal them hereafter, though they have not

as yet met with them ; to labour to overcome them beforehand, to suppose the hardest things that may be incident
to them, and to put on the strongest resolutions they can
attain unto. Yet all that is but an imaginary effort ; and
therefore there is no assurance that the victory is any more
than imaginary too, till it come to action, and then, they
that have spoken and thought very confidently, may prove
but (as one said of the Athenians) *fortes in tabula*, patient
and courageous in picture or fancy ; and, notwithstanding
all their arms, and dexterity in handling them by way of
exercise, may be foully defeated when they are to fight in
earnest.

APHORISM XIV.

The Language of Scripture.

The Word of God speaks to men, and therefore it speaks
the language of the Children of Men. This just and pregnant thought was suggested to Leighton by *Gen.* xxii. 12.
The same text has led me to unfold and expand the
remark.—On moral subjects, the Scriptures speak in the
language of the affections which they excite in us ; on
sensible objects, neither metaphysically, as they are known
by superior intelligences ; nor theoretically, as they would
be seen by us were we placed in the sun ; but as they are
represented by our human senses in our present relative
position. Lastly, from no vain, or worse than vain, ambition of seeming *to walk on the sea* of Mystery in my way
to Truth, but in the hope of removing a difficulty that
presses heavily on the minds of many who· in heart and
desire are believers, and which long pressed on my own
mind, I venture to add : that on *spiritual* things, and allu-
sively to the mysterious union or conspiration of the Divine
with the Human in the Spirits of the Just, spoken of in
Romans viii. 27, the word of God attributes the language
of the Spirit sanctified to the Holy One, the Sanctifier.

Now the Spirit in Man (that is, the Will) knows its
own State in and by its Acts alone : even as in geometrical

reasoning the Mind knows its constructive *faculty* in the *act* of constructing, and contemplates the act in the *product* (that is, the mental figure or diagram) which is inseparable from the act and co-instaneous.

Let the reader join these two positions : first, that the Divine Spirit acting *in* the Human Will is described as *one with* the Will so filled and actuated : secondly, that our actions are the means, by which alone the Will becomes assured of its own state ; and he will understand, though he may not perhaps adopt my suggestion, that the verse, in which God *speaking of himself*, says to Abraham, *Now I know that thou fearest God, seeing thou hast not withheld thy son, thy only son, from me* [1]—may be more than merely *figurative.* An *accommodation* I grant; but in the *thing expressed*, and not altogether in the Expressions. In arguing with infidels, or with the weak in faith, it is a part of religious Prudence, no less than of religious Morality, to avoid whatever looks *like* an evasion. To retain the literal sense, wherever the harmony of Scripture permits, and reason does not forbid, is ever the honester, and, nine times in ten, the more rational and pregnant interpretation. The contrary plan is an easy and approved way of *getting rid* of a difficulty; but nine times in ten a bad way of solving it. But alas ! there have been too many Commentators who are content not to understand a text themselves, if only they can make the reader believe that they do.

Of the figures of speech in the sacred volume, that are only figures of speech, the one of most frequent occurrence is that which describes an effect by the name of its most usual and best known cause : the passages, for instance, in which grief, fury, repentance, &c., are attributed to the Deity.—But these are far enough from justifying the (I had almost said, dishonest) fashion of metaphorical glosses, in as well as out of the Church ; and which our fashionable divines have carried to such an extent, as in the doctrinal part of their creed, to leave little else but metaphors. But the reader who wishes to find this latter subject, and that of the Aphorism, treated more at large, is referred to Mr. Southey's ' Omniana,' Vol. II.

---

[1] Gen. xxii. 12.—Ed.

p. 7—12 ; and to the Note in p. 62—67, of the author's second 'Lay-Sermon.'[1]

APHORISM XV.

The Christian no Stoic.

LEIGHTON AND COLERIDGE.

Seek not altogether to dry up the stream of Sorrow, but to bound it, and keep it within its banks. Religion doth not destroy the life of nature, but adds to it a life more excellent ; yea, it doth not only permit, but requires some feeling of afflictions. Instead of patience, there is in some men an affected pride of spirit suitable only to the doctrine of the Stoics as it is usually taken. They strive not to feel at all the afflictions that are on them ; but where there is no feeling at all, there can be no patience.

Of the sects of ancient philosophy the Stoic is, perhaps the nearest to Christianity. Yet even to this sect Christianity is fundamentally opposite. For the Stoic attaches the highest honour (or rather, attaches honour *solely*) to the person that acts virtuously in spite of his feelings, or who has raised himself above the conflict by their extinction ; while Christianity instructs us to place small reliance on a virtue that does not *begin* by bringing the Feelings to a conformity with the commands of the Conscience. Its especial aim, its characteristic operation, is to moralize the affections. The Feelings, that oppose a right act, must be wrong feelings. The *act*, indeed, whatever the agent's *feelings* might be, Christianity would command ; and under certain circumstances would both command and commend it—commend it, ·as a healthful symptom in a sick patient ; and command it, as one of the ways and means of changing the feelings, or displacing them by calling up the opposite.

---

[1] An edition of the 'Lay Sermons' is published with Bohn's edition of Coleridge's 'Biographia Literaria.' The corresponding pages to those referred to would be pp. 409-10. The passages in 'Omniana' referred to are in Coleridge's own contributions to that work, and are reprinted in his 'Remains' (1836, v. 1, pp. 321—330), under the heads "Pelagianism" and "The Soul and its Organs of Sense."—ED.

Corollaries to Aphorism XV.

I. The more *consciousness* in our Thoughts and Words, and the less in our Impulses and general Actions, the better and more healthful the state both of head and heart. As the flowers from an orange tree in its time of blossoming, that burgeon forth, expand, fall and are momently replaced, such is the sequence of hourly and momently charities in a pure and gracious soul. The modern fiction which depictures the son of Cytherea with a bandage round his eyes, is not without a spiritual meaning. There is a sweet and holy blindness in Christian LOVE, even as there is a blindness of Life, yea and of Genius too, in the moment of productive Energy.

II. Motives are symptoms of weakness, and supplements for the deficient Energy of the living PRINCIPLE, the LAW within us. Let them then be reserved for those momentous Acts and Duties, in which the strongest and best balanced natures must feel themselves deficient, and where Humility, no less than Prudence, prescribes Deliberation. We find a similitude of this, I had almost said a remote analogy, in organized bodies. The lowest class of animals or *protozoa*, the *polypi* for instance, have neither brain nor nerves. Their motive powers are all from without. The sun, light, the warmth, the air are their nerves and brain. As life ascends, nerves appear; but still only as the conductors of an *external* influence; next are seen the knots or ganglions, as so many *foci* of *instinctive* agency, that imperfectly imitate the yet wanting *centre*.—And now the promise and token of a true Individuality are disclosed; both the reservoir of Sensibility and the imitative power that actuates the organs of Motion (the muscles) with the net-work of conductors, are all taken inward and appropriated; the Spontaneous rises into the Voluntary, and finally after various steps and a long ascent, the Material and Animal Means and Conditions are prepared for the manifestations of a Free Will, having its Law within itself and its motive in the Law—and thus bound to originate its own Acts, not only without, but even against, alien Stimulants. That in our present state we have only the

Dawning of this inward Sun (the perfect Law of Liberty) will sufficiently limit and qualify the preceding position if only it have been allowed to produce its twofold consequence—the excitement of Hope and the repression of Vanity.[1]

APHORISM XVI.

Leighton.

As excessive eating or drinking both makes the body sickly and lazy, fit for nothing but sleep, and besots the mind, as it clogs up with crudities the way through which the spirits should pass,[2] bemiring them, and making them move heavily, as a coach in a deep way; thus doth all immoderate use of the world and its delights wrong the soul in its spiritual condition, makes it sickly and feeble, full of spiritual distempers and inactivity, benumbs the graces of the Spirit, and fills the soul with sleepy vapours, makes it grow secure and heavy in spiritual exercises, and obstructs the way and motion of the Spirit of God, in the soul. Therefore, if you would be spiritual, healthful, and vigorous, and enjoy much of the consolations of Heaven, be sparing and sober in those of the earth, and what you abate of the one, shall be certainly made up in the other.

APHORISM XVII.

Inconsistency.

Leighton and Coleridge.

It is a most unseemly and unpleasant thing, to see a man's life full of ups and downs, one step like a Christian,

[1] See Prof. J. H. Green's ' Vital Dynamics,' 1840.—Ed.

[2] Technical phrases of an obsolete System will yet retain their places, nay, acquire universal currency, and become sterling in the language, when they at once represent the feelings, and give an apparent solution of them by visual images easily managed by the fancy. Such are many terms and phrases from the *Humoral* Physiology long exploded, but which are far more popular then any description would be from the theory that has taken its place.

and another like a worldling; it cannot choose but both
pain himself and mar the edification of others.

The same sentiment, only with a special application
to the maxims and measures of our Cabinet and Statesmen,
has been finely expressed by a sage Poet of the preceding
generation, in lines which no generation will find inappli-
cable or superannuated.

> God and the World we worship both together,
>   Draw not our Laws to Him, but His to ours;
> Untrue to both, so prosperous in neither,
>   The imperfect Will brings forth but barren Flowers!
> Unwise as all distracted Interests be,
> Strangers to God, Fools in Humanity:
> Too good for great things, and too great for good,
> While still "I dare not" waits upon "I wou'd."

APHORISM XVII. CONTINUED.

The Ordinary Motive to Inconsistency.

LEIGHTON.

What though the polite man count thy fashion a little
odd and too precise, it is because he knows nothing above
that model of goodness which he hath set himself, and
therefore approves of nothing beyond it: he knows not
God, and therefore doth not discern and esteem what is
most like Him. When courtiers come down into the
country, the common home-bred people possibly think their
habit strange; but they care not for that, it is the fashion
at court. What need, then, that Christians should be so
tender-foreheaded, as to be put out of countenance because
the world looks on holiness as a singularity? It is the
only fashion in the highest court, yea, of the King of
Kings himself.

APHORISM XVIII.

Superficial Reconciliations, and Self-deceit in Forgiving.

LEIGHTON.

When, after variances, men are brought to an agreement, they are much subject to this, rather to cover their remaining malices with superficial verbal forgiveness, than to dislodge them, and free the heart of them. This is a poor self-deceit. As the philosopher said to him, who being ashamed that he was espied by him in a tavern in the outer room, withdrew himself to the inner, he called after him, " That is not the way out, the more you go that way, you will be the further in ! " So when hatreds are upon admonition not thrown out, but retire inward to hide themselves, they grow deeper and stronger than before ; and those constrained semblances of reconcilement are but a false healing, do but skin the wound over, and therefore it usually breaks forth worse again.

APHORISM XIX.

Of the Worth and the Duties of the Preacher.

LEIGHTON.

The stream of custom and our profession bring us to the Preaching of the Word, and we sit out our hour under the sound ; but how few consider and prize it as the great ordinance of God for the salvation of souls, the beginner and the sustainer of the Divine life of grace within us ! And certainly, until we have these thoughts of it, and seek to feel it thus ourselves, although we hear it most frequently, and let slip no occasion, yea, hear it with attention and some present delight, yet still we miss the right use of it, and turn it from its true end, while we take it not as *that ingrafted word which is able to save our souls* (*James* i. 21).

Thus ought they who preach to speak the word; to endeavour their utmost to accommodate it to this end, that sinners may be converted, begotten again, and believers nourished and strengthened in their spiritual life; to regard no lower end, but aim steadily at that mark. Their hearts and tongues ought to be set on fire with holy zeal for God and love to souls, kindled by the Holy Ghost, that came down on the apostles in the shape of fiery tongues.

And those that hear, should remember this as the end of their hearing, that they may receive spiritual life and strength by the word. For though it seems a poor despicable business, that a frail sinful man like yourselves should speak a few words in your hearing, yet, look upon it as the way wherein God communicates happiness to those who believe, and works that believing unto happiness, alters the whole frame of the soul, and makes a new creation, as it begets it again to the inheritance of glory. Consider it thus, which is its true notion; and then, what can be so precious?

APHORISM XX.

Leighton.

The difference is great in our natural life, in some persons especially; that they who in infancy were so feeble, and wrapped up as others in swaddling clothes, yet, afterwards come to excel in wisdom and in the knowledge of sciences, or to be commanders of great armies, or to be kings: but the distance is far greater and more admirable, betwixt the small beginnings of grace, and our after perfection, that fulness of knowledge that we look for, and that crown of immortality which all they are born to who are born of God.

But as in the faces or actions of some children, characters and presages of their after-greatness have appeared (as a singular beauty in Moses's face, as they write of him, and as Cyrus was made king among the shepherds' children with whom he was brought up, &c.) so also, certainly, in these children of God, there be some characters and evidences that they are born for Heaven by their new birth. That holiness and meekness, that patience and faith which shine in the actions and sufferings of the saints, are characters of their Father's image, and show their high original, and foretell their glory to come ; such a glory as doth not only surpass the world's thoughts, but the thoughts of the children of God themselves. 1 *John* iii. 2.

COMMENT.

On an Intermediate State, or State of Transition from Morality to Spiritual Religion.

This Aphorism would, it may seem, have been placed more fitly in the Chapter following. In placing it here, I have been determined by the following convictions : 1. Every state, and consequently that which we have described as the state of Religious Morality, which is not progressive, is dead, or retrograde. 2. As a pledge of this progression, or, at least, as the form in which the propulsive tendency shows itself, there are certain Hopes, Aspirations, Yearnings, that, with more or less of consciousness, rise and stir in the Heart of true Morality as naturally as the sap in the full-formed stem of a rose flows towards the bud, within which the flower is maturing. 3. No one, whose own experience authorizes him to confirm the truth of this statement, can have been conversant with the volumes of religious biography, can have perused (for instance) the lives of Cranmer, Ridley, Latimer, Wishart, Sir Thomas More, Bernard Gilpin, Bishop Bedel, or of Egede, Swartz, and the missionaries of the frozen world, without an occasional conviction, that these men lived under extraordinary influences, which in each instance and in all ages of the Christian æra bear the same characters, and both in the accompaniments and the results evidently refer to a common origin. And what can this be ? is the question that must needs force itself on the mind in the first moment of reflection on a phenomenon so interesting and apparently so anomalous. The answer is as necessarily contained in one or the other of two assumptions. These influences are either the Product of Delusion (*insania amabilis*, and the

re-action of disordered nerves), or they argue the existence
of a relation to some real agency, distinct from what is
experienced or acknowledged by the world at large, for
which as not merely *natural* on the one hand, and yet not
assumed to be *miraculous* [1] on the other, we have no apter
name than *spiritual*. Now if neither analogy justifies nor
the moral feelings permit the former assumption, and we
decide therefore in favour of the reality of a State other
and higher than the mere Moral Man, whose Religion [2]
consists in Morality, has attained under these convictions,
can the existence of a *transitional* state appear other than
probable? or that these very convictions, when accompanied by correspondent dispositions and stirrings of the
heart, are among the marks and indications of such a
state? And thinking it not unlikely that among the
readers of this volume, there may be found some Individuals, whose inward state, though disquieted by doubts
and oftener still perhaps by blank misgivings, may, nevertheless, betoken the commencement of a Transition from a
not irreligious Morality to a Spiritual Religion, with a
view to their interests I placed this Aphorism under the
present head.

APHORISM XXI.

LEIGHTON.

The most approved teachers of wisdom, in a human way,
have required of their scholars, that to the end their minds
might be capable of it, they should be purified from vice
and wickedness. And it was Socrates' custom, when any
one asked him a question, seeking to be informed by him,

[1] In check of fanatical pretensions, it is expedient to confine the term
miraculous, to cases where the *senses* are appealed to in proof of something that transcends, or can be a part of the Experience derived from
the senses.

[2] For let it not be forgotten, that Morality, as distinguished from
Prudence, implying (it matters not under what name, whether of Honour,
or Duty, or Conscience, still, I say, implying), and being grounded in,
an awe of the Invisible and a Confidence therein beyond (nay, occasionally in apparent contradiction to) the inductions of outward Experience,
is essentially religious.

before he would answer them, he asked them concerning their own qualities and course of life.

APHORISM XXII.

Knowledge not the ultimate End of Religious Pursuits.

LEIGHTON AND COLERIDGE.

The Hearing and Reading of the Word, under which I comprise theological studies generally, are alike defective when pursued *without* increase of Knowledge, and when pursued chiefly *for* increase of Knowledge. To seek no more than a present delight, that evanisheth with the sound of the words that die in the air, is not to desire the Word as meat, but as music, as God tells the prophet Ezekiel of his people, *Ezek.* xxxiii. 32. *And lo, thou art unto them as a very lovely song of one that hath a pleasant voice, and can play well upon an instrument; for they hear thy words, and they do them not.* To desire the word for the increase of knowledge, although this is necessary and commendable, and, being rightly qualified, is a part of spiritual accretion, yet, take it as going no further, it is not the true end of the Word. Nor is the venting of that knowledge in speech and frequent discourse of the Word and the divine truths that are in it; which, where it is governed with Christian prudence, is not to be despised, but commended; yet, certainly, the highest knowledge, and the most frequent and skilful speaking of the Word, severed from the growth here mentioned, misses the true end of the Word. If any one's head or tongue should grow apace, and all the rest stand at a stay, it would certainly make him a monster; and they are no other, who are knowing and discoursing Christians, and grow daily in that respect, but not at all in holiness of heart, and life, which is the proper growth of the children of God. Apposite to their case is Epictetus's comparison of the sheep; they return not what they eat in grass, but in wool.

F

APHORISM XXIII.

The sum of Church History.

LEIGHTON.

In times of peace, the Church may dilate more, and build as it were into breadth, but in times of trouble, it arises more in height; it is then built upwards; as in cities where men are straitened, they build usually higher than in the country.

APHORISM XXIV.

Worthy to be framed and hung up in the Library of every Theological Student.

LEIGHTON AND COLERIDGE.

When there is a great deal of smoke, and no clear flame, it argues much moisture in the matter, yet it witnesseth certainly that there is fire there; and therefore dubious questioning is a much better evidence, than that senseless deadness which most take for believing. Men that know nothing in sciences, have no doubts. He never truly believed, who was not made first sensible and convinced of unbelief.

Never be afraid to doubt, if only you have the disposition to believe, and doubt in order that you may end in believing the Truth. I will venture to add in my own name and from my own conviction the following:

APHORISM XXV.

He, who begins by loving Christianity better than Truth, will proceed by loving his own Sect or Church better than Christianity, and end in loving himself better than all.

APHORISM XXVI.

The Absence of Disputes, and a general Aversion to Religious Controversies, no proof of True Unanimity.

LEIGHTON AND COLERIDGE.

The boasted peaceableness about questions of Faith too often proceeds from a superficial temper, and not seldom from a supercilious disdain of whatever has no marketable use or value, and from indifference to religion itself. Toleration is a herb of spontaneous growth in the Soil of Indifference; but the weed has none of the virtues of the medicinal plant, reared by Humility in the Garden of Zeal. Those, who regard religions as matters of taste, may consistently include all religious differences in the old adage, *De gustibus non est disputandum*. And many there be among these of Gallio's temper, who *care for none of these things*, and who account all questions in religion, as he did, but matter of words and names. And by this all religions may agree together. But that were not a natural union produced by the active heat of the spirit, but a confusion rather, arising from the want of it; not a knitting together, but a freezing together, as cold congregates all bodies, how heterogeneous soever, sticks, stones, and water; but heat makes first a separation of different things, and then unites those that are of the same nature.

Much of our common union of minds, I fear, proceeds from no other than the afore-mentioned causes, want of knowledge, and want of affection to religion. You that boast you live conformably to the appointments of the Church, and that no one hears of your noise, we may thank the ignorance of your minds for that kind of quietness.

The preceding extract is particularly entitled to our serious reflections, as in a tenfold degree more applicable to the present times than to the age in which it was written. We all know, that Lovers are apt to take offence and wrangle on occasions that perhaps are but trifles, and which assuredly would appear such to those who regard Love itself as folly. These quarrels may, indeed, be no proof of wisdom; but

still, in the imperfect state of our nature the entire absence
of the same, and this too on far more serious provocations,
would excite a strong suspicion of a comparative indifference
in the parties who can love so coolly where they profess to
love so well. I shall believe our present religious tolerancy
to proceed from the abundance of our charity and good
sense, when I see proofs that we are equally cool and for-
bearing as litigants and political partizans.

APHORISM XXVII.

*The Influence of Worldly Views (or what are called a Man's
Prospects in Life), the Bane of the Christian Ministry.*

LEIGHTON.

It is a base, poor thing for a man to seek himself; far
below that royal dignity that is here put upon Christians,
and that priesthood joined with it. Under the Law, those
who were squint-eyed were incapable of the priesthood :
truly, this squinting toward our own interest, the looking
aside to that, in God's affairs especially, so deforms the
face of the soul, that it makes it altogether unworthy the
honour of this spiritual priesthood. Oh! this is a large
task, an infinite task. The several creatures bear their
part in this ; the sun says somewhat, and moon and stars,
yea, the lowest have some share in it ; the very plants and
herbs of the field speak of God ; and yet, the very highest
and best, yea all of them together, the whole concert of
Heaven and earth, cannot show forth all His praise to the
full. No, it is but a part, the smallest part of that glory,
which they can reach.

APHORISM XXVIII.

Despise none : Despair of none.

LEIGHTON.

The Jews would not willingly tread upon the smallest
piece of paper in their way, but took it up; for possibly,

said they, the name of God may be on it. Though there was a little superstition in this, yet truly there is nothing but good religion in it, if we apply it to men. Trample not on any; there may be some work of grace there, that thou knowest not of. The name of God may be written upon that soul thou treadest on; it may be a soul that Christ thought so much of, as to give His precious blood for it; therefore despise it not.

APHORISM XXIX.

Men of Least Merit most apt to be Contemptuous, Because most Ignorant and most Overweening of Themselves.

Leighton.

Too many take the ready course to deceive themselves; for they look with both eyes on the failings and defects of others, and scarcely give their good qualities half an eye, while on the contrary, in themselves, they study to the full their own advantages, and their weaknesses and defects, (as one says), they skip over, as children do their hard words in their lesson, that are troublesome to read; and making this uneven parallel, what wonder if the result be a gross mistake of themselves!

APHORISM XXX.

Vanity may strut in rags, and Humility be arrayed in purple and fine linen.

Leighton.

It is not impossible that there may be in some an affected pride in the meanness of apparel, and in others, under either neat or rich attire, a very humble unaffected mind: using it upon some of the afore-mentioned engagements, or such like, and yet the heart not at all upon it. *Magnus qui fictilibus utitur tanquam argento, nec ille minor qui argento tanquam fictilibus*, says Seneca: Great is he who enjoys his earthenware as if it were plate, and not less great is the man to whom all his plate is no more than earthenware.

APHORISM XXXI.

Of the Detraction among Religious Professors.

LEIGHTON AND COLERIDGE.

They who have attained to a self-pleasing pitch of civility or formal religion, have usually that point of presumption with it, that they make their own size the model and rule to examine all by. What is below it, they condemn indeed as profane; but what is beyond it, they account needless and affected preciseness; and therefore are as ready as others to let fly invectives or bitter taunts against it, which are the keen and poisoned shafts of the tongue, and a persecution that shall be called to a strict account.

The slanders, perchance, may not be altogether forged or untrue; they may be the implements, not the inventions, of Malice. But they do not on this account escape the guilt of detraction. Rather, it is characteristic of the evil spirit in question, to work by the advantage of real faults; but these stretched and aggravated to the utmost. IT IS NOT EXPRESSIBLE HOW DEEP A WOUND A TONGUE SHARPENED TO THIS WORK WILL GIVE, WITH NO NOISE AND A VERY LITTLE WORD. This is the true *white* gunpowder, which the dreaming Projectors of silent Mischiefs and insensible Poisons sought for in the Laboratories of Art and Nature, in a World of Good; but which was to be found, in its most destructive form, in "the World of Evil, the Tongue."

APHORISM XXXII.

The Remedy.

LEIGHTON.

All true remedy must begin at the heart; otherwise it will be but a mountebank cure, a false imagined conquest.

The weights and wheels are *there*, and the clock strikes according to their motion. Even he that speaks contrary to what is within him, guilefully contrary to his inward conviction and knowledge, yet speaks conformably to what is within him in the temper and frame of his heart, which is double, *a heart and a heart*, as the Psalmist hath it: *Psalm* xii. 2.

APHORISM XXXIII.

LEIGHTON AND COLERIDGE.

It is an argument of a candid ingenuous mind, to delight in the good name and commendations of others; to pass by their defects, and take notice of their virtues; and to speak and hear of those willingly, and not endure either to speak or hear of the other; for in this indeed you may be little less guilty than the ·evil speaker, in taking pleasure in it, though you speak it not. He that willingly drinks in tales and calumnies, will, from the delight he hath in evil hearing, slide insensibly into the humour of evil speaking. It is strange how most persons dispense with themselves in this point, and that in scarcely any societies shall we find a hatred of this ill, but rather some tokens of taking pleasure in it; and until a Christian sets himself to an inward watchfulness over his heart, not suffering in it any thought that is uncharitable, or vain self-esteem, upon the sight of others' frailties, he will still be subject to somewhat of this, in the tongue or ear at least. So, then, as for the evil of guile in the tongue, a sincere heart, *truth in the inward parts*, powerfully redresses it; therefore it is expressed, *Psal.* xv. 2, *That speaketh the truth from his heart;* thence it flows. Seek much after this, to speak nothing with God, nor men, but what is the sense of a single unfeigned heart. O sweet truth! excellent but rare sincerity! he that *loves that truth within*, and who is himself at once THE TRUTH and THE LIFE, He alone can work it there! Seek it of him.

It is characteristic of the Roman dignity and sobriety, that, in the Latin, *to favour with the* tongue (*favere lingua*) means *to be silent*. We say, Hold your tongue! as if it were an injunction, that could not be carried into effect but by manual force, or the pincers of the Forefinger and Thumb! And verily—I blush to say it—it is not Women and Frenchmen only that would rather have their tongues bitten than bitted, and feel their souls in a strait-waist-coat, when they are obliged to remain silent.

APHORISM XXXIV.

On the Passion for New and Striking Thoughts.

LEIGHTON.

In conversation seek not so much either to vent thy knowledge, or to increase it, as to know more spiritually and effectually what thou dost know. And in this way those mean despised truths, that everyone thinks he is sufficiently seen in, will have a new sweetness and use in them, which thou didst not so well perceive before (for these flowers cannot be sucked dry), and in this humble sincere way thou shalt *grow in grace and in knowledge* too.

APHORISM XXXV.

The Radical Difference between the Good Man and the Vicious Man.

LEIGHTON AND COLERIDGE.

The godly man hates the evil he possibly by temptation hath been drawn to do, and loves the good he is frustrated of, and, having intended, hath not attained to do. The sinner, who hath his denomination from sin as his course, hates the good which sometimes he is forced to do, and loves that sin which many times he does not, either wanting occasion and means, so that he cannot do it, or through the check of an enlightened conscience possibly dares not do; and though so bound up from the act, as a dog in a chain, yet the habit, the natural inclination and desire in him, is still the same, the strength of his affection is carried to sin. So in the weakest *sincere* Christian, there is that predominant sincerity and desire of holy walking, according to which he is called a *righteous person*, the Lord is pleased to give him that name, and account him so, being upright in heart, though often failing.

Leighton adds, " There is a Righteousness of a higher strain." I do not ask the reader's full assent to this position : I do not suppose him as yet prepared to yield it. But thus much he will readily admit, that here, *if* any where, we are to seek the fine Line which, like stripes of Light in Light, distinguishes, not divides, the summit of religious Morality from Spiritual Religion.

" A Righteousness " (Leighton continues) " that is not *in* him, but *upon* him. He is *clothed* with it." This, reader ! is the controverted Doctrine, so warmly asserted and so bitterly decried under the name of " IMPUTED RIGHTEOUS-NESS." Our learned Archbishop, you see, adopts it ; and it is on this account principally, that by many of our leading Churchmen his orthodoxy has been more than questioned, and his name put in the list of proscribed divines, as a Calvinist. That Leighton attached a definite sense to the words above quoted, it would be uncandid to doubt ; and the general spirit of his writings leads me to presume that it was compatible with the eternal distinction between *things* and *persons*, and therefore opposed to *modern* Calvinism. But what it was, I have not (I own) been able to discover. The sense, however, in which I think he *might* have received this doctrine, and in which I avow myself a believer in it, I shall have an opportunity of showing in another place. My present object is to open out the road by the removal of prejudices, so far at least as to throw some disturbing *doubts* on the secure *taking-for-granted*, that the peculiar Tenets of the Christian Faith asserted in the articles and homilies of our National Church are in contradiction to the common sense of mankind. And with this view, (and not in the arrogant expectation or wish, that a mere *ipse dixit* should be received for argument) I here avow my conviction, that the doctrine of IMPUTED Righteousness, rightly and scripturally interpreted, is so far from being either *irrational* or *immoral*, that Reason itself prescribes the idea in order to give a *meaning* and an ultimate object to Morality ; and that the Moral Law in

the Conscience demands its reception in order to give
reality and substantive existence to the idea presented by
the Reason.

APHORISM XXXVI.

LEIGHTON.

Your blessedness is not,—no, believe it, it is not where
most of you seek it, in things below you. How can that
be ? It must be a higher good to make you happy.

COMMENT.

Every rank of creatures, as it ascends in the scale of
creation, leaves death behind it or under it. The metal
at its height of being seems a mute prophecy of the
coming vegetation, into a mimic semblance of which it
crystallizes. The blossom and flower, the acme of vegetable life, divides into correspondent organs with reciprocal functions, and by instinctive motions and approxima-
tions seems impatient of that fixure, by which it is differenced in kind from the flower-shaped Psyche, that flutters
with free wing above it. And wonderfully in the insect
realm doth the Irritability, the proper seat of Instinct,
while yet the nascent Sensibility is subordinated thereto—
most wonderfully, I say, doth the muscular life in the
insect, and the musculo-arterial in the bird, imitate and
typically rehearse the adaptive Understanding, yea, and
the moral affections and charities, of man. Let us carry
ourselves back, in spirit, to the mysterious Week, the
teeming Work-days of the Creator : as they rose in vision
before the eye of the inspired historian *of the Generations of the Heaven and the Earth, in the days that the
Lord God made the Earth and the Heavens.*[1] And who
that hath watched their ways with an understanding heart,
could, as the vision evolving, still advanced towards him,
contemplate the filial and loyal bee; the home-building,
wedded, and divorceless swallow ; and above all the mani-

[1] Gen. ii. 4.—ED.

foldly intelligent [1] ant tribes, with their Commonwealths and Confederacies, their warriors and miners, the husbandfolk, that fold in their tiny flocks on the honeyed leaf, and the virgin sisters, with the holy instincts of maternal love, detached and in selfless purity—and not say to himself, Behold the Shadow of approaching Humanity, the Sun rising from behind, in the kindling Morn of Creation! Thus all lower Natures find their highest Good in semblances and seekings of that which is higher and better. All things strive to ascend, and ascend in their striving. And shall man alone stoop? Shall his pursuits and desires, the *reflections* of his inward life, be like the reflected image of a tree on the edge of a pool, that grows downward, and seeks a mock heaven in the unstable element beneath it, in neighbourhood with the slim water-weeds and oozy bottom-grass that are yet better than itself and more noble, in as far as Substances that appear as Shadows are preferable to Shadows mistaken for Substance! No! it must be a higher good to make you happy. While you labour for any thing below your proper Humanity, you seek a happy Life in the region of Death. Well saith the moral poet—

> Unless above himself he can
> Erect himself, how mean a thing is man! [2]

APHORISM XXXVII.

LEIGHTON.

There is an imitation of men that is impious and wicked, which consists in taking a copy of their sins. Again, there is an imitation which though not so grossly evil, yet is poor and servile, being in mean things, yea, sometimes descending to imitate the very imperfections of others, as fancying some comeliness in them : as some of Basil's

[1] See Hüber on Bees, and on Ants.
[2] Samuel Daniel, 1562—1619 :—

> Unless above himself he can
> Erect himself, how poor a thing is man!
> *To the Countess of Cumberland*, stanza 12.—ED.

scholars, who imitated his slow speaking, which he had a little in the extreme, and could not help. But this is always laudable, and worthy of the best minds, to be *imitators of that which is good*, wheresoever they find it; for that stays not in any man's person, as the ultimate pattern, but rises to the highest grace, being man's nearest likeness to God, His image and resemblance, bearing his stamp and superscription, and belonging peculiarly to Him, in what hand soever it be found, as carrying the mark of no other owner than Him.

APHORISM XXXVIII.

Leighton.

Those who think themselves high-spirited, and will bear least, as they speak, are often, even by that, forced to bow most, or to burst under it; while humility and meekness escape many a burden, and many a blow, always keeping peace within, and often without too.

APHORISM XXXIX.

Leighton.

Our condition is universally exposed to fears and troubles, and no man is so stupid but he studies and pro-jects for some fence against them, some bulwark to break the incursion of evils, and so to bring his mind to some ease, ridding it of the fear of them. Thus men seek safety in the greatness, or multitude, or supposed faithfulness of friends; they seek by any means to be strongly underset this way; to have many, and powerful, and trust-worthy friends. But wiser men, perceiving the unsafety and vanity of these and all external things, have cast about for some higher course. They see a necessity of withdrawing a man from externals, which do nothing but mock and deceive those most who trust most to them; but they cannot tell whither to direct him. The best of them bring him *into himself*, and think to quiet him so; but the truth is, he finds as little to support him there; there is nothing truly strong enough within him, to hold out against the many sorrows and fears which still from without do assault him. So then, though it is well done, to call off a man from outward things, as moving sands, that he build not on them, yet, this is not enough; for his own spirit is as unsettled a piece as is in all the world, and must have some higher strength than its own, to fortify and fix it. This is the way that is here taught, *Fear not their fear, but sanctify the Lord your God in your hearts;* and if you can attain this latter, the former will follow of itself.

APHORISM XL.

Worldly Troubles Idols.

LEIGHTON.

The too ardent love or self-willed desire of power, or wealth, or credit in the world, is (an Apostle has assured us) Idolatry. Now among the words or synonimes for idols, in the Hebrew language, there is one that in its primary sense signifies *troubles* (*tegirim*), other two that signify *terrors* (*miphletzeth* and *emim*). And so it is certainly. All our idols prove so to us. They fill us with nothing but anguish and troubles, with cares and fears, that are good for nothing but to be fit punishments of the folly, out of which they arise.

APHORISM XLI.

On the right Treatment of Infidels.

LEIGHTON AND COLERIDGE.

A regardless contempt of infidel writings is usually the fittest answer; *Spreta vilescerent.* But where the holy profession of Christians is likely to receive either the main or the indirect blow, and a word of defence may do any thing to ward it off, there we ought not to spare to do it.

Christian prudence goes a great way in the regulating of

this. Some are not capable of receiving rational answers, especially in Divine things ; they were not only lost upon them, but religion dishonoured by the contest.

Of this sort are the vulgar railers at religion, the foul-mouthed beliers of the Christian faith and history. Impudently false and slanderous assertions can be met only by assertions of their impudent and slanderous falsehood : and Christians will not, must not, condescend to this. How can mere railing be answered by them who are forbidden to return a railing answer ? Whether, or on what provocations, such offenders may be punished or coerced on the score of incivility, and ill-neighbourhood, and for abatement of a nuisance, as in the case of other scolds and endangerers of the public peace, must be trusted to the discretion of the civil magistrate. Even then, there is danger of giving them importance, and flattering their vanity, by attracting attention to their works, if the punishment be slight; and if severe, of spreading far and wide their reputation as martyrs, as the smell of a dead dog at a distance is said to change into that of musk. Experience hitherto seems to favour the plan of treating these *bêtes puantes* and *enfans de diable*, as their four-footed brethren, the skink and squash, are treated [1] by the American woodmen, who turn their backs upon the fetid intruder, and make appear not to see him, even at the cost of suffering him to regale on the favourite viand of these animals, the brains of a stray goose or crested *thraso* of the dunghill. At all events, it is degrading to the majesty, and injurious to the character of Religion, to make its safety the plea for their punishment, or at all to connect the name of Christianity with the castigation of indecencies

---

[1] About the end of the same year (says Kalm), another of these Animals (*Mephitis Americana*) crept into our cellar; but did not exhale the smallest scent, *because it was not disturbed. A foolish old woman, however, who perceived it at night, by the shining, and thought, I suppose, that it would set the world on fire, killed it : and at that moment its stench began to spread.*

We recommend this anecdote to the consideration of sundry old women, on this side of the Atlantic, who, though they do not wear the appropriate garment, are worthy to sit in their committee-room, like Bickerstaff in the Tatler, under the canopy of their grandam's hoop-petticoat.

that properly belong to the beadle, and the perpetrators of which would have equally deserved his lash, though the religion of their fellow-citizens, thus assailed by them, had been that of Fo or Juggernaut.

On the other hand, we are to answer every one that *inquires a reason*, or an account; which supposes something receptive of it. We ought to judge ourselves engaged to give it, be it an enemy, if he will hear; if it gain him not, it may in part convince and cool him; much more, should it be one who ingenuously inquires for satisfaction, and possibly inclines to receive the truth, but has been prejudiced by misrepresentations of it.

APHORISM XLII.

Passion no Friend to Truth.

LEIGHTON.

Truth needs not the service of passion; yea, nothing so disserves it, as passion when set to serve it. The *Spirit of truth* is withal the *Spirit of meekness*. The Dove that rested on that great champion of truth, who is The Truth itself, is from Him derived to the lovers of truth, and they ought to seek the participation of it. Imprudence makes some kind of Christians lose much of their labour, in speaking for religion, and drive those further off, whom they would draw into it.

The confidence that attends a Christian's belief makes the believer not fear men, to whom he answers, but still he fears his God, for whom he answers, and whose interest is chief in those things he speaks of. The soul that hath the deepest sense of spiritual things, and the truest knowledge of God, is most afraid to miscarry in speaking of Him, most tender and wary how to acquit itself when engaged to speak of and for God.[1]

---

[1] To the same purpose are the two following sentences from Hilary : *Etiam quæ pro Religione dicimus, cum grandi metu et disciplina dicere debemus.*—Hilarius de Trinit. Lib. 7.

Non relictus est hominum eloquiis de Dei rebus alius quam Dei sermo. —Idem.

The latter, however, must be taken with certain *qualifications* and

APHORISM XLIII.

On the Conscience.

LEIGHTON.

It is a fruitless verbal debate, whether Conscience be a Faculty or a Habit. When all is examined, Conscience will be found to be no other than *the mind of a man, under the notion of a particular reference to himself* and his own actions.

COMMENT.

What Conscience is, and that it is the ground and antecedent of human (or *self-*) consciousness, and not any modification of the latter, I have shown at large in a work announced for the press, and described in the Chapter following.[1] I have selected the preceding extract as an Exercise for Reflection; and *because* I think that in too closely following Thomas à Kempis, the Archbishop has strayed from his own judgment. The definition, for instance, seems to say all, and in fact says nothing; for if I asked, How do you define the *human mind?* the answer must at least *contain*, if not consist of, the words, "a mind capable of *Conscience.*" For Conscience is no synonime of Consciousness, nor any mere expression of the same as modified by the particular Object. On the contrary, a Consciousness properly human (that is, *Self*-consciousness), with the sense of moral responsibility, presupposes the Conscience, as its antecedent condition and ground. Lastly, the sentence, "It is a fruitless verbal debate," is an assertion of the same complexion with the contemptuous sneers at verbal criticism by the contemporaries of Bentley. In questions of Philosophy or Divinity, that have occupied

exceptions; as when any two or more texts are in apparent contradiction, and it is required to state a Truth that comprehends and reconciles both, and which, of course, cannot be expressed in the words of either,—for example, the filial subordination (*My Father is greater than I*), in the equal Deity (*My Father and I are one*).

[1] See Aphorisms on Spiritual Religion, p. 103.—ED.

the learned and been the subjects of many successive controversies, for one instance of mere logomachy I could bring ten instances of *logodædaly*, or verbal legerdemain, which have perilously confirmed prejudices, and withstood the advancement of truth in consequence of the neglect of *verbal debate*, that is, strict discussion of terms. In whatever sense, however, the term Conscience may be used, the following Aphorism is equally true and important. It is worth noticing, likewise, that Leighton himself in a following page (vol. ii. p. 97), tells us that a good Conscience is the *root* of a good Conversation : and then quotes from St. Paul a text, *Titus* i. 15, in which the Mind and the Conscience are expressly distinguished.

APHORISM XLIV.

The Light of Knowledge a necessary accompaniment of a Good Conscience.

LEIGHTON.

If you would have a good conscience, you must by all means have so much light, so much knowledge of the will of God, as may regulate you, and show you your way, may teach you how to do, and speak, and think, as in His presence.

APHORISM XLV.

Yet the Knowledge of the Rule, though Accompanied by an endeavour to accommodate our conduct to this Rule, will not of itself form a Good Conscience.

LEIGHTON.

To set the outward actions right, though with an honest intention, and not so to regard and find out the inward disorder of the heart, whence that in the actions flows, is but to be still putting the index of a clock right with your finger, while it is foul, or out of order within, which is a continual business, and does no good. Oh ! but a purified

G

conscience, a soul renewed and refined in its temper and affections, will make things go right without, in all the duties and acts of our calling.

APHORISM XLVI.

The Depth of the Conscience.

How deeply seated the conscience is in the human soul is seen in the effect which sudden calamities produce on guilty men, even when unaided by any determinate notion or fears of punishment after death. The wretched Criminal, as one rudely awakened from a long sleep, bewildered with the new light, and half recollecting, half striving to recollect, a fearful something, he knows not what, but which he will recognize as soon as he hears the name, already interprets the calamities into *judgments*, executions of a sentence passed by an *invisible* Judge; as if the vast pyre of the Last Judgment were already kindled in an unknown distance, and some flashes of it, darting forth at intervals beyond the rest, were flying and lighting upon the face of his soul. The calamity may consist in loss of fortune, or character, or reputation; but you hear no *regrets* from him. Remorse extinguishes all Regret; and Remorse is the *implicit* Creed of the Guilty.

APHORISM XLVII.

LEIGHTON AND COLERIDGE.

God hath suited every creature He hath made with a convenient good to which it tends, and in the obtainment of which it rests and is satisfied. Natural bodies have all their own natural place, whither, if not hindered, they move incessantly till they be in it; and they declare, by resting there, that they are (as I may say) where they would be. Sensitive creatures are carried to seek a sensitive good, as agreeable to their rank in being, and, attaining that, aim no further. Now, in this is the excellency of

Man, that he is made capable of a communion with his Maker, and, because capable of it, is unsatisfied without it: the soul, being cut out (so to speak) to that largeness, cannot be filled with less.   Though he is fallen from his right to that good, and from all right desire of it, yet, not from a capacity of it, no, nor from a necessity of it, for the answering and filling of his capacity.

Though the heart once gone from God turns continually further away from Him, and moves not towards Him till it be renewed, yet, even in that wandering, it retains that natural relation to God, as its centre, that it hath no true rest elsewhere, nor can by any means find it.   It is made for Him, and is therefore still restless till it meet with Him.

It is true, the natural man takes much pains to quiet his heart by other things, and digests many vexations with hopes of contentment in the end and accomplishment of some design he hath; but still the heart misgives.   Many times he attains not the thing he seeks; but if he do, yet he never attains the satisfaction he seeks and expects in it, but only learns from that to desire something further, and still hunts on after a fancy, drives his own shadow before him, and never overtakes it; and if he did, yet it is but a shadow.   And so, in running from God, besides the sad end, he carries an interwoven punishment with his sin, the natural disquiet and vexation of his spirit, fluttering to and fro, and *finding no rest for the sole of his foot; the waters* of inconstancy and vanity *covering the whole face of the earth.*

These things are too gross and heavy.   The soul, the immortal soul, descended from heaven, must either be more happy, or remain miserable.   The Highest, the Increated Spirit, is the proper good, *the Father of Spirits,* that pure and full good which raises the soul above itself; whereas all other things draw it down below itself.   So, then, it is never well with the soul but when it is near unto God, yea, in its union with Him, married to Him : mismatching itself elsewhere, it hath never anything but shame and sorrow. *All that forsake Thee shall be ashamed,* says the Prophet, *Jer.* xvii. 13; and the Psalmist, *They that are far off from thee shall perish, Psalm* lxxiii. 27.   And this is indeed our natural miserable condition, and it is often expressed this way, by estrangedness and distance from God.

The same sentiments are to be found in the works of Pagan philosophers and moralists. Well then may they be made a subject of Reflection in our days. And well may the pious deist, if such a character now exists, reflect that Christianity alone both teaches the way, and provides the means, of fulfilling the obscure promises of this great Instinct for all men, which the Philosophy of boldest pretensions confined to the sacred few.

APHORISM XLVIII.

A contracted Sphere, or what is called Retiring from the Business of the World, no Security from the Spirit of the World.

LEIGHTON.

The heart may be engaged in a little business, as much, if thou watch it not, as in many and great affairs. A man may drown in a little brook or pool, as well as in a great river, if he be down and plunge himself into it, and put his head under water. Some care thou must have, that thou mayest not care. Those things that are thorns indeed, thou must make a hedge of them, to keep out those temptations that accompany sloth, and extreme want that waits on it; but let them be the hedge; suffer them not to grow within the garden.

APHORISM XLIX.

On Church-going, as a part of Religious Morality, when not in reference to a Spiritual Religion.

LEIGHTON.

It is a strange folly in multitudes of us, to set ourselves no mark, to propound no end in the hearing of the Gospel. —The merchant sails not merely that he may sail, but for traffic, and traffics that he may be rich. The husbandman plows not merely to keep himself busy, with no further end, but plows that he may sow, and sows that he may reap with advantage. And shall we do the most excellent and fruitful work fruitlessly,—hear only to hear, and look no further? This is indeed a great vanity, and a great misery, to lose that labour, and gain nothing by it, which, duly used, would be of all others most advantageous and gainful: and yet all meetings are full of this!

APHORISM L.

On the Hopes and Self-Satisfaction of a religious Moralist, independent of a Spiritual Faith—on what are they grounded?

LEIGHTON.

There have been great disputes one way or another, about the merit of good works; but I truly think they who have laboriously engaged in them have been very idly, though very eagerly, employed about nothing, since the more sober of the schoolmen themselves acknowledge there can be no such thing as meriting from the blessed God, in the human, or, to speak more accurately, in any created nature whatsoever: nay, so far from any possibility of merit, there can be no room for reward any otherwise than of the sovereign pleasure and gracious kindness of God; and the more ancient writers, when they use the word merit, mean nothing by it but a certain *correlate* to that reward which God both promises and bestows of mere grace and benignity. Otherwise, in order to constitute what is properly called merit, many things must concur, which no man in his senses will presume to attribute to human works, though ever so excellent; particularly, that the thing done must not previously be matter of debt, and that it be entire, or our own act, unassisted by foreign aid; it must also be perfectly good, and it must bear an adequate proportion to the reward claimed in consequence of it. If all these things do not concur, the act cannot possibly amount to merit. Whereas I think no one will venture to assert, that any one of these can take place in any human action whatever. But why should I enlarge here, when one single circumstance overthrows all those titles: the most righteous of mankind would not be able to stand, if his works were weighed in the balance of strict justice; how much less then could they deserve that immense glory which is now in question! Nor is this to be denied only concerning the unbeliever and the sinner, but concerning the righteous and pious believer, who is not only free from all the guilt of his former impenitence and rebellion, but endowed with the gift of the Spirit. "For the time *is come* that judgment must begin at the house of God: and if *it* first *begin* at us, what shall the end *be* of them that obey not the Gospel of God? And if the righteous scarcely be saved, where shall the ungodly and the sinner appear?" 1 *Peter*, iv. 17, 18. The Apostle's interrogation expresses the most vehement negation, and signifies that no mortal, in whatever degree he is placed, if he be called to the strict examination of Divine Justice, without daily and repeated forgiveness, could be able to keep his standing, and much less could he arise to that glorious height. "That merit," says Bernard, "on which my hope relies, consists in these three things; the love of adoption, the truth of the promise, and the power of its performance." This is the threefold cord which cannot be broken.

COMMENT.

Often have I heard it said by advocates for the Socinian scheme—True! we are all sinners; but even in the Old Testament God has promised forgiveness on repentance. One of the Fathers (I forget which) supplies the retort— True! God has promised pardon on penitence: but has he promised penitence on sin?—He that repenteth shall be forgiven: but where is it said, He that sinneth shall repent? But repentance, perhaps, the repentance required in Scripture, *the Passing into a new mind*, into a new and contrary Principle of Action, this METANOIA,[1] is in the sinner's own power? at his own liking? He has but to open his eyes to the sin, and the tears are close at hand to wash it away!—Verily, the exploded tenet of *Transubstan-*

---

[1] Μετανοιὰ, the New Testament word which we render by Repentance, compounded of μετὰ, *trans*, and νȣς, *mens*, the Spirit, or practical Reason.

tiation is scarcely at greater variance with the common sense and experience of mankind, or borders more closely on a contradiction in terms, than this volunteer *Transmentation*, this Self-change, as the easy [1] means of Self-salvation! But the reflections of our evangelical author on this subject will appropriately commence the Aphorisms relating to Spiritual Religion.

[1] May I without offence be permitted to record the very appropriate title, with which a stern Humorist *lettered* a collection of Unitarian Tracts ?—" Salvation made easy ; or, Every Man his own Redeemer."

ELEMENTS

OF

RELIGIOUS PHILOSOPHY,

PRELIMINARY TO THE

APHORISMS ON SPIRITUAL RELIGION.

PHILIP saith unto him : Lord, *show* us the Father, and it sufficeth us. Jesus saith unto him, He that hath seen me hath seen the Father ; and how sayest thou then, *Show* us the Father ? Believest thou not, that I am in the Father, and the Father in me ? And I will pray the Father and he shall give you another Comforter, even the *Spirit* of Truth : whom the world *cannot* receive, because it seeth him not, neither knoweth him. But ye know him, for he dwelleth *with* you and *shall* be *in* you. And in that day ye shall know that I am in my Father, and ye in me, and I in you. *John* xiv. 8, 9, 10, 16, 17, 20.

PRELIMINARY.

IF there be aught *Spiritual* in Man, the Will must be such.

If there be a Will, there must be a Spirituality in Man.

I suppose both positions granted. The Reader admits the reality of the power, agency, or mode of Being expressed in the term, Spirit; and the actual existence of a Will. He sees clearly, that the idea of the former is necessary to the conceivability of the latter; and that, *vice versâ*, in asserting the *fact* of the latter he presumes and instances the truth of the former—just as in our common and re-

ceived Systems of Natural Philosophy, the Being of imponderable Matter is assumed to render the lode-stone
intelligible, and the Fact of the lode-stone adduced to
prove the reality of imponderable Matter.

In short, I suppose the reader, whom I now invite to
the third and last division of the work, already disposed
to reject for himself and his human brethren the insi-
dious title of " Nature's noblest *animal*," or to retort it as
the unconscious irony of the Epicurean poet on the anima-
lizing tendency of his own philosophy.   I suppose him
convinced, that there is more in man than can be rationally
referred to the life of Nature and the mechanism of Organization ; that he has a will not included in this mechanism ; and that the Will is in an especial and pre-eminent
sense the spiritual part of our Humanity.

Unless, then, we have some distinct notion of the Will,
and some acquaintance with the prevalent errors respecting
the same, an insight into the nature of Spiritual Religion
is scarcely possible ; and our reflections on the particular
truths and evidences of a Spiritual State will remain obscure, perplexed, and unsafe.   To place my reader on this
requisite vantage-ground, is the purpose of the following
exposition.

We have begun, as in geometry, with defining our Terms ;
and we proceed, like the Geometricians, with stating our
POSTULATES ; the difference being, that the postulates of
Geometry *no* man *can* deny, those of Moral Science are
such as no *good* man *will* deny.   For it is *not* in our power
to disclaim our nature, as *sentient* beings ; but it *is* in our
power to disclaim our nature as *moral* beings.[1]   It is possible (barely possible, I admit) that a man may have remained ignorant or unconscious of the Moral Law within
him : and a man need only persist in disobeying the Law
of Conscience to *make* it possible for himself to deny its
existence, or to reject or repel it as a phantom of Superstition.   Were it otherwise, the Creed would stand in the
same relation to Morality as the multiplication table.

This then is the distinction of Moral Philosophy—*not*

---

[1] In a leaf of corrections to the text of the first edition Coleridge
directed that " prerogative as *moral* beings" should be read here.   The
correction seems to have been overlooked by Coleridge's editors.—ED.

that I begin with one or more *assumptions:* for this is common to *all* science; but—that I assume a something, the proof of which no man can *give* to another, yet every man may *find* for himself. If any man assert, that he *can* not find it, I am *bound* to disbelieve him. I cannot do otherwise without unsettling the very foundations of my own moral nature. For I either find it as an *essential* of the Humanity *common* to him and me : or I have not *found* it at all, except as an hypochondriast finds *glass* legs. If, on the other hand, he *will* not find it, he excommunicates himself. He forfeits his *personal* rights, and becomes a *Thing:* that is, one who may rightfully be *employed*, or *used* as[1] means to an end, against his will, and without regard to his interest.

All the significant objections of the Materialist and Necessitarian are contained in the term, Morality, all the objections of the infidel in the term, Religion. The very terms, I say, imply a something *granted*, which the Objection supposes *not* granted. The term *presumes* what the objection denies, and in denying *presumes* the contrary. For it is most important to observe, that the reasoners on *both* sides commence by taking something for granted, our assent to which they ask or demand : that is, both set off with an Assumption in the form of a Postulate. But the Epicurean assumes what according to himself he neither is nor can be under any *obligation* to assume, and demands what he *can* have no *right* to demand : for *he* denies the reality of *all* moral Obligation, the existence of *any* Right. If he use the *words*, Right and Obligation, he does it deceptively, and means only Power and Compulsion. To overthrow the Faith in aught higher or other than Nature and physical Necessity, is the very purpose of his

---

[1] On this principle alone is it possible to justify *capital*, or *ignominious* punishments (or indeed any punishment not having the reformation of the Criminal, as *one* of its objects). Such punishments, like those inflicted on Suicides, must be regarded as *posthumous:* the wilful extinction of the moral and personal life being, for the purposes of punitive Justice, equivalent to a wilful destruction of the natural life. If the speech of Judge Burnet to the horse-stealer (You are not hanged for stealing a horse ; but, that horses may not be stolen) can be vindicated at all, it must be on *this* principle ; and not on the all-unsettling scheme of *Expedience*, which is the anarchy of Morals.

argument. He desires you only to *take for granted*, that *all* reality is *in*cluded in Nature, and he may then safely defy you to ward off his conclusion—that *nothing* is *ex*cluded !

But as he cannot morally demand, neither can he rationally expect, your assent to this premiss : for he cannot be ignorant, that the best and greatest of men have devoted their lives to the enforcement of the contrary, that the vast majority of the human race in all ages and in all nations have believed in the contrary ; and there is not a language on earth, in which he could argue, for ten minutes, in support of his scheme, without sliding into words and phrases, that imply the contrary. It has been said, that the Arabic has a thousand names for a lion ; but this would be a trifle compared with the number of superfluous words and useless synonyms that would be found in an *Index Expurgatorius* of any European dictionary constructed on the principles of a consistent and strictly consequential Materialism.

The *Christian* likewise grounds *his* philosophy on assertions ; but with the best of all *reasons* for making them— namely, that he *ought* so to do. He asserts what he can neither prove, nor account for, nor himself comprehend ; but with the strongest *inducements,* that of understanding thereby whatever else it most concerns him to understand aright. And yet his assertions have nothing in them of theory or hypothesis : but are in immediate reference to three ultimate *facts ;* namely, the Reality of the LAW OF CONSCIENCE ; the existence of a RESPONSIBLE WILL, as the subject of that law ; and lastly, the existence of EVIL—of Evil essentially such, not by accident of outward circumstances, not derived from its physical consequences, nor from any cause, out of itself. The first is a Fact of Consciousness ; the second a Fact of Reason necessarily concluded from the first ; and the third a Fact of History interpreted by both.

Omnia exeunt in mysterium, says a schoolman ; that is, *There is nothing, the absolute ground of which is not a Mystery*. The contrary were indeed a contradiction in terms : for how can that, which is to explain all things, be susceptible of an explanation ? It would be to suppose the same thing first and second at the same time.

If I rested here, I should merely have placed my Creed

in direct opposition to that of the Necessitarians, who assume (for observe *both* Parties begin in an *Assumption*, and cannot do otherwise) that motives act on the Will, as bodies act on bodies ; and that whether mind and matter are essentially the same, or essentially different, they are both alike under one and the same law of compulsory Causation. But this is far from exhausting my intention. I mean at the same time to oppose the disciples of SHAFTES-BURY and those who, substituting one Faith for another, have been well called the pious Deists of the last century, in order to distinguish them from the Infidels of the present age, who *persuade* themselves, (for the thing itself is not possible) that they reject all Faith. I declare my dissent from these too, because they imposed upon themselves an *idea* for a fact : a most sublime idea indeed, and so necessary to human nature, that without it no virtue is conceivable : but still an idea. In contradiction to their splendid but delusory tenets, I profess a deep conviction that man was and is a *fallen* creature, not by accidents of bodily constitution, or any other cause, which *human* wisdom in a course ·of ages might be supposed capable of removing ; but as diseased in his *Will*, in that Will which is the true and only strict synonime of the word, I, or the intelligent Self. Thus at each of these two opposite roads (the philosophy of Hobbes and that of Shaftesbury), I have placed a directing post, informing my fellow-travellers, that on neither of these roads can they see the Truths to which I would direct their attention.

But the place of starting was at the meeting of *four* roads, and one only was the right road. I proceed, therefore, to preclude the opinion of those likewise, who indeed agree with me as to the moral Responsibility of man in opposition to Hobbes and the Anti-Moralists, and that he is a fallen creature, essentially diseased, in opposition to Shaftesbury and the misinterpreters of Plato ; but who differ from me in exaggerating the diseased *weakness* of the Will into an absolute privation of all Freedom, thereby making moral responsibility, not a mystery *above* comprehension, but a direct contradiction, of which we do distinctly comprehend the absurdity. Among the consequences of this doctrine, is that direful one of swallowing up all

the attributes of the Supreme Being in the one Attribute of
infinite Power, and thence deducing that things are good
and wise because they were created, and not created through
Wisdom and Goodness. Thence too the awful Attribute
of *Justice* is explained away into a mere right of absolute
Property; the sacred distinction between things and persons is erased; and the selection of persons for virtue and
vice in this life, and for eternal happiness or misery in
the next, is represented as the result of a mere *Will*, acting
in the blindness and solitude of its own Infinity. The
title of a work written by the great and pious Boyle is
" Of the Awe, which the human Mind owes to the Supreme
Reason." This, in the language of these gloomy doctors,
must be translated into—" The horror, which a Being
capable of eternal Pleasure or Pain is compelled to feel at
the idea of an Infinite Power, about to inflict the latter on
an immense majority of human Souls, without any power
on their part either to prevent it or the actions which are
(not indeed its causes but) its assigned *signals*, and preceding links of the same iron chain ! "

Against these tenets I maintain, that a Will conceived
separately from Intelligence is a Non-entity and a mere
phantasm of abstraction; and that a Will, the state of
which does in *no sense* originate in its own act, is an absolute contradiction. It might be an Instinct, an Impulse,
a plastic Power, and, if accompanied with consciousness, a
Desire; but a Will it *could* not be. And this *every* human
being *knows* with equal *clearness*, though different minds
may *reflect* on it with different degrees of *distinctness;* for
who would not smile at the notion of a rose *willing* to put
forth its buds and expand them into flowers ? That such
a phrase would be deemed a *poetic* licence proves the
difference in the things : for all metaphors are grounded on
an apparent likeness of things essentially different. I utterly
disclaim the notion, that any *human* Intelligence, with
whatever power it might manifest itself, is *alone* adequate
to the office of restoring health to the Will: but at the
same time I deem it impious and absurd to hold, that the
Creator would have *given* us the faculty of Reason, or that
the Redeemer would in so many varied forms of argument
and persuasion have *appealed* to it, if it had been either

totally useless or wholly impotent. Lastly, I find all these
several Truths reconciled and united in the belief, that the
imperfect human understanding can be effectually exerted
only in *subordination* to, and in a dependent *alliance* with,
the means and aidances supplied by the All-perfect and
Supreme Reason; but that under these conditions it is not
only an admissible, but a necessary, instrument of better-
ing both ourselves and others.

We may now proceed to our reflections on the *Spirit* of
Religion. The first three or four Aphorisms I have selected
from the Theological Works of Dr. Henry More, a contemporary of Archbishop Leighton, and like him, holden in
suspicion by the Calvinists of that time as a Latitudinarian
and Platonizing Divine, and who probably, like him, would
have been arraigned as a Calvinist by the Latitudinarians
(I cannot say, Platonists) of this day, had the suspicion
been equally groundless. One or two I have ventured to
add from my own Reflections. The purpose, however, is
the same in all—that of declaring, in the first place, what
Spiritual Religion is *not*, what is *not* a Religious Spirit, and
what are *not* to be deemed influences of the Spirit. If
after these declaimers I shall without proof be charged by
any with renewing or favouring the errors of the *Familists*,
Vanists, *Seekers*, *Behmenists*, or by whatever other names
Church History records the poor bewildered Enthusiasts,
who in the swarming time of our Republic turned the
facts of the Gospel into allegories, and superseded the
written ordinances of Christ by a pretended Teaching and
sensible Presence of the Spirit, I appeal against them to
their own consciences, as wilful slanderers. But if with
proof, I have in these Aphorisms signed and sealed my own
condemnation.

"These things I could not forbear to write. For *the
Light within me*, that is, *my Reason and Conscience*, does
assure me, that the Ancient and Apostolic Faith according
to the *historical* meaning thereof, and in the *literal* sense

of the Creed, is solid and true : and that *Familism*[1] in its fairest form and under whatever disguise, is a smooth tale to seduce the simple from their Allegiance to Christ."

HENRY MORE.[2]

[1] The religion of the Dutch sect called the "Family of Love," originated by Henry Nicholas about 1540.—ED.
[2] More's ' Mystery of Godliness.'—ED.

APHORISMS ON SPIRITUAL RELIGION.

And here it will not be impertinent to observe, that what the eldest Greek Philosophy entitled *the Reason* (ΝΟΥΣ) and *Ideas*, the philosophic Apostle names *the Spirit* and *Truths spiritually* discerned : while to those who in the pride of learning or in the over-weening meanness of modern metaphysics decry the doctrine of the Spirit in Man and its possible communion with the Holy Spirit, as *vulgar* enthusiasm, I submit the following sentences from a Pagan philosopher, a nobleman and a minister of state—"Ita dico, Lucili! SACER INTRA NOS SPIRITUS SEDET, malorum bonorumque nostrorum observator et custos. Hic prout a nobis tractatus est, ita nos ipse tractat. BONUS VIR SINE DEO NEMO EST." SENECA, *Epist.* xli.

APHORISM I. ·

H. MORE.

EVERY one is *to give a reason of his faith;* but Priests and Ministers more punctually than any, their province being to make good every sentence of the Bible to a rational inquirer into the truth of these Oracles. Enthusiasts find it an easy thing to heat the fancies of unlearned and unreflecting hearers; but when a sober man would be satisfied of the *grounds* from whence they speak, he shall not have one syllable or the least tittle of a pertinent answer. Only they will talk big of THE SPIRIT, and inveigh against *Reason* with bitter reproaches, calling it carnal or fleshly, though it be indeed no soft flesh, but ·enduring and penetrant steel, even the sword of the Spirit, and such as pierces to the heart.

APHORISM II.

H. MORE.

There are two very bad things in this resolving of men's Faith and Practice into *the immediate suggestion* of a Spirit not acting on our understandings, or rather into the illumination of such a Spirit as they can give no account of, such as does not enlighten their reason or enable them to render their doctrine intelligible to others. First, it defaces and makes useless that part of the Image of God in us, which we call REASON; and secondly, it takes away that advantage, which raises Christianity above all other religions, that she dare appeal to so solid a faculty.

APHORISM III.

It is the glory of the Gospel Charter and the Christian Constitution, that its Author and Head is the Spirit of Truth, Essential Reason as well as Absolute and Incomprehensible Will. Like a just Monarch, he refers even his own causes to the Judgment of his high Courts. He has his King's Bench in the Reason, his Court of Equity in the Conscience: *that* the Representative of his majesty and universal justice, *this* the nearest to the King's heart, and the dispenser of his particular decrees. He has likewise his Court of Common Pleas in the Understanding, his Court of Exchequer in the Prudence. The Laws are *his* Laws. And though by Signs and Miracles he has mercifully condescended to interline here and there with his own hand the great Statute-book, which he had dictated to his Amanuensis, Nature; yet has he been graciously pleased to forbid our receiving as the *King's* Mandates aught that is not stamped with the Great Seal of the Conscience, and countersigned by the Reason.

H

APHORISM IV.

On an Unlearned Ministry, under pretence of a Call of the Spirit, and inward Graces superseding Outward helps.

H. MORE.

Tell me, Ye high-flown *Perfectionists*, ye boasters of the *Light within* you, could the highest perfection of your inward Light ever show to you the history of past ages, the state of the world at present, the knowledge of arts and tongues, without books or teachers ? How then can you understand the Providence of God, or the age, the purpose, the fulfilment of Prophecies, or distinguish such as have been fulfilled from those to the fulfilment of which we are to look forward ? How can you judge concerning the authenticity and uncorruptedness of the Gospels, and the other sacred Scriptures ? And how without this knowledge can you support the truth of Christianity ? How can you either have, or give a reason for the faith which you profess ? This *Light within*, that loves darkness, and would exclude those excellent Gifts of God to Mankind, Knowledge and Understanding, what is it but a sullen self-sufficiency within you, engendering contempt of superiors, pride and a spirit of division, and inducing you to reject for yourselves and to undervalue in others the *helps without*, which the Grace of God has provided and appointed for his Church—nay, to make them grounds or pretexts of your dislike or suspicion of Christ's Ministers who have fruitfully availed themselves of the Helps afforded them ?

APHORISM V.

H. MORE.

There are wanderers, whom neither pride nor a perverse humour have led astray ; and whose condition is such, that I think few more worthy of a man's best directions. For the more imperious sects having put such unhandsome vizards on Christianity, and the sincere milk of the *Word* having been every where so sophisticated by the humours and inventions of men, it has driven these anxious melancholists to seek for *a teacher* that cannot deceive, the voice of the *eternal* Word within them; to which if they be faithful, they assure themselves it will be faithful to them in return. Nor would this be a groundless presumption, if they had sought this voice in the Reason and the Conscience, with the Scripture articulating the same, instead of giving heed to their fancy and mistaking bodily disturbances, and the vapours resulting therefrom, for inspiration and the teaching of the Spirit.

APHORISM VI.

Bishop Hacket.

When every man is his own end, all things will come to a bad end. Blessed were those days, when every man thought himself rich and fortunate by the good success of the public wealth and glory. We want public souls, we want them. I speak it with compassion : there is no sin and abuse in the world that affects my thought so much. Every man thinks, that he is a whole Commonwealth in his private family. *Omnes quæ sua sunt quærunt.* All seek their own.[1]

Comment.

Selfishness is common to all ages and countries. In all ages Self-seeking is the Rule, and Self-sacrifice the Exception. But if to seek our private advantage in harmony with, and by the furtherance of, the public prosperity, and to derive a portion of our happiness from sympathy with the prosperity of our fellow-men—if this be Public Spirit, it would be morose and querulous to pretend that there is any want of it in this country and at the present time. On the contrary, the number of "public souls"

[1] Hacket's Sermons, p. 449.—Ed.

and the general readiness to contribute to the public good,
in science and in religion, in patriotism and in philanthropy, stand prominent [1] among the characteristics of this
and the preceding generation. The habit of referring actions
and opinions to fixed laws ; convictions rooted in principles ; thought, insight, system ;—these, had the good
Bishop lived in our times, would have been his *desiderata,*
and the theme of his complaints.—" We want *thinking*
Souls, we *want them.*"

This and the three preceding extracts will suffice as
precautionary Aphorisms. And here again, the reader
may exemplify the great advantages to be obtained from
the habit of tracing the *proper* meaning and history of
words. We need only recollect the common and idiomatic
phrases in which the word " spirit " occurs in a physical
or material sense (as, fruit has lost its *spirit* and flavour),
to be convinced that its property is to improve, enliven,
actuate some other thing, not to constitute a thing in its
own name. The enthusiast may find one exception to this
where the material itself is called *Spirit.* And when
he calls to mind, how *this* spirit acts when taken *alone*
by the unhappy persons who in their first exultation will
boast that it is meat, drink, fire, and clothing to them,
all in one—when he reflects, that its properties are to
inflame, intoxicate, madden, with exhaustion, lethargy,
and atrophy for the sequels—well for him, if in some

---

[1] The very marked *positive* as well as comparative, magnitude and
prominence of the bump, entitled BENEVOLENCE (*see Spurzheim's Map
of the Human Skull*) on the head of the late Mr. John Thurtel, has
woefully unsettled the faith of many ardent Phrenologists, and
strengthened the previous doubts of a still greater number into utter
disbelief. On MY mind this fact (for a *fact* it is) produced the directly
contrary effect ; and inclined me to suspect, for the first time, that there
may be some truth in the Spurzheimian Scheme. Whether future
Craniologists may not see cause to *new-name* this and one or two other
of these convex gnomons, is quite a different question. At present, and
according to the present use of words, any such change would be
premature ; and we must be content to say, that Mr. Thurtel's Benevolence was insufficiently modified by the unprotrusive and unindicated
convolutes of the brain, that secrete honesty and common-sense. The
organ of Destructiveness was indirectly *potentiated* by the absence or
imperfect development of the glands of Reason and Conscience in this,
" *unfortunate Gentleman !* "

lucid interval he should fairly put the question to his own mind, how far this is *analogous* to his own case, and whether the exception does not confirm the rule. The *Letter* without the Spirit killeth; but does it follow, that the Spirit is to kill the Letter? To kill that which it is its appropriate office to enliven?

However, where the Ministry is not invaded, and the plain sense of the Scriptures is left undisturbed, and the Believer looks for the suggestions of the Spirit only or chiefly in applying particular passages to his own individual case and exigences; though in this there may be much weakness, some delusion and imminent danger of more, I cannot but join with Henry More in avowing, that I feel knit to such a man in the bonds of a common faith far more closely, than to those who receive neither the Letter nor the Spirit, turning the one into metaphor, and oriental hyperbole, in order to explain away the other into the influence of motives suggested by their own understandings, and realized by their own strength.

APHORISMS

ON THAT

WHICH IS INDEED SPIRITUAL RELIGION.

IN the selection of the extracts that form the remainder of this volume and of the comments affixed, I had the following objects principally in view :—first, to exhibit the true and scriptural meaning and intent of several Articles of Faith, that are rightly classed among the Mysteries and peculiar Doctrines of Christianity :—secondly, to show the perfect rationality of these Doctrines, and their freedom from all just objection when examined by their proper organs, the Reason and Conscience of Man :—lastly, to exhibit from the works of Leighton, who perhaps of all our learned Protestant Theologians best deserves the title of a Spiritual Divine, an instructive and affecting picture of the contemplations, reflections, conflicts, consolations and monitory experiences of a philosophic and richly-gifted mind, amply stored with all the knowledge that books and long intercourse with men of the most discordant characters could give, under the convictions, impressions, and habits of a Spiritual Religion.

To obviate a possible disappointment in any of my readers, who may chance to be engaged in theological studies, it may be well to notice, that in vindicating the peculiar tenets of our Faith, I have not entered on the Doctrine of the Trinity, or the still profounder Mystery of the Origin of Moral Evil—and this for the reasons following. 1. These Doctrines are not (strictly speaking) subjects of *Reflection*, in the proper sense of this word : and both of them demand a power and persistency of Abstraction, and a previous discipline in the highest forms of human thought, which it would be unwise, if not presumptuous, to expect from any, who require "*Aids* to Reflection," or would be likely to seek them in the present work. 2. In my intercourse with men of various ranks and ages, I have found the far larger number of serious and inquiring persons little, if at all, disquieted by doubts respecting Articles of Faith, that are simply above their comprehension. It is only where the belief required of them jars with their *moral* feelings; where a doctrine in the sense, in which they have been taught to receive it, appears to contradict their clear notions of right and wrong, or to be at variance with the divine attributes of goodness and justice; that these men are surprised, perplexed, and alas! not seldom offended and alienated. Such are the Doctrines of Arbitrary Election and Reprobation ; the Sentence to everlasting Torment by an eternal and necessitating decree ; vicarious Atonement, and the necessity of the Abasement, Agony and ignominious Death of a most holy and meritorious Person, to appease the wrath of God. Now it is more especially for such persons, unwilling sceptics, who believing earnestly ask help for their unbelief, that this volume was compiled, and the comments written : and therefore to the Scripture Doctrines, *intended* by the above-mentioned, my principal attention has been directed.

But lastly, the whole Scheme of the Christian Faith, including *all* the Articles of Belief common to the Greek and Latin, the Roman and the Protestant Churches, with the threefold proof, that it is *ideally, morally,* and *historically* true, will be found exhibited and vindicated in a proportionally larger work, the principal labour of my life since manhood, and which I am now preparing for the press under the title, 'Assertion of Religion, as necessarily *involving* Revelation ; and of Christianity, as the only Revelation of permanent and universal validity.' [1]

---

[1] A work left incomplete by Coleridge, and not yet given to the world. —ED.

APHORISM I.

Leighton.

Where, if not in Christ, is the Power that can persuade a Sinner to return, that can *bring home a heart to God?*

Common mercies of God, though they have a leading faculty to repentance, (*Rom.* ii. 4.) yet, the rebellious heart will not be led by them. The judgments of God, public or personal, though they ought to drive us to God, yet the heart, unchanged, runs the further from God. Do we not see it by ourselves and other sinners about us? They look not at all towards Him who smites, much less do they return; or if any more serious thoughts of returning arise upon the surprise of an affliction, how soon vanish they, either the stroke abating, or the heart, by time, growing hard and senseless under it! Leave Christ out, I say, and all other means work not this way; neither the works nor the word of God sounding daily in his ear, *Return return.* Let the noise of the rod speak it too, and both join together to make the cry the louder, *yet the wicked will do wickedly: Dan.* xii. 10.

Comment.

By the phrase "in Christ," I understand all the supernatural aids vouchsafed and conditionally promised in the Christian dispensation; and among them the Spirit of Truth, which the world cannot receive, were it only that the knowledge of *spiritual* Truth is of necessity immediate and *intuitive:* and the World or Natural Man possesses no higher intuitions than those of the pure *Sense,* which are the subjects of *mathematical* science. But *aids,* observe! Therefore, not *by* Will of man alone; but neither *without* the Will. The doctrine of modern Calvinism as laid down by Jonathan Edwards and the late Dr. Williams, which represents a Will absolutely passive, clay in the hands of a potter, destroys all Will, takes away its essence and definition, as effectually as in saying: This circle is square—I should deny the figure to be a circle at all. It was in strict consistency therefore, that these writers supported the Necessitarian scheme, and made the relation of Cause and Effect the Law of the Universe, subjecting to its mechanism the moral World no less than the material or physical. It follows, that all is Nature. Thus, though few writers use the term Spirit more frequently, they in effect deny its existence, and evacuate the term of all its proper meaning. With such a system not the wit of man nor all the Theodicies ever framed by human ingenuity before and since the attempt of the celebrated Leibnitz, can reconcile the Sense of Responsibility, nor the fact of the difference *in kind* between REGRET AND REMORSE. The same compulsion of consequence drove the Fathers of Modern (or Pseudo-) Calvinism to the origination of Holiness in power, of Justice in right of Property, and whatever other outrages on the common sense and moral feelings of mankind they have sought to cover, under the fair name of *Sovereign Grace*.

I will not take on me to defend sundry harsh and inconvenient expressions in the works of Calvin. Phrases equally strong and assertions not less rash and startling are no rarities in the writings of Luther; for catachresis was the favourite figure of speech in that age. But let not the opinions of either on this most fundamental subject be confounded with the New England System, now entitled Calvinistic. The fact is simply this. Luther considered the pretensions to Free-will *boastful*, and better suited to the "budge doctors of the Stoic Fur," than to the preachers of the Gospel, whose great theme is the Redemption of the Will from Slavery; the restoration of the Will to perfect Freedom being the *end* and consummation of the redemptive process, and the same with the entrance of the Soul into Glory, that is, its union with Christ: "GLORY" (*John* xvii. 5.) being one of the names or tokens or symbols of the Spiritual Messiah. Prospectively to this we are to understand the words of our Lord. "At that day ye shall know that I am in my Father, and ye in me," *John* xiv. 20: the freedom of a finite will being possible under this condition only, that it has become one with the will of God. Now as the difference of a captive and enslaved Will, and

no Will at all, such is the difference between the *Lutheranism*
of Calvin and the Calvinism of Jonathan Edwards.

APHORISM II.

LEIGHTON.

There is nothing in religion farther out of Nature's reach,
and more remote from the natural man's liking and
believing, than the doctrine of Redemption by a Saviour,
and by a crucified Saviour. It is comparatively easy to
persuade men of the necessity of an amendment of conduct; it is more difficult to make them see the necessity of
Repentance in the *Gospel* sense, the necessity of a change
in the *principle* of action; but to convince men of the
necessity of the Death of Christ is the most difficult of all.
And yet the first is but varnish and white-wash without
the second; and the second but a barren notion without
the last. Alas! of those who admit the doctrine in words,
how large a number evade it in fact, and empty it of all its
substance and efficacy, making the effect the efficient cause,
or attributing their election to Salvation to a supposed
Foresight of their Faith and Obedience.—But it is most
vain to imagine a faith in such and such men, which being
foreseen by God, determined him to elect them for salvation: were it only that nothing at all is *future*, or can have
this imagined *futurition*, but *as* it is decreed, and *because* it
is decreed by God so to be.

COMMENT.

No impartial person, competently acquainted with the
history of the Reformation, and the works of the earlier
Protestant Divines, at home and abroad, even to the close
of Elizabeth's reign, will deny that the doctrines of Calvin
on Redemption and the natural state of fallen man, are in
all essential points the same as those of Luther, Zuinglius,
and the first Reformers collectively. These Doctrines
have, however, since the re-establishment of the Episcopal

Church at the return of Charles II., been as generally [1] exchanged for what is commonly entitled Arminianism, but which, taken as a complete and explicit Scheme of Belief, it would be both historically and theologically more accurate to call *Grotianism*, or Christianity according to Grotius. The change was not, we may readily believe, effected without a struggle. In the Romish Church this latitudinarian system, patronized by the Jesuits, was manfully resisted by Jansenius, Arnauld, and Pascal; in our own Church by the Bishops Davenant, Sanderson, Hall, and the Archbishops Usher and Leighton: and in the latter half of the preceding' Aphorism the reader has a *specimen* of the *reasonings* by which Leighton strove to

---

[1] At a period, in which Doctors Marsh and Wordsworth have, by the Zealous on one side, being charged with Popish principles on account of their *Anti-bibliolatry*, and the sturdy adherents of the doctrines common to Luther and Calvin, and the literal interpreters of the Articles and Homilies, are, (I wish I could say, altogether without any fault of their own) regarded by the Clergy generally as virtual Schismatics, dividers *of*, though not *from*, the Church, it is serving the cause of charity to assist in circulating the following instructive passage from the Life of Bishop Hackett respecting the dispute between the Augustinians, or Luthero-Calvinistic divines and the Grotians of his age: in which Controversy (says his biographer) he, Hackett, " was ever very moderate."

" But having been bred under Bishop Davenant and Dr. Ward in Cambridge, he was addicted to their sentiments. Archbishop Usher would say, that Davenant understood those controversies better than ever any man did since St. Augustine. But he (Bishop Hackett) used to say, that he was *sure* he had *three* excellent men of his mind in this controversy: 1. *Padre Paolo* (Father Paul) whose letter is extant in Heinsius, *anno* 1604: 2. *Thomas Aquinas:* 3. St. Augustine. But besides and above them all, he believed in his Conscience that St. Paul was of the same mind likewise. Yet at the same time he would profess, that he disliked no Arminians, but such as revile and defame every one who is *not so:* and he would often commend Arminius himself for his excellent wit and parts, but only tax his want of reading and knowledge in Antiquity. And he ever held, it was the foolishest thing in the world to say the Arminians were *Popishly* inclined, when so many Dominicians and Jansenists were rigid followers of Augustine in these points: and no less foolish to say that the *Anti-Arminians* were Puritans or Presbyterians, when *Ward*, and *Davenant*, and Prideaux, and Brownrig, those stout champions for Episcopacy, were decided Anti-Arminians; while Arminius himself was ever a Presbyterian. Therefore he greatly commended the moderation of our Church, which extended equal Communion to both."

invalidate or counterpoise the *reasonings* of the inno-
vators.

Passages of this sort are, however, of rare occurrence in
Leighton's works. Happily for thousands, he was more
usefully employed in making his readers feel that the
doctrines in question, *scripturally treated, and taken as co-
organized parts of a great organic whole*, need no such reasonings. And better still would it have been, had he left
them altogether for those, who severally detaching the
great features of Revelation from the living context of
Scripture, do by that very act destroy their life and purpose. And then, like the eyes of the Indian spider,[1] they
become clouded microscopes, to exaggerate and distort all
the other parts and proportions.—No offence then will be
occasioned, I trust, by the frank avowal that I have given
to the preceding passage a place among the Spiritual
Aphorisms for the sake of the Comment: the following
Remarks having been the first marginal note I had pencilled
on Leighton's pages, and thus (remotely, at least) the
occasion of the present work.

Leighton, I observed, throughout his inestimable work,
avoids all metaphysical views of Election, relatively to God,
and confines himself to the doctrine in its relation to Man:
and in that sense too, in which every Christian may judge
of it who strives to be sincere with his own heart. The
following may, I think, be taken as a safe and useful Rule
in religious inquiries. Ideas, that derive their origin and
substance from the *Moral* Being, and to the reception of
which as true *objectively* (that is, as corresponding to a
reality out of the human mind) we are determined by a
practical interest exclusively, may not, like theoretical or
speculative Positions, be pressed onward into all their possible *logical* consequences.[2] The Law of Conscience, and

---

[1] *Aranca prodigiosa.* See Baker's Microscopic Experiments.

[2] May not this Rule be expressed more intelligibly (to a mathematician
at least) thus:—Reasoning from *finite* to *finite*, on a basis of truth, also,
reasoning from *infinite* to *infinite*, on a basis of truth, will always lead
to truth, as intelligibly as the basis on which such truths respectively
rest.—While, reasoning from *finite* to *infinite*, or from *infinite* to *finite*,
will lead to apparent absurdity, although the basis be true: and is not
such apparent absurdity, another expression for " truth unintelligible by
a *finite* mind " ?

not the Canons of discursive Reasoning, must decide in such cases. At least, the latter have no validity, which the single *veto* of the former is not sufficient to nullify. The most pious conclusion is here the most legitimate.

It is too seldom considered though most worthy of consideration, how far even those Ideas or Theories of pure Speculation, that bear the same name with the Objects of Religious Faith, are indeed the same. Out of the principles necessarily presumed in all discursive thinking, and which being, in the first place *universal*, and secondly, antecedent to every particular exercise of the understanding, are therefore referred to the reason, the human mind (wherever its powers are sufficiently developed, and its attention strongly directed to speculative or theoretical inquiries,) forms certain essences, to which for its own purposes it gives a sort of notional *subsistence*. Hence they are called *entia rationalia*: the conversion of which into *entia realia*, or real objects, by aid of the imagination, has in all times been the fruitful stock of empty theories, and mischievous superstitions, of surreptitious premises and extravagant conclusions. For as these substantiated notions were in many instances expressed by the same terms, as the objects of religious Faith; as in most instances they were applied, though deceptively, to the explanation of real experiences; and lastly, from the gratifications, which the pride and ambition of man received from the supposed extension of his knowledge and insight; it was too easily forgotten or overlooked, that the stablest and most indispensable of these notional beings were but the necessary *forms* of thinking, taken abstractedly : and that like the breadthless lines, depthless surfaces, and perfect circles of geometry, they subsist wholly and solely in and for the mind, that contemplates them. Where the evidence of the senses fails us, and beyond the precincts of sensible experience, there is no *reality* attributable to any notion, but what is given to it by Revelation, or the Law of Conscience, or the necessary interests of Morality.

Take an instance :

It is the office, and, as it were, the instinct of Reason to bring a unity into all our conceptions and several knowledges. On this all system depends ; and without this we

could reflect connectedly neither on nature nor our own
minds. Now this is possible only on the assumption or
hypothesis of a ONE as the ground and cause of the Universe,
and which in all succession and through changes is the
subject neither of Time nor Change. The ONE must be
contemplated as Eternal and Immutable.

Well! the Idea, which is the basis of Religion, commanded by the Conscience and required by Morality, contains the same truths, or at least truths that can be expressed in no other terms; but this idea presents itself to
our mind with additional attributes, and these too not
formed by mere Abstraction and Negation—with the attributes of Holiness, Providence, Love, Justice, and Mercy.
It comprehends, moreover, the independent (*extra-mundane*)
existence and personality of the supreme ONE, as our Creator,
Lord, and Judge.

The hypothesis of a *one* Ground and Principle of the
Universe (necessary as an *hypothesis;* but having only a
logical and *conditional* necessity) is thus raised into the Idea
of the LIVING GOD, the supreme Object of our Faith, Love,
Fear, and Adoration. Religion and Morality do indeed
constrain us to declare him Eternal and Immutable. But
if from the Eternity of the Supreme Being a Reasoner
should deduce the impossibility of a Creation; or conclude
with Aristotle, that the Creation was co-eternal; or, like
the latter Platonists, should turn Creation into *Emanation*,
and make the universe proceed from Deity, as the Sun-
beams from the Solar Orb;—or if from the divine Immutability he should infer, that all prayer and supplication
must be vain and superstitious : then however evident and
logically necessary such conclusions may appear, it is
scarcely worth our while to examine, whether they are so
or not. The positions themselves *must* be false. For were
they true, the Idea would lose the sole ground of its *reality*.
It would be no longer the Idea intended by the Believer in
his premise—in the premise, with which alone Religion
and Morality are concerned. The very subject of the discussion would be changed. It would no longer be the God
in whom we *believe;* but a stoical FATE, or the superessential
ONE of Plotinus, to whom neither Intelligence, nor Self-
consciousness, nor Life, nor even *Being* can be attributed;

nor lastly, the world itself, the indivisible one and only substance (*substantia una et unica*) of Spinoza, of which all *phœnomena*, all particular and individual things, lives, minds, thoughts, and actions are but modifications.

Let the believer never be alarmed by objections wholly speculative, however plausible on speculative grounds such objections may appear, if he can but satisfy himself, that the *result* is repugnant to the dictates of conscience, and irreconcilable with the interests of morality. For to baffle the objector we have only to demand of him, by what right and under what authority he converts a thought into a substance, or asserts the existence of a real somewhat corresponding to a notion not derived from the experience of his senses. It will be of no purpose for him to answer, that it is a *legitimate* notion. The *notion* may have its mould in the understanding; but its realization must be the work of the FANCY.

A reflecting reader will easily apply these remarks to the subject of Election, one of the stumbling stones in the ordinary conceptions of the Christian Faith, to which the infidel points in scorn, and which far better men pass by in silent perplexity. Yet surely, from mistaken conceptions of the doctrine. I suppose the person, with whom I am arguing, already so far a believer, as to have convinced himself, both that a state of enduring bliss is attainable under certain conditions; and that these conditions consist in his compliance with the directions given and rules prescribed in the Christian Scriptures. These rules he likewise admits to be such, that, by the very law and constitution of the human mind, a full and faithful compliance with them cannot but have *consequences*, of some sort or other. But these *consequences* are moreover distinctly described, enumerated, and promised in the same Scriptures, in which the conditions are recorded; and though some of them may be apparent to God only, yet the greater number of them are of such a nature that they cannot exist unknown to the individual, in and for whom they exist. As little possible is it, that he should find these consequences in himself, and not find in them the sure marks and the safe pledges, that he is at the time in the right road to the Life promised under these conditions. Now I dare assert, that no such man, however fervent his charity, and however deep his humility may be, can peruse the records of History with a reflecting spirit, or look round the world with an observant eye, and not find himself compelled to admit, that *all* men are *not* on the right road. He cannot help judging, that even in Christian countries, many, a fearful many! have not their faces turned toward it.

This then is a mere matter of fact. Now comes the question. Shall the believer, who thus hopes on the appointed *grounds* of hope, attribute this distinction exclusively to his own resolves and strivings? or if not exclusively, yet primarily and principally? Shall he refer the first movements and preparations to his own Will and Understanding, and bottom his claim to the promises on his own comparative excellence? If not, if no man dare take this honour to himself, to whom shall he assign it, if not to that Being in whom the promise originated, and on whom its fulfilment depends? If he stop here, who shall blame him? By what argument shall his reasoning be invalidated, that might not be urged with equal force against any essential difference between obedient and disobedient, Christian and worldling? that would not imply that both *sorts* alike are, in the sight of God, the Sons of God by adoption? If he stop here, I say, who shall drive him from his position? For thus far he is practically concerned—this the Conscience requires, this the highest interests of Morality demand. It is a question of facts, of the will and the deed, to argue against which on the abstract notions and possibilities of the speculative reason, is as unreasonable, as an attempt to decide a question of colours by pure Geometry, or to unsettle the classes and specific characters of Natural History by the Doctrine of Fluxions.

But if the self-examinant will abandon this position, and exchange the safe circle of Religion and practical Reason for the shifting sand-wastes and *mirages* of Speculative Theology; if instead of seeking after the *marks* of Election in himself he undertakes to determine the ground and origin, the possibility and mode of election itself *in relation to God;*—in this case, and whether he does it for the satisfaction of curiosity, or from the ambition of answering those, who would call God himself to account, why and by what right certain souls were born in Africa instead of England:—or why (seeing that it is against all reason and goodness to choose a worse, when being omnipotent He could have created a better) God did not create beasts men, and men angels:—or why God created any men but with fore-knowledge of their obedience, and left any occasion for Election?—in this case, I say, we can only regret, that the inquirer had not been better instructed in the nature, the bounds, the true purposes and proper objects of his intellectual faculties, and that he had not previously asked himself, by what appropriate sense, or organ of knowledge, he hoped to secure an insight into a Nature which was neither an object of his senses, nor a part of his self-consciousness; and so leave him to ward off shadowy spears with the shadow of a shield, and to retaliate the nonsense of blasphemy with the *abracadabra* of presumption. He that will fly without wings must fly in his dreams : and till he awakes, will not find out, that to fly in a dream is but to dream of flying.

Thus then the doctrine of Election is in itself a necessary inference from an undeniable fact—necessary at least for all who hold that the best of men are what they are through the grace of God. In relation to the believer it is a *hope*, which if it spring out of Christian principles, be examined by the tests and nourished by the means prescribed in Scripture, will become a *lively*, an *assured* hope, but which cannot in this life pass into *knowledge*, much less certainty of fore-knowledge. The contrary belief does indeed make the article of Election both tool and parcel of a mad and mischievous fanaticism. But with what force and clearness does not the Apostle confute, disclaim, and prohibit the pretence, treating it as a downright contradiction in terms ! See *Romans*, viii. 24.

But though I hold the doctrine handled as Leighton handles it (that is practically, morally, *humanly*) rational, safe, and of essential importance, I see many [1] reasons

---

[1] For example : at the date of St. Paul's Epistles, the (Roman) world may be resembled to a mass in the furnace in the first moment of fusion, here a speck and there a spot of the melted metal shining pure

I

resulting from the peculiar circumstances, under which St. Paul preached and wrote, why a discreet minister of the Gospel should avoid the frequent use of the *term*, and express the *meaning* in other words perfectly equivalent and equally Scriptural; lest in *saying* truth he may convey error.

Had my purpose been confined to one particular tenet, an apology might be required for so long a Comment. But the reader will, I trust, have already perceived, that my object has been to establish a general rule of interpretation and vindication applicable to *all* doctrinal tenets, and especially to the (so called) mysteries of the Christian Faith : to provide a *Safety-lamp* for religious inquirers. Now this I find in the principle, that all Revealed Truths are to be judged of by us, as far as they are possible subjects of human conception, or grounds of practice, or in some way connected with our moral and spiritual interests. In order to have a reason *for* forming a judgment on any given article, we must be sure that we possess a reason, by and according to which a judgment may be formed. Now in respect of all Truths, to which a *real* independent existence is assigned, and which yet are not contained in, or to be imagined under, any form of space or time, it is strictly demonstrable, that the human reason, considered abstractly, as the source of positive *science* and theoretical *insight*, is *not* such a reason. At the utmost, it has only a *negative* voice. In other words, nothing can be allowed as true for the human mind, which directly contradicts this reason. But even here, before we admit the existence of any such contradiction, we must be careful to ascertain,

---

and brilliant amid the scum and dross. To have received the *name* of Christian was a privilege, a high and distinguishing favour. No wonder therefore, that in St. Paul's writings the words, elect, and election, often, nay, most often, mean the same as *eccalumeni, ecclesia,* that is, those who have been *called out* of the world : and it is a dangerous perversion of the Apostle's word to interpret it in the sense, in which it was used by our Lord, viz. in *opposition to the called.* (Many are *called* but few *chosen.*) In St. Paul's sense and at that time the believers collectively formed a small and select number ; and every Christian real or nominal, was one of the Elect. Add too, that this ambiguity is increased by the accidental circumstance, that the *kyriak, Ædes Dominicæ,* Lord's House, *kirk ;* and *ecclesia,* the sum total of the *eccalumeni, evocati, called out ;* are both rendered by the same word Church.

that there is no equivocation in play, that two different
subjects are not confounded under one and the same word.
A striking instance of this has been adduced in the difference between the notional ONE of the Ontologists, and the
idea of the Living God.

But if not the abstract or speculative reason, and yet a
reason there must be in order to a rational belief—then
it must be the *practical* reason of man, comprehending
the Will, the Conscience, the Moral Being with its inseparable Interests and Affections—that Reason, namely, which
is the Organ of *Wisdom*, and (as far as man is concerned)
the source of living and actual Truths.

From these premises we may further deduce, that every
doctrine is to be interpreted in reference to those, to whom
it has been revealed, or who have or have had the means
of knowing or hearing the same. For instance : the Doctrine that *there is no name under Heaven, by which a man
can be saved, but the name of Jesus*. If the word here
rendered *name*, may be understood (as it well may, and as
in other texts it must be) as meaning the Power, or originating Cause, I see no objection on the part of the practical
reason to our belief of the declaration in its whole extent.
It is true universally or not true at all. If there be any
redemptive Power not contained in the Power of Jesus,
then Jesus is not *the* Redeemer : not the Redeemer of the
World, not the Jesus (*i.e.* Saviour) of mankind. But if with
Tertullian and Augustine we make the Text assert the condemnation and misery of all who are not Christians by
Baptism and explicit belief in the Revelation of the
New Covenant—then I say, the doctrine is true *to all in-
tents and purposes*. It is true, in every respect, in which
any practical, moral, or spiritual interest or end can be
connected with its truth. It is true in respect to every
man who has had, or who might have had, the Gospel
preached to him. It is true and obligatory for every Christian community and for every individual believer, wherever the opportunity is afforded of spreading the *Light* of
the Gospel, and making *known* the name of the only Saviour
and Redeemer. For even though the uninformed Heathens
should *not* perish, the *guilt* of their perishing will attach to
those who not only had no certainty of their safety, but

who are commanded to *act* on the supposition of the contrary. But if, on the other hand, a theological dogmatist
should attempt to persuade me, that this text was intended
to give us an historical knowledge of God's future actions
and dealings—and for the gratification of our curiosity to
inform us, that Socrates and Phocion, together with all the
savages in the woods and wilds of Africa and America,
will be sent to keep company with the devil and his angels
in everlasting torments—I should remind him, that the
purpose of Scripture was to teach us our duty, not to
enable us to sit in judgment on the souls of our fellow
creatures.

One other instance will, I trust, prevent all misconception of my meaning. I am clearly convinced, that the
scriptural and only true [1] Idea of God will, in its development, be found to involve the Idea of the Tri-unity. But
I am likewise convinced, that previously to the promulgation of the Gospel the doctrine had no claim on the
faith of mankind ; though it might have been a legitimate
contemplation for a speculative philosopher, a theorem in
metaphysics valid in the Schools.

I form a certain notion in my mind, and say :—This is
what *I* understand by the term, God. From books and
conversation I find, that the learned generally connect
the same notion with the same word. I then apply the
rules, laid down by the masters of logic, for the involu-
tion and evolution of terms, and prove (to as many as
agree with me in my premises) that the notion, God, involves the notion, Trinity. I now pass out of the Schools,
and enter into discourse with some friend or neighbour,
unversed in the *formal* sciences, unused to the process of
abstraction, neither Logician nor Metaphysician ; but sensible and single-minded, *an Israelite indeed,* trusting in
*the Lord God of his Fathers, even the God of Abraham,
of Isaac, and of Jacob.* If I speak of God to *him,* what
will *he* understand me to be speaking of ? What does he
mean, and suppose me to mean, by the word ? An accident

---

[1] Or (I may add) *any* Idea which does not either identify the Creator
with the Creation ; or else represent the Supreme Being as a mere
impersonal Law or *ordo ordinans,* differing from the Law of Gravitation
only by its *universality.*

or product of the reasoning faculty, or an abstraction which the human mind forms by reflecting on its own thoughts and forms of thinking? No. By God he understands me to mean an existing and self-subsisting reality,[1]

[1] I have elsewhere remarked on the assistance which those that labour after distinct conceptions would receive from the re-introduction of the terms *objective*, and *subjective*, *objective* and *subjective reality*, and the like, as substitutes for *real* and *notional*, and to the exclusion of the false antithesis between *real* and *ideal*. For the Student in that noblest of the sciences, the *scire teipsum*, the advantage would be especially great.* The few sentences that follow, in illustration of the terms here advocated, will not, I trust, be a waste of the reader's time.

The celebrated Euler having demonstrated certain properties of arches, adds : " All experience is in contradiction to this; but this is no reason for doubting its truth." The words *sound* paradoxical ; but mean no more than this—that the mathematical properties of figure and space are not less certainly the properties of figure and space because they can never be perfectly realized in wood, stone, or iron. Now this assertion of Euler's might be expressed at once, briefly and simply, by saying, that the properties in question were *subjectively* true, though not objectively—or that the mathematical arch possessed a *subjective reality* though incapable of being realized *objectively*.

In like manner if I had to express my conviction, that space was not itself a *thing*, but a *mode* or *form* of perceiving, or the inward ground and condition in the percipient, in consequence of which things are seen as outward and co-existing, I convey this at once by the words, space is *subjective*, or space is real in and for the *subject* alone.

If I am asked, Why not say in and for the *mind*, which every one would understand ? I reply : we know indeed, that all minds are Subjects ; but are by no means certain, that all subjects are minds. For a mind is a subject that knows itself, or a subject that is its own object. The inward principle of Growth and individual Form in every seed and plant is a *subject*, and without any exertion of poetic privilege poets may speak of the *soul* of the flower. But the man would be a dreamer, who otherwise than poetically should speak of roses and lilies as *self-conscious* subjects. Lastly, by the assistance of the terms, Object and Subject, thus used as correspondent opposites, or as negative and positive in physics (for example, negative and positive electricity) we may arrive at the distinct import and proper use of the strangely misused word, idea. And as the forms of logic are all borrowed from geometry (*Ratiocinatio discursiva formas suas sive canonas recipit ab intuitu*) I may be permitted to elucidate my present meaning. Every line may be, and by the ancient Geometricians *was*, considered as a point *produced*, the two extreme sbeing its poles, while the point itself remains in, or is at least represented by, the midpoint, the indifference of the two poles or

---

* See the ' Selection from Mr. Coleridge's Literary Correspondence ' in *Blackwood's Magazine*, 1821, Letter II.—ED.

a real and personal Being—even the *Person*, the I AM, who sent Moses to his forefathers in Egypt. Of the actual existence of this divine Being he has the same historical as-

correlative opposites. Logically applied, the two extremes or poles are named Thesis and Antithesis : thus in the line

$$\text{T}\underset{\text{A}}{\overset{\text{I}}{\rule{4cm}{0.4pt}}}$$

we have T = Thesis, A = Antithesis, and I = Punctum Indifferens sive *amphotericum*, which latter is to be conceived as *both* in as far as it may be *either* of the two former. Observe : not both at the same time in the same relation : for this would be the *identity* of T and A, not the *indif-ference:*—but so, that relatively to A, I is equal to T, and relatively to T it becomes = A. For the purposes of the universal *Noetic*, in which we require terms of most comprehension and least specific import, might not the Noetic Pentad be,—

	1. Prothesis.	
2. Thesis.	4. Mesothesis.	3. Antithesis.
	5. Synthesis.	

	Prothesis.	
	Sum.	
Thesis.	Methosesis.	Antithesis.
Res.	Agere.	Ago, Patior.
	Synthesis.	
	Agens.	

1. Verb Substantive = Prothesis, as expressing the *identity* or co-inherence of Act and Being.

2. Substantive = Thesis, expressing Being. 3. Verb = Antithesis, expressing, Act. 4. Infinite = Mesothesis, as being either Substantive or Verb, or both at once, only in different relations. 5. Participle = Synthesis. Thus in Chemistry Sulphuretted Hydrogen is an Acid relatively to the more powerful Alkalis, and an Alkali relatively to a powerful Acid. Yet one other remark, and I pass to the question. In order to render the constructions of pure Mathematics applicable to Philosophy, the Pythagoreans, I imagine, represented the Line as *generated*, or, as it were, radiated, by a Point not contained in the Line but independent, and (in the language of that School) transcendent to all production, which it caused but did not partake in. *Facit, non patitur.* This was the *punctum invisible, et presuppositum:* and in this way the Pythagoreans guarded against the error of Pantheism, into which the later schools fell. The assumption of this Point I call the logical PROTHESIS. We have now therefore four Relations of Thought expressed : 1. Prothesis, or the Identity of T and A, which is neither, because in it, as the transcendent of both, both are contained and exist as one. Taken *absolutely*, this finds its application in the Supreme Being alone, the Pythagorean TETRACTYS ; the INEFFABLE NAME, to which no Image can be attached ; the Point, which has no (real) Opposite or Counter-point. But *relatively* taken and inadequately, the ger-

surance as of theirs; confirmed indeed by the Book of Nature, as soon and as far as that stronger and better light has taught him to read and construe it—confirmed by it, I say, but not derived from it. Now by what right can I require this man (and of such men the great majority of serious believers consisted, previously to the light of the Gospel) to receive a *notion* of mine, wholly alien from his habits of thinking, because it may be logically deduced from another notion, with which he was almost as little acquainted, and not at all concerned ? Grant for a moment, that the latter (that is, the notion, with which I first set out) as soon as it is combined with the assurance of a corresponding Reality becomes identical with the true and effective Idea of God ! Grant, that in thus *realizing* the notion I am warranted by Revelation, the Law of Conscience, and the interests and necessities of my Moral Being ! Yet by what authority, by what inducement, am I entitled to attach the same reality to a second notion, a notion drawn from a notion ? It is evident, that if I have the same right, it must

minal power of every seed * might be generalized under the relation of Identity. 2. Thesis, or position. 3. Antithesis, or Opposition. 4. Indifference. To which when we add the Synthesis or Composition, in its several forms of Equilibrium, as in quiescent Electricity ; of Neutralization, as of Oxygen and Hydrogen in water ; and of Predominance, as of Hydrogen and Carbon with Hydrogen, predominant, in pure alcohol ; or of Carbon and Hydrogen, with the comparative predominance of the Carbon, in Oil ; we complete the five most general Forms or Preconceptions of Constructive Logic.

And now for the answer to the question, What is an IDEA, if it mean neither an Impression on the Senses, nor a definite Conception, nor an abstract Notion ? (And if it does mean either of these, the word is superfluous : and while it remains undetermined which of these is meant by the word, or whether it is not *which you please*, it is worse than superfluous. See the 'Statesman's Manual,' Appendix *ad finem*.) But supposing the word to have a meaning of its own, what does it mean ?—What is an IDEA ?—In answer to this I commence with the *absolutely* Real as the PROTHESIS ; the *subjectively* Real as the THESIS ; the *objectively* Real as the ANTITHESIS : and I affirm, that Idea is the INDIFFERENCE of the two—so namely, that if it be conceived as in the Subject, the Idea is an Object, and possesses Objective Truth ; but if in an Object, it is then a Subject and is necessarily thought of as exercising the powers of a Subject. Thus an IDEA conceived as subsisting in an Object becomes a LAW ; and a Law contemplated *subjectively* (in a mind) is an Idea.

---

* See Comment on Moral and Religious Aphorism VI., p. 40.—ED.

be on the same grounds. Revelation must have assured it,
my Conscience required it—or in some way or other I
must have an *interest* in this belief. It must *concern* me,
as a moral and responsible Being. Now these grounds
were first given in the Redemption of Mankind by Christ,
the Saviour and Mediator : and by the utter incompatibility
of these offices with a mere creature. On the doctrine of
Redemption depends the *Faith*, the *Duty*, of believing in
the Divinity of our Lord. And this again is the strongest
Ground for the reality of that Idea, in which alone this
Divinity can be received without breach of the faith in the
unity of the Godhead. But such is the Idea of the Trinity.
Strong as the motives are that induce me to defer the full
discussion of this great Article of the Christian creed, I
cannot withstand the request of several divines, whose
situation and extensive services entitle them to the utmost
deference, that I should so far deviate from my first intention as at least to indicate the point on which I stand, and
to prevent the misconception of my purpose : as if I held
the doctrine of the Trinity for a truth which Men could be
called on to believe by mere force of reasoning, independently of any positive *Revelation*. In short, it had been
reported in certain circles, that I considered this doctrine as
a demonstrable part of the Religion of Nature. Now
though it might be sufficient to say, that I regard the very
phrase " *Revealed* Religion " as a pleonasm, inasmuch as a
religion not revealed is, in my judgment, no religion at all ;
I have no objection to announce more particularly and distinctly what I do and what I do not maintain on this point :
provided that in the following paragraph, with this view
inserted, the reader will look for nothing more than a plain
statement of my opinions. The grounds on which they rest,
and the arguments by which they are to be vindicated, are
for another place.

I hold then, it is true, that all the (so called) demonstrations of a God either prove too little, as that from the order
and apparent purpose in Nature ; or too much, namely, that
the World is itself God : or they clandestinely involve the
conclusion in the premises, passing off the mere analysis or
explication of an Assertion for the Proof of it,—a species of
logical legerdemain not unlike that of the jugglers at a fair,

who putting into their mouths what seems to be a walnut, draw out a score yards of ribbon—as in the Postulate of a First Cause. And lastly, in all these demonstrations the demonstrators presuppose the Idea or Conception of a God without being able to authenticate it, that is, to give an account whence they obtained it. For it is clear, that the proof first mentioned and the most natural and convincing of all (the Cosmological I mean, or that from the Order in Nature) presupposes the Ontological—that is, the proof of a God from the necessity and necessary *Objectivity* of the Idea. *If* the latter can assure us of a God as an existing Reality, the former will go far to prove his power, wisdom, and benevolence. All this I hold. But I also hold, that this truth, the hardest to demonstrate, is the one which of all others least needs to be demonstrated; that though there may be no conclusive demonstrations of a good, wise, living, and personal God, there are so many convincing reasons for it, within and without—a grain of sand sufficing, and a whole universe at hand to echo the decision !—that for every mind not devoid of all reason, and desperately conscience-proof, the Truth which it is the least possible to prove, it is little less than impossible not to believe! only indeed just so much short of impossible, as to leave some room for the will and the moral election, and thereby to keep it a truth of Religion, and the possible subject of a Commandment.[1]

On this account I do not demand of a *Deist*, that he should adopt the doctrine of the Trinity. For he might very well

---

[1] In a letter to a friend on the mathematical atheists of the French Revolution, La Lande and others, or rather on a young man of distinguished abilities, but an avowed and proselyting partizan of their tenets, I concluded with these words: " The man who will believe nothing but by force of demonstrative evidence (even though it is strictly demonstrable that the demonstrability required would countervene all the purposes of the truth in question, all that render the belief of the same desirable or obligatory) is not in a state of mind to be reasoned with on any subject. But if he further denies the *fact* of the Law of Conscience, and the essential difference between right and wrong, I confess, he puzzles me. I cannot without gross inconsistency appeal to his Conscience and Moral Sense, or I should admonish him that, as an honest man, he ought to *advertize* himself, with a *Cavete omnes! Scelus sum.* And as an honest man myself, I dare not advise him on prudential grounds to keep his opinions secret, lest I should make myself his accomplice, and *be helping him on with a wrap-rascal.*"

be justified in replying, that he rejected the doctrine, *not* because it could not be *demonstrated*, nor yet on the score of any incomprehensibilities and seeming contradictions that might be objected to it, as knowing that these might be, and in fact had been, urged with equal force against a personal God under any form capable of love and veneration ; *but* because he had not the same theoretical necessity, the same interests and instincts of reason for the one hypothesis as for the other. It is not enough, the Deist might justly say, that there is no cogent reason why I should *not* believe the Trinity ; you must show me some cogent reason why I *should*.

But the case is quite different with a Christian, who accepts the Scriptures as the Word of God, yet refuses his assent to the plainest declarations of these Scriptures, and explains away the most express texts into metaphor and hyperbole, *because* the literal and obvious interpretation is (according to *his* notions) absurd and contrary to reason. *He* is bound to show, that it is so in any sense, not equally applicable to the texts asserting the Being, Infinity, and Personality of God the Father, the Eternal and Omnipresent ONE, who *created* the Heaven and the Earth. And the more is he bound to do this, and the greater is my right to demand it of him, because the doctrine of Redemption from sin supplies the Christian with motives and reasons for the divinity of the Redeemer far more *concerning* and coercive *subjectively*, that is, in the economy of his own soul, than are all the inducements that can influence the Deist *objectively*, that is, in the interpretation of Nature.

Do I then utterly exclude the speculative Reason from Theology ? No ! It is its office and rightful privilege to determine on the *negative* truth of whatever we are required to believe. The Doctrine must not *contradict* any universal principle : for this would be a Doctrine that contradicted itself. Or Philosophy ? No. It may be and has been the servant and pioneer of Faith by convincing the mind, that a doctrine is cogitable, that the soul can present the *Idea* to itself ; and that *if* we determine to contemplate, or *think* of, the subject at all, so and in no other form can this be effected. So far are both logic and philosophy to be received and trusted. But the *duty*, and in some cases and for some persons even the *right*, of thinking on subjects beyond the bounds of sensible experience; the grounds of the *real* truth; the *life*, the *substance*, the *hope*, the *love*, in one word, the *Faith:* these are Derivatives from the practical, moral, and spiritual Nature and Being of Man.

APHORISM III.

BURNET AND COLERIDGE.

That Religion is designed to improve the nature and faculties of man, in order to the right governing of our actions, to the securing the peace and progress, external and internal, of individuals and of communities, and lastly, to the rendering us capable of a more perfect state, entitled the kingdom of God, to which the present life is *probationary*—this is a Truth, which all who have truth only in view, will receive on its own evidence. If such then be the main end of religion altogether (the improvement namely of our nature and faculties), it is plain, that every part of religion is to be judged by its relation to this main end. And since the Christian scheme is religion in its most perfect and effective form, a revealed religion, and therefore, in a *special* sense proceeding from that Being who made us and knows what we are, of course therefore adapted to the needs and capabilities of human nature; nothing can be a part of this holy faith that is not duly proportioned to this end.[1]

COMMENT.

This Aphorism should be borne in mind, whenever a theological *Resolve* is proposed to us as an article of Faith. Take, for instance, the determinations passed at the Synod of Dort, concerning the Absolute Decrees of God in connection with his Omniscience and Fore-knowledge. Or take the decision in the Council of Trent on the difference between the two kinds of Transubstantiation, the one in

[1] Slightly altered from Burnet's Preface to Part ii. of his ' History of the Reformation.' See pp. 26, 27, v. ii. Clarendon Press edition, 1865. —ED.

which both the substance and the accidents are changed, the same matter remaining—as in the conversion of water to wine at Cana : the other, in which the matter and the substance are changed, the accidents remaining unaltered, as in the Eucharist—this latter being Transubstantiation *par eminence!* Or rather take the still more tremendous dogma, that it is indispensable to a saving faith carefully to distinguish the one kind from the other, and to believe both, and to believe the necessity of believing both in order to Salvation ! For each or either of these *extra-scriptural* Articles of Faith the preceding Aphorism supplies a safe criterion. Will the belief tend to the improvement of any of my moral or intellectual faculties ? But before I can be convinced that a faculty will be *improved*, I must be assured that it *exists.* On all these dark sayings, therefore, of Dort or Trent, it is quite sufficient to ask, by what *faculty*, *organ*, or *inlet* of knowledge, we are to assure ourselves that the words *mean* any thing, or correspond to any object out of our own mind or even in it : unless indeed the mere craving and striving to think *on*, after all the materials for thinking have been exhausted, can be called an *object.* When a number of trust-worthy persons assure me, that a portion of fluid which they saw to be water, by some change in the fluid itself or in their senses, suddenly acquired the colour, taste, smell, and exhilarating property of wine, I perfectly understand what they tell me, and likewise by what faculties they might have come to the knowledge of the fact. But if any one of the number not satisfied with my acquiescence in the fact, should insist on my believing, that the *matter* remained the same, the substance and the accidents having been removed in order to make way for a different substance with different accidents, I must entreat his permission to wait till I can discover in myself any faculty, by which there can be presented to me a matter distinguishable from accidents, and a substance that is different from both. It is true, I have a faculty of articulation ; but I do not see that it can be *improved* by my using it for the formation of words without meaning, or at best, for the utterance of thoughts, that mean only the act of so thinking, or of trying so to think. But the end of Religion is the improvement of our Nature and Faculties. *Ergo*, &c.

I sum up the whole in one great practical Maxim.   The Object of *religious* Contemplation, and of a truly Spiritual Faith, is " THE WAYS OF GOD TO MAN."   Of the Workings of the Godhead, God himself has told us, *My Ways are not as your Ways, nor my Thoughts as your Thoughts.*

APHORISM IV.

The characteristic Difference between the Discipline of the Ancient Philosophers and the Dispensation of the Gospel.

By undeceiving, enlarging, and informing the Intellect, Philosophy sought to purify, and to elevate the Moral Character.   Of course, those alone could receive the latter and incomparably greater benefit, who by natural capacity and favourable contingencies of fortune were fit recipients of the former.   How small the number, we scarcely need the evidence of history to assure us.   Across the night of Paganism, Philosophy flitted on, like the lantern-fly of the Tropics, a light to itself, and an ornament, but alas ! no more than an ornament of the surrounding darkness.

Christianity reversed the order.   By means accessible to all, by inducements operative on all, and by convictions, the grounds and materials of which all men might find in themselves, her first step was to cleanse the *heart*.   But the benefit did not stop here.   In preventing the rank vapours that steam up from the corrupt *heart*, Christianity restores the *intellect* likewise to its natural clearness.   By relieving the mind from the distractions and importunities of the unruly passions, she improves the *quality* of the Understanding : while at the same time she presents for its contemplations, objects so great and so bright as cannot but enlarge the organ, by which they are contemplated. The fears, the hopes, the remembrances, the anticipations, the inward and outward Experience, the belief and the Faith, of a Christian, form of themselves a philosophy and a Sum of Knowledge, which a life spent in the Grove of Academus, or the " painted Porch," could not have attained or collected.   The result is contained in the fact of a wide and still widening CHRISTENDOM.

Yet I dare not say, that the effects have been proportionate to the divine wisdom of the scheme. Too soon did the Doctors of the Church forget that the *heart*, the *moral* nature, was the beginning and the end; and that truth, knowledge, and insight were comprehended in its expansion. This was the true and first apostasy—when in council and synod the Divine Humanities of the Gospel gave way to speculative Systems, and Religion became a Science of Shadows under the name of Theology, or at best a bare Skeleton of Truth, without life or interest, alike inaccessible and unintelligible to the majority of Christians. For these therefore there remained only rites and ceremonies and spectacles, shows and semblances. Thus among the learned *the substance of things hoped for* (Heb. xi. 1.) passed off into *Notions;* and for the unlearned the Surfaces of things became [1] Substance. The Christian world was for centuries divided into the Many, that did not think at all, and the Few who did nothing but think—both alike *unreflecting*, the one from defect of the *act*, the other from the absence of an *object*.

APHORISM V.

There is small chance of Truth at the goal where there is not a child-like Humility at the starting-post.

COMMENT.

Humility is the safest Ground of Docility : and Docility the surest Promise of Docibility. Where there is no working of self-love in the heart that secures a leaning beforehand; where the great magnet of the planet is not overwhelmed or obscured by partial masses of Iron in close neighbourhood to the compass of the judgment, though hidden or unnoticed; there will this great *desideratum* be found of a child-like Humility. Do I then say, that I am to be influenced by *no* interest ? Far from it ! There is an Interest of Truth : or how could there be a Love of Truth ?

---

[1] *Virium et proprietatum, quæ non nisi de substantibus predicari possunt, formis superstantibus attributio, est* SUPERSTITIO.

And that a love of truth for its own sake, and merely as truth, is possible, my soul bears witness to itself in its inmost recesses. But there are other interests—those of goodness, of beauty, of utility. It would be a sorry proof of the humility I am extolling, were I to ask for angel's wings to overfly my own human nature. I exclude none of these. It is enough if the *lene clinamen*, the gentle bias, be given by no interest that concerns myself other than as I am a man, and included in the great family of mankind; but which does therefore especially concern me, because being a common interest of *all* men it must needs concern the very *essentials* of my being, and because these essentials, as existing in *me*, are especially intrusted to my particular charge.

Widely different from this social and truth-attracted bias, different both in its nature and its effects, is the interest connected with the desire of *distinguishing* yourself from other men, in order to be distinguished by them. Hoc revera *est inter* te et veritatem. This Interest does indeed stand between thee and truth. I might add between thee and thy own soul. It is scarcely more at variance with the love of truth than it is unfriendly to the attainment that deserves that name. By your own act you have appointed the Many as your judges and appraisers: for the anxiety to be admired is a loveless passion, ever strongest with regard to those by whom we are least known and least cared for, loud on the hustings, gay in the ball-room, mute and sullen at the family fireside. What you have acquired by patient thought and cautious discrimination, demands a portion of the same effort in those who are to receive it from you. But applause and preference are things of barter; and if you trade in them, Experience will soon teach you that there are easier and less unsuitable ways to win golden judgments than by at once taxing the patience and humiliating the self-opinion of your judges. To obtain your end, your words must be as indefinite as their thoughts: and how vague and general these are even on objects of sense, the few who at a mature age have seriously set about the discipline of their faculties, and have honestly *taken stock*, best know by recollection of their own state. To be admired you must make your auditors believe at least that they understand what you say.; which, be assured, they never will, under such circumstances, if it be worth understanding, or if you understand your own soul. But while your prevailing motive is to be compared and appreciated, is it credible, is it possible, that you should in earnest seek for a knowledge which is and must remain a hidden light, a secret treasure? Have you children, or have you lived among children, and do you not know, that in all things, in food, in medicine, in all their doings and abstainings they must believe in order to acquire a reason for their belief? But so is it with religious truths for all men. These we must all learn as children. The ground of the prevailing error on this point is the ignorance, that in spiritual concernments to believe and to understand are not diverse things, but the same thing in different periods of its growth. Belief is the seed, received into the will, of which the Understanding or Knowledge is the Flower, and the thing believed is the fruit. Unless ye believe ye cannot understand: and unless ye be humble as children, ye not only *will* not, but ye *cannot* believe. Of such therefore is the Kingdom of Heaven. Yea, blessed is the calamity that makes us humble: though. so repugnant thereto is our nature, in our present state, that after a while, it is to be feared, a second and sharper calamity would be wanted to cure us of our pride in having become so humble.

Lastly, there are among us, though fewer and less in fashion than among our ancestors, persons who, like Shaftesbury, do not belong to "the herd of Epicurus," yet prefer a philosophic Paganism to the morality of the Gospel. Now it would conduce, methinks, to the child-like humility, we have been discoursing of, if the use of the term, Virtue, in that high, comprehensive, and *notional* sense in which it was used by the ancient Stoics, were abandoned, as a relic of Paganism, to these modern Pagans: and if Christians restoring the word to its original import, namely, Manhood or Manliness, used it exclusively to express the quality of Fortitude; Strength of Character in relation to the resistance opposed by Nature and the irrational Passions to the Dictates of Reason; Energy of Will in preserving the Line of Rectitude tense and firm against the warping forces and treacheries of temptation. Surely, it were far less unseemly to value ourselves on this moral strength than on strength of body, or even strength of intellect. But we will rather value *it* for ourselves: and bearing in mind the old adage, *Quis custodiet ipsum custodem ?*—we will value it the more, yea, then only will we allow it true spiritual *worth*, when we possess it as a gift of *grace*, a boon of mercy undeserved, a fulfilment of a free *promise* (1 *Corinth*. x. 13.). What more is meant in this last paragraph, let the venerable HOOKER say for me in the following.

APHORISM VI.

HOOKER.

What is virtue but a medicine, and vice but a wound ?— Yea, we have so often deeply wounded ourselves with medicine, that God hath been fain to make wounds medicinable; to cure by vice where virtue hath stricken; to suffer the just man to fall, that being raised he may be taught what power it was which upheld him standing. I am not afraid to affirm it boldly with St. Augustine, that men puffed up through a proud opinion of their own sanctity and holiness receive a benefit at the hands of God, and are assisted with his grace when with his grace they are *not* assisted, but permitted (and that grievously) to transgress. Whereby, as they were through over-great liking of themselves supplanted (*tripped up*), so the dislike of that which did supplant them may establish them afterwards the surer. Ask the very soul of Peter, and it shall undoubtedly itself make you this answer: My eager protestations made in the glory of my spiritual strength I am ashamed of. But my shame and the tears, with which my presumption and my weakness were bewailed, recur in the songs of my thanksgiving. My Strength had been my ruin, my Fall hath proved my stay.[1]

[1] Hooker 'On the Nature of Pride,' Works, p. 521.—ED.

APHORISM VII.

The Being and Providence of One Living God, holy, gracious, merciful, the creator and preserver of all things, and a father of the righteous; the Moral Law in its [1] utmost height, breadth, and purity, a State of Retribution after Death; the [2] Resurrection of the Dead; and a Day of Judgment—all these were known and received by the Jewish people, as established articles of the national faith, at or before the proclaiming of Christ by the Baptist. They are the ground-work of Christianity, and essentials in the Christian Faith, but not its characteristic and peculiar Doctrines: except indeed as they are confirmed, enlivened, realized and brought home to the *whole being* of man, head, heart, and spirit, by the truths and influences of the Gospel.

Peculiar to Christianity are:

I. The belief that a Means of Salvation has been effected and provided for the human race by the incarnation of the Son of God in the person of Jesus Christ; and that his life on earth, his sufferings, death, and resurrection, are not only proofs and manifestations, but likewise essential and effective parts of the great redemptive Act, whereby also the Obstacle from the corruption of our Nature is rendered no longer insurmountable.

II. The belief in the possible appropriation of this benefit by Repentance and Faith, including the aids that render an effective faith and repentance themselves possible.

III. The belief in the reception (by as many as *shall be heirs of salvation*) of a living and spiritual principle, a seed of life capable of surviving this natural life, and of existing in a divine and immortal state.

IV. The belief in the awakening of the spirit [3] in them

---

[1] and [2]. These reference marks are the author's own, for which, however, he supplied no notes here; but further on, in the Comment, at pp. 132-3, he gives them *in the text*.—ED.

[3] See Comment on Moral and Religious Aphorism VI., p. 45.—ED.

that truly believe, and in the communion of the spirit, thus awakened, with the Holy Spirit.

V. The belief in the accompanying and consequent gifts, graces, comforts, and privileges of the Spirit, which acting primarily on the heart and will, cannot but manifest themselves in suitable works of love and obedience, that is, in right acts with right affections, from right principles.

VI. Further, as Christians we are taught, that these WORKS are the appointed signs and evidences of our FAITH; and that, under limitation of the power, the means, and the opportunities afforded us individually, they are the rule and measure, by which we are bound and enabled to judge, of *what spirit we are.*

VII. All these, together with the doctrine of the Fathers re-proclaimed in the everlasting Gospel, we receive in the full assurance, that God beholds and will finally judge us with a merciful consideration of our infirmities, a gracious acceptance of our sincere though imperfect strivings, a forgiveness of our defects through the mediation, and a completion of our deficiencies by the perfect righteousness, of the Man Christ Jesus, even the Word that was in the beginning with God, and who, being God, became Man for the redemption of Mankind.

COMMENT.

I earnestly entreat the reader to pause awhile, and to join with me in reflecting on the preceding Aphorism. It has been my aim throughout this work to enforce two points: 1. That MORALITY arising out of the Reason and Conscience of Men, and PRUDENCE, which in like manner flows out of the Understanding and the natural Wants and Desires of the Individual, are two distinct things. 2. That Morality with Prudence as its instrument has, considered abstractedly, not only a value but a *worth* in itself. Now the question is (and it is a question which every man must answer for himself)—From what you know of yourself; of your own heart and strength; and from what history and personal experience have led you to conclude of mankind generally; dare you *trust* to it? Dare *you* trust to it? To *it,* and to it alone? If so, well! It is at your own risk.   I

judge you not. Before Him, who cannot be mocked, you
stand or fall. But if not, if you have had too good reason
to know, that your heart is deceitful and your strength
weakness : if you are disposed to exclaim with Paul—the
Law indeed is holy, just, good, spiritual ; but I am carnal,
sold under sin : for that which I do, I allow not ; and what
I would, that I do not !—in this case, there is a voice that
says, *Come unto me : and I will give you rest.* This is the
Voice of Christ: and the conditions, under which the
promise was given by him, are that you believe *in* him,
and believe his words. And he has further assured you,
that *if* you do so, you will obey him. You are, in short, to
embrace the *Christian* Faith as your Religion—those Truths
which St. Paul believed *after* his conversion, and not those
only which he believed no less undoubtingly while he was
persecuting Christ, and an enemy of the Christian Religion. With what consistency could I offer you this
volume as Aids to Reflection, if I did not call on you to
ascertain in the first instance what these truths are ? But
these I could not lay before you without first enumerating
certain other points of belief, which though truths, indispensable truths, and truths comprehended or rather pre-
supposed in the Christian scheme, are yet not *these* truths.
(*John* i. 17.)

While doing this, I was aware that the Positions, in the
first paragraph of the preceding Aphorism, to which the
numerical *marks* are affixed, will startle some of my Readers.
Let the following sentences serve for the notes corresponding
to the marks :

[1] *Be you holy : even as God is holy.*—*What more does he
require of thee, O man! than to do justice, love mercy,
and walk humbly with the Lord thy God?* * To these summary passages from Moses and the Prophets (the first
exhibiting the closed, the second the expanded, Hand of
the Moral Law) I might add the Authorities of Grotius
and other more orthodox and not less learned Divines,
for the opinion that the Lord's Prayer was a *selection*, and
the famous passage [The hour is now coming, &c., *John* v.
28, 29.] a *citation* by our Lord from the liturgy of the

---

* *Lev.* xix. 2, and *Micah*, vi. 8.—ED.

Jewish Church. But it will be sufficient to remind the reader, that the apparent difference between the prominent *moral* truths of the Old and those of the New Testament results from the latter having been written in Greek; while the conversations recorded by the Evangelists took place in Hebrew or Syro-Chaldaic or Aramaic.—Hence it happened that where our Lord cited the original text, his biographers substituted the Septuagint version, while our English version is in *both* instances immediate and literal—in the Old Testament from the Hebrew Original, in the New Testament from the freer Greek translation. The text, *I give you a new commandment*, has no connection with the present subject.

² There is a current mistake on this point likewise, though this article of the Jewish Belief is not only asserted by St. Paul, but is elsewhere spoken of as common to the Twelve Tribes. The mistake consists in supposing the Pharisees to have been a distinct *sect*, and in strangely over-rating the number of the Sadducees. The former were distinguished not by holding, as matters of religious belief, articles different from the Jewish Church at large; but by their pretences to a more rigid orthodoxy, a more scrupulous performance. They were, in short (if I may dare use a phrase which I dislike as profane, and denounce as uncharitable), the *Evangelicals* and strict *professors* of the day. The latter, the Sadducees, whose opinions much more nearly resembled those of the *Stoics* than the Epicureans (a remark that will appear paradoxical to those only who have abstracted their notions of the Stoic Philosophy from Epictetus, Mark Antonine, and certain brilliant inconsistencies of Seneca), were a handful of rich men, *Romanized* Jews, not more numerous than infidels among us, and holden by the People at large in at least equal abhorrence. Their great argument was : that the belief of a future state of rewards and punishments injured or destroyed the purity of the Moral Law for the more enlightened classes, and weakened the influence of the Laws of the Land for the people, the vulgar multitude.

I will now suppose the reader to have thoughtfully re-perused the paragraph containing the tenets peculiar to Christianity, and if he have his religious principles yet to form, I should expect to overhear a troubled murmur: How can I comprehend this? How is this to be proved? To the first question I should answer: Christianity is not a Theory, or a Speculation; but a *Life;*—not a *Philosophy* of Life, but a Life and a living Process. To the second: TRY IT. It has been eighteen hundred years in existence: and has one individual left a record, like the following? " I tried it; and it did not answer. I made the experiment faithfully according to the directions; and the result has been, a conviction of my own credulity." Have you, in your own experience, met with any one in whose words you could place full confidence, and who has seriously affirmed:— " I have given Christianity a fair trial. I was aware, that its promises were made only *conditionally.* But my heart bears me witness, that I have to the utmost of my power complied with these conditions. Both outwardly and in the discipline of my inward acts and affections, I have performed the duties which it enjoins, and I have used the means, which it prescribes. Yet my assurance of its truth has received no increase. Its promises have not been fulfilled: and I repent me of my delusion!" If neither your own experience nor the History of almost two thousand years has presented a single testimony to this purport; and if you have read and heard of many who have lived and died bearing witness to the contrary: and if you have yourself met with some *one*, in whom on any other point you would place unqualified trust, who has on his own experience made report to you, that He is faithful who promised, and what he promised He has proved Himself able to perform; is it bigotry, if I fear that the Unbelief, which prejudges and prevents the experiment, has its source elsewhere than in the uncorrupted judgment; that not the strong free mind, but the enslaved will, is the true original infidel in this instance? It would not be the first time, that a treacherous bosom-sin had suborned the understandings of men to bear false witness against its avowed enemy, the right though unreceived owner of the house, who had long *warned it out*, and waited only for its ejection to enter and take possession of the same.

I have elsewhere in the present work explained the difference between the Understanding and the Reason, by reason meaning exclusively the speculative or scientific power so called, the νοῦς or *mens* of the ancients. And wider still is the distinction between the Understanding and the Spiritual Mind. But no gift of God does or can contradict any other gift, except by misuse or misdirection. Most readily therefore do I admit, that there can be no contrariety between Revelation and the Understanding; unless you call the fact, that the skin, though sensible of the warmth of the sun, can convey no notion of its figure or its joyous light, or of the colours, which it impresses on the clouds, a contrariety between the skin and the eye; or infer that the cutaneous and the optic nerves *contradict* each other.

But we have grounds to believe, that there are yet other rays or effluences from the sun, which neither feeling nor sight can apprehend, but which are to be inferred from the effects. And were it even so with regard to the Spiritual Sun, how would this contradict the Understanding or the Reason? It is a sufficient proof of the contrary, that the mysteries in question are not *in the direction* of the understanding or the (speculative) reason. They do not move on the same line or plane with them, and therefore cannot contradict them. But besides this, in the mystery that most immediately concerns the believer, that of the birth into a new and spiritual life, the common sense and experience of mankind come in aid of their faith. The analogous facts, which we know to be true, not only facilitate the apprehension of the facts promised to us, and expressed by the same words in conjunction with a distinctive epithet; but being confessedly not less incomprehensible, the certain *knowledge* of the one disposes us to the *belief* of the other. It removes at least all objections to the truth of the doctrine derived from the mysteriousness of its subject. The life, we seek after, is a mystery; but so both in itself and in its origin is the life we have. In order to meet this question, however, with minds duly prepared, there are two preliminary inquiries to be decided ; the first respecting the *purport*, the second respecting the *language* of the Gospel.

First then of the *purport*, namely, what the Gospel does

not, and what it *does* profess to be. The Gospel is not a system of Theology, nor a *syntagma* of theoretical propositions and conclusions for the enlargement of speculative knowledge, ethical or metaphysical. But it is a history, a series of facts and events related or announced. These do indeed involve, or rather I should say they at the same time *are*, most important doctrinal Truths; but still *Facts* and Declaration of *Facts*.

Secondly of the *language*. This is a wide subject. But the point, to which I chiefly advert, is the necessity of thoroughly understanding the distinction between *analogous*, and *metaphorical* language. *Analogies* are used in aid of *Conviction*: Metaphors, as means of *Illustration*. The language is analogous, wherever a thing, power, or principle in a higher dignity is expressed by the same thing, power, or principle in a lower but more known form. Such, for instance, is the language of *John* iii. 6. *That which is born of the flesh, is flesh; that which is born of the Spirit, is Spirit.* The latter half of the verse contains the fact *asserted;* the former half the *analogous* fact, by which it is rendered intelligible. If any man choose to call this *metaphorical* or figurative, I ask him whether with Hobbes and Bolingbroke he applies the same rule to the moral attributes of the Deity? Whether he regards the divine Justice, for instance, as a *metaphorical* term, a mere figure of speech? If he disclaims this, then I answer, neither do I regard the words, *born again*, or *spiritual life*, as figures or metaphors. I have only to add, that these analogies are the material, or (to speak chemically) the *base*, of Symbols and symbolical expressions; the nature of which is always *tau*tegorical, that is, expressing the *same* subject but with a *difference*, in contra-distinction from metaphors and similitudes, that are always *alle*gorical, that is, expressing a *different* subject but with a resemblance.

Of *metaphorical* language, on the other hand, let the following be taken as instance and illustration. I am speaking, we will suppose, of an act, which in its own nature, and as a producing and efficient *cause*, is transcendent; but which produces sundry *effects*, each of which is the same in kind with an effect produced by a cause well known and of ordinary occurrence. Now when I characterize or designate this transcendent act, in exclusive reference to these its *effects*, by a succession of names bor- rowed from their ordinary causes; not for the purpose of rendering the act itself, or the manner of the agency, conceivable, but in order to show the nature and magnitude of the benefits received from it, and thus to excite the due admiration, gratitude, and love in the receivers; in this case I should be rightly described as speaking *metaphori- cally*. And in this case to confound *the similarity*, in respect of the effects relatively to the recipients, with *an identity* in respect of the causes or modes of causation rela- tively to the transcendent act or the Divine Agent, is a confusion of metaphor with analogy, and of figurative with literal; and has been and continues to be a fruitful source of superstition or enthusiasm in believers, and of objec- tions and prejudices to infidels and sceptics. But each of these points is worthy of a separate consideration: and apt occasions will be found of reverting to them severally in the following Aphorisms, or the comments thereto attached.

APHORISM VIII.

LEIGHTON.

FAITH elevates the soul not only above sense and sensible things, but above reason itself. As reason corrects the errors which sense might occasion, so supernatural faith corrects the errors of natural reason judging according to sense.

COMMENT.

My remarks on this Aphorism from Leighton cannot be better introduced, or their purport more distinctly an- nounced, than by the following sentence from Harrington, with no other change than was necessary to make the words express, without aid of the context, what from the context it is evident was the writer's meaning. " The definition and proper character of Man—that, namely, which should contra-distinguish him from the Animals—

is to be taken from his reason rather than from his understanding : in regard that in other creatures there may
be something of understanding, but there is nothing of
reason.[1]

Sir Thomas Browne, in his *Religio Medici*, complains,
that there are not impossibilities enough in Religion for his
active faith ; and adopts by choice and in free preference,
such interpretations of certain texts and declarations of
Holy Writ, as place them in irreconcilable contradiction to
the demonstrations of science and the experience of mankind, because (says he) " I love to lose myself in a
mystery, and 'tis my solitary recreation to pose my apprehension with those involved enigmas and riddles of the
Trinity and Incarnation ; "—and because he delights (as
thinking it no vulgar part of faith) to believe a thing not
only above but contrary to reason, and against the evidence of our proper senses. For the worthy knight could
answer all the objections of the devil and reason " with
the odd resolution he had learnt of Tertullian : *Certum
est quia impossibile est*. It is certainly true because it is
quite impossible ! "   Now this I call ULTRAFIDIANISM.[2]

---

[1] See 'The Friend,' vol. i., p. 263 ; or p. 95 in Bohn's one vol. edition ;
and 'The Statesman's Manual,' Appendix (Note C.).—ED.

[2] There is this advantage in the occasional use of a newly minted term
or title, expressing the doctrinal schemes of particular sects or parties,
that it avoids the inconvenience that presses on either side, whether we
adopt the name which the party itself has taken up by which to express
its peculiar tenets, or that by which the same party is designated by its
opponents. If we take the latter, it most often happens that either the
persons are invidiously aimed at in the designation of the principles, or
that the name implies some consequence or occasional accompaniment
of the principles denied by the parties themselves, as applicable to them
collectively. On the other hand, convinced as I am, that current
appellations are never wholly indifferent or inert ; and that, when employed to express the characteristic belief or object of a *religious*
confederacy, they exert on the many a great and constant, though
insensible, influence ; I cannot but fear that in adopting the former I
may be sacrificing the interests of Truth beyond what the duties of
courtesy can demand or justify. I have elsewhere stated my objections
to the word *Unitarians :* as a name which in its proper sense can belong
only to the maintainers of the truth impugned by the persons, who have
chosen it as their designation. For *Unity* or Unition, and indistinguish-
able *Unicity* or Sameness, are incompatible terms. We never speak of the
unity of attraction, or the unity of repulsion ; but of the unity of attraction
and repulsion in each corpuscle. Indeed, the essential diversity of the

Again, there is a scheme constructed on the principle of retaining the social sympathies, that attend on the name of

conceptions, Unity and Sameness, was among the elementary principles of the old logicians; and Leibnitz, in his critique on Wissowatius, has ably exposed the sophisms grounded on the confusion of the two terms. But in the exclusive sense, in which the name, Unitarian, is appropriated by the sect, and in which they mean it to be understood, it is a presumptuous boast, and an uncharitable calumny. No one of the Churches to which they on this article of the Christian Faith stand opposed, Greek or Latin, ever adopted the term, Trini—or Tri-uni-tarians as their ordinary and proper name: and had it been otherwise, yet Unity is assuredly no logical Opposite to Tri-unity, which expressly includes it. The triple alliance is *a fortiori* alliance. The true designation of their characteristic Tenet, and which would simply and inoffensively express a fact admitted on all sides, is Psilanthropism, or the assertion of the *mere* humanity of Christ.*

I dare not hesitate to avow my regret, that any scheme of doctrines or tenets should be the subject of penal law: though I can easily conceive, that any scheme, however excellent in itself, may be propagated, and however false or injurious, may be assailed, in a manner and by means that would make the advocate or assailant justly punishable. But then it is the *manner*, the *means*, that constitute the *crime*. The merit or demerit of the opinions themselves depends on their originating and determining causes, which may differ in every different believer, and are certainly known to Him alone, who commanded us, *Judge not, lest ye be judged*. At all events, in the present state of the law, I do not see where we can begin, or where we can stop, without inconsistency and consequent hardship. Judging by all that *we* can pretend to know or are entitled to infer, who among us will take on himself to deny that the late Dr. Priestley was a good and benevolent man, as sincere in his love, as he was intrepid and indefatigable in his pursuit, of truth? Now let us construct three parallel tables, the first containing the Articles of Belief, moral and theological, maintained by the venerable Hooker, as the representative of the Established Church, each article being distinctly lined and numbered; the second the Tenets and Persuasions of Lord Herbert, as the representative of the platonizing Deists; and the third, those of Dr. Priestley. Let the points, in which the second and third agree with or differ from the first, be considered as to the comparative number modified by the comparative weight and importance of the several points—and let any competent and upright man be appointed the arbiter, to decide according to his best judgment, without any reference to the truth of the opinions, which of the two differed from the first the more widely. I say this, well aware that it would be abundantly more prudent to leave it unsaid. But I say it in the conviction, that the *liberality* in the adoption of admitted *misnomers* in the naming of doctrinal systems, if only they have been negatively

---

* See the second 'Lay Sermon,' Bohn's edition, pp. 406-7.—ED.

Believer, at the least possible expenditure of Belief; a
scheme of picking and choosing Scripture texts for the

legalized, is but an equivocal proof of liberality towards the *persons* who
dissent from us. On the contrary, I more than suspect that the former
liberality does in too many men arise from a latent pre-disposition to
transfer their reprobation and intolerance from the doctrines to the
doctors, from the belief to the believers. Indecency, abuse, scoffing
on subjects dear and awful to a multitude of our fellow-citizens, appeals
to the vanity, appetites, and malignant passions of ignorant and incompetent judges—these are flagrant overt-acts, condemned by the law
written in the heart of every honest man, Jew, Turk, and Christian.
These are points respecting which the humblest honest man feels it his
duty to hold himself infallible, and dares not hesitate in giving utterance
to the verdict of his conscience, in the jury-box as fearlessly as by his
fireside. It is far otherwise with respect to matters of faith and inward
conviction : and with respect to *these* I say—Tolerate no Belief, that
you judge false and of injurious tendency : and arraign no Believer.
The Man is more and other than his Belief : and God only knows, how
small or how large a part of him the Belief in question may be, for good
or for evil. Resist every false doctrine : and call no man heretic. The
false doctrine does not necessarily make the man a heretic ; but an evil
heart can make any doctrine heretical.

Actuated by these principles, I have objected to a false and deceptive
designation in the case of one System. Persuaded that the doctrines,
enumerated in p. 123, 124, are not only *essential* to the Christian Religion,
but those which contra-distinguish the religion as *Christian*, I merely
repeat this persuasion in another form, when I assert, that (in *my* sense
of the word, Christian) Unitarianism is not Christianity. But do I say,
that those, who call themselves Unitarians, are not Christians ? God
forbid ! I would not think, much less promulgate, a judgment at once
so presumptuous and so uncharitable.* Let a friendly antagonist retort
on *my* scheme of faith, in the like manner : I shall respect him all the
more for his consistency as a reasoner, and not confide the less in his
kindness towards me as his neighbour and fellow-Christian. This
latter and most endearing name I scarcely know how to withhold even
from my friend, HYMAN HURWITZ, as often as I read what every
Reverer of Holy Writ and of the English Bible ought to read, his admirable VINDICIÆ HEBRAICÆ! It has trembled on the verge, as it were,
of my lips, every time I have conversed with that pious, learned, strong-
minded, and single-hearted Jew, an Israelite indeed, and without guile,—

> *Cujus cura sequi naturam, legibus uti,*
> *Et mentem vitiis, ora negare dolis;*
> *Virtutes opibus, verum præponere falso,*
> *Nil vacuum sensu dicere, nil facere.*

---

* See Coleridge's ' Table Talk,' April 4, 1832, On Unitarianism.—ED.

support of doctrines, that had been learned beforehand from the higher oracle of Common Sense ; which, as applied

Post obitum vivam * secum, secum requiescam,
Nec fiat melior sors mea sorte suâ !

From a poem of Hildebert on his Master,
the persecuted Berengarius.

Under the same feelings I conclude this *Aid to Reflection* by applying the principle to another misnomer not less inappropriate and far more influential. Of those whom I have found most reason to respect and value, many have been members of the Church of Rome : and certainly I did not honour those the least, who scrupled even in common parlance to call our Church a reformed Church. A similar scruple would not, methinks, disgrace a Protestant as to the use of the words, Catholic or Roman Catholic; and if (tacitly at least, and in thought) he remembered that the Romish Anti-catholic Church would more truly express the fact.—*Romish*, to mark that the corruptions in discipline, doctrine, and practice do, for the larger part, owe both their origin and perpetuation to the Romish *Court*, and the local Tribunals of the *City* of Rome ; and neither are or ever have been *Catholic*, that is, universal, throughout the Roman *Empire*, or even in the whole Latin or Western Church— and *Anti*-catholic, because no other Church acts on so narrow and excommunicative a principle, or is characterized by such a jealous spirit of monopoly. Instead of a Catholic (universal) spirit, it may be truly described as a spirit of Particularism counterfeiting Catholicity by a *negative* totality and heretical self-circumscription—in the first instances cutting off, and since then cutting herself off from, all the other members of Christ's body For the rest, I think as that man of true catholic spirit and apostolic zeal, Richard Baxter, thought ; and my readers will thank me for conveying my reflections in his own words, in the following golden passage from his Life, "faithfully published from his own original MSS. by Matthew Silvester, 1696."

"My censures of the Papists do much differ from what they were at first. I then thought that their errors in the *doctrines of faith* were their most dangerous mistakes. But now I am assured that their misexpressions and misunderstanding us, with our mistakings of them and inconvenient expressing of our own opinions, have made the difference in most points appear much greater than it is ; and that in some it is next to none at all. But the great and unreconcileable differences lie in their Church Tyranny ; in the usurpations of their Hierarchy, and Priesthood, under the name of spiritual authority exercising a temporal Lordship ; in their corruptions and abasement of God's Worship ; but above all their systematic befriending of Ignorance and Vice.

"At first I thought that Mr. Perkins well proved, that a Papist cannot go beyond a reprobate ; but now I doubt not that God hath many sanctified ones among them, who have received the true doctrine of

---

* I do not answer for the corrupt Latin.

to the truths of Religion, means the popular part of the philosophy in fashion. Of course, the scheme differs at different times and in different individuals in the number of articles excluded; but, it may always be recognized by this permanent character, that its object is to draw religion down to the believer's intellect, instead of raising his intellect up to religion. And this extreme I call MINIMI-FIDIANISM.

Now if there be one preventive of both these extremes more efficacious than another, and preliminary to all the rest, it is the being made fully aware of the diversity of Reason and Understanding. And this is the more expedient, because though there is no want of authorities ancient and modern for the distinction of the faculties, and the distinct appropriation of the terms, yet our best writers too often confound the one with the other. Even Lord Bacon himself, who in his *Novum Organum* has so incomparably set forth the nature of the difference, and the unfitness of the latter faculty for the objects of the former, does nevertheless in sundry places use the term Reason where he means the Understanding, and sometimes, though less frequently, Understanding for Reason.[1] In consequence of thus confounding the two terms, or rather of wasting both words for the expression of one and the same faculty, he left himself no appropriate term for the other and higher gift of Reason, and was thus under the necessity of adopting fantastical and mystical phrases, for example, the dry light (*lumen siccum*), the lucific vision, and the like, meaning thereby nothing more than Reason in contra-distinction from the Understanding. Thus too in the preceding Aphorism,

Christianity so practically, that their contradictory errors prevail not against them, to hinder their love of God and their salvation: but that their errors are like a conquerable dose of poison, which a healthful nature doth overcome. *And I can never believe that a man may not be saved by that religion, which doth but bring him to the true Love of God and to a heavenly mind and life; nor that God will ever cast a Soul into hell, that truly loveth him.* Also at first it would disgrace any doctrine with me, if I did but hear it called Popery and Anti-Christian; but I have long learned to be more impartial, and to know that Satan can use even the names of Popery and Antichrist, to bring a truth into suspicion and discredit."—Baxter's Life, part I. p. 131.

[1] See 'The Friend,' Bohn's edition, pp. 95-100, and 319-27.—ED.

by Reason Leighton means the human Understanding, the explanation annexed to it being (by a noticeable coincidence), word for word, the very definition which the founder of the Critical Philosophy gives of the Understanding—namely, "the faculty judging according to sense."

ON THE DIFFERENCE IN KIND OF REASON AND THE UNDERSTANDING.

SCHEME OF THE ARGUMENT.

On the contrary, Reason is the Power of Universal and necessary Convictions, the Source and Substance of Truths above Sense, and having their evidence in themselves. Its presence is always marked by the *necessity* of the position affirmed: this necessity being *conditional*, when a truth of Reason is applied to Facts of Experience, or to the rules and maxims of the Understanding; but *absolute*, when the subject matter is itself the growth or offspring of the Reason. Hence arises a distinction in the Reason itself, derived from the different mode of applying it, and from the objects to which it is directed: accordingly as we consider one and the same gift, now as the ground of formal principles, and now as the origin of *ideas*. Contemplated distinctively in reference to *formal* (or abstract) truth, it is the *speculative* reason; but in reference to *actual* (or moral) truth, as the fountain of ideas, and the *light* of the conscience, we name it the *practical* reason. Whenever by self-subjection to this universal light, the will of the individual, the *particular* will, has become a will of reason, the man is regenerate: and reason is then the *spirit* of the regenerated man, whereby the person is capable of a quickening inter-communion with the Divine Spirit. And herein consists the mystery of Redemption, that this has been rendered possible for us. *And so it is written: the first man Adam was made a living soul, the last Adam a quickening Spirit.* (1 *Cor.* xv. 45.) We need only compare the passages in the writings of the Apostles Paul and John, concerning the *spirit* and spiritual Gifts, with those in the Proverbs and in the Wisdom of Solomon respecting *reason*, to be convinced that the terms are synonymous.[1] In this at once most comprehensive and most appropriate acceptation of the word, reason is preeminently spiritual, and a spirit, even *our* spirit, through an effluence of the same grace by which we are privileged to say Our Father!

On the other hand, the Judgments of the Understanding are binding only in relation to the objects of our Senses, which we *reflect* under the forms of the Understanding. It is, as Leighton rightly defines it, "the faculty judging according to sense." Hence we add the epithet *human*, without tautology: and speak of the *human* understanding, in disjunction from that of beings higher or lower than man. But there is, in this sense, no *human* reason. There neither is nor can be but one reason, one and the same: even the light that lighteth every man's individual Understanding (*Discursus*), and thus maketh it a reasonable understanding, *discourse of reason—one only*, yet *manifold: it goeth through all understanding, and remaining in itself regenerateth all other powers.* The same writer calls it likewise *an influence from the Glory of the Almighty*, this being one of the names of the Messiah, as the *Logos*, or coeternal Filial Word. And most noticeable for its coincidence is a fragment of Heraclitus, as I have indeed already noticed elsewhere;—"To discourse rationally it behoves us to derive strength from that which is common to all men: for all human Understandings are nourished by the one DIVINE WORD."

Beasts, we have said, partake of understanding. If any man deny this, there is a ready way of settling the question. Let him give a careful perusal to Hüber's two small volumes, on bees and ants (especially the latter), and to Kirby and Spence's Introduction to Entomology; and one or other of two things must follow. He will either change his opinion as irreconcilable with the facts; or he must deny the facts, which yet I cannot suppose, inasmuch as the denial would be tantamount to the no less extravagant than uncharitable assertion, that Hüber, and the several eminent naturalists, French and English, Swiss, German,

---

[1] See Wisd. of Sol., c. vii. 22, 23, 27.—H. N. C.

and Italian, by whom Hüber's observations and experiments
have been repeated and confirmed, had all conspired to
impose a series of falsehoods and fairy-tales on the world.
I see no way at least, by which he can get out of this
dilemma, but by over-leaping the admitted rules and
fences of all legitimate discussion, and either transferring
to the word, Understanding, the definition already appropriated to Reason, or defining Understanding *in genere* by
the *specific* and *accessional* perfections which the *human*
understanding derives from its co-existence with reason
and free-will in the same individual person; in plainer
words, from its being exercised by a self-conscious and
responsible creature. And, after all, the supporter of Harrington's position would have a right to ask him, by what
other name he would designate the faculty in the instances
referred to ? If it be not Understanding, what is it ?

In no former part of this volume has the author felt the
same anxiety to obtain a patient attention. For he does
not hesitate to avow, that on his success in establishing
the validity and importance of the distinction between
Reason and Understanding, he rests his hopes of carrying
the reader along with him through all that is to follow.
Let the student but clearly see and comprehend the diversity in the things themselves, the expediency of a correspondent distinction and appropriation of the *words* will
follow of itself. Turn back for a moment to the Aphorism,
and having re-perused the first paragraph of this Comment
thereon, regard the two following narratives as the illustration. I do not say proof : for I take these from a multitude of facts equally striking for the one only purpose of
placing my *meaning* out of all doubt.

I. Hüber put a dozen humble-bees under a bell-glass
along with a comb of about ten silken cocoons so unequal
in height as not to be capable of standing steadily. To
remedy this two or three of the humble-bees got upon the
comb, stretched themselves over its edge, and with their
heads downwards fixed their fore-feet on the table on which
the comb stood, and so with their hind-feet kept the comb
from falling. When these were weary, others took their
places. In this constrained and painful posture, fresh bees
relieving their comrades at intervals, and each working in

its turn, did these affectionate little insects support the
comb for nearly three days: at the end of which they had
prepared sufficient wax to build pillars with. But these
pillars having accidentally got displaced, the bees had
recourse again to the same manœuvre till Hüber, pitying
their hard case, &c.

II. " I shall at present describe the operations of a single
ant that I observed sufficiently long to satisfy my curiosity.
One rainy day, I observed a labourer digging the ground
near the aperture which gave entrance to the ant-hill.
It placed in a heap the several fragments it had scraped
up, and formed them into small pellets, which it deposited
here and there upon the nest. It returned constantly
to the same place, and appeared to have a marked design, for it laboured with ardour and perseverance. I remarked a slight furrow, excavated in the ground in a
straight line, representing the plan of a path or gallery.
The Labourer, the whole of whose movements fell under
my immediate observation, gave it greater depth and
breadth, and cleared out its borders: and I saw at length,
in which I could not be deceived, that it had the intention
of establishing an avenue which was to lead from one of
the stories to the underground chambers. This path, which
was about two or three inches in length, and formed by a
single ant, was opened above and bordered on each side by
a buttress of earth; its concavity *en forme de gouttière* was
of the most perfect regularity, for the architect had not
left an atom too much. The work of this ant was so well
followed and understood, that I could almost to a certainty
guess its next proceeding, and the very fragment it was
about to remove. At the side of the opening where this
path terminated, was a second opening to which it was
necessary to arrive by some road. The same ant engaged
in and executed alone this undertaking. It furrowed out
and opened another path, parallel to the first, leaving
between each a little wall of three or four lines in height.
Those ants who lay the foundation of a wall, chamber, or
gallery, from working separately occasion now and then a
want of coincidence in the parts of the same or different
objects. Such examples are of no unfrequent occurrence,
but they by no means embarrass them. What follows

proves that the workman, on discovering his error, knew how to rectify it. A wall had been erected with the view of sustaining a vaulted ceiling, still incomplete, that had been projected from the wall of the opposite chamber. The workman who began constructing it, had given it too little elevation to meet the opposite partition upon which it was to rest. Had it been continued on the original plan, it must infallibly have met the wall at about one half of its height, and this it was necessary to avoid. This state of things very forcibly claimed my attention, when one of the ants arriving at the place, and visiting the works, appeared to be struck by the difficulty which presented itself; but this it as soon obviated, by taking down the ceiling and raising the wall upon which it reposed. It then, in my presence, constructed a new ceiling with the fragments of the former one."—*Hüber's Natural History of Ants*, p. 38-41.

Now I assert, that the faculty manifested in the acts here narrated does not differ *in kind* from Understanding, and that it *does* so differ from Reason. What I conceive the former to be, physiologically considered, will be shown hereafter. In this place I take the understanding as it exists in *men*, and in exclusive reference to its *intelligential* functions; and it is in this sense of the word that I am to prove the necessity of contra-distinguishing it from reason.

Premising then, that two or more subjects having the same essential characters are said to fall under the same general definition, I lay it down, as a self-evident truth,— (it is, in fact, an identical proposition) that whatever subjects fall under one and the same general definition are of one and the same kind: consequently, that which does *not* fall under this definition, must differ in kind from each and all of those that *do*. Difference in degree does indeed suppose sameness in kind; and difference in kind precludes distinction from difference of degree. *Heterogenea non comparari, ergo nec distingui, possunt.* The inattention to this rule gives rise to the numerous sophisms comprised by Aristotle under the head of μετάβασις εἰς ἄλλο γένος, that is, transition into a new kind, or the falsely applying to X what had been truly asserted of A, and might have been true of X, had it differed from A in its degree only. The sophistry consists in the omission to notice what not being noticed will be supposed not to exist; and where the silence respecting the difference in kind is tantamount to an assertion that the difference is merely in degree. But the fraud is especially gross, where the heterogeneous subject, thus clandestinely *slipt in*, is in its own nature insusceptible of degree : such as, for instance, Certainty, or Circularity, contrasted with Strength, or Magnitude.

To apply these remarks for our present purpose, we have only to describe Understanding and Reason, each by its characteristic qualities. The comparison will show the difference.

UNDERSTANDING.	REASON.
1. Understanding is discursive.	1. Reason is fixed.
2. The Understanding in all its judgments refers to some other Faculty as its ultimate Authority.	2. The Reason in all its decisions appeals to itself, as the ground and *substance* of their truth. (*Hebrews* vi. 13.)
3. Understanding is the Faculty of *Reflection*.	3. Reason of Contemplation. Reason indeed is much nearer to SENSE than to Understanding : for Reason (says our great HOOKER) is a direct aspect of Truth, an inward Beholding, having a similar relation to the Intelligible or Spiritual, as SENSE has to the Material or Phenomenal.

The Result is : that neither falls under the definition of the other. They differ *in kind* : and had my object been confined to the establishment of this fact, the preceding columns would have superseded all further disquisition. But I have ever in view the especial interest of my youthful readers, whose reflective *power* is to be cultivated, as well as their particular reflections to be called forth and guided. Now the main chance of their *reflecting* on religious subjects *aright*, and of their attaining to the *contemplation* of spiritual truths *at all*, rests on their insight into

the *nature* of this disparity still more than on their conviction of its existence. I now, therefore, proceed to a brief
analysis of the Understanding, in elucidation of the definitions already given.

The Understanding then (considered exclusively as an
organ of human intelligence,) is the Faculty by which we
reflect and generalize. Take, for instance, any objects con-
sisting of many parts, a house, or a group of houses : and if it
be contemplated, as a Whole, that is, as many constituting
a one, it forms what in the technical language of Psycho-
logy, is called a *total impression*. Among the various component parts of this, we direct our attention especially to such
as we recollect to have noticed in other total impressions.
Then, by a voluntary act, we withhold our attention from all
the rest to reflect exclusively on these ; and these we henceforward use as *common characters*, by virtue of which the
several objects are referred to one and the same sort.[1] Thus,
the whole process may be reduced to three acts, all depend-
ing on and supposing a previous impression on the senses :
first, the appropriation of our Attention; second, (and in
order to the continuance of the first) Abstraction, or the
voluntary withholding of the Attention ; and third, Generalization. And these are the proper Functions of the Understanding : and the power of so doing, is what we mean,
when we say we possess Understanding, or are created
with the faculty of Understanding.

[It is obvious, that the third function includes the act
of comparing one object with another. In a note (for, not
to interrupt the argument, I avail myself of this most useful contrivance,) I have shown, that the act of comparing
supposes in the comparing faculty, certain inherent forms,
that is, modes of reflecting not referable to the objects
reflected on, but pre-determined by the constitution and
(as it were) mechanism of the Understanding itself. And
under some one or other of these forms,[2] the resemblances

---

[1] Accordingly as we attend more or less to the differences, the *sort*
becomes, of course, more or less comprehensive. Hence there arises for
the systematic naturalist, the necessity of subdividing the sorts into
orders, classes, families, &c. : all which, however, resolve themselves
for the mere logician into the conception of *genus* and *species*, *i.e.* the
comprehending and the comprehended.

[2] Were it not so, how could the first comparison have been possible ?—

and differences must be subsumed in order to be conceivable, and *a fortiori* therefore in order to be comparable.

It would involve the absurdity of measuring a thing by itself. But if
we think on some one thing, the length of our own foot, or of our hand
and arm from the elbow joint, it is evident that in *order* to do this, we
must have the conception of measure. Now these antecedent and most
general conceptions are what is meant by the constituent *forms* of the
Understanding : we call them *constituent* because they are not *acquired*
by the Understanding, but are implied in its constitution. As rationally
might a circle be said to acquire a centre and circumference, as the
Understanding to acquire these, its inherent *forms*, or ways of conceiving.
This is what Leibnitz meant, when to the old adage of the Peripatetics,
Nihil in intellectu quod non prius in sensu (There is nothing in the
Understanding not derived from the Senses, or—There is nothing *con-*
ceived that was not previously *perceived* ;) he replied—*præter intellectum
ipsum* (except the Understanding itself).

And here let me remark for once and all : whoever would *reflect* to
any purpose—whoever is in earnest in his pursuit of Self-knowledge, and
of one of the principal means to this, an insight into the meaning of the
words he uses, and the different meanings properly or improperly conveyed by one and the same word, accordingly as it is used in the schools or
the market, accordingly as the *kind* or a high *degree* is intended (for example,
heat, weight, and the like, as employed scientifically, compared with the
same word used popularly)—whoever, I say, seriously proposes this as
his object, must so far overcome his dislike of pedantry, and his dread
of being sneered at as a pedant, as not to quarrel with an uncouth word
or phrase, till he is quite sure that some other and more familiar one
would not only have expressed the *precise* meaning with equal clearness,
but have been as likely to draw attention to *this* meaning exclusively.
The ordinary language of a Philosopher in conversation or popular
writings, compared with the language he uses in strict reasoning, is as
his watch compared with the chronometer in his observatory. He sets
the former by the Town-clock, or even, perhaps, by the Dutch clock in
his kitchen, not because he believes it right, but because his neighbours
and his cook *go* by it. To afford the reader an opportunity for exercising the forbearance here recommended, I turn back to the phrase,
" most general conceptions," and observe, that in strict and severe propriety of language I should have said *generalific* or *generific* rather than
general, and *concipiences* or *conceptive* acts rather than conceptions.

It is an old complaint, that a man of genius no sooner appears, but
the host of dunces are up in arms to repel the invading alien. This
observation would have made more converts to its truth, I suspect, had
it been worded more dispassionately, and with a less contemptuous
antithesis. For " dunces," let us substitute " the many," or the " οὗτος
κόσμος " (*this world*) of the Apostle, and we shall perhaps find no great
difficulty in accounting for the fact. To arrive at the *root*, indeed, and
last ground of the problem, it would be necessary to investigate the
nature and effects of the sense of difference on the human mind where
it is not holden in check by reason and reflection. We need not go to

The senses do not compare, but merely furnish the materials for comparison.   But this the reader will find ex-

the savage tribes of North America, or the yet ruder natives of the Indian Isles, to learn, how slight a degree of difference will, in uncultivated minds, call up a sense of diversity, and inward perplexity and contradiction, as if the strangers were, and yet were not, of the same *kind* with themselves.   Who has not had occasion to observe the effect which the gesticulations and nasal tones of a Frenchman produce on our own vulgar ?   Here we may see the origin and primary import of our *unkindness*.   It is a sense of *un*kind, and not the mere negation but the positive Opposite of the sense of *kind*.   Alienation, aggravated now by fear, now by contempt, and not seldom by a mixture of both, aversion, hatred, enmity, are so many successive shapes of its growth and metamorphosis.—In application to the present case, it is sufficient to say, that Pindar's remark on sweet music holds equally true of genius : as many as are not delighted by it are disturbed, perplexed, irritated.   The beholder either recognizes it as a projected form of his own Being, that moves before him with a Glory round its head, or recoils from it as from a Spectre.   But this speculation would lead me too far ; I must be content with having referred to it as the ultimate ground of the fact, and pass to the more obvious and proximate causes.   And as the first, I would rank the person's *not* understanding what yet he expects to understand, and as if he had a right to do so.   An original mathematical work, or any other that requires peculiar and (so to say) technical marks and symbols, will excite no uneasy feelings—not in the mind of a competent reader, for he understands it ; and not with others, because they neither expect nor are expected to understand it.   The second place we may assign to the *mis*understanding, which is almost sure to follow in cases where the incompetent person, finding no outward marks (diagrams, arbitrary signs, and the like) to inform him at first sight, that the subject is one which he does not pretend to understand, and to be ignorant of which does not detract from his estimation as a man of abilities generally, *will* attach some meaning to what he hears or reads ; and as he is out of humour with the author, it will most often be such a meaning as he can quarrel with and exhibit in a ridiculous or offensive point of view.

But above all, the whole world almost of minds, as far as we regard intellectual efforts, may be divided into two classes of the Busy-Indolent and Lazy-indolent.   To both alike all Thinking is painful, and all attempts to rouse them to think, whether in the re-examination of their existing convictions, or for the reception of new light, are irritating. " It *may* all be very deep and clever ; but really one ought to be quite sure of it before one wrenches one's brain to find out what it is.   I take up a Book as a Companion, with whom I can have an easy cheerful chit-chat on what we both know beforehand, or else matters of fact.   In our leisure hours we have a right to relaxation and amusement."

Well ! but in their *studious* hours, when their bow is to be bent, when they are *apud Musas*, or amidst the Muses ? Alas ! it is just the same ! The same craving for *amusement*, that is, to be away from the Muses ! for re-

plained in the note; and will now cast his eye back to the sentence immediately preceding this parenthesis.]

Now when a person speaking to us of any particular Object or Appearance refers it by means of some common character to a known class (which he does in giving it a Name), we say, that we understand him; that is, we understand his words. The Name of a thing, in the original sense of the word Name, (*nomen, νούμενον, τὸ intelligible, id quod intelligitur*) expresses that which is *understood* in an appearance, that which we place (or make to *stand*) *under* it, as

laxation, that is, the unbending of a bow which in fact had never been strung! There are two ways of obtaining their applause. The first is: Enable them to reconcile in one and the same occupation the love of Sloth and the hatred of Vacancy! Gratify indolence, and yet save them from *ennui*—in plain English, from themselves! For, spite of their antipathy to *dry* reading, the keeping company with themselves is, after all, the insufferable annoyance: and the true secret of their dislike to a work of thought and inquiry lies in its tendency to make them acquainted with their own permanent Being. The other road to their favour is, to introduce to them their own thoughts and predilections, tricked out in the *fine* language, in which it would gratify their vanity to express them in their own conversation, and with which they can imagine themselves *showing off:* and this (as has been elsewhere remarked) is the characteristic difference between the second-rate writers of the last two or three generations, and the same class under Elizabeth and the Stuarts. In the latter we find the most far-fetched and singular thoughts in the simplest and most native language; in the former, the most obvious and common-place thoughts in the most far-fetched and motley language. But lastly, and as the *sine quâ non* of their patronage, a sufficient arc must be left for the Reader's mind to *oscillate* in—freedom of choice,

To make the shifting cloud be what you please,

save only where the attraction of curiosity determines the line of motion. The attention must not be fastened down: and this every work of genius, not simply narrative, must do before it can be justly appreciated.

In former times a *popular* work meant one that adapted the *results* of studious meditation or scientific research to the capacity of the people, presenting in the concrete, by instances and examples, what had been ascertained in the abstract and by discovery of the Law. *Now*, on the other hand, that is a popular work which gives back to the people their own errors and prejudices, and flatters the many by creating them, under the title of THE PUBLIC, into a supreme and inappellable Tribunal of intellectual Excellence. P.S. In a continuous work, the frequent insertion and length of Notes would need an Apology: in a book like this of Aphorisms and detached Comments none is necessary, it being understood beforehand, that the sauce and the garnish are to occupy the greater part of the dish.

the condition of its real existence, and in proof that it is
not an accident of the senses, or affection of the individual,
not a phantom or *apparition*, that is, an appearance that is
only an appearance. (See *Gen.* ii. 19, 20, and in *Psalm* xx. 1,
and in many other places of the Bible, the identity of *nomen*
with *numen*, that is, invisible power and presence, the *nomen
substantivum* of all real objects, and the ground of their
reality, independently of the affections of sense in the percipient). In like manner, in a connected succession of names,
as the speaker passes from the one to the other, we say that
we can understand his *discourse* (*discursio intellectûs, discursus*,
his passing rapidly from one thing to another). Thus, in all
instances, it is words, names, or, if images, yet images used
as words or names, that are the only and exclusive subjects
of Understanding. In no instance do we understand a thing
in itself; but only the name to which it is referred. Sometimes indeed, when several classes are recalled conjointly, we
identify the words with the object—though by courtesy of
idiom rather than in strict propriety of language. Thus
we may say that we *understand* a rainbow, when recalling
successively the several Names for the several sorts of
colours, we know that they are to be applied to one and the
same *phenomenon*, at once distinctly and simultaneously;
but even in common speech we should not say this of a
single colour. No one would say he understands red or
blue. He *sees* the colour, and had seen it before in a vast
number and variety of objects; and he understands the
word red, as referring his fancy or memory to this his col-
lective experience.

If this be so, and so it most assuredly is—if the proper
functions of the Understanding be that of generalizing the
notices received from the senses in order to the construction
of *names:* of referring particular notices (that is, impressions
or sensations) to their proper names; and, *vice versâ*, names
to their correspondent class or kind of notices—then it follows of necessity, that the Understanding is truly and accurately defined in the words of Leighton and Kant, a
"faculty judging according to sense."

Now whether in defining the speculative Reason (that is,
the Reason considered abstractedly as an *intellective* power)
we call it " the source of necessary and universal principles,

according to which the notices of the senses are either affirmed or denied ; " or describe it as " the power by which we are enabled to draw from particular and contingent appearances universal and necessary conclusions : " [1] it is equally evident that the two definitions differ in their

---

[1] Take a familiar illustration. My sight and touch convey to me a certain impression, to which my Understanding applies its pre-conceptions (*conceptus antecedentes et generalissimi*) of quantity and relation, and thus refers it to the class and name of three-cornered bodies—we will suppose it the iron of a turf-spade. It compares the sides, and finds that any two measured as one are greater than the third ; and according to a law of the imagination, there arises a presumption that in all other bodies of the same figure (that is, three-cornered and equilateral) the same proportion exists. After this, the senses have been directed successively to a number of three-cornered bodies of *unequal* sides—and in these too the same proportion has been found without exception, till at length it becomes a fact of *experience*, that in *all* triangles hitherto seen, the two sides together are greater than the third : and there will exist no ground or analogy for anticipating an exception to a rule, generalized from so vast a number of particular instances. So far and no farther could the Understanding carry us : and as far as this " the faculty, judging according to sense," conducts many of the *inferior* animals, if not in the same, yet in instances analogous and fully equivalent.

The Reason supersedes the whole process, and on the first conception presented by the Understanding in consequence of the first sight of a tri-angular figure, of whatever sort it might chance to be, it affirms with an assurance incapable of future increase, with a perfect *certainty*, that in all possible triangles any two of the inclosing lines *will* and *must* be greater than the third. In short, Understanding in its highest form of experience remains commensurate with the experimental notices of the senses from which it is generalized. Reason, on the other hand, either predetermines Experience, or avails itself of a past Experience to supersede its necessity in all future time ; and affirms truths which no sense could perceive, nor experiment verify, nor experience confirm.

Yea, this is the test and character of a truth so affirmed, that in its own proper form it is *inconceivable*. For *to conceive* is a function of the Understanding, which can be exercised only on subjects subordinate thereto. And yet to the forms of the Understanding all truth must be reduced, that is to be fixed as an object of reflection, and to be rendered *expressible*. And here we have a second test and sign of a truth so affirmed, that it can come forth out of the moulds of the Understanding only in the disguise of two contradictory conceptions, each of which is partially true, and the conjunction of both conceptions becomes the representative or *expression* (the *exponent*) of a truth *beyond* conception and inexpressible. Examples : Before Abraham *was*, I *am*.—God is a Circle, the centre of which is everywhere, and circumference nowhere. The soul is all in every part.

If this appear extravagant, it is an extravagance which no man can indeed learn from another, but which, (were this possible,) I might have

essential characters, and consequently the subjects differ in *kind*.

The dependence of the Understanding on the representations of the senses, and its consequent posteriority thereto, as contrasted with the independence and antecedency of

learnt from Plato, Kepler, and Bacon; from Luthur, Hooker, Pascal, Leibnitz, and Fénélon. But in this last paragraph I have, I see, unwittingly overstepped my purpose, according to which we were to take Reason as a simply intellectual power. Yet even as such, and with all the disadvantage of a technical and arbitrary Abstraction, it has been made evident—1. that there is an *Intuition* or *im*mediate Beholding, accompanied by a conviction of the necessity and universality of the truth so beholden not derived from the senses, which intuition, when it is *construed* by *pure* sense, gives birth to the Science of Mathematics, and when applied to objects supersensuous or spiritual is the organ of Theology and Philosophy :—and 2. that there is likewise a reflective and discursive faculty, or *mediate* Apprehension which, taken by itself and uninfluenced by the former, depends on the senses for the materials on which it is exercised, and is contained within the sphere of the senses. And this faculty it is, which in generalizing the notices of the senses constitutes Sensible Experience, and gives rise to Maxims or Rules which may become more and more *general*, but can never be raised into universal Verities, or beget a consciousness of absolute Certainty ; though they may be sufficient to extinguish all doubt. (Putting Revelation out of view, take our first progenitor in the 50th or 100th year of his existence. His experience would probably have freed him from all doubt, as the sun sank in the horizon that it would re-appear the next morning. But compare this state of assurance with that which the same man would have had of the 37th Proposition of Euclid, supposing him, like Pythagoras, to have discovered the *Demonstration*.) Now is it expedient, I ask, or conformable to the laws and purposes of language, to call two so altogether disparate subjects by one and the same name ? Or, having two names in our language, should we call each of the two diverse subjects by both—that is, by either name, as caprice might dictate ? If not, then, as we have the two words, Reason and Understanding (as indeed what language of cultivated man has not ?) what should prevent us from appropriating the former to the Power distinctive of humanity ?   We need only place the derivatives from the two terms in opposition (for example, " A and B are both rational beings; but there is no comparison between them in point of *intelligence ;*" or " She always concludes *rationally*, though not a woman of much *understanding* ") to see that we cannot reverse the order—*i. e.* call the higher gift Understanding, and the lower Reason. What *should* prevent us ?   I asked.   Alas ! that which *has* prevented us—the *cause* of this confusion in the terms—is only too obvious ; namely, inattention to the momentous distinction in the *things*, and (generally) to the duty and habit recommended in the fifth Introductory Aphorism of this volume, (*see* p. 2).   But the cause of this, and of all its lamentable effects and subcauses, *false doctrine, blindness of heart and contempt of the word*, is best declared by the philosophic

Reason, are strikingly exemplified in the Ptolemaic System (that truly wonderful product and highest boast of the faculty, judging according to the senses!) compared with the Newtonian, as the offspring of a yet higher power, arranging, correcting, and annulling the representations of the senses according to its own inherent laws and constitutive ideas.

APHORISM IX.

In Wonder all Philosophy began: in Wonder it ends: and Admiration fills up the interspace. But the first Wonder is the offspring of Ignorance: the last is the parent of Adoration. The first is the birth-throe of our knowledge: the last is its euthanasy and *apotheosis*.

Sequelæ: or Thoughts suggested by the preceding Aphorism.

As in respect of the first wonder we are all on the same level, how comes it that the philosophic mind should, in all ages, be the privilege of a few? The most obvious reason is this: The wonder takes place before the period of reflection, and (with the great mass of mankind) long before the individual is capable of directing his attention freely and consciously to the feeling, or even to its exciting causes. Surprise (the form and dress which the Wonder of Ignorance usually puts on) is worn away, if not precluded, by custom and familiarity. So is it with the objects of the senses, and the ways and fashions of the world around us; even as with the beat of our own hearts, which we notice only in moments of fear and perturbation. But with regard to the concerns of our inward being, there is yet another cause that acts in concert with the power in

Apostle: *they did not* like *to retain God in their knowledge,* (*Rom.* i. 28,) and though they could not *extinguish the light that lighteth every man,* and which *shone in the darkness;* yet because the darkness could not *comprehend* the light, they refused to bear witness of the light, and worshipped, instead, the shaping mist, which the light had drawn upward from *the ground* (that is, from the mere animal nature and instinct), and which that light alone had made visible, that is, by superinducing on the animal instinct the principle of Self-consciousness.

custom to prevent a fair and equal exertion of reflective thought. The great fundamental truths and doctrines of religion, the existence and attributes of God, and the life after death, are in Christian countries taught so early, under such circumstances, and in such close and vital association with whatever makes or marks *reality* for our infant minds, that the words ever after represent sensations, feelings, vital assurances, sense of reality—rather than thoughts, or any distinct conception. Associated, I had almost said *identified*, with the parental voice, look, touch, with the living warmth and pressure of the Mother, on whose lap the child is first made to kneel, within whose palms its little hands are folded, and the motion of whose eyes *its* eyes follow and imitate—(yea, what the blue sky is to the mother, the mother's upraised eyes and brow are to the child, the Type and Symbol of an invisible Heaven!)— from within and without, these great First Truths, these good and gracious Tidings, these holy and humanizing Spells, in the preconformity to which our very humanity may be said to consist, are so infused, that it were but a tame and inadequate expression to say, we all take them for granted. At a later period, in youth or early man- hood, most of us, indeed, (in the higher and middle classes at least) read or hear certain PROOFS of these truths— which we commonly listen to, when we listen at all, with much the same feelings as a popular Prince on his Corona- tion Day, in the centre of a fond and rejoicing nation, may be supposed to hear the Champion's challenge to all the non-existents, that deny or dispute his Rights and Royalty. In fact, the order of Proof is most often reversed or trans- posed. As far, at least as I dare judge from the goings on in my own mind, when with keen delight I first read the works of Derham, Nieuwentiet, and Lyonet, I should say, that the full and life-like conviction of a gracious Creator is the Proof (at all events, performs the office and answers all the purpose of a Proof) of the wisdom and benevolence in the construction of the Creature.

Do I blame this? Do I wish it to be otherwise? God forbid! It is only one of its accidental, but too frequent consequences, of which I complain, and against which I protest. I regret nothing that tends to make the Light

become the Life of men, even as the Life in the eternal
Word is their only and single true light.   But I do regret,
that in after years—when by occasion of some new dispute
on some old heresy, or any other accident, the attention has
for the first time been distinctly attracted to the superstructure raised on these fundamental truths, or to truths
of later revelation supplemental of these and not less
important—all the doubts and difficulties, that cannot but
arise where the Understanding, *the mind of the flesh*, is
made the measure of spiritual things; all the sense of
strangeness and seeming contradiction in terms; all the
marvel and the mystery, that belong equally to both, are
first thought of and applied in objection exclusively to the
latter.   I would disturb no man's faith in the great articles
of the (falsely so called) Religion of Nature.   But before
the man rejects, and calls on other men to reject, the reve-
lations of the Gospel and the Religion of all Christendom, I
would have him place himself in the state and under all the
privations of a Simonides, when in the fortieth day of his
meditation the sage and philosophic poet abandoned the
problem in despair.   Ever and anon he seemed to have
hold of the truth; but when he asked himself what he
meant by it, it escaped from him, or resolved itself into
meanings, that destroyed each other.   I would have the
sceptic, while yet a sceptic only, seriously consider whether
a doctrine, of the truth of which a Socrates could obtain no
other assurance than what he derived from his strong *wish*
that it should be true; and which Plato found a mystery
hard to discover, and when discovered, communicable only
to the fewest of men; can, consonantly with history or
common sense, be classed among the articles, the belief of
which is ensured to all men by their mere common sense?
Whether, without gross outrage to fact, they can be said to
constitute a Religion of Nature, or a Natural Theology
antecedent to Revelation, or superseding its necessity?
Yes! in prevention (for there is little chance, I fear, of
a *cure*) of the pugnacious dogmatism of *partial* reflection,
I would prescribe to every man, who feels a commencing
alienation from the Catholic Faith, and whose studies and
attainments authorise him to argue on the subject at all, a
patient and thoughtful perusal of the arguments and repre-

sentations which Bayle supposes to have passed through the mind of Simonides.   Or I should be fully satisfied if I could induce these eschewers of mystery to give a patient, manly, and impartial perusal to the single Treatise of Pomponatius, *De Fato*.[1]

When they have fairly and satisfactorily overthrown the objections and cleared away the difficulties urged by this sharp-witted Italian against the doctrines which they profess to retain, then let them commence their attack on those which they reject.   As far as the supposed irrationality of the latter is the ground of argument, I am much deceived if, on reviewing their forces, they would not find the ranks woefully thinned by the success of their own fire in the preceding engagement—unless, indeed, by pure heat of controversy, and to storm the lines of their antagonists, they can bring to life again the arguments which they had themselves killed off in the defence of their own positions.   In vain shall we seek for any other mode of meeting the broad facts of the scientific Epicurean, or the requisitions and queries of the all-analysing Pyrrhonist, than by challenging the tribunal to which they appeal, as incompetent to try the question.   In order to *non-suit* the infidel plaintiff, we must remove the cause from the faculty, that judges according to sense, and whose judgments, therefore, are valid only on objects of sense, to the Superior Courts of Conscience and intuitive Reason !   *The words I speak unto you, are Spirit*, and such only *are life*, that is, have an inward and actual power abiding in them.

But the same truth is at once shield and bow.   The shaft of Atheism glances aside from it to strike and pierce the breast-plate of the heretic.   Well for the latter, if plucking the weapon from the wound he recognizes an arrow from his own quiver, and abandons a cause that connects him with such confederates !   Without further rhetoric, the sum and substance of the argument is this :—

---

[1] The philosopher, whom the Inquisition would have burnt alive as an atheist, had not Leo X. and Cardinal Bembo decided that the work might be formidable to those semi-pagan Christians who regarded Revelation as a mere make-weight to their boasted Religion of Nature ;   but contained nothing dangerous to the Catholic Church or offensive to a true believer.   [He was born in 1462, and died in 1525.—H. N. C.]

an insight into the proper functions and subaltern rank of
the Understanding may not, indeed, disarm the Psilanthro-
pist of his metaphorical glosses, or of his *versions* fresh
from the forge, and with no other stamp than the private
mark of the individual manufacturer; but it will deprive
him of the only rational pretext for having recourse to
tools so liable to abuse, and of such perilous example.

COMMENT.

Since the preceding pages were composed, and during an
interim of depression and disqualification, I heard with a
delight and an interest, that I might without hyperbole
call medicinal, that the contra-distinction of Understanding
from Reason, for which during twenty years I have been
contending, *casting my bread upon the waters* with a perseverance, which in the existing state of the public taste
nothing but the deepest conviction of its importance could
have inspired—has been lately adopted and sanctioned by
the present distinguished Professor of Anatomy, in the
Course of Lectures given by him at the Royal College of
Surgeons, on the zoological part of Natural History; and,
if I am rightly informed, in one of the eloquent and
impressive introductory Discourses.[1] In explaining the
Nature of Instinct, as deduced from the actions and
tendencies of animals successively presented to the observation of the comparative physiologist in the ascending
scale of organic life—or rather, I should have said, in an
attempt to determine that precise import of the *term*, which
is required by the facts [2]—the Professor explained the

---

[1] A discourse by Prof. J. H. Green. This, "On Instinct," was
afterwards printed by Prof. Green with his 'Vital Dynamics,' 1840.
We give it as so published in the Appendix to the present edition;
though, of course, the " report," apparently verbal, on which Coleridge's
remarks of 1825 are founded, may have differed somewhat from the
Professor's text as published in 1840.—ED.

[2] The word, Instinct, brings together a number of facts into one class
by the assertion of a common ground, the nature of which ground it
determines *negatively* only—that is, the word does not explain *what* this
common ground is; but simply indicates that there *is* such a ground,
and that it is different in kind from that in which the responsible and
consciously voluntary actions of men originate. Thus, in its true and
primary import, Instinct stands in antithesis to Reason; and the

nature of what I have elsewhere called the *adaptive power*, that is, the faculty of adapting means to proximate ends. [N. B. I mean here a *relative* end—that which relatively to one thing is an *end*, though relatively to some other it is in itself a *mean*. It is to be regretted, that we have no single word to express those ends, that are not *the* end : for the distinction between those and an end in the proper sense of the term is an important one.] The Professor, I say, not only explained, first, the nature of the adaptive power *in genere*, and, secondly, the distinct character of the *same* power as it exists *specifically* and exclusively in the *human* being, and acquires the name of Understanding; but he did it in a way which gave the whole sum and sub-stance of my convictions, of all I had so long wished, and so often, but with such imperfect success, attempted to convey, free from all semblance of paradoxy, and from all occasion of offence—*omnem offendiculi*[1] *ansam præcidens*. It is, indeed, for the *fragmentary* reader only that I have any scruple. In those who have had the patience to accompany me so far on the up-hill road to manly prin-ciples, I can have no reason to guard against that disposi-tion to hasty offence from anticipation of *consequences*,—that faithless and loveless spirit of fear which plunged Galileo

perplexity and contradictory statements into which so many meritorious naturalists, and popular writers on natural history (Priscilla Wake-field, Kirby, Spence, Hüber, and even Reimarus) have fallen on this subject, arise wholly from their taking the word in opposition to Under-standing. I notice this, because I would not lose any opportunity of impressing on the mind of my youthful readers the important truth that language (as the embodied and articulated Spirit of the Race, as the growth and emanation of a People, and not the work of any individual wit or will) is often inadequate, sometimes deficient, but never false or delusive. We have only to master the true origin and original import of any native and abiding word, to find in it, if not the *solution* of the facts expressed by it, yet a finger-mark pointing to the road on which this solution is to be sought.

[1] *Neque quicquam addubito, quin ea candidis omnibus faciat satis. Quid autem facias istis qui vel ob ingenii pertinaciam sibi satisfieri nolint, vel stupidiores sint quam ut satisfactionem intelligant? Nam quemad-modum Simonides dixit, Thessalos hebetiores esse quam ut possint a se decipi, ita quosdam videas stupidiores quam ut placari queant. Adhuc non mirum est invenire quod calumnietur qui nihil aliud quærit nisi quod calumnietur.* (Erasmi Epist. ad Dorpium.) At all events, the paragraph passing through the medium of my own prepossessions, if any fault

M

into a prison [1]—a spirit most unworthy of an educated man,
who ought to have learnt that the mistakes of scientific
men have never injured Christianity, while every new truth
discovered by them has either added to its evidence, or
prepared the mind for its reception.

On Instinct in Connexion with the Understanding.

It is evident, that the definition of a Genus or class is
an *adequate* definition only of the lowest *species* of that
Genus: for each higher species is distinguished from the
lower by some additional character, while the general
definition includes only the characters common to *all* the
species. Consequently it *describes* the lowest only. Now
I distinguish a genus or *kind* of Powers under the name of
Adaptive power, and give as its generic definition—the
power of selecting, and adapting means to proximate ends;
and as an instance of the lowest *species* of this genus, I take
the stomach of a caterpillar. I ask myself, under what
words I can generalize the action of this organ; and I see,
that it selects and adapts the appropriate means (that is, the
assimilable part of the vegetable *congesta*) to the proximate

be found with it, the fault probably, and the blame certainly, belongs
to the reporter.

[1] And which (I may add) in a more enlightened age, and in a
Protestant country, impelled more than one German University to
anathematize Fr. Hoffman's discovery of carbonic acid gas, and of its
effects on animal life, as hostile to religion, and tending to atheism!
Three or four students at the university of Jena, in the attempt to raise
a spirit for the discovery of a supposed hidden treasure, were strangled
or poisoned by the fumes of the charcoal they had been burning in a
close garden-house of a vineyard near Jena, while employed in their
magic fumigations and charms. One only was restored to life: and
from his account of the noises and spectres (*in* his ears and eyes) as he
was losing his senses, it was taken for granted that *the bad spirit* had
destroyed them. Frederic Hoffman admitted that it was a *very bad*
spirit that had *tempted* them, the Spirit of Avarice and Folly ; and that
a very *noxious* Spirit (gas, or *geist*,) was the immediate cause of their
death. But he contended that this latter spirit was the *spirit* of charcoal, which would have produced the same effect, had the young men
been chaunting psalms instead of incantations : and acquitted the devil
of all *direct* concern in the business. The Theological Faculty took
the alarm : even physicians pretended to be horror-stricken at Hoffman's
audacity. The controversy and its appendages embittered several
years of this great and good man's life.

end, that is, the growth or reproduction of the insect's body. This we call VITAL POWER, or *vita propria* of the stomach ; and this being the *lowest* species, its definition is the same with the definition of the *kind*.

Well! from the power of the stomach, I pass to the power exerted by the whole animal. I trace it wandering from spot to spot, and plant to plant, till it finds the appropriate vegetable ; and again on this chosen vegetable, I mark it seeking out and fixing on the part of the plant, bark, leaf, or petal, suited to its nourishment : or (should the animal have assumed the butterfly form), to the deposition of its eggs, and the sustentation of the future *larva*. Here I see a power of selecting and adapting means to proximate ends *according to circumstances :* and this higher species of Adaptive Power we call INSTINCT.

Lastly, I reflect on the facts narrated and described in the preceding extracts from Hüber, and see a power of selecting and adapting the proper means to the proximate ends, according to *varying* circumstances. And what shall we call this yet higher species ? We name the former, Instinct : we must call this INSTINCTIVE INTELLIGENCE.

Here then we have three Powers of the same kind ; Life, Instinct, and instinctive Intelligence : the essential characters that define the genus existing equally in all three. But in addition to these, I find one other character common to the highest and lowest : namely, that the purposes are all manifestly predetermined by the peculiar organization of the animals ; and though it may not be possible to discover any such immediate dependency in all the actions, yet the actions being determined by the purposes, the *result* is equivalent : and both the actions and the purposes are all in a necessitated reference to the preservation and continuance of the particular animal or the progeny. There is selection, but not *choice :* volition rather than will. The possible *knowledge* of a thing, or the desire to have that *thing* representable by a distinct correspondent *thought*, does not, in the animal, suffice to render the thing an *object*, or the ground of a purpose. I select and adapt the proper means to the separation of a stone from a rock, which I neither can, or desire to make use of, for food, shelter, or ornament : because, perhaps, I wish to measure the angles

of its primary crystals, or, perhaps, for no better reason
than the apparent *difficulty* of loosening the stone—*sit pro
ratione voluntas*—and thus make a motive out of the absence
of all motive, and a reason out of the arbitrary will to act
without any reason.

Now what is the conclusion from these premises?
Evidently this: that if I suppose the Adaptive Power in
its highest *species*, or form of Instinctive Intelligence, to
co-exist with Reason, *Free* will, and Self-consciousness, it
instantly becomes UNDERSTANDING : in other words, that
Understanding differs indeed from the noblest form of
Instinct, but not in itself or in its own essential properties,
but in consequence of its co-existence with far higher
Powers of a diverse kind in one and the same subject.
INSTINCT in a rational, responsible, and self-conscious
Animal, is Understanding.

Such I apprehend to have been the Professor's view and
Exposition of Instinct—and in confirmation of its truth, I
would merely request my readers, from the numerous well-
authenticated instances on record, to recall some one of the
extraordinary actions of dogs for the preservation of their
masters' lives, and even for the avenging of their deaths.
In these instances we have the third *species* of the Adaptive
Power, in connexion with an apparently *moral* end—with
an *end* in the proper sense of the word. *Here* the Adaptive
Power co-exists with a purpose apparently *voluntary*, and
the action seems neither pre-determined by the organization
of the animal, nor in any direct reference to his own
preservation, or to the continuance of his race. It is
united with an imposing semblance of gratitude, fidelity,
and disinterested love. We not only *value* the faithful
brute : we attribute *worth* to him. This, I admit, is a problem, of which I have no solution to offer. One of the
wisest of uninspired men has not hesitated to declare the
dog a great mystery, on account of this dawning of a *moral*
nature unaccompanied by any the least evidence of *reason*,
in whichever of the two senses we interpret the word—
whether as the *practical* reason, that is, the power of pro-
posing an *ultimate* end, the determinability of the Will by
IDEAS ; or as the *sciential* reason, that is, the faculty of concluding universal and necessary truths from particular and

contingent appearances. But in a question respecting the possession of reason, the absence of all truth is tantamount to a proof of the contrary. It is, however, by no means equally clear to me, that the dog may not possess an *analogon* of WORDS, which I have elsewhere shown to be the proper objects of the "faculty, judging according to sense."

But to return to my purpose: I intreat the reader to reflect on any one fact of this kind, whether occurring in his own experience, or selected from the numerous anecdotes of the dog preserved in the writings of zoologists. I will then confidently appeal to him, whether it is in his power not to consider the faculty displayed in these actions as the same *in kind* with the Understanding, however inferior *in degree*.—Or should he even in these instances prefer calling it *Instinct*, and this in *contra*-distinction from *Understanding*, I call on him to point out the boundary between the two, the chasm or partition-wall that divides or separates the one from the other. If he can, he will have done what none before him have been able to do, though many and eminent men have tried hard for it : and my recantation shall be among the first trophies of his success. If he cannot, I must infer that he is controlled by his dread of the *consequences*, by an apprehension of some injury resulting to Religion or Morality from this opinion ; and I shall console myself with the hope, that in the sequel of this work he will find proofs of the directly contrary tendency.—Not only is this view of the Understanding, as differing in *degree* from Instinct and *in kind* from Reason, innocent in its possible influences on the religious character, but it is an indispensable preliminary to the removal of the most formidable obstacles to an intelligent Belief of the *peculiar* doctrines of the Gospel, of the *characteristic* Articles of the Christian Faith, with which the Advocates of the truth in Christ have to contend ;—the evil *heart* of Unbelief alone excepted.

Reflections Introductory to Aphorism X.

The most *momentous* question a man can ask is, Have I a Saviour ? And yet as far as the individual querist is con-

cerned, it is premature and to no purpose, unless another
question has been previously put and answered, (alas! too
generally put after the wounded conscience has already
given the answer!) namely, Have I any need of a Saviour?
For him who *needs* none, (O bitter irony of the evil Spirit,
whose whispers the proud Soul takes for its own thoughts,
and knows not how the Tempter is scoffing the while!)
there *is* none, as long as he feels no need. On the other
hand, it is scarcely possible to have answered this question
in the affirmative, and not ask—first, *in what* the necessity
consists? secondly, *whence* it proceeded? and, thirdly,
how far the answer to this second question is or is not
contained in the answer to the first? I intreat the intelligent reader, who has taken me as his temporary guide on
the straight, but yet, from the number of cross roads,
difficult way of religious Inquiry, to halt a moment, and
consider the main points, that, in this last division of my
work, have been already offered for his reflection. I have
attempted then to fix the proper meaning of the words,
Nature and Spirit, the one being the *antithesis* to the
other: so that the most general and *negative* definition of
Nature is, Whatever is not Spirit; and *vice versâ* of Spirit,
That which is not comprehended in Nature: or in the
language of our elder divines, that which transcends
Nature. But nature is the term in which we comprehend
all things that are representable in the forms of time and
space, and subjected to the relations of cause and effect:
and the cause of the existence of which, therefore, is to be
sought for perpetually in something antecedent. The
word itself expresses this in the strongest manner possible:
Natura, that which is *about to be* born, that which is always
becoming. It follows, therefore, that whatever originates
its own acts, or in any sense contains in itself the cause of
its own state, must be *spiritual*, and consequently *super-
natural*: yet not on that account necessarily *miraculous*.
And such must the responsible WILL in us be, if it be
at all.

A prior step had been to remove all misconceptions from
the subject; to show the reasonableness of a belief in the
reality and real influence of a universal and divine Spirit;
the compatibility and possible communion of such a Spirit

with the Spiritual principle in individuals; and the analogy offered by the most undeniable truths of Natural Philosophy.[1]

These views of the Spirit, and of the Will as Spiritual, form the ground-work of my scheme. Among the numerous corollaries or appendents, the first that presented itself respects the question, Whether there is any faculty in man by which a knowledge of spiritual truths, or of any truths not abstracted from nature, is rendered possible? and an Answer is attempted in the Comment on Aphorism VIII. And here I beg leave to remark, that in this comment the only novelty, and, if there be merit, the only merit is—that there being two very different Meanings, and two different Words, I have here and in former Works appropriated one meaning to one of the Words, and the other to the other—instead of using the words indifferently and by haphazard: a confusion, the ill effects of which in this instance are so great and of such frequent occurrence in the works of our ablest philosophers and divines, that I should select it before all others in proof of Hobbes's Maxim:—that it is a short, downhill passage from errors in words to errors in things. The difference of the Reason from the Understanding, and the imperfection and limited sphere of the latter, have been asserted by many both before and since Lord Bacon;[2] but still the habit of using Reason and Understanding as synonyms, acted as a disturbing force. Some it led into mysticism, others it set

---

[1] It has in its consequences proved no trifling evil to the Christian world, that Aristotle's Definitions of Nature are all grounded on the petty and rather rhetorical than philosophical Antithesis of Nature to Art—a conception inadequate to the demands even of *his* philosophy. Hence in the progress of his reasoning, he confounds the *natura naturata* (that is, the sum total of the facts and phænomena of the Senses) with an hypothetical *natura naturans*, a *Goddess* Nature, that has no better claim to a place in any sober system of Natural Philosophy than the Goddess *Multitudo;* yet to which Aristotle not rarely gives the name and attributes of the Supreme Being. The result was, that the idea of God thus identified with this hypothetical *Nature* becomes itself but an *hypothesis,* or at best but a precarious inference from incommensurate premises and on disputable principles: while in other passages, God is confounded with (and every where, in Aristotle's *genuine* works, *included in*) the Universe: which most grievous error it is the great and characteristic merit of Plato to have avoided and denounced.

[2] Take one passage among many from the posthumous Tracts (1660)

on explaining away a clear difference *in kind* into a mere superiority in degree : and it partially eclipsed the truth for all.

In close connexion with this, and therefore forming the Comment on the Aphorism next following, is the subject of the legitimate exercise of the Understanding and its limitation to Objects of Sense; with the errors both of un-belief and of misbelief, which result from its extension beyond the sphere of possible Experience. Wherever the forms of reasoning appropriate only to the *natural* world are applied to *spiritual* realities, it may be truly said, that the more strictly logical the reasoning is in all its *parts*, the more irrational it is as a *whole*.

To the reader thus armed and prepared, I now venture to present the so called mysteries of Faith, that is, the peculiar tenets and especial constituents of Christianity, or Religion in spirit and in truth. In right order I must have com-menced with the Articles of the Trinity and Apostacy, including the question respecting the Origin of Evil, and the Incarnation of the WORD. And could I have followed this order, some difficulties that now press on me would have been obviated.—But (as has already been explained) the limits of the present volume rendered it alike imprac-ticable and inexpedient; for the necessity of my argument would have called forth certain hard though most true sayings, respecting the hollowness and tricksy sophistry of the so called "Natural Theology," "Religion of Nature," "Light of Nature," and the like, which a brief exposition could not save from innocent misconceptions, much less protect against plausible misinterpretation.—And yet both

of John Smith,[*] not the least star in that bright constellation of Cam-bridge men, the contemporaries of Jeremy Taylor. "While we reflect on our own idea of Reason, we know that our Souls are not it, but only partake of it ; and that we have it κατὰ μέθεξιν and not κατ᾽ οὐσίην. Neither can it be called a Faculty, but far rather a Light, which we enjoy, but the Source of which is not in ourselves, nor rightly by any individual to be denominated *mine*." This *pure* intelligence he then pro-ceeds to contrast with the *Discursive* Faculty, that is, the Understanding.

---

[*] There is a Note on John Smith and his ' Select Discourses' in Coleridge's ' Literary Remains,' 1838, v. iii. pp. 415-19.—ED.

Reason and Experience have convinced me, that in the greater number of our ALOGI, who feed on the husks of Christianity, the disbelief of the Trinity, the Divinity of Christ included, has its origin and support in the assumed self-evidence of this Natural Theology, and in their ignorance of the insurmountable difficulties which (on the same mode of reasoning) press upon the fundamental articles of their own Remnant of a Creed. But arguments, which would prove the falsehood of a known truth, must themselves be false, and can prove the falsehood of no other position in *eodem genere.*

This *hint* I have thrown out as a *spark* that may perhaps fall where it will kindle. And worthily might the wisest of men make inquisition into the three momentous points here spoken of, for the purposes of speculative insight, and for the formation of enlarged and systematic views of the destination of man, and the dispensation of God. But the *practical* Inquirer (I speak not of those who inquire for the gratification of curiosity, and still less of those who labour as students only to shine as disputants; but of one, who seeks the truth, because he feels the want of it,) the practical Inquirer, I say, hath already placed his foot on the rock, if he have satisfied himself that whoever needs not a Redeemer is more than human. Remove for him the difficulties and objections, that oppose or perplex his belief of a crucified Saviour; convince him of the reality of sin, which is impossible without a knowledge of its true nature and inevitable consequences; and then satisfy him as to the *fact* historically, and as to the truth spiritually, of a redemption therefrom by Christ; do this for him, and there is little fear that he will permit either logical quirks or metaphysical puzzles to contravene the plain dictate of his common sense, that the Sinless One that redeemed mankind from sin, must have been more than man; and that He who brought Light and Immortality into the world, could not in his own nature have been an inheritor of Death and Darkness. It is morally impossible that a man with these convictions should suffer the objection of Incomprehensibility (and this on a subject of *Faith*) to overbalance the manifest absurdity and contradiction in the notion of a mediator between God and the human race, at the same infinite distance from God as the race for whom he mediates.

The origin of evil, meanwhile, is a question interesting only to the metaphysician, and in a system of moral and religious philosophy. The man of sober mind, who seeks for truths that possess a moral and practical interest, is content to be *certain*, first, that evil must have had a beginning, since otherwise it must either be God, or a co-eternal and co-equal rival of God ; both impious notions, and the latter foolish to boot :—secondly, that it could not originate in God ; for if so, it would be at once evil and not evil, or God would be at once God (that is, infinite Goodness) and not God—both alike impossible positions. Instead therefore of troubling himself with this barren controversy, he more profitably turns his inquiries to *that* evil which most concerns himself, and of which he *may* find the origin.

The entire Scheme of *necessary* Faith may be reduced to two heads ;—first, the object and occasion, and, secondly, the fact and effect,—of our redemption by Christ : and to this view does the order of the following Comments correspond. I have begun with ORIGINAL SIN, and proceeded in the following Aphorism to the doctrine of Redemption. The Comments on the remaining Aphorisms are all subsidiary to these, or written in the hope of making the minor tenets of general belief be believed in a spirit worthy of these. They are, in short, intended to supply a febrifuge against aguish scruples and horrors, the hectic of the soul ;—and "for servile and thrall-like fear to substitute that adoptive and cheerful boldness, which our new alliance with God requires of us as Christians." (*Milton.*) NOT the Origin of Evil, NOT the *Chronology* of Sin, or the chronicles of the original Sinner ; but Sin originant, underived from without, and no passive link in the adamantine chain of Effects, each of which is in its turn an *instrument* of Causation, but no one of them a Cause ;—NOT with Sin *inflicted*, which would be a Calamity ;—NOT with Sin (that is, an evil tendency) *implanted*, for which let the planter be responsible ; but I begin with *Original* Sin. And for this purpose I have selected the Aphorism from the ablest and most formidable antagonist of this doctrine, Bishop JEREMY TAYLOR, and from the most eloquent work of this most eloquent of divines.[1] Had I said, of men, Cicero would forgive me, and Demosthenes nod assent![2]

[1] See Coleridge on Jeremy Taylor : 'Literary Remains,' 1838, v. iii. pp. 295-334, &c.—ED.

[2] We have the assurance of Bishop Horsley, that the Church of England does not demand the literal understanding of the document contained in the second (from verse 8) and third Chapters of Genesis as a point of faith, or regard a different interpretation as affecting the orthodoxy of the interpreter ; divines of the most unimpeachable orthodoxy, and the most averse to the allegorizing of Scripture history in general, having from the earliest ages of the Christian Church adopted or permitted it in this instance. And indeed no unprejudiced man can pretend to doubt, that if in any other work of Eastern origin he met with Trees of Life and of Knowledge ; talking and conversable snakes :

Inque rei signum *serpentem serpere* jussum ;

he would want no other proofs that it was an allegory he was reading, and intended to be understood as such. Nor, if we suppose him conversant with Oriental works of any thing like the same antiquity, could it surprise him to find events of true history in connexion with, or historical personages among the actors and interlocutors of, the parable. In the temple-language of Egypt the serpent was the symbol of the understanding in its twofold function, namely as the faculty of *means* to *proximate* or *medial*, ends, analogous to the *instinct* of the more intelligent animals, ant, bee, beaver, and the like, and opposed to the practical reason, as the determinant of the *ultimate* end ; and again, it typifies the understanding as the discursive and logical faculty possessed individually by each individual—the λόγος ἐν ἑκάστω, in distinction from the νοῦς, that is, intuitive reason, the source of ideas and ABSOLUTE Truths, and the principle of the necessary and the universal in our affirmations and conclusions. Without or in contra-vention to the reason (*i. e. the spiritual mind* of St. Paul, and *the light that lighteth every man* of St. John) this understanding (φρόνημα σαρκὸς, or carnal mind) becomes the *sophistic* principle, the wily tempter to evil by counterfeit good ; the pander and advocate of the passions and appetites ; ever in league with, and always first applying to, the *Desire*, as the inferior nature in man, the *woman* in our humanity ; and through the DESIRE prevailing on the WILL) the *Man*-hood, *Vir*tus) against the command of the universal reason, and against the light of reason in the WILL itself. This essential inherence of an intelligential principle (φῶς νοερὸν) in the Will (ἀρχὴ φελητικὴ,) or rather the Will itself thus considered, the Greeks expressed by an appropriate word βουλή. This, but little differing from Origen's interpretation or hypothesis, is supported and confirmed by the very old tradition of the *homo androgynus*, that is, that the original man, the individual first created, was bi-sexual : a chimæra, of which and of many other mythological traditions the most probable explanation is, that they were originally symbolical *glyphs* or sculptures, and afterwards translated into *words*, yet *literally*, that is

APHORISM X.

On Original Sin.

JEREMY TAYLOR.

Is there any such thing ? That is not the question. For it is a fact acknowledged on all hands almost : and even

into the common names of the several figures and images composing the symbol, while the symbolic *meaning* was left to be deciphered as before, and sacred to the initiate. As to the abstruseness and subtlety of the conceptions, this is so far from being an objection to this oldest *gloss* on this venerable relic of Semitic, not impossibly ante-diluvian, philosophy, that to those who have carried their researches farthest back into Greek, Egyptian, Persian, and Indian antiquity, it will seem a strong confirmation. Or if I chose to address the sceptic in the language of the day, I might remind him, that as alchemy went before chemistry, and astrology before astronomy, so in all countries of civilized man have metaphysics outrun common sense. Fortunately for us that they have so ! For from all we know of the *un*metaphysical tribes of New Holland and elsewhere, a common sense not preceded by metaphysics is no very enviable possession. O be not cheated, my youthful reader, by this shallow prate ! The creed of true common sense is composed of the *results* of scientific meditation, observation, and experiment, as far as they are *generally* intelligible. It differs therefore in different countries and in every different age of the same country. The common sense of a people is the moveable *index* of its average judgment and information. Without metaphysics science could have had no language, and common sense no materials.

But to return to my subject. It cannot be denied, that the Mosaic Narrative thus interpreted gives a just and faithful exposition of the birth and parentage and successive moments of *phænomenal* sin (*peccatum phænomenon ; crimen primarium et commune*), that is, of sin as it reveals itself *in time,* and is an immediate object of consciousness. And in this sense most truly does the Apostle assert, that in Adam we all fell. The first human sinner is the adequate representative of all his successors. And with no less truth may it be said, that it is the same Adam that falls in every man, and from the same reluctance to abandon the too dear and undivorceable Eve : and the same EVE tempted by the same serpentine and perverted understanding, which, framed originally to be the interpreter of the reason and the ministering angel of the Spirit, is henceforth sentenced and bound over to the service of the Animal Nature, its needs and its cravings, dependent on the senses for all its materials, with the World of Sense for its appointed sphere : *Upon thy belly shalt thou go, and dust shalt thou eat all the days of thy life.* I have shown elsewhere, that as the Instinct of the mere intelligence differs in degree not in kind, and circumstantially, not essentially, those who will not confess it in words, confess it in their complaints. For my part I cannot but confess that *to be*, which I feel and groan under, and by which all the world is miserable.

Adam turned his back on the sun, and dwelt in the dark and the shadow. He sinned, and brought evil into his *supernatural* endowments, and lost the Sacrament and Instrument of Immortality, the Tree of Life in the centre of

from the *vis vitæ*, or vital power in the assimilative and digestive functions of the stomach and other organs of nutrition, even so the Understanding, in itself and distinct from the Reason and Conscience, differs in degree only from the Instinct in the animal. It is still but *a beast of the field*, though *more subtle than any beast of the field*, and therefore in its corruption and perversion *cursed above any*—a pregnant word! of which, if the reader wants an exposition or paraphrase, he may find one more than two thousand years old among the fragments of the poet Menander. (See Cumberland's Observer, No. CL. vol. iii. p. 289, 290.) This is the *Understanding* which in its *every thought* is to be brought *under obedience to Faith;* which it can scarcely fail to be, if only it be first subjected to the Reason, of which spiritual Faith is even the blossoming and the fructifying process. For it is indifferent whether I say that Faith is the interpenetration of the Reason and the Will, or that it is at once the Assurance and the Commencement of the approaching Union between the Reason and the *intelligible* realities, the *living* and *substantial* truths, that are even in this life its most proper objects.

I have thus put the reader in possession of my own opinions respecting the narrative in *Gen.* ii. and iii. Ἔστιν οὖν δὴ, ὡς ἐμοίγε δοκεῖ, ἱερὸς μῦθος, ἀληθέστατον καὶ ἀρχαιότατον φιλοσόφημα, εὐσέβεσι μὲν σέβασμα, συνετοῖς τε φωνᾶν· ἐς δὲ τὸ πᾶν ἑρμήνεως χατίζει. Or I might ask with Augustine, Why not both? Why not at once symbol and history? or rather how should it be otherwise? Must not of necessity the FIRST MAN be a SYMBOL of Mankind, in the fullest force of the word, Symbol, rightly defined—that is, a sign included in the idea, which it represents;—an actual *part* chosen to represent the *whole*, as a lip with a chin prominent is a symbol of man; or a *lower* form or species used as the representative of a higher in the same *kind:* thus Magnetism is the Symbol of Vegetation, and of the vegetative and reproductive power in animals; the Instinct of the ant-tribe, or the bee, is a symbol of the human understanding. And this definition of the word is of great practical importance, inasmuch as the symbolical is hereby distinguished *toto genere* from the allegoric and metaphorical. But, perhaps, parables, allegories, and allegorical or typical applications, are incompatible with *inspired* Scripture! The writings of St. Paul are sufficient proof of the contrary. Yet I readily acknowledge, that allegorical *applications* are one thing, and allegorical *interpretation* another: and that where there is no ground for supposing such a sense to have entered into the intent and purpose of the sacred penman, they are not to be commended. So far, indeed, am I from entertaining any

the garden.[1] He then fell under the evils of a sickly body, and a passionate and ignorant soul. His sin made him sickly, his sickness made him peevish: his sin left him ignorant, his ignorance made him foolish and unreasonable. His sin left him to his *nature:* and by nature, whoever was to be born at all, was to be born a child, and to do before he could understand, and to be bred under laws to which he was always bound, but which could not always be exacted ; and he was to choose when he could not reason, and had passions most strong when he had his understanding most weak ; and the more need he had of a curb, the less strength he had to use it ! And this being the case of all the world, what was *every* man's evil became *all* men's greater evil; and though alone it was very bad, yet when they came together it was made much worse. Like ships in a storm, every one alone hath enough to do to outride it ; but when they meet, besides the evils of the storm, they find the intolerable calamity of their mutual concussion; and every ship that is ready to be oppressed with the tempest, is a worse tempest to every vessel against which it is violently dashed. So it is in mankind. Every man hath evil enough of his own, and it is hard for a man to live up to the rule of his own reason and conscience. But when he hath parents and children, friends and enemies, buyers and sellers, lawyers and clients, a family and a neighbourhood—then it is that every man

predilection for them, or any favourable opinion of the Rabbinical commentators and traditionists, from whom the fashion was derived, that in carrying it as far as our own Church has carried it, I follow her judgment, not my own. But in the first place, I know but one other part of the Scriptures not universally held to be parabolical, which, not without the sanction of great authorities, I am disposed to regard as an Apologue or Parable, namely, the book of Jonah ; the reasons for believing the Jewish nation collectively to be therein impersonated, seeming to me unanswerable. Secondly, as to the Chapters now in question—that such interpretation is at least tolerated by our Church, I have the word of one of her most zealous champions. And lastly it is my deliberate and conscientious conviction, that the proofs of such having been the intention of the inspired writer or compiler of the book of Genesis, lie on the face of the narrative itself.

[1] *Rom.* v. 14. Who were they, who *had* not *sinned after the similitude of Adam's transgression ;* and over whom, notwithstanding, *death reigned?*

dashes against another, and one relation requires what another denies ; and when one speaks another will contradict him ; and that which is well spoken is sometimes innocently mistaken ; and that upon a good cause produces an evil effect ; and by these, and ten thousand other concurrent causes, man is made more than most miserable.[1]

Comment.

The first question we should put to ourselves, when we have to read a passage that perplexes us in a work of authority, is; What does the writer *mean* by all this ? And the second question should be, What does he intend by all this ? In the passage before us, Taylor's *meaning* is not quite clear. A sin is an evil which has its ground or origin in the agent, and not in the compulsion of circumstances. Circumstances are compulsory from the absence of a power to resist or control them : and if this absence likewise be the effect of Circumstance (that is, if it have been neither directly nor indirectly caused by the agent himself) the evil *derives* from the circumstances ; and therefore (in the Apostle's sense of the word, sin, when he speaks of the exceeding sinfulness of sin) such *evil* is not *sin;* and the person who suffers it, or who is the compelled instrument of its infliction on others, may feel *regret*, but cannot feel *remorse*. So likewise of the word origin, original, or originant. The reader cannot too early be warned that it is not applicable, and, without abuse of language, can never be applied, to a mere *link* in a chain of effects, where each, indeed, stands in the relation of a *cause* to those that follow, but is at the same time the *effect* of all that precede. For in these cases a cause amounts to little more than an antecedent. At the utmost it means only a *conductor* of the causative influence ; and the old axiom, *causa causæ causa causati*, applies, with a never-ending regress to each several link, up the whole chain of nature. But this *is* Nature : and no *natural* thing or act can be called originant, or be

---

[1] Slightly altered from Jeremy Taylor's 'Deus Justificatus ; or a Vindication of the Glory of the Divine Attributes in the Question of Original Sin, Against the Presbyterian way of Understanding it.' See Heber's edition of Taylor's works, 1822, v. ix. pp. 315·16.—Ed.

truly said to have an *origin* [1] in any other. The moment
we assume an origin in nature, a true *beginning*, an actual
first—that moment we rise *above* nature, and are compelled
to assume a *supernatural* power. (*Gen.* i. 1.)

It will be an equal convenience to myself and to my

---

[1] This sense of the word is implied even in its metaphorical or figurative use. Thus we may say of a *river* that it *originates* in such or such
a *fountain ;* but the water of a *canal* is *derived* from such or such a river.
The Power which we call Nature, may be thus defined : A Power
subject to the Law of Continuity (*lex continui ; nam in naturâ non datur
saltus*) which law the human understanding, by a necessity arising out
of its own constitution, can *conceive* only under the form of Cause and
Effect. That this *form* (or law) of Cause and Effect is (relatively to the
world *without*, or to things as they subsist independently of our per-
ceptions) only a form or mode of *thinking ;* that it is a law inherent in
the Understanding itself (just as the symmetry of the miscellaneous
objects seen by the kaleidoscope inheres in, or results from, the
mechanism of the kaleidoscope itself)—this becomes evident as soon as
we attempt to apply the pre-conception directly to any operation of
nature. For in this case we are forced to represent the cause as being
at the same instant the effect, and *vice versâ* the effect as being the
cause—a relation which we seek to express by the terms Action and
Re-action ; but for which the term Reciprocal Action or the law of
Reciprocity (*Wechselwirkung*) would be both more accurate and more
expressive.

These are truths which can scarcely be too frequently impressed on
the mind that is in earnest in the wish to *reflect* aright. Nature is a
line in constant and continuous evolution. Its *beginning* is lost in the
super-natural : and *for our understanding*, therefore, it must appear as
a continuous line without beginning or end. But where there is no
discontinuity there can be no origination, and every appearance of
origination in *nature* is but a shadow of our own casting. It is a
reflection from our own *Will* or Spirit. Herein, indeed, the Will
consists. This is the essential character by which WILL is *opposed* to
Nature, as *Spirit*, and raised *above* Nature, as *self-determining* Spirit—
this namely, that it is a power of *originating* an act or state.

A young friend or, as he was pleased to describe himself, *a pupil of
mine, who is beginning to learn to think*, asked me to explain by an
instance what is meant by " *originating* an act or state." My answer
was—This morning I awoke with a dull pain, which I knew from experience the getting up would remove ; and yet by adding to the
drowsiness and by weakening or depressing the *volition* (*voluntas
sensorialis seu mechanica*) the very pain seemed to *hold me back*, to fix
me (as it were) to the bed. After a peevish ineffectual quarrel with
this ᵢ ainful disinclination, I said to myself : Let me count twenty,
and; ι ọ moment I come to nineteen I will leap out of bed. So said,
and so done. Now should you ever find yourself in the same or in
a similar state, and should attend to *the goings-on* within you, you

readers, to let it be agreed between us, that we will generalize the word Circumstance, so as to understand by it, as
often as it occurs in this Comment, all and every thing not
connected with the Will, past or present, of a Free Agent.
Even though it were the blood in the chambers of his heart,

will learn what I mean by *originating* an act. At the same time you
will see that it belongs *exclusively* to the Will (*arbitrium*) ; that there
is nothing analogous to it in outward experiences ; and that I had,
therefore, no way of explaining it but by referring you to an *act* of
your own, and to the peculiar self-consciousness preceding and accompanying it. As we know what Life is by *Being*, so we know what Will
is by *Acting*. That in *willing* (replied my young friend) we *appear*
to ourselves to constitute an actual *Beginning* and that this seems
unique, and without any example in our *sensible* experience, or in the
phænomena of nature, is an undeniable *fact*. But may it not be an
illusion arising from our ignorance of the antecedent causes ? You
may suppose this (I rejoined) :—that the soul of every man should impose a *Lie* on itself ; and that this Lie, and the acting on the faith of
its being the most important of all truths and the most real of all
realities, should form the main contra-distinctive character of Humanity,
and the only basis of that distinction between Things and Persons on
which our whole moral and criminal Law is grounded ;—you may
suppose this ; I cannot, as I could in the case of an arithmetical or
geometrical proposition, render it *impossible* for you to suppose it.
Whether you can reconcile such a supposition with the belief of an all-
wise Creator, is another question. But, taken singly, it is doubtless
in your power to suppose this. Were it not, the belief of the contrary
would be no subject of a *command*, no part of a moral or religious
duty. You would not, however, suppose it *without a reason*. But all
the pretexts that ever have been or ever can be offered for this supposition, are built on certain *notions* of the Understanding that have
been generalized from *conceptions;* which conceptions, again, are
themselves generalized or abstracted from objects of sense. Neither
the one nor the other, therefore, have any force except in application to
objects of sense and within the sphere of sensible Experience. What
but absurdity can follow, if you decide on Spirit by the laws of Matter ?
if you judge that which, if it be at all, must be *super*-sensual, by that
faculty of your mind, the very definition of which is " the faculty
judging *according* to sense " ? These then are unworthy the name of
reasons : they are only pretexts. But *without* reason to contradict your
own consciousness in defiance of your own conscience, is *contrary* to
reason. Such and such writers, you say, have made a great *sensation*.
If so, I am sorry for it ; but the fact I take to be this. From a
variety of causes the more austere Sciences have fallen into discredit,
and impostors have taken advantage of the general ignorance to give a
sort of mysterious and terrific importance to a parcel of trashy sophistry,
the authors of which would not have employed themselves more irra-
tionally in submitting the works of Raffaelle or Titian to canons of

N

or his own inmost sensations, we will regard them as *circumstantial, extrinsic,* or *from without.*

In this sense of the word Original, and in the sense before given of Sin, it is evident that the phrase, original sin, is a pleonasm, the epithet not adding to the thought, but only enforcing it.   For if it be sin, it must be *original;* and a state or act, that has not its origin in the will, may be calamity, deformity, disease, or mischief; but a *sin* it cannot be.   It is not enough that the act appears voluntary, or that it is intentional; or that it has the most hateful passions or debasing appetite for its proximate cause and accompaniment.   All these may be found in a mad-house, where neither law nor humanity permit us to condemn the actor of sin.   The reason of law declares the maniac not a free-agent; and the verdict follows of course—Not guilty.   Now mania, as distinguished from idiocy, frenzy, delirium, hypochondria, and derangement (the last term used specifically to express a suspension or disordered state of the understanding or adaptive power) is the occultation or eclipse of reason, as the power of ultimate ends.   The maniac, it is well known, is often found clever and inventive in the selection and adaptation of means to *his* ends; but his *ends* are madness.   He has lost his reason.   For though Reason, in finite Beings, is not the Will—or how could the Will be opposed to the Reason?—yet it is the *condition*, the *sine qua non* of a *Free*-will.

---

criticism deduced from the sense of smell. Nay, less so. For here the objects and the organs are only disparate: while in the other case they are absolutely diverse. I conclude this note by reminding the reader, that my first object is to make myself *understood.* When he is in full possession of my *meaning*, then let him consider whether it deserves to be received as *the truth.* Had it been my immediate purpose to make him *believe* me as well as *understand* me, I should have thought it necessary to warn him that a *finite* Will does indeed originate an *act*, and may originate a *state* of being; but yet only *in* and *for* the Agent himself. A finite Will *constitutes* a true Beginning; but with regard to the series of motions and changes by which the free act is manifested and made *effectual*, the *finite* Will *gives* a beginning only by co-incidence with that *absolute* WILL, which is at the same time *Infinite* POWER! Such is the language of Religion, and of Philosophy too in the last instance. But I express the same truth in ordinary language when I say, that a finite Will, or the Will of a finite free-agent, acts outwardly by confluence with the laws of nature.

We will now return to the extract from Jeremy Taylor on a theme of deep interest in itself, and trebly important from its *bearings*. For without just and distinct views respecting the Article of Original Sin, it is impossible to understand aright any one of the peculiar doctrines of Christianity. Now my first complaint is, that the eloquent Bishop, while he admits the *fact* as established beyond controversy by universal experience, yet leaves us wholly in the dark as to the main point, supplies us with no answer to the principal question—why he names it Original Sin. It cannot be said, We know what the Bishop *means*, and what matters the name? for the *nature* of the fact, and in what light it should be regarded by us, depends on the nature of our answer to the question, whether Original Sin is or is not the right and proper designation. I can imagine the same quantum of *sufferings*, and yet if I had reason to regard them as symptoms of a commencing change, as pains of growth, the temporary deformity and misproportions of immaturity, or (as in the final sloughing of the caterpillar) the throes and struggles of the waxing or evolving PSYCHE, I should think it no Stoical flight to doubt, how far I was authorized to declare the Circumstance an *evil* at all. Most assuredly I would not express or describe the fact as an evil having an origin in the sufferers themselves or as sin.

Let us, however, waive this objection. Let it be supposed that the Bishop uses the word in a different and more comprehensive sense, and that by sin he understands evil of all kind connected with or resulting from *actions*—though I do not see how we can represent the properties even of inanimate bodies (of poisonous substances for instance) except as *acts* resulting from the constitution of such bodies. Or if this sense, though not unknown to the Mystic divines, should be *too* comprehensive and remote, we will suppose the Bishop to comprise under the term sin, the evil accompanying or consequent on *human* actions and purposes:—though here too, I have a right to be informed, for what reason and on what grounds Sin is thus limited to *human* agency? And truly, I should be at no loss to assign the reason. But then this reason would instantly bring me back to my first definition; and any other reason, than that the human agent is endowed with Reason, and with a Will which can place itself either in subjection or in opposition to his Reason—in other words, that man is alone of all known animals a responsible creature—I neither know nor can imagine.

Thus, then, the sense which Taylor—and with him the antagonists generally of this Article as propounded by the first Reformers—attaches to the words, Original Sin, needs only be carried on into its next consequence, and it will be found to *imply* the sense which I have given—namely, that Sin is Evil having an *Origin*. But inasmuch as it is *evil*, in God it cannot originate : and yet in some *Spirit* (that is, in some *supernatural* power) it *must*. For in *Nature* there is no origin. Sin therefore is spiritual Evil : but the spiritual in man is the Will. Now when we do not refer to any particular sins, but to that state and constitution of the Will, which is the ground, condition, and common Cause of all Sins ; and when we would further express the truth, that this corrupt *nature* of the Will must in some sense or other be considered as its own act, that the corruption must have been self-originated ;—in this case and for this purpose we may, with no less propriety than force, entitle this dire spiritual evil and source of all evil, that is absolutely such, Original Sin. I have said, " the corrupt *nature* of the Will." I might add, that the admission of a *nature* into a spiritual essence by its own act is a corruption.

Such, I repeat, would be the inevitable conclusion, *if* Taylor's sense of the term were carried on into its immediate consequences. But the whole of his most eloquent Treatise makes it certain that Taylor did not carry it on : and consequently Original Sin, according to his conception, is a calamity which being common to all men must be supposed to result from their common nature : in other words, the universal Calamity of Human *Nature*.

Can we wonder, then, that a mind, a heart like Taylor's should reject, that he should strain his faculties to explain away, the belief that this calamity, so dire in itself, should appear to the All-merciful God a rightful cause and motive for inflicting on the wretched sufferers a calamity infinitely more tremendous; nay, that it should be incompatible with Divine Justice *not* to punish it by everlasting torment ? Or

need we be surprised if he found nothing that could reconcile his mind to such a belief, in the circumstance that the
acts now *consequent* on this calamity and either directly or
indirectly *effects* of the same, were, five or six thousand years
ago in the instance of a certain individual and his accomplice, *anterior* to the calamity, and the *Cause* or *Occasion* of
the same;—that what in all other men is *disease*, in these
two persons was *guilt;*—that what in us is *hereditary*, and
consequently *nature*, in *them* was *original*, and consequently
sin? Lastly, might it not be presumed, that so enlightened,
and at the same time so affectionate, a divine, would even
fervently disclaim and reject the pretended justifications of
God grounded on flimsy analogies drawn from the imperfections of human ordinances and human justice-courts—
some of very doubtful character even as human institutes,
and all of them just only as far as they are necessary, and
rendered necessary chiefly by the weakness and wickedness,
the limited powers and corrupt passions, of mankind? The
more confidently might this be presumed of so acute and
practised a logician, as Taylor, in addition to his other
extraordinary gifts, is known to have been, when it is demonstrable that the most current of these justifications
rests on a palpable equivocation: namely, the gross misuse
of the word right.[1] An instance will explain my meaning.
In as far as, from the known frequency of dishonest or mis-

---

[1] It may conduce to the readier comprehension of this point if I say,
that the equivoque consists in confounding the almost technical sense of
the *noun substantive*, right, (a sense most often determined by the genitive case following, as the right of property, the right of husbands to
chastise their wives, and so forth) with the popular sense of the *adjective*, right: though this likewise has, if not a double sense, yet a double
application;—the first, when it is used to express the fitness of a mean to
a relative end, for example, " the *right* way to obtain the *right* distance
at which a picture should be examined," and the like ; and the other,
when it expresses a perfect conformity and commensurateness with the
immutable idea of equity, or perfect rectitude. Hence the close connexion between the words righteousness and *god*liness, that is, godlikeness.

I should be tempted to subjoin a few words on a predominating doctrine closely connected with the present argument—the Paleyan principle
of GENERAL CONSEQUENCES ; but the inadequacy of this Principle as a
criterion of Right and Wrong, and above all its utter unfitness as a
Moral *Guide*, have been elsewhere so fully stated (' The Friend,' vol. ii.

chievous persons, it may have been found *necessary*, in so
far is the law *justifiable* in giving landowners the right of
proceeding against a neighbour or fellow-citizen for even a
slight trespass on that which the law has made their property :—nay, of proceeding in sundry instances criminally
and even capitally. But surely, either there is no religion
in the world, and nothing obligatory in the precepts of the
Gospel, or there are occasions in which it would be very
wrong in the proprietor to exercise the *right*, which yet it
may be highly *expedient* that he should possess. On this
ground it is, that Religion is the sustaining opposite of
Law.

That Taylor, therefore, should have striven fervently
against the Article so interpreted and so vindicated, is,
(for me, at least) a subject neither of surprise nor of complaint. It is the doctrine which he *substitutes*, it is the
weakness and inconsistency betrayed in the defence of this
substitute ; it is the unfairness with which he blackens the
established Article—for to give it, as it had been caricatured
by a few Ultra-Calvinists during the fever of the (so called)
Quinquarticular controversy, was in effect to blacken it—
and then imposes another scheme, to which the same objections apply with even increased force, a scheme which

Essay xi.*), that even in again referring to the subject, I must shelter
myself under Seneca's rule, that what we cannot too frequently think of,
we cannot too often be made to recollect. It is, however, of immediate
importance to the point in discussion, that the reader should be made to
see how altogether incompatible the principle of judging by General
Consequences is with the Idea of an Eternal, Omnipresent, and Omni-
scient Being ;—that he should be made aware of the absurdity of attributing *any* form of Generalization to the All-perfect Mind. To *generalize*
is a faculty and function of the human understanding, and from the
imperfection and limitation of the understanding are the use and the
necessity of generalizing derived. Generalization is a Substitute for
Intuition, for the power of *intuitive* (that is, immediate) knowledge.
As a substitute, it is a gift of inestimable value to a finite intelligence,
such as *man* in his present state is endowed with and capable of exercising ; but yet a *substitute* only, and an imperfect one to boot. To attribute it to God is the grossest anthropomorphism : and grosser instances
of anthropomorphism than are to be found in the controversial writings
on Original Sin and Vicarious Satisfaction, the records of superstition
do not supply.

---

* Essay xv. p. 204, Bohn's edition.—Ed.

seems to differ from the former only by adding fraud and mockery to injustice: these are the things that excite my wonder; it is of these that I complain. For what does the Bishop's scheme amount to?—God, he tells us, required of Adam a perfect obedience, and made it possible by endowing him " with perfect rectitudes and super-natural heights of grace " proportionate to the obedience which he required. As a *consequence* of his disobedience, Adam lost this rectitude, this perfect sanity and proportionateness of his intellectual, moral and corporeal state, powers and impulses; and as the *penalty* of his crime, he was deprived of all super-natural aids and graces. The death, with whatever is comprised in the Scriptural sense of the word, death, began from that moment to work in him, and this *consequence* he conveyed to his offspring, and through them to all his posterity, that is, to all mankind. They were *born* diseased in mind, body and will. For what less than disease can we call a necessity of error and a predisposition to sin and sickness? Taylor, indeed, *asserts*, that though perfect obedience became incomparably more difficult, it was not, however, absolutely *impossible*. Yet he himself admits that the contrary was *universal*; that of the countless millions of Adam's posterity, not a single individual ever realized, or approached to the realization of, this possibility; and (if my memory [1] does not deceive me) Taylor himself has elsewhere exposed—and if he has not, yet Common Sense will do it for him—the sophistry in asserting of a whole what may be true of the whole, but—is in fact true only, of each of its component parts. Any one may snap a horse-hair: therefore, any one may perform the same feat with the horse's tail. On a level floor (on the hardened sand, for instance, of a sea-beach) I chalk two parallel straight lines, with a width of eight inches. It is *possible* for a man, with a bandage over his eyes, to keep

---

[1] I have since this page was written, met with several passages in the Treatise on Repentance, the Holy Living and Dying, and the Worthy Communicant, in which the Bishop asserts without scruple the *impossibility* of total obedience; and on the same grounds as I have given. [See Taylor's ' Doctrine and Practice of Repentance,' c. I. sec. ii., " On the Possibility or Impossibility of Keeping the Precepts of the Gospel; " Heber's ed. of the ' Works,' v. 8, p. 265.—ED.]

within the path for two or three paces : therefore, it is *possible* for him to walk blindfold for two or three leagues without a single deviation ! And this *possibility* would suffice to acquit me of *injustice*, though I had placed man-traps within an inch of one line, and knew that there were pit-falls and deep wells beside the other !

This *assertion*, therefore, without adverting to its discordance with, if not direct contradiction to, the tenth and thirteenth Articles of our Church, I shall not, I trust, be thought to rate below its true value, if I treat it as an *infinitesimal* possibility that may be safely dropped in the calculation :—and so proceed with the argument. The consequence then of Adam's crime was, by a natural necessity, inherited by persons who could not (the Bishop affirms) in any sense have been accomplices in the crime or partakers in the guilt : and yet consistently with the divine holiness, it was not possible that the same perfect obedience should not be required of them. Now what would the idea of equity, what would the law inscribed by the Creator in the heart of man, seem to dictate in this case ? Surely, that the supplementary aids, the super-natural graces correspondent to a law above nature, should be increased in proportion to the diminished strength of the agents, and the increased resistance to be overcome by them. But no ! not only the consequence of Adam's act, but the penalty due to his crime, was perpetuated. His descendants were despoiled or left destitute of these aids and graces, while the obligation to perfect obedience was continued ; an obligation too, the non-fulfilment of which brought with it death and the unutterable woe that cleaves to an immortal soul for ever alienated from its Creator.

Observe, that all these *results* of Adam's fall enter into Bishop Taylor's scheme of Original Sin equally as into that of the first Reformers. In this respect the Bishop's doctrine is the same with that laid down in the Articles and Homilies of the Established Church. The only difference that has hitherto appeared, consists in the aforesaid *mathematical* possibility of fulfilling the whole law, which in the Bishop's scheme is affirmed to remain still in human nature, or (as it is elsewhere expressed) in the nature of the human Will.[1] But though it were possible to grant this existence of a power in all men, which in no man was ever exemplified, and where the *non*-actualization of such power is, *a priori*, so certain, that the belief or imagination of the contrary in any individual is expressly given us by the Holy Spirit as a test, whereby it may be known that *the truth is not in him*, as an infallible sign of imposture or self-delusion! Though it were possible to grant this, which, consistently with Scripture and the principles of reasoning which we apply in all other cases, it is not possible to grant;—and though it were possible likewise to overlook the glaring sophistry of concluding in relation to a series of indeterminate length, that whoever can do any one, can therefore do all; a conclusion, the futility of which must force itself on the common-sense of every man who understands the proposition;—still the question will arise —Why, and on what principle of equity, were the unoffending sentenced to be born with so fearful a disproportion of their powers to their duties? Why were they subjected to a law, the fulfilment of which was all but impos-

[1] Availing himself of the equivocal sense and (I most readily admit) the injudicious use, of the word " free " in the—even on this account— *faulty* phrase, " *free only to sin*," Taylor treats the notion of a power in the Will of determining itself to evil without an equal power of determining itself to good, as a " *foolery*." I would this had been the only instance in his " Deus Justificatus " of that inconsiderate contempt so frequent in the polemic treatises of minor divines, who will have ideas of reason, spiritual truths that can only be spiritually discerned, translated for them into adequate conceptions of the understanding. The great articles of Corruption and Redemption are *propounded* to us as spiritual mysteries; and every interpretation, that pretends to explain them into comprehensible notions, does by its very success furnish presumptive proof of its failure. The acuteness and logical dexterity, with which Taylor has brought out the falsehood or semblance of falsehood in the Calvinistic scheme, are truly admirable. Had he next concentered his thoughts in tranquil meditation, and asked himself: What then *is* the truth? If a Will *be* at all, what must a will be ?—he might, I think, have seen that a *nature* in a Will implies already a *corruption* of that Will; that a *nature* is as inconsistent with *freedom* as free choice with an incapacity of choosing aught but evil. And lastly, a free power in a *nature* to fulfil a law *above* nature!—I, who love and honour this good and great man with all the reverence that can dwell " on this side idolatry," dare not retort on this assertion the charge of *foolery;* but I find it a paradox as startling to my *reason* as any of the hard sayings of the Dort divines were to his *understanding*.

sible, yet the penalty on the failure tremendous ?   Admit
that for those who had never enjoyed a happier lot, it was
no punishment to be made to inhabit a ground which the
Creator had cursed, and to have been born with a body
prone to sickness, and a soul surrounded with temptation,
and having the worst temptation within itself in its own
temptibility ;—to have the duties of a spirit with the wants
and appetites of an animal ! Yet on such imperfect Creatures, with means so scanty and impediments so numerous,
to impose the same task-work that had been required of a
Creature with a pure and entire nature, and provided with
super-natural aids—if this be not to inflict a penalty ;—
yet to be placed under a law, the difficulty of obeying
which is infinite, and to have momently to struggle with
this difficulty, and to live momently in hazard of these consequences—if this be no punishment ;—words have no
correspondence with thoughts, and thoughts are but shadows of each other, shadows that own no substance for
their anti-type !

Of such an outrage on common-sense, Taylor was incapable. He himself calls it a penalty ; he admits that in
effect it is a punishment : nor does he seek to suppress the
question that so naturally arises out of this admission ;—on
what principle of equity were the innocent offspring of
Adam *punished* at all ? He meets it, and puts-in an answer.
He states the problem, and gives his solution—namely,
that " God on Adam's account was so exasperated with mankind, that being angry he would still continue the punishment " !   " The case " (says the Bishop) " is this : Jonathan
and Michal were Saul's children. It came to pass, that
seven of Saul's issue were to be hanged : all equally innocent, equally culpable."   [*Before I quote further, I feel
myself called on to remind the reader, that these two last words
were added by Jeremy Taylor without the least grounds in
Scripture, according to which,* (2 Samuel, xxi.) *no crime was
laid to their charge, no blame imputed to them. Without any
pretence of culpable conduct on their part, they were arraigned
as children of Saul, and sacrificed to a point of state-expe-
dience. In recommencing the quotation, therefore, the reader
ought to let the sentence conclude with the words—*] " all
equally innocent. David took the five sons of Michal, for

she had left him unhandsomely. Jonathan was his friend : and therefore he spared *his* son, Mephibosheth. Here it was indifferent as to the guilt of the persons " (*Bear in mind, reader, that no guilt was attached to either of them!*) " whether David should take the sons of Michal or of Jonathan ; but it is likely that as upon the kindness that David had to Jonathan, he spared his son ; so upon the just provocation of Michal, he made that evil fall upon them, which, it may be, they should not have suffered, if their mother had been kind. Adam was to God, as Michal to David." [1]

This answer, this solution proceeding too from a divine so pre-eminently gifted, and occurring (with other passages not less startling) in a vehement refutation of the received doctrine on the express ground of its opposition to the clearest conceptions and best feelings of mankind— this it is that surprises me ! It is of this that I complain ! The Almighty Father *exasperated* with those, whom the Bishop has himself in the same treatise described as " innocent and most unfortunate "—the two things best fitted to conciliate love and pity ! Or though they did not remain innocent, yet those whose abandonment to a mere nature, while they were left amenable to a law above nature, he affirms to be the irresistible cause, that they one and all *did* sin ! And this decree illustrated and justified by its analogy to one of the worst actions of an imperfect mortal ! From such of my readers as will give a thoughtful perusal to these works of Taylor, I dare anticipate a concurrence with the judgment which I here transcribe from the blank space at the end of the *Deus Justificatus* in my own copy ; and which, though twenty years [2] have elapsed since it was written, I have never seen reason to recant or modify. " This most eloquent Treatise may be compared to a statue of Janus, with the one face, which we must suppose fronting the Calvinistic tenet, entire and fresh, as from the master's hand : beaming with life and force, witty scorn on the lip, and a brow at once bright and weighty

---

[1] Vol. ix. pp. 5, 6, Heber's edit. [' Doctrine and Practice of Repentance,' c. vi. sec. 1.—Ed.]
[2] This passage appears as here in the first edition of the ' Aids,' 1825. —Ed.

with satisfying reason :—the other, looking toward the
" something to be put in its place," maimed, featureless,
and weather-bitten into an almost visionary confusion and
indistinctness." [1]

With these expositions I hasten to contrast the *Scriptural*
article respecting Original Sin, or the corrupt and sinful
Nature of the Human Will, and the belief which alone is
required of us, as Christians.   And here the first thing to
be considered, and which will at once remove a world of
error, is ; that this is no tenet first introduced or imposed
by Christianity, and which, should a man see reason to
disclaim the authority of the Gospel, would no longer have
any claim on his attention.   It is no perplexity that a man
may get rid of by ceasing to be a Christian, and which has
no existence for a philosophic Deist.   It is a FACT, affirmed,
indeed, in the Christian Scriptures alone with the force and
frequency proportioned to its consummate importance ; but
a fact acknowledged in *every* religion that retains the
least glimmering of the patriarchal faith in a God infinite,
yet *personal*—a Fact assumed or implied as the basis of
every religion, of which any relics remain of earlier date
than the last and total apostacy of the Pagan world, when
the faith in the great I AM, the *Creator*, was extinguished
in the sensual Polytheism, which is inevitably the final
result of Pantheism or the worship of nature; and the
only form under which the Pantheistic scheme—that,
according to which the world is God, and the material
universe itself the one only *absolute* Being—can exist for a
people, or become the popular creed.   Thus in the most
ancient books of the Brahmins, the deep sense of this Fact,
and the doctrines grounded on obscure traditions of the
promised remedy, are seen struggling, and now gleaming,
now flashing, through the mist of Pantheism, and producing
the incongruities and gross contradictions of the Brahmin
Mythology : while in the rival sect—in that most strange
phœnomenon, the religious atheism of the Buddhists : with
whom God is only universal matter considered abstractedly
from all particular forms—the Fact is placed among the

---

[1] The same, slightly different, appears in Coleridge's 'Literary
Remains,' 1838, v. iii., p. 328.—ED.

delusions natural to man, which, together with other superstitions grounded on a supposed *essential* difference between right and wrong, *the sage* is to decompose and precipitate from the *menstruum* of *his* more refined apprehensions! Thus in denying the Fact, they virtually acknowledge it.

From the remote East turn to the mythology of Lesser Asia, to the descendants of Javan who dwelt in the tents of Shem, and possessed the Isles. Here again, and in the usual form of an historic solution we find the same *Fact*, and as characteristic of the human *race*, stated in that earliest and most venerable *mythus* (or symbolic parable) of Prometheus—that truly wonderful Fable, in which the characters of the rebellious Spirit and of the Divine Friend of Mankind (Θεὸς φιλάνθρωπος) are united in the same person; and thus in the most striking manner noting the forced amalgamation of the Patriarchal tradition with the incongruous scheme of Pantheism. This and the connected tale of Io, which is but the sequel of the Prometheus, stand alone in the Greek Mythology, in which elsewhere both gods and men are mere powers and products of nature. And most noticeable it is, that soon after the promulgation and spread of the Gospel had awakened the moral sense, and had opened the eyes even of its wiser enemies to the necessity of providing some solution of this great problem of the Moral World, the beautiful Parable of Cupid and Psyche was brought forward as a *rival* FALL OF MAN: and the fact of a moral corruption connatural with the human race was again recognized. In the assertion of ORIGINAL SIN the Greek Mythology rose and set.

But not only was the *fact* acknowledged of a law in the nature of man resisting the law of God; (and whatever is placed in active and direct oppugnancy to the good is, *ipso facto*, positive evil;) it was likewise an acknowledged MYSTERY, and one which by the nature of the subject must ever remain such—a problem, of which any other solution, than the statement of the *Fact* itself, was demonstrably *impossible*. That it is so, the least reflection will suffice to convince every man, who has previously satisfied himself that he is a responsible being. It follows necessarily from the postulate of a responsible Will. Refuse to grant this, and I have not a word to say. Concede this and you concede all. For this is the essential attribute of a Will, and contained in the very *idea*, that whatever determines the Will acquires this power from a previous determination of the Will itself. The Will is ultimately self-determined, or it is no longer a *Will* under the law of perfect freedom, but a *nature* under the mechanism of cause and effect. And if by an act, to which it had determined itself, it has subjected itself to the determination of nature (in the language of St. Paul, to the law of the flesh), it receives a nature into itself, and so far it becomes a nature : and this is a corruption of the Will and a corrupt nature. It is also a *Fall* of Man, inasmuch as his Will is the condition of his personality ; the ground and condition of the attribute which constitutes him *man*. And the ground work of *personal* Being is a capacity of acknowledging the Moral Law (the Law of the Spirit, the Law of Freedom, the Divine Will) as that which should, of itself, suffice to determine the Will to a free obedience of the law, the law working therein by its own exceeding lawfulness.[1] This, and this alone, is *positive* Good ; good in itself, and independent of all relations. Whatever resists, and, as a positive force, opposes *this* in the Will is therefore evil. But an evil in the Will is an evil Will ; and as all moral evil (that is, all evil that is evil without reference to its contingent physical consequences) is *of* the Will, this evil Will must have its source in the Will. And thus we might go back from act to act, from evil to evil, *ad infinitum*, without advancing a step.

We call an individual a *bad* man, not because an action is contrary to the law, but because it has led us to conclude from it some *Principle* opposed to the law, some private maxim, or by-law in the Will contrary to the universal law of right reason in the conscience, as the *ground* of the action. But this evil principle again must be grounded in some other principle which has been made determinant of the Will by the Will's own self-determination. For if not, it must have its ground in some necessity of nature, in some instinct or propensity imposed, not

---

[1] If the Law worked *on* the Will, it would be the working of an extrinsic and alien force, and, as St. Paul profoundly argues, would prove the Will sinful.

acquired, another's work not our own.   Consequently, neither act nor principle could be imputed ; and relatively to the agent, not *original*, not *sin*.

Now let the grounds on which the fact of an evil inherent in the Will is affirmable in the instance of any one man, be supposed equally applicable in *every* instance, and concerning all men : so that the fact is asserted of the individual, *not*, because he has committed this or that crime, or because he has shown himself to be *this* or *that* man, but simply because he is *a* man.   Let the evil be supposed such as to imply the impossibility of an individual's referring to any particular time at which it might be conceived to have commenced, or to any period of his existence at which it was not existing.   Let it be supposed, in short, that the subject stands in no relation whatever to time, can neither be called *in* time nor *out of* time ; but that all relations of time are as alien and heterogeneous in this question, as the relations and attributes of space (north or south, round or square, thick or thin) are to our affections and moral feelings.   Let the reader suppose this, and he will have before him the precise import of the Scriptural *doctrine* of Original Sin ; or rather of the Fact acknowledged in all ages, and recognized but not originating, in the Christian Scriptures.

In addition to this it will be well to remind the inquirer, that the stedfast conviction of the existence, personality, and moral attributes of God, is pre-supposed in the acceptance of the Gospel, or required as its indispensable preliminary.   It is taken for granted as a point which the hearer had already decided for himself, a point finally settled and put at rest: not by the removal of all difficulties, or by any such increase of insight as enabled him to meet every objection of the Epicurean or the sceptic with a full and precise answer ; but because he had convinced himself that it was folly as well as presumption in so imperfect a creature to expect it ; and because these difficulties and doubts disappeared at the beam, when tried against the weight and convictive power of the reasons in the other scale.   It is, therefore, most unfair to attack Christianity, or any article which the Church has declared a Christian doctrine, by arguments, which, if valid, are valid against all religion.   Is there a disputant who scorns a mere *pos-tulate*, as the basis of any argument in support of the Faith; who is too high-minded *to beg* his ground, and will take it by a strong hand ?   Let him fight it out with the Atheists, or the Manichæans; but not stoop to pick up their arrows, and then run away to discharge them at Christianity or the Church !

The only true way is to state the doctrine, believed as well by Saul of Tarsus, *yet breathing out threatenings and slaughter against* the Church of Christ, as by Paul the Apostle *fully preaching the Gospel of Christ*.   A moral Evil is an evil that has its origin in a Will.   An evil common to all must have a ground common to all.   But the actual existence of moral evil we are bound in con-science to admit; and that there is an evil common to all is a fact; and this evil must therefore have a common ground.   Now this evil ground cannot originate in the Divine Will : it must therefore be referred to the will of man.   And this evil ground we call Original Sin.   It is a *mystery*, that is, a fact, which we see, but cannot explain ; and the doctrine a truth which we apprehend, but can neither comprehend nor communicate.   And such by the quality of the subject (namely, a responsible *Will*) it must be, if it be truth at all.

A sick man, whose complaint was as obscure as his sufferings were severe and notorious, was thus addressed by a humane stranger : " My poor Friend ! I find you dan-gerously ill, and on this account only, and having certain information of your being so, and that you have not where-withal to pay for a physician, I have come to you.   Respect-ing your disease, indeed, I can tell you nothing, that you are capable of understanding, more than you know already, or can only be taught by reflection on your own experience. But I have rendered the disease no longer irremediable. I have brought the remedy with me : and I now offer you the means of immediate relief, with the assurance of gradual convalescence, and a final perfect cure; nothing more being required on your part, but your best endeavours to follow the prescriptions I shall leave with you.   It is, indeed, too probable, from the nature of your disease, that you will occasionally neglect or transgress them.   But even this has been calculated on in the plan of your cure, and the remedies provided, if only you are sincere and in right earnest with yourself, and have your *heart* in the work. Ask me not how such a disease can be conceived possible. Enough for the present that you know it to be real: and I come to cure the disease not to explain it."

Now, what if the patient or some of his neighbours should charge this good Samaritan, with having given rise to the mischievous notion of an inexplicable disease, involving the honour of the King of the country;—should inveigh against *him* as the author and first introducer of the notion, though of the numerous medical works composed ages before *his* arrival, and by physicians of the most venerable authority, it was scarcely possible to open a single volume without finding some description of the disease, or some lamentation of its malignant and epidemic character :—and, lastly, what if certain pretended friends of this good Samaritan, in their zeal to vindicate him against this absurd charge, should assert that he was a perfect stranger to this disease, and boldly deny that he had ever said or done any thing connected with it, or that implied its existence ?

In this Apologue or imaginary case, reader, you have the true bearings of Christianity on the fact and doctrine of Original Sin. The doctrine (that is, the confession of a known fact) Christianity has only in common with every religion, and with every philosophy, in which the reality of a responsible Will and the *essential* difference between good and evil have been recognised. *Peculiar* to the Christian religion are the remedy and (for all purposes but those of a merely speculative curiosity) the solution. By the annunciation of the remedy it affords all the solution which our *moral* interests require; and even in that which remains, and must remain, unfathomable, the Christian finds a new motive to walk humbly with the Lord his God.

Should a professed Believer ask you whether that, which is the ground of responsible action in *your* will, could in any way be responsibly present in the Will of Adam,—answer him in these words: " *You*, Sir ! can no more demonstrate the negative, than I can conceive the affirmative. The corruption of my will may very warrantably be

o

spoken of as a *consequence* of Adam's fall, even as my
birth of Adam's existence; as a consequence, a link in the
historic chain of instances, whereof Adam is the first.
But that it is *on account* of Adam; or that this evil principle was, *a priori*, inserted or infused into my Will by the
will of another—which is indeed a contradiction in terms,
my Will in such case being no *Will*—*this* is nowhere asserted in Scripture explicitly or by implication." It belongs
to the very essence of the doctrine, that in respect of
Original Sin *every* man is the adequate representative of
all men.   What wonder, then, that where no inward ground
of preference existed, the choice should be determined by
outward relations, and that the first *in time* should be taken
as the diagram ?   Even in Genesis the word, Adam, is
distinguished from a proper name by an Article before it.
It is *the* Adam, so as to express the *genus*, not the individual—or rather, perhaps, I should say, *as well as* the
individual.   But that the word with its equivalent, *the old
man*, is used symbolically and universally by St. Paul,
(1 *Cor.* xv. 22. 45.   *Eph.* iv. 22.   *Col.* iii. 9.   *Rom.* vi. 6.)
is too evident to need any proof.

I conclude with this remark.   The doctrine of Original
Sin concerns all men.   But it concerns Christians *in particular* no otherwise than by its connexion with the doctrine
of Redemption; and with the Divinity and Divine Humanity of the Redeemer as a corollary or necessary inference from both mysteries.   BEWARE OF ARGUMENTS
AGAINST CHRISTIANITY, WHICH CANNOT STOP THERE, AND CON-
SEQUENTLY OUGHT NOT TO HAVE COMMENCED THERE.   Something I might have added to the clearness of the preceding
views, if the limits of the work had permitted me to clear
away the several delusive and fanciful assertions respecting
the state [1] of our first parents, their wisdom, science, and
angelic faculties, assertions without the slightest ground
in Scripture :—Or, if consistently with the wants and preparatory studies of those for whose use the volume was
especially intended, I could have entered into the mo-

---

[1] For a specimen of these Rabbinical dotages I refer, not to the
writings of mystics and enthusiasts, but to the shrewd and witty Dr.
South, one of whose most elaborate sermons stands prominent among
the many splendid extravaganzas on this subject.

mentous subject of a Spiritual Fall or Apostacy *antecedent* to the formation of man—a belief, the scriptural grounds of which are few and of diverse interpretation, but which has been almost universal in the Christian Church. Enough, however, has been given, I trust, for the Reader to see and (as far as the subject is capable of being understood) to understand this long controverted Article, in the sense in which alone it is binding on his faith. Supposing him therefore, to know the meaning of original sin, and to have decided for himself on the fact of its actual existence, as the antecedent ground and occasion of Christianity, we may now proceed to Christianity itself, as the Edifice raised on this ground, that is, to the great Constituent Article of the Faith in Christ, as the Remedy of the Disease—The Doctrine of Redemption.

But before I proceed to this momentous doctrine let me briefly remind the young and friendly pupil, to whom I would still be supposed to address myself, that in the following Aphorism the word science is used in its strict and narrowest sense. By a Science I here mean any chain of truths which are either absolutely certain, or necessarily true for the human mind, from the laws and constitution of the mind itself. In neither case is our conviction derived, or capable of receiving any addition, from outward experience, or empirical *data*—that is, matters of fact *given* to us through the medium of the senses—though these *data* may have been the occasion, or may even be an indispensable condition, of our reflecting on the former, and thereby becoming *conscious* of the same. On the other hand, a connected series of conclusions grounded on empirical *data*, in contra-distinction from science, I beg leave (no better term occurring) in this place and for this purpose, to denominate a scheme.

APHORISM XI.

In whatever age and country it is the prevailing mind and character of the nation to regard the present life as subordinate to a life to come, and to mark the present state, *the World of their Senses*, by signs, instruments, and

mementos of its connexion with a future state and a
spiritual world;—where the Mysteries of Faith are brought
within the *hold* of the people at large, not by being explained away in the vain hope of accommodating them to
the average of their understanding, but by being made
the objects of love by their combination with events and
epochs of history, with national traditions, with the monu-
ments and dedications of ancestral faith and zeal, with
memorial and symbolical observances, with the realizing
influences of social devotion, and above all, by early and
habitual association with Acts of the Will, *there* Religion
is. *There*, however obscured by the hay and straw of
human Will-work, the foundation is safe. In *that* country,
and under the predominance of such maxims the National
Church is no mere State-*Institute*. It is the State itself in
its intensest federal union; yet at the same moment the
Guardian and Representative of all personal Individuality.
For the Church is the Shrine of Morality; and in Morality
alone the citizen asserts and reclaims his personal independence, his *integrity*. Our outward acts are efficient,
and most often possible, only by coalition. As an efficient
power, the agent, is but *a fraction* of unity: he becomes
an *integer* only in the recognition and performance of the
Moral Law. Nevertheless it is most true (and a truth
which cannot with safety be overlooked) that morality *as*
morality, has no existence for *a people*. It is either absorbed and lost in the quicksands of prudential *calculus*,
or it is taken up and transfigured into the duties and
mysteries of religion. And no wonder: since morality
(including the *personal* being, the I AM, as its subject) is
itself a mystery, and the ground and *suppositum* of all
other mysteries, relatively to man.

APHORISM XII.

Paley not a Moralist.

Schemes of conduct, grounded on calculations of self-
interest; or on the average consequences of actions, supposing them *general;* form a branch of Political Economy,

to which let all due honour be given. Their utility is not here questioned. But however estimable within their own sphere, such schemes, or any one of them in particular, may be, they do not belong to Moral Science, to which both in kind and purpose, they are in all cases *foreign*, and, when substituted for it, *hostile*. Ethics, or the *Science* of Morality, does indeed in no wise exclude the consideration of *action*; but it contemplates the same in its originating spiritual *source*, without reference to space or time or sensible existence. Whatever springs out of *the perfect law of freedom*, which exists only by its unity with the will of God, its inherence in the Word of God, and its communion with the Spirit of God—*that* (according to the principles of Moral Science) is GOOD—it is light and righteousness and very truth. Whatever seeks to separate itself from the Divine Principle, and proceeds from a false centre in the agent's particular will, is EVIL—a work of darkness and contradiction. It is sin and essential falsehood. Not the outward deed, constructive, destructive, or neutral,—not the deed as a possible object of the senses,—is the object of Ethical Science. For this is no compost, *collectorium* or inventory of single duties; nor does it seek in the multitudinous sea, in the pre-determined waves, and tides and currents of *nature* that freedom, which is exclusively an attribute of *spirit*. Like all other pure sciences, whatever it enunciates, and whatever it concludes, it enunciates and concludes *absolutely*. Strictness is its essential character: and its first Proposition is, *Whosoever shall keep the whole law, and yet offend in one point, he is guilty of all*. For as the Will or Spirit, the Source and Substance of Moral Good, is one and all in every part; so must it be the totality, the whole articulated series of single acts, taken as unity, that can alone, in the severity of science, be recognised as the proper counterpart and adequate representative of a good Will. Is it in this or that limb, or not rather in the whole body, the entire *organismus* that the law of life reflects itself?—Much less, then, can the law of the Spirit work in fragments.

APHORISM XIII.

Wherever there exists a permanent[1] learned class, having authority and possessing the respect and confidence of the country ; and wherever the Science of Ethics is acknowledged, and taught in *this* class as a regular part of a learned education, to its future members generally, but as the special study and indispensable ground-work of such as are intended for holy orders ;—*there* the Article of Original Sin will be an AXIOM of Faith in *all* classes. Among the learned an undisputed *truth*, and with the people a fact, which no man imagines it possible to deny : and the doctrine, thus inwoven in the faith of all, and coeval with the consciousness of each, will for each and all, possess a reality, *subjective* indeed, yet virtually equivalent to that which we intuitively give to the objects of our senses.

With the learned this will be the case, because the Article is the first—I had almost said, *spontaneous*—product of the application of moral science to history, of which it is the interpreter. A mystery in its own right, and by the necessity and essential character of its subject —(for the Will, like the Life, in every act and product pre-supposes to itself, a Past always present, a Present that evermore resolves itself into a Past) — the doctrine of Original Sin gives to all the other mysteries of religion a common basis, a connection of dependency, an intelligibility of relation, and total harmony, that supersede extrinsic proof. There is here that same proof from unity of purpose, that same evidence of symmetry, which, in the

---

[1] A learned order must be supposed to consist of three classes. First, those who are employed in adding to the existing sum of power and knowledge. Second, and most numerous class, those whose office it is to diffuse through the community at large the practical Results of science, and that kind and degree of knowledge and cultivation, which for all is requisite or clearly useful. Third, the formers and instructors of the second—in schools, halls, and universities, or through the medium of the press. The second class includes not only the parochial clergy, and all others duly ordained to the ministerial office; but likewise all the members of the legal and medical professions, who have received a learned education under accredited and responsible teachers. [See ' The Church and State, p. 45, &c., third edition.—H. N. C.]

contemplation of a human skeleton, flashed conviction on the mind of Galen, and kindled meditation into a hymn of praise.

Meanwhile the People, not goaded into doubt by the lessons and examples of their teachers and superiors; not drawn away from the fixed stars of heaven, the form and magnitude of which are the same for the naked eye of the shepherd as for the telescope of the sage—from the immediate truths, I mean, of Reason and Conscience to an exercise to which they have not been trained,—of a faculty which has been imperfectly developed,—on a subject not within the sphere of the faculty, nor in any way amenable to its judgment;—the PEOPLE will need no arguments to receive a doctrine confirmed by their own experience from within and from without, and intimately blended with the most venerable traditions common to all races, and the traces of which linger in the latest twilight of civilization.

Among the revulsions consequent on the brute bewilderments of a Godless revolution, a great and active zeal for the interests of religion may be one. I dare not trust it, till I have seen what it is that gives religion this interest, till I am satisfied that it is not the interests of this world; necessary and laudable interests, perhaps, but which may, I dare believe, be secured as effectually and more suitably by the prudence of this world, and by this world's powers and motives. At all events, I find nothing in the fashion of the day to deter me from adding, that the reverse of the preceding—that where religion is valued and patronized as a supplement of law, or an aid extraordinary of police; where Moral SCIENCE is exploded as the mystic jargon of dark ages; where a lax System of Consequences, by which every iniquity on earth may be (and how many *have* been!) denounced and defended with equal plausibility, is publicly and authoritatively taught as Moral Philosophy; where the mysteries of religion, and truths supersensual, are either cut and squared for the comprehension of the understanding, "the faculty judging according to sense," or desperately torn asunder from the reason, nay, fanatically opposed to it; lastly, where Private[1] Interpretation is every

---

[1] The author of 'The Statesman's Manual' must be the most inconsistent of men, if he can be justly suspected of a leaning to the Romish

thing and the Church nothing—*there* the mystery of
Original Sin will be either rejected, or evaded, or perverted
into the monstrous fiction of Hereditary Sin,—guilt inherited; in the mystery of Redemption metaphors will be
obtruded for the reality; and in the mysterious appur-
tenants and symbols of Redemption (Regeneration, Grace,
the Eucharist, and Spiritual Communion) the realities will
be evaporated into metaphors.

APHORISM XIV.

LEIGHTON.

As in great maps or pictures you will see the border
decorated with meadows, fountains, flowers, and the like,
represented in it, but in the middle you have the main
design: so amongst the works of God is it with the fore-
ordained Redemption of Man. All his other works in the
world, all the beauty of the creatures, the succession of ages,
and the things that come to pass in them, are but as the
border to this as the mainpiece. But as a foolish unskilful

Church; or if it be necessary for him to repeat his fervent Amen to the
wish and prayer of our late good old King, that "every adult in the
British Empire should be able to read his Bible, and have a Bible to
read!" Nevertheless, it may not be superfluous to declare, that in thus
protesting against the *license* of private interpretation, I do not mean to
condemn the exercise or deny the right of individual judgment. I
condemn only the pretended right of every individual, competent and
incompetent, to interpret Scripture in a sense of his own, in opposition
to the judgment of the Church, without knowledge of the originals or
of the languages, the history, the customs, opinions, and controversies
of the age and country in which they were written; and where the interpreter judges in ignorance or contempt of uninterrupted tradition, the
unanimous consent of Fathers and Councils, and the universal Faith of
the Church in all ages. It is not the attempt to form a judgment, which
is here called in question; but the grounds, or rather the *no-grounds* on
which the judgment is formed and relied on.

My fixed principle is: that A CHRISTIANITY WITHOUT A CHURCH
EXERCISING SPIRITUAL AUTHORITY IS VANITY AND DISSOLUTION. And
my *belief* is, that when Popery is rushing in on us like an inundation,
the nation will find it to be so. I say *Popery;* for this too I hold for a
delusion, that Romanism or *Roman* Catholicism is separable from
Popery. Almost as readily could I suppose a circle without a centre.

beholder, not discerning the excellency of the principal piece in such maps or pictures, gazes only on the fair border, and goes no farther—thus do the greatest part of us as to this great Work of God, the redemption of our personal Being, and the re-union of the Human with the Divine, by and through the Divine Humanity of the Incarnate Word.

APHORISM XV.

LUTHER.

It is a hard matter, yea, an impossible thing for thy human strength, whosoever thou art (without God's assistance), at such a time when Moses setteth on thee with the Law (see Aphorism XII.),—when the holy Law written in thy heart accuseth and condemneth thee, forcing thee to a comparison of thy heart therewith, and convicting thee of the incompatibleness of thy will and nature with Heaven and holiness and an immediate God — that then thou shouldest be able to be of such a mind as if no Law nor sin had ever been! I say it is in a manner impossible that a human creature, when he feeleth himself assaulted with trials and temptations, and the conscience hath to do with God, and the tempted man knoweth that the root of temptation is within him, should obtain such mastery over his thoughts as then to think no otherwise than that from everlasting nothing hath been but only and alone Christ, altogether Grace and Deliverance!

COMMENT.

In irrational agents, namely, the brute animals, the will is hidden or absorbed in the law. The law is their *nature*. In the original purity of a rational agent the uncorrupted will is identical with the law. Nay, inasmuch as a Will perfectly identical with the Law is one with the *divine* Will, we may say, that in the unfallen rational agent the Will *constitutes* the Law.[1] But it is evident that the holy and spiritual

[1] In fewer words thus: For the brute animals, their nature is their law; —for what other third law can be imagined, in addition to the law of

power and light, which by a *prolepsis* or anticipation we have *named* law, is a grace, an inward perfection, and without the commanding, binding and menacing character which belongs to a law, acting as a master or sovereign distinct from, and existing, as it were, externally for, the agent who is bound to obey it. Now this is St. Paul's sense of the word; and on this he grounds his whole reasoning. And hence too arises the obscurity and apparent paradoxy of several texts. That the Law is a *Law* for you; that it acts *on* the Will not *in* it; that it exercises an agency *from without*, by fear and coercion; proves the corruption of your Will, and presupposes it. Sin in this sense came by the law: for it has its essence, as sin, in that counter-position of the holy principle to the will, which occasions this principle to be a LAW. Exactly (as in all other points) consonant with the Pauline doctrine is the assertion of John, when speaking of the re-adoption of the redeemed to be sons of God, and the consequent resumption (I had almost said re-absorption) of the Law into the Will (νόμον τέλειον τὸν τῆς ἐλευθερίας, James i. 25.,)—he says—*For the law was given by Moses, but Grace and Truth came by Jesus Christ.* That by the Law St. Paul meant only the *ceremonial* law, is a notion that could originate only in utter inattention to the whole strain and bent of the Apostle's argument.

APHORISM XVI.

LEIGHTON AND COLERIDGE.

Christ's death was both voluntary and violent. There was external violence: and that was the accompaniment, or at most the occasion, of his death. But there was in-

nature, and the law of reason? Therefore: in irrational agents the law constitutes the will. In moral and rational agents the will constitutes, or ought to constitute, the law: I speak of moral agents, unfallen. For the personal Will comprehends the *idea*, as a Reason, and it gives causative force to the Idea, as a *practical* Reason. But Idea with the power of realizing the same is a Law; or say :—the Spirit comprehends the Moral Idea, by virtue of its rationality, and it gives to the Idea causative Power, as a Will: In every sense therefore, it *constitutes* the Law, supplying both the Elements of which it consists—namely, the Idea, and the realizing Power.

ternal willingness, the spiritual Will, the Will of the Spirit, and this was the proper cause. By this Spirit he was restored from death : neither indeed *was it possible for him to be holden of it ; being put to death in the flesh, but quickened by the Spirit*, says St. Peter. But he is likewise declared elsewhere to have died by that same Spirit, which here, in opposition to the violence, is said to quicken him. Thus *Hebrews* ix. 14. *Through the eternal Spirit he offered himself.* And even from Peter's words, and without the epithet, eternal, to aid the interpretation, it is evident that *the Spirit*, here opposed to the flesh, body or animal life, is of a higher nature and power than the individual *soul*, which cannot of itself return to re-inhabit or quicken the body.

If these points were niceties, and an over-refining in doctrine, is it to be believed that the Apostles, John, Peter and Paul, with the author of the Epistle to the Hebrews, would have laid so great stress on them ? But the true life of Christians is to eye Christ in every step of his life— not only as their Rule but as their Strength : looking to him as their Pattern both in doing and in suffering, and drawing power from him for going through both : being *without him* able for nothing. Take comfort then, thou that believest ! *It is he that lifts up the Soul from the Gates of Death :* and he hath said, *I will raise thee up at the last day.* Thou that believest *in* him, believe him and take comfort. Yea, when thou art most sunk in thy sad apprehensions, and he far off to thy thinking, then is he nearest to raise and comfort thee : as sometimes it grows darkest immediately before day.

APHORISM XVII.

LEIGHTON AND COLERIDGE.

Would any of you be cured of that common disease, the fear of death ? Yet this is not the right name of the disease, as a mere reference to our armies and navies is sufficient to prove : nor can the fear of death, either as loss of life or pain of dying, be justly held a *common* disease. But would you be cured of the fear and fearful questionings connected with the approach of death ? Look this way, and you shall find more than you seek. Christ, the Word that was from the beginning and was made flesh and dwelt among men, died. And he, who dying conquered death in his own person, conquered Sin, and Death which is the Wages of Sin, for thee. And of this thou mayest be assured, if only thou believe in him, and love him. I need not add, keep his commandments : since where Faith and Love are, Obedience in its threefold character, as Effect, Reward, and Criterion, follows by that moral necessity which is the highest form of freedom. The Grave is thy bed of rest, and no longer the *cold* bed : for thy Saviour has warmed it, and made it fragrant.

If then it be health and comfort to the Faithful that Christ descended into the grave, with especial confidence may we meditate on his return from thence, *quickened by the Spirit:* this being to those who are in him the certain pledge, yea, the effectual cause of that blessed resurrection, for which they themselves hope. There is that union betwixt them and their Redeemer, that they shall rise by the communication and virtue of his rising : not simply by his *power*—for so the *wicked* likewise to their grief shall be raised : but *they by his life as their life.*

COMMENT
On the three Preceding Aphorisms.

To the reader, who has consented to submit his mind to my temporary guidance, and who permits me to regard him as my pupil, or junior fellow-student, I continue to address myself. Should he exist only in my imagination, let the bread float on the waters ! If it be the Bread of Life, it will not have been utterly cast away.

Let us pause a moment, and review the road we have passed over since the transit from Religious Morality to Spiritual Religion. My first attempt was to satisfy you, that there *is* a Spiritual principle in Man,[1] and to expose the sophistry of the arguments in support of the contrary. Our next step was to clear the road of all counterfeits, by showing what is *not* the Spirit, what is *not* Spiritual

[1] Elements of Religious Philosophy, *ante*, p. 88.—Ed.

Religion.[1]   And this was followed by an attempt to establish a difference in kind between religious truths and
the deductions of speculative science; yet so as to prove,
that the former are not only equally rational with the
latter, but that they alone appeal to reason in the fulness
and living reality of their power.   This and the state
of mind requisite for the formation of right convictions
respecting spiritual truths, afterwards employed our attention.   Having then enumerated the Articles of the Christian Faith *peculiar* to Christianity, I entered on the great
object of the present work; namely, the removal of all valid
objections to these articles on grounds of right reason or
conscience.   But to render this practicable it was necessary,
first, to present each article in its true Scriptural purity, by
exposure of the caricatures of misinterpreters; and this,
again, could not be satisfactorily done till we were agreed
respecting the faculty entitled to sit in judgment on such
questions.   I early foresaw, that my best chance (I will not
say, of giving an *insight* into the surpassing worth and
transcendent reasonableness of the Christian scheme, but)
of rendering the very question intelligible, depended on my
success in determining the true nature and limits of the
human UNDERSTANDING, and in evincing its *diversity* from
REASON.   In pursuing this momentous subject, I was
tempted in two or three instances into disquisitions, which
if not beyond the comprehension, were yet unsuited to the
taste, of the persons for whom the work was principally
intended.   These, however, I have separated from the
running text, and compressed into notes.   The reader will
at worst, I hope, pass them by as a leaf or two of waste
paper, willingly given by him to those for whom it may
not be paper *wasted*.   Nevertheless, I cannot conceal, that
the subject itself supposes, on the part of the reader, a
steadiness in *self-questioning*, a pleasure in referring to his
own inward experience for the facts asserted by the author,
which can only be expected from a person who has fairly set
his heart on arriving at clear and fixed conclusions in
matters of Faith.   But where this interest is felt, nothing
more than a common capacity, with the ordinary advantages of education, is required for the complete comprehen-

[1] See *ante*, pp. 96—101.—ED.

sion both of the argument and the result. Let but one thoughtful hour be devoted to the pages 143-165. In all that follows, the reader will find no difficulty in *understanding* the author's meaning, whatever he may have in *adopting* it.

The two great moments of the Christian Religion are, Original Sin and Redemption; *that* the Ground, *this* the Superstructure of our faith. The former I have exhibited, first, according to the scheme of the Westminster Divines and the Synod of Dort; then, according to the [1] scheme of

---

[1] To escape the consequences of this scheme, some Arminian divines have asserted that the penalty inflicted on Adam, and continued in his posterity, was simply the loss of immortality, Death as the utter extinction of personal Being: immortality being regarded by them (and not, I think, without good reason) as a supernatural attribute, and its loss therefore involved in the forfeiture of supernatural graces. This theory has its golden side; and as a private opinion, is said to have the countenance of more than one dignitary of our Church, whose general orthodoxy is beyond impeachment. For here the *penalty* resolves itself into the *consequence*, and this the natural and *naturally* inevitable consequence of Adam's crime. For Adam, indeed, it was a *positive* punishment: a punishment of his guilt, the justice of which who could have dared arraign? While for the Offspring of Adam it was simply a *not* super-adding to their nature the privilege by which the original man was contra-distinguished from the brute creation—a mere negation, of which they had no more right to complain than any other species of animals. God in this view appears only in his attribute of mercy, as averting by supernatural interposition a consequence naturally inevitable. This is the golden side of the theory. But if we approach to it from the opposite direction, it first excites a just scruple, from the countenance it seems to give to the doctrine of Materialism. The supporters of this scheme do not, I presume, contend, that Adam's offspring would not have been born *men*, but have formed a new species of beasts! And if not, the notion of a rational, and self-conscious soul, perishing utterly with the dissolution of the organized body, seems to require, nay, almost involves, the opinion that the soul is a quality or accident of the body—a mere harmony resulting from organization.

But let this pass unquestioned. Whatever else the descendants of Adam might have been without the intercession of Christ, yet (this intercession having been effectually made) they are now endowed with souls that are not extinguished together with the material body. Now unless these divines teach likewise the Romish figment of Purgatory, and to an extent in which the Church of Rome herself would denounce the doctrine as an impious heresy: unless they hold, that a punishment temporary and remedial is the *worst* evil that the impenitent have to apprehend in a future state; and that the spiritual Death declared and foretold by Christ, *the death eternal where the worm never dies*, is

a contemporary Arminian divine; and lastly, in contrast with both schemes, I have placed what I firmly believe to be the *Scriptural* sense of this article, and vindicated its entire conformity with reason and experience. I now proceed to the other momentous article—from the necessitating *Occasion* of the Christian Dispensation to Christianity itself. For Christianity and Redemption are equivalent terms. And here my Comment will be comprised in a few sentences : for I confine my views to the one object of clearing this awful mystery from those too current misrepresentations of its nature and import that have laid it open to scruples and objections, not to such as shoot forth from an unbelieving heart—(against these a sick bed will be a more effectual antidote than all the argument in the world)—but to such scruples as have their birth-place in the reason and moral sense. Not that it is a mystery—

neither Death nor eternal, but a certain *quantum* of suffering in a state of faith, hope, and progressive amendment—unless they go these lengths (and the divines here intended are orthodox Churchmen, men who would not knowingly advance even a step on the road towards them)— then I fear, that any advantage their theory might possess over the Calvinistic scheme in the article of Original Sin, would be dearly purchased by increased difficulties, and an ultra-Calvinistic narrowness in the article of Redemption. I at least find it impossible, with my present human feelings, not to imagine otherwise than that even in heaven it would be a fearful thing to know, that in order to my elevation to a lot infinitely more desirable than by nature it would have been, the lot of so vast a multitude had been rendered infinitely more calamitous ; and that my felicity had been purchased by the everlasting misery of the majority of my fellow-men, who if no redemption had been provided, after inheriting the pains and pleasures of earthly existence during the numbered hours, and the few and evil—evil yet *few*—days of the years of their mortal life, would have fallen asleep to wake no more,—would have sunk into the dreamless sleep of the grave, and have been as the murmur and the plaint, and the exulting swell and the sharp scream, which the unequal gust of yesterday snatched from the strings of a wind-harp !

In another place I have ventured to question the spirit and tendency of Taylor's work on Repentance.* But I ought to have added, that to discover and keep the true medium in expounding and applying the Efficacy of Christ's Cross and Passion, is beyond comparison the most difficult and delicate point of practical divinity—and that which especially needs a guidance from above.

---

* Perhaps in his " Unum Necessarium ; or the Doctrine and Practice of Repentance," part of his " Notes on Jeremy Taylor," pp. 295—325, v. iii., of the ' Remains,' 1838.—ED.

not that *it passeth all understanding* ;—if the doctrine be
more than an hyperbolical phrase, it *must* do so ;—but that
it is at variance with the Law revealed in the conscience ;
that it contradicts our moral instincts and intuitions—*this* is
the difficulty, which alone is worthy of an answer. And
what better way is there of correcting the misconceptions
than by laying open the source and occasion of them ?
What surer way of removing the scruples and prejudices,
to which these misconceptions have given rise, than by pro-
pounding the mystery itself—namely THE REDEMPTIVE ACT,
as the transcendent *Cause* of Salvation—in the express and
definite words, in which it was enunciated by the Redeemer
himself ?

But here, in addition to the three Aphorisms preceding,
I interpose a view of redemption as appropriated by faith,
coincident with Leighton's, though for the greater part expressed in my own words. *This* I propose as the right
view. Then follow a few sentences transcribed from Field
(an excellent divine of the reign of James I., of whose
work on the Church it would be difficult to speak too
highly) [1] containing the questions to be solved, and which is
numbered, as an Aphorism, rather to preserve the uniformity of appearance, than as being strictly such. Then
follows the Comment : as part and commencement of which
the Reader will consider the two paragraphs of pp. 135, 136,
written for this purpose and in the foresight of the present
inquiry : and I entreat him therefore to begin the Comment
by re-perusing these.

APHORISM XVIII.

Stedfast by Faith. This is absolutely necessary for resistance to the Evil Principle. There is no standing out
without some firm ground to stand on : and this Faith
alone supplies. By Faith in the Love of Christ the power
of God becomes ours. When the soul is beleaguered by
enemies, weakness on the walls, treachery at the gates,
and corruption in the citadel, then by Faith she says—

---

[1] See also " Notes on Field on the Church " (1628), in Coleridge's
' Remains,' 1838, v. iii., pp. 57—92.—ED.

Lamb of God, slain from the foundation of the World!
thou art my strength! I look to thee for deliverance!
And thus she overcomes. The pollution (*miasma*) of sin
is precipitated by his blood, the power of sin is conquered
by his Spirit. The Apostle says not—stedfast by your
own resolutions and purposes; but—*stedfast by faith.* Nor
yet stedfast in your Will, but *stedfast in the faith.* We
are not to be looking to, or brooding over ourselves, either
for accusation or for confidence, or (by a deep yet too
frequent self-delusion) to obtain the latter by making a
merit to ourselves of the former. But we are to look to
CHRIST and *him crucified.* The Law *that is very nigh to
thee, even in thy heart;* the Law that condemneth and hath
no promise; that stoppeth the guilty PAST in its swift
flight, and maketh it disown its name; the Law will
accuse thee enough. Linger not in the Justice-court, listening to thy indictment! Loiter not in waiting to hear the
Sentence! No! Anticipate the verdict! *Appeal to Cæsar!*
Haste to the King for a pardon! Struggle thitherward,
though in fetters; and cry aloud, and collect the whole
remaining strength of thy Will in the outcry—*I believe!
Lord! help my unbelief!* Disclaim all right of property
in thy fetters. Say, that they belong to the *old man,* and
that thou dost but carry them to the Grave, to be buried
with their owner! Fix thy thought on what *Christ* did,
what *Christ* suffered, what *Christ* is—as if thou wouldst fill
the hollowness of thy Soul with Christ! If he emptied
himself of glory to become sin for thy salvation, must not
thou be emptied of thy sinful Self to become Righteousness
in and through his agony and the effective merits of his
Cross? [1] By what other means, in what other form, is it

---

[1] *God manifested in the flesh* is Eternity in the form of Time. But
Eternity in relation to Time is the absolute to the conditional, or the
real to the apparent, and Redemption must partake of both;—always
perfected, for it is a *Fiat* of the Eternal;—continuous, for it is a process
in relation to man; the former, the alone objectively, and therefore
universally, true. That Redemption in an *opus perfectum,* a finished
work, the claim to which is conferred in Baptism; that a Christian
cannot speak or think as if his Redemption by the blood, and his Justification by the Righteousness of Christ alone, were future or contingent
events, but must both say and think, I *have been* redeemed, I am justified; lastly, that for as many as are received into his Church by baptism,

possible for thee to stand in the presence of the Holy One ?
With *what* mind wouldst thou come before God, if not with

Christ has condemned sin in the flesh, has made it *dead in law*, that
is, no longer imputable as *guilt*, has destroyed the *objective reality*
of sin :— these are truths, which all the Reformed Churches,
Swedish, Danish, Evangelical, (or Lutheran,) the Reformed (the Calvinistic in mid-Germany, France, and Geneva, so called,) lastly, the
Church of England, and the Church of Scotland—nay, the best and
most learned divines of the Roman Catholic Church have united in
upholding as most certain and necessary articles of faith, and the
effectual preaching of which Luther declares to be the appropriate
criterion, *stantis vel cadentis Ecclesiæ*. The Church is standing or
falling, according as this doctrine is supported, or overlooked, or counter-
vened. Nor has the contrary doctrine, according to which the baptized are yet, each individually, to be called, converted, and chosen,
with all the corollaries from this assumption, the watching for signs and
sensible assurances, " the frames," and " the states," and " the feelings,"
and "the sudden conversions," the contagious fever-boils, of the (most
unfitly, so called) Evangelicals, and Arminian Methodists of the day,
been in any age taught or countenanced by any known and accredited
Christian Church, or by any body and succession of learned divines.
On the other hand it has rarely happened, that the Church has not
been troubled by pharisaic and fanatical individuals, who have sought,
by working on the fears and feelings of the weak and unsteady that
celebrity, which they could not obtain by learning and orthodoxy : and
alas ! so subtle is the poison, and so malignant in its operation, that it
is almost hopeless to attempt the cure of any person, once infected,
more particularly when, as most often happens, the patient is a woman.
Nor does Luther in his numerous and admirable discourses on this
point, conceal or palliate the difficulties, which the carnal mind, that
works under many and different disguises, throws in the way to
prevent the laying firm hold of the truth. One most mischievous and
very popular mis-belief must be cleared away in the first instance—the
presumption, I mean, that whatever is not *quite* simple, and what any
plain body can understand at the first hearing, cannot be of necessary
belief, or among the fundamental articles or essentials of Christian
faith. A docile, child-like mind, a deference to the authority of the
Churches, a presumption of the truth of doctrines that have been received and taught as true by the whole Church in all times; reliance on
the positive declarations of the Apostle—in short, all the convictions of
the truth of a doctrine that are previous to a perfect *insight* into its
truth, because these convictions, with the affections and dispositions
accompanying them, are the very means and conditions of attaining to
that insight—and study of, and quiet meditation on, them, with a gradual
growth of spiritual knowledge, and earnest prayer for its increase ; all
these, to each and all of which the young Christian is so repeatedly and
fervently exhorted by St. Paul, are to be superseded, because, forsooth,
truths needful for all men, must be quite simple and easy, and adapted
to the capacity of all, even of the plainest and dullest understanding !

the mind of Him, in whom *alone* God loveth the world ?
With good advice, perhaps, and a little assistance, thou
wouldst rather cleanse and patch up a mind of thy own,
and offer it as thy *admission-right*, thy *qualification*, to Him
who *charged his angels with folly !* [1] Oh ! take counsel
of thy Reason ! It will show thee how impossible it is, that
even a world should merit the love of Eternal Wisdom and
all sufficing Beatitude, otherwise than as it is contained in
that all-perfect Idea, in which the Supreme Spirit contem-
plateth itself and the plenitude of its infinity—the Only-
Begotten before all ages ! *the beloved Son, in whom the Father
is* indeed *well pleased !*

And as the Mind, so the Body with which it is to be
clothed ! as the Indweller, so the House in which it is to
be the Abiding-place ! [2] There is but one wedding-
garment, in which we can sit down at the marriage-feast
of Heaven : and that is the Bridegroom's own gift, when

What cannot be poured all at once on a man, can only be supererogatory
drops from the emptied shower-bath of religious instruction! But
surely, the more rational inference would be, that the faith, which is to
save the whole man, must have its roots and justifying grounds in the
very depths of our being. And he who can read the Writings of the
Apostles, John and Paul, without finding in almost every page a confirmation of this, must have looked at them, as at the sun in an eclipse,
through blackened glasses.

[1] Job. iv. 18.—ED.

[2] St. Paul blends both forms of expression, and asserts the same doctrine when speaking of the *celestial body* provided for *the new man* in
the spiritual flesh and blood, (that is, the informing power and vivific
life of the incarnate Word : for the Blood is the Life, and the Flesh
the Power)—when speaking, I say, of this *celestial body*, as a *house not
made with hands, eternal in the heavens*, yet brought down to us, made
appropriable by faith, and *ours*—he adds, *for in this earthly house* (that
is, this mortal life, as the inward principle or energy of our Tabernacle,
or outward and sensible body) *we groan, earnestly desiring to be clothed
upon with our house which is from heaven : not that we would be unclothed,
but clothed upon, that mortality might be swallowed up of life.* 2 Cor.
v. 1—4.

The four last words of the first verse (*eternal in the heavens*) compared
with the conclusion of v. 2, (*which is from heaven*) present a coincidence
with *John* iii. 13, " And no man hath ascended up to heaven, but he
that came down from heaven, even the Son of Man, which is in
heaven." [Would not the coincidence be more apparent, if the words
of John had been rendered word for word, even to a disregard of the
English idiom, and with what would be servile and superstitious fidelity
in the translation of a common classic ? I can see no reason why the

he gave himself for us that we might live in him and he in us. There is but one robe of Righteousnes, even the

ούδείς, so frequent in St. John, should not be rendered literally, *no one;* and there may be a reason why it should. I have some doubt likewise respecting the omission of the definite articles τὸν, τοῦ, τῶ—and a greater, as to the ὁ ῶν, both in this place and in *John* i. 18, being *adequately* rendered by our *which is.* What sense some of the Greek Fathers attached to, or inferred from, St. Paul's *in the Heavens,* the theological student (and to theologians is this note principally addressed) may find in Waterland's Letters to a Country Clergyman— a divine, whose judgment and strong sound sense are as unquestionable as his learning and orthodoxy. A clergyman in full orders, who has never read the works of Bull and Waterland, has a duty yet to perform.]

Let it not be objected, that, forgetful of my own professed aversion to allegorical interpretations, I have, in this note, fallen into "the fond humour of the mystic divines, and *allegorizers* of Holy Writ." * There is, believe me, a wide difference between *symbolical* and *allegorical.* If I say that the flesh and blood (*corpus noumenon*) of the Incarnate Word are power and life, I say likewise that this mysterious power and life are *verily* and *actually* the flesh and blood of Christ. *They* are the allegorizers, who turn the 6th chapter of the Gospel according to St. John,—*the hard saying,—who can hear it?*—after which time many of Christ's disciples, who had been eye-witnesses of his mighty miracles, who had heard the sublime morality of his Sermon on the Mount, had glorified God for the wisdom which they had heard, and had been prepared to acknowledge, *This is indeed the Christ,*—went back and walked no more with him!—the hard sayings, which even THE TWELVE were not yet competent to understand farther than that they were to be spiritually understood; and which the chief of the Apostles was content to receive with an implicit and anticipative faith!—*they,* I repeat, are the allegorizers who moralize these hard sayings, these high words of mystery, into a hyperbolical metaphor *per catachresin,* which only means a belief of the doctrine which Paul believed, an obedience to the law, respecting which Paul *was blameless,* before the voice called him on the road to Damascus! What every parent, every humane preceptor, would do when a child had misunderstood a metaphor or apologue in a literal sense, we all know. But the meek and merciful Jesus suffered *many* of HIS disciples to fall off from eternal life, when, to retain them, he had only to say,—O ye simple-ones! why are ye offended? My words, indeed, sound strange; but I mean no more than what you have often and often heard from me before, with delight and entire acquiescence!—*Credat Judæus! Non ego.* It is sufficient for me to know that I have used the language of Paul and John, as it was understood and interpreted by Justin Martyr, Tertullian, Irenæus, and (if he does not err) by the whole Christian Church then existing.

---

* See Introductory Aphorisms, xxix., p. 19.—ED.

Spiritual Body, formed by the assimilative power of faith for whoever eateth the flesh of the Son of Man and drinketh his blood.   Did Christ come from Heaven, did the Son of God leave the glory *which he had with his Father before the world began*, only to *show* us a way to life, to *teach* truths, to *tell* us of a resurrection ?   Or saith he not, I *am* the way—I *am* the truth—I *am* the Resurrection and the Life ?

APHORISM XIX.

FIELD.

The *Romanists* teach that sins committed after baptism (that is, for the immense majority of Christians having Christian parents, all their sins from the cradle to the grave) are not so remitted for Christ's sake, but that we must suffer that extremity of punishment which they deserve : and therefore either we must afflict ourselves in such sort and degree of extremity as may answer the demerit of our sins, or be punished by God, here or in the world to come, in such degree and sort that his Justice may be satisfied. [*As the encysted venom, or poison-bag, beneath the Adder's fang, so does this doctrine lie beneath the tremendous power of the Romish Hierarchy.   The demoralizing influence of this dogma, and that it curdled the very life-blood in the veins of Christendom, it was given to Luther beyond all men since Paul to see, feel, and promulgate.   And yet in his large Treatise on Repentance, how near to the spirit of this doctrine—even to the very walls and gates of Babylon—was Jeremy Taylor driven, in recoiling from the fanatical extremes of the opposite error!*]   But they that are orthodox, teach that it is injustice to require the payment of one debt twice. * * * It is no less absurd to say, as the Papists do, that *our* satisfaction is required as a condition, without which *Christ's* satisfaction is not applicable unto us, than to say, Peter hath paid the debt of John, and He, to whom it was due, accepteth of the same payment on the condition that John pay it himself also. * * * The satisfaction of Christ is communicated and applied unto us without suffering the punishment that sin deserveth, [*and essentially*

involveth,] upon the condition of our faith and repentance.
[To which I would add : Without faith there is no power
of repentance : without a commencing repentance no power
to faith : and that it is in the power of the will either
to repent or to have faith in the Gospel sense of the words,
is itself a consequence of the redemption of mankind, a
free gift of the Redeemer : the guilt of its rejection, the
refusing to avail ourselves of the power, being all that we
can consider as exclusively attributable to our own act.] [1]

COMMENT.

(*Containing an Application of the Principles laid down in pp.* 135, 136.)

Forgiveness of sin, the abolition of guilt, through the
redemptive power of Christ's love, and of his perfect
obedience during his voluntary assumption of humanity,
is expressed, on account of the resemblance of the consequences in both cases, by the payment of a debt for
another, which debt the payer had not himself incurred.
Now the *impropriation* of this metaphor—(that is, the taking
it *literally*) by transferring the sameness from the consequents to the antecedents, or inferring the identity of
the causes from a resemblance in the effects—this is the
point on which I am at issue : and the view or scheme of
redemption grounded on this confusion I believe to be
altogether un-Scriptural.

Indeed, I know not in what other instance I could better
exemplify the species of sophistry noticed in p. 147, as the
Aristotelean μετάβασις εἰς ἄλλο γένος, or clandestine passing
over into a diverse kind. The purpose of a metaphor is to
illustrate a something less known by a partial identification
of it with some other thing better understood, or at least
more familiar. Now the article of Redemption may be
considered in a two-fold relation—in relation to the *antecedent*, that is, the Redeemer's act as the efficient cause and
condition of redemption; and in relation to the *consequent*,
that is, the effects in and for the Redeemed. Now it is the

[1] Dr. Richard Field's " Of the Church," folio ed., Oxford, 1628,
p. 58.—ED.

latter relation, in which the subject is treated of, set forth, expanded, and enforced by St. Paul. The mysterious act, the operative cause is *transcendent*. *Factum est:* and beyond the information contained in the enunciation of the *Fact*, it can be characterized only by the *consequences*. It is the *consequences* of the Act of Redemption, which the zealous Apostle would bring home to the minds and affections both of Jews and Gentiles. Now the Apostle's opponents and gainsayers were principally of the former class. They were Jews: not only Jews unconverted, but such as had partially received the Gospel, and who, sheltering their national prejudices under the pretended authority of Christ's original apostles and the Church in Jerusalem, set themselves up against Paul as followers of Cephas. Add too, that Paul himself was *a Hebrew of the Hebrews;* intimately versed *in the Jews' religion above many, his equals, in his own nation, and above measure zealous of the traditions of his fathers.* It might, therefore, have been anticipated, that his reasoning would receive its outward forms and language, that it would take its predominant colours, from his own *past*, and his opponents' present, habits of thinking; and that his figures, images, analogies, and references would be taken preferably from objects, opinions, events, and ritual observances ever uppermost in the imaginations of his own countrymen. And such we find them;—yet so judiciously selected, that the prominent forms, the figures of most frequent recurrence, are drawn from points of belief and practice, forms, laws, rites and customs, that then prevailed through the whole Roman world, and were common to Jew and Gentile.

Now it would be difficult if not impossible to select points better suited to this purpose, as being equally familar to all, and yet having a special interest for the Jewish converts, than those are from which the learned Apostle has drawn the four principal metaphors, by which he illustrates the blessed *consequences* of Christ's redemption of mankind. These are: 1. Sin-offerings, sacrifical expiation. 2. Reconciliation, atonement, καταλλαγὴ.[1] 3. Ran-

---

[1] This word occurs but once in the New Testament, *Romans* v. 11, the marginal rendering being *reconciliation*. The personal noun, καταλλακτὴς, is still in use with the modern Greeks for a money-changer,

som from slavery, Redemption, the buying back again, or
being bought back. 4. Satisfaction of a creditor's claims
by a payment of the debt. To one or other of these four
heads all the numerous forms and exponents of Christ's
mediation in St. Paul's writings may be referred. And the
very number and variety of the words or *periphrases* used
by him to express one and the same thing furnish the
strongest presumptive proof, that all alike were used *metaphorically*. [In the following notation, let the small letters
represent the *effects* or *consequences*, and the capitals the
efficient *causes* or *antecedents*. Whether by causes we mean
acts or agents, is indifferent. Now let X signify a *transcendent*, that is, a cause beyond our comprehension and not
within the sphere of sensible experience; and on the other
hand, let A, B, C, and D represent each some one known
and familiar cause, in reference to some single and charac-

---

or one who takes the debased currency, so general in countries under a
despotic or other dishonest government, in exchange for sterling coin
or bullion; the purchaser paying the *catallage*, that is, the difference. In
the elder Greek writers, the verb means *to exchange for an opposite*, as,
καταλλάσσετο τὴν ἐχθρην τοῖς στασιώταις.—He exchanged within himself enmity for friendship, (that is, he reconciled himself) with his party;
—or, as we say, *made it up* with them, an idiom which (with whatever
loss of dignity) gives the exact force of the word. He made *up the
difference*. The Hebrew word of very frequent occurrence in the Pen-
tateuch, which we render by the substantive, *atonement*, has its radical
or visual image, in *copher*, pitch. Gen. vi. 14: *Thou shalt pitch it within
and without with pitch*. Hence to unite, to fill up a breach, or leak, the
word expressing both the *act*, namely, the bringing together what had been
previously separated, and the *means*, or material, by which the re-union
is effected, as in our English verbs, *to caulk, to solder, to poy* or *pay*
(from *poix*, pitch), and the French *suiver*. Thence, metaphorically,
expiation, the *piacula* having the same root, and being grounded on
another property or use of gums and resins, the supposed *cleansing*
powers of their fumigation. *Numbers* viii. 21: *made atonement for
the Levites to cleanse them.*"—Lastly (or if we are to believe the Hebrew
Lexicons, *properly* and most *frequently*) it means *ransom*. But if by *proper*
the Interpreters mean *primary* and *radical*, the assertion does not need a
confutation: all radicals belonging to one or other of three classes. 1.
Interjections, or sounds expressing sensations or passions. 2. Imitations
of sounds, as splash, roar, whiz, &c. 3. and principally, visual images,
objects of sight. But as to *frequency*, in all the numerous (fifty, I
believe,) instances of the word in the Old Testament, I have not found
one in which it can, or at least need, be rendered by *ransom:* though
beyond all doubt *ransom* is used in the Epistle to Timothy, as an
equivalent term.

teristic effect : namely, A in reference to k, B to l, C to m, and D to n. Then I say X + k l m n is in different places expressed by A + k ; B + l ; C + m ; D + n.—And these I should call *metaphorical* exponents of X.]

Now John, the beloved Disciple, who leaned on the Lord's bosom, the Evangelist κατὰ πνεῦμα, that is, according to the *Spirit*, the inner and substantial truth of the Christian creed—John, recording the Redeemer's own words, enunciates the fact itself, to the full extent in which it is enunciable for the human mind, simply and *without any metaphor*, by identifying it *in kind* with a fact of hourly occurrence—*expressing* it, I say, by a familiar fact the same *in kind* with that intended, though of a far lower *dignity* ;— by a fact of every man's experience, *known* to all, yet not better *understood* than the fact described by it. In the Redeemed it is a re-*generation*, a *birth*, a spiritual seed impregnated and evolved, the germinal principle of a higher and enduring life, of a *spiritual* life—that is, a life the actuality of which is not dependent on the material body, or limited by the circumstances and processes indispensable to its organization and subsistence. Briefly, it is the *differential* of immortality, of which the assimilative power of faith and love is the *integrant*, and the life in Christ the *integration*.

But even this would be an imperfect statement, if we omitted the awful truth, that besides that dissolution of our earthly tabernacle which we call death, there is another death, not the mere negation of life, but its positive opposite. And as there is a mystery of life and an assimilation to the principle of life, even to him who is *the* Life; so is there a mystery of death and an assimilation to the principle of evil; a fructifying of the corrupt seed, of which death is the germination. Thus the regeneration to spiritual life is at the same time a redemption from the spiritual death.

Respecting the redemptive act itself, and the Divine Agent, we know from revelation that he *was made a quickening* (ζωοποιοῦν, *life-making) spirit* : and that in order to this it was necessary, that God should be *manifested in the flesh*, that the Eternal Word, through whom and by whom the world (κόσμος, the order, beauty, and sustaining law of

visible natures) was and is, should be made flesh, assume
our humanity personally, fulfil all righteousness, and so
suffer and so die for us as in dying to conquer death for as
many as should receive him. More than this, the mode, the
possibility, we are not competent to know. It is, as hath
been already observed concerning the primal act of apostacy,
a mystery by the necessity of the subject—a mystery, which
at all events it will be time enough for us to seek and
expect to understand, when we understand the mystery of
our *natural* life, and *its* conjunction with mind and will and
personal identity. Even the truths that are given to us to
know, we can know only through faith in the spirit. They
are spiritual things which must be spiritually discerned.
Such, however, being the means and the effects of our
Redemption, well might the fervent Apostle associate it
with whatever was eminently dear and precious to erring
and afflicted mortals, and (where no expression could be
commensurate, no single title be other than imperfect) seek
from similitude of *effect* to describe the superlative boon by
successively transferring to it, as by a superior claim, the
name of each several act and ordinance, habitually connected in the minds of *all* his hearers with feelings of joy,
confidence, and gratitude.

Do you rejoice when the atonement made by the priest
has removed the civil stain from your name, restored you
to your privileges as a son of Abraham, and replaced you
in the respect of your brethren?—Here is an atonement
which takes away a deeper and worse stain, an eating
canker-spot in the very heart of your personal being. This,
to as many as receive it, gives the privilege to become sons
of God (*John* i. 12) ; this will admit you to the society of
angels, and insure to you the rights of brotherhood with
spirits made perfect.—(*Heb.* xii. 22.) Here is a sacrifice,
a sin-offering for the whole world : and a High Priest, who
is indeed a Mediator, who not in type or shadow but in very
truth and in his own right stands in the place of Man to
God, and of God to Man ; and who receives as a Judge
what he offered as an Advocate.

Would you be grateful to one who had ransomed you
from slavery under a bitter foe, or who brought you out of
captivity ? Here is redemption from a far direr slavery, the

slavery of sin unto death; and he, who gave himself for the ransom, has taken captivity captive.

Had you by your own fault alienated yourself from your best, your only sure friend;—had you, like a prodigal, cast yourself out of your father's house;—would you not love the good Samaritan, who should reconcile you to your friend? Would you not prize above all price the intercession, which had brought you back from husks, and the tending of swine, and restored you to your father's arms, and seated you at your father's table?

Had you involved yourself in a heavy DEBT for certain gew-gaws, for high seasoned meats, and intoxicating drinks, and glistering apparel, and in default of payment had made yourself over as a bondsman to a hard creditor, who it was foreknown, would enforce the bond of judgment to the last tittle;—with what emotions would you not receive the glad tidings, that a stranger, or a friend whom in the days of your wantonness you had neglected and reviled, had paid the DEBT for you, had made SATISFACTION to your creditor? But you have incurred a debt of Death to the EVIL NATURE! you have sold yourself over to SIN! and relatively to *you*, and to all *your* means and resources, the seal on the bond is the seal of necessity! Its stamp is the *nature* of evil. But the stranger has appeared, the forgiving friend has come, even the Son of God from heaven: and to as many as have faith in his name, I say—the Debt is paid for you. The Satisfaction has been made.

Now to simplify the argument and at the same time to bring the question to the test, we will confine our attention to the figure last mentioned, viz. the satisfaction of a debt. Passing by our modern *Alogi* who find nothing but metaphors in either Apostle, let us suppose for a moment with certain divines, that our Lord's words, recorded by John, and which in all places repeat and assert the same analogy, are to be regarded as metaphorical; and that it is the varied expressions of St. Paul that are to be literally interpreted:—for example, that sin is, or involves, an infinite debt, (in the proper and law-court sense of the word debt) —a debt owing by us to the vindictive justice of God the Father, which can only be liquidated by the everlasting misery of Adam and all his posterity, or by a sum of suffering equal to this. Likewise, that God the Father by his absolute decree, or (as some divines teach) through the necessity of his unchangeable justice, had determined to exact the full sum; which must, therefore, be paid either by ourselves or by some other in our name and behalf. But besides the debt which *all* mankind contracted in and through Adam, as a *homo publicus*, even as a nation is bound by the acts of its head or its plenipotentiary, every man (say these divines) is an insolvent debtor on his own score. In this fearful predicament the Son of God took compassion on mankind, and resolved to pay the debt for us, and to satisfy the divine justice by a perfect equivalent. Accordingly, by a strange yet strict *consequence*, it has been holden by more than one of these divines, that the agonies suffered by Christ were equal in amount to the sum total of the torments of all mankind here and hereafter, or to the infinite debt, which in an endless succession of instalments we should have been paying to the divine justice, had it not been paid in full by the Son of God incarnate!

It is easy to say—" O but I do not hold this, or *we* do not make this an article of our belief!" The true question is: "Do you take any *part* of it: and can you reject the rest without being *inconsequent?*" Are debt, satisfaction, payment in full, creditor's *rights*, and the like, *nomina propria*, by which the very nature of Redemption and its occasion is expressed;—or are they, with several others, figures of speech for the purpose of illustrating the nature and extent of the consequences and effects of the redemptive Act, and to excite in the receivers a due sense of the magnitude and manifold operation of the Boon, and of the Love and gratitude due to the Redeemer? If still you reply, the former : *then*, as your whole theory is grounded on a notion of *justice*, I ask you—Is this justice a *moral* attribute? But morality commences with, and begins in, the sacred distinction between thing and person : on this distinction all law human and divine is grounded : consequently, the law of justice. If you attach any meaning to the term justice, as applied to God, it must be the same to which you refer when you affirm or deny it of any other personal agent— save only, that in its attribution to God, you speak of it as unmixed and perfect. For if not, what *do* you mean? And why do you call it by the same name ? I may, therefore, with all right and reason, put the case as between man and man. For should it be found irreconcilable with the justice, which the light of reason, made *law* in the conscience, dictates to *man*, how much more must it be incongruous with the all-perfect justice of God ! Whatever case I should imagine would be felt by the reader as below the dignity of the subject, and in some measure jarring with his feelings ; and in other respects the more familiar the case, the better suited to the present purpose.

A sum of £1,000 is owing from James to Peter, for which James has given a bond. He is insolvent, and the bond is on the point of being put in suit against him, to James's utter ruin. At this moment Matthew steps in, pays Peter the thousand pounds and discharges the bond. In this case, no man would hesitate to admit, that a complete *satisfaction* had been made to Peter. Matthew's £1,000 is a perfect equivalent for the sum which James was bound to have paid, and which Peter had lent. *It is the same thing :* and this is altogether a question of *things.* Now instead of James's being indebted to Peter for a sum of money, which (he having become insolvent) Matthew pays for him, we will put the case, that James had been guilty of the basest and most hard-hearted ingratitude to a most worthy and affectionate mother, who had not only performed all the duties and tender offices of a mother, but whose whole heart was bound up in this her only child—who had foregone all the pleasures and amusements of life in watching over his sickly childhood, had sacrificed her health and the far greater part of her resources to rescue him from the consequences of his follies and excesses during his youth and early manhood ; and to procure for him the means of his present rank and affluence—all which he had repaid by neglect, desertion, and open profligacy. Here the mother stands in the relation of the creditor : and here too I will suppose the same generous friend to interfere, and to peform with the greatest tenderness and constancy all those duties of a grateful and affectionate son, which James ought to have performed. Will this satisfy the Mother's claims on James, or entitle him to her esteem, approbation, and blessing ? Or what

if Matthew, the vicarious son, should at length address
her in words to this purpose:—"Now, I trust, you are
appeased, and will be henceforward reconciled to James.
I have satisfied all your claims on him. I have paid his
debt in full : and you are too just to require the same
debt to be paid twice over. You will therefore regard
him with the same complacency, and receive him into your
presence with the same love, as if there had been no difference between him and you. For I have *made it up*."
What other reply could the swelling heart of the mother
dictate than this ? " O misery ! and is it possible that *you*
are in league with my unnatural child to insult me ? Must
not the very necessity of *your* abandonment of your proper
sphere form an additional evidence of *his* guilt ? Must
not the sense of your goodness teach me more fully to
comprehend, more vividly to feel, the evil in him ? Must
not the contrast of your merits magnify his demerit in his
mother's eye, and at once recall and embitter the conviction
of the canker-worm in his soul ? "

If indeed by the force of Matthew's example, by persuasion or by additional and more mysterious influences, or
by an inward co-agency, compatible with the existence of
a personal will, James should be led to repent; if through
admiration and love of this great goodness gradually
assimilating his mind to the mind of his benefactor, he
should in his own person become a grateful and dutiful
child—*then* doubtless the mother would be wholly satisfied !
But then the case is no longer a question of *things*, or
a matter of *debt* payable by another. Nevertheless, the
effect,—and the reader will remember, that it is the *effects*
and *consequences* of Christ's mediation, on which St. Paul
is dilating—the effect to *James* is similar in both cases,
that is, in the case of James the debtor, and of James the
undutiful son. In both cases, James is liberated from a
grievous burthen ; and in both cases he has to attribute his
liberation to the act and free grace of another. The only
difference is, that in the former case (namely, the payment
of the debt) the beneficial act is *singly*, and without
requiring any re-action or co-agency on the part of James,
the efficient *cause* of his liberation : while in the latter
case (namely, that of Redemption) the beneficial act

is the *first*, the indispensable *condition*, and *then* the *co-*efficient.

The professional student of theology will, perhaps, understand the different positions asserted in the preceding argument more readily if they are presented *synoptically*, that is, brought at once within his view, in the form of answers to four questions, comprising the constituent parts of the Scriptural Doctrine of Redemption. And I trust that my lay readers of both sexes will not allow themselves to be scared from the perusal of the following short catechism by half a dozen Latin words, or rather words with Latin endings, that translate themselves into English, when I dare assure them, that they will encounter no other obstacle to their full and easy comprehension of the contents.

Synopsis of the Constituent Points in the Doctrine of Redemption, in Four Questions, with Correspondent Answers.

Questions.

Who (or What) is the
1. *Agens Causator ?*
2. *Actus Causativus ?*
3. *Effectum Causatum ?*
4. *Consequentia ab Effecto ?*

Answers.

I. The Agent and Personal Cause of the Redemption of Mankind is—the co-eternal Word and only begotten Son of the Living God, incarnate, tempted, agonizing (*agonistes* ἀγωνιζόμενος), crucified, submitting to death, resurgent, communicant of his Spirit, ascendent, and obtaining for his Church the Descent, and Communion of the Holy Spirit, the Comforter.

II. The causative act is—a spiritual and transcendent Mystery, *that passeth all understanding.*

III. The Effect caused is—the being born anew : as before in the *flesh* to the world, so now born in the *spirit* to Christ.

IV. The Consequences from the Effect are—Sanctification from Sin, and Liberation from the inherent and penal consequences of Sin in the World to come, with all the means and processes of Sanctification by the Word and the Spirit : these Consequents being the same for the Sinner relatively to God and his own Soul, as the satisfaction of a debt for a debtor relatively to his creditor ; as the sacrificial atonement made by the priest for the transgressor of the Mosaic Law ; as the reconciliation to an alienated parent for a son who had estranged himself from his father's house and presence ; and as a redemptive ransom for a slave or captive.

Now I complain that this metaphorical *naming* of the transcendent causative act through the *medium* of its proper effects from actions and causes of familiar occurrence connected with the former by similarity of result, has been mistaken for an intended designation of the essential character of the causative act itself ; and that thus divines have interpreted *de omni* what was spoken *de singulo*, and magnified a *partial equation* into a *total identity*.

I will merely hint, to my more *learned* readers, and to the professional students of theology, that the origin of this error is to be sought for in the discussions of the Greek Fathers, and (at a later period) of the Schoolmen, on the obscure and *abysmal* subject of the divine *A-seity*, and the distinction between the θέλημα and the βουλὴ, that is, the Absolute Will, as the universal *ground* of *all* Being, and the election and purpose of God in the personal idea, as the Father. And this view would have allowed me to express what I believe to be the true import and scriptural idea of Redemption in terms much more nearly resembling those used ordinarily by the Calvinistic divines, and with a conciliative *show* of coincidence. But this motive was outweighed by the reflection, that I could not rationally have expected to be understood by those to whom I most wish to be intelligible : *et si non vis intelligi, cur vis legi ?*

Not to countervene the purpose of a Synopsis, I have detached the confirmative or explanatory remarks from the Answers to Questions II. and III., and place them below as *scholia*. A single glance of the eye will enable the reader to re-connect each with the sentence it is supposed to follow.

SCHOLIUM TO ANSWER II.

Nevertheless, *the fact or actual truth having been assured to us by Revelation,* it is not impossible, by stedfast meditation on the idea and super-natural character of a personal WILL, for a mind spiritually disciplined to satisfy itself, that the redemptive act *supposes* (and that our redemption is even negatively *conceivable* only on the supposition of) an agent who can at once act *on* the Will as an exciting cause, *quasi ab extra;* and *in* the Will, as the *condition* of its potential, and the *ground* of its actual, being.

SCHOLIUM TO ANSWER III.

Where two subjects, that stand to each other in the relation of *antithesis* or contradistinction, are connected by a middle term common to *both,* the sense of this middle term is indifferently determinable by *either;* the preferability of the one or the other in any given case being decided by the circumstance of our more frequent experience of, or greater familiarity with, the Term, in *this* connexion. Thus, if I put hydrogen and oxygen gas, as opposite poles, the term *gas* is common to both; and it is a matter of indifference, by which of the two bodies I ascertain the sense of the term. But if for the conjoint purposes of connexion and contrast, I oppose transparent crystallized alumen to opaque derb, or uncrystallized alumen;—it may easily happen to be far more *convenient* for me to show the sense of the middle term, that is, alumen, by a piece of pipe-clay than by a sapphire or ruby ; especially if I should be describing the beauty and preciousness of the latter to a peasant woman, or in a district where a ruby was a rarity which the fewest only had an opportunity of seeing. This is a plain rule of common logic directed in its application by common sense.

Now let us apply this to the case in hand. The two opposites *here* are Flesh and Spirit, *this* in relation to *Christ, that* in relation to the *World;* and these two opposites are connected by the middle term, *Birth,* which is of course common to both. But for the same reason, as in the instance last mentioned, the interpretation of the common term is to be ascertained from its known sense, in the

Q

more familiar connexion—birth, namely, in relation to our
natural life and to the organized body, by which we belong
to the present world.—Whatever the word signifies in this
connexion, the same *essentially* (in *kind* though not in
dignity and value) must be its signification in the other.
How else could it be (what yet in this text it undeniably
is), the *punctum indifferens*, or *nota communis*, of the *thesis*,
Flesh ; or the World, and the *antithesis* Spirit ; or Christ ?
We might therefore, upon the supposition of a writer having
been speaking of river-water in distinction from rain-water,
as rationally pretend that in the latter phrase the term,
water, was to be understood metaphorically, as that the
word, birth, is a metaphor, and means only so and so, in
the Gospel according to St. John.

There is, I am aware, a numerous and powerful party in
our Church, so numerous and powerful as not seldom to be
entitled *the* Church, who hold and publicly teach, that
" Regeneration is only Baptism." Nay, the writer of the
article on the Lives of Scott and Newton in our ablest and
most respectable Review [1] is but one among many who
do not hesitate to brand the contrary opinion as heterodoxy, and schismatical superstition. I trust, that I think
as seriously as most men, of the evil of schism ; but with
every disposition to pay the utmost deference to an acknowledged majority including, it is said, a very large proportion of the present dignitaries of our Church, I cannot but
think it a sufficient reply, that if Regeneration means
Baptism, Baptism must mean Regeneration ; and this too,
as Christ himself has declared, a Regeneration in the
Spirit. Now I would ask these divines this simple
question : Do they believingly suppose a spiritual regene-
rative power and agency inhering in or accompanying the
sprinkling a few drops of water on an infant's face ? They
cannot evade the question by saying that Baptism is a *type*
or *sign*. For this would be to supplant their own assertion,
that Regeneration means Baptism, by the contradictory
admission, that Regeneration is the *significatum*, of which
Baptism is the significant. Unless, indeed, they would
incur the absurdity of saying, that Regeneration is a type

[1] Review of the Memoirs of the Rev. J. Scott and Rev. J. Newton,
' Quarterly Review,' April, 1824.—ED.

of Regeneration, and Baptism a type of itself—or that Baptism only means Baptism! And this indeed is the plain consequence to which they might be driven, should they answer the above question in the negative.

But if their answer be, "Yes! we do suppose and believe this efficiency in the Baptismal act"—I have not another word to say. Only, perhaps, I might be permitted to express a hope, that for consistency's sake they would speak less slightingly of the *insufflation*, and *extreme unction*, used in the Romish Church; notwithstanding the not easily to be answered arguments of our Christian Mercury, the all-eloquent Jeremy Taylor, respecting the latter, which, "since it is used when the man is above half dead, when he can exercise no act of understanding, it must needs be nothing; for no rational man can think that any ceremony can make a spiritual change without a spiritual act of him that is to be changed; nor work by way of nature, or by charm, but morally and after the manner of reasonable creatures." [1]

It is too obvious to require suggestion, that these words here quoted apply with yet greater force and propriety to the point in question: as the babe is an unconscious subject, which the dying man need not be supposed to be. My avowed convictions respecting Regeneration with the spiritual Baptism, as its condition and initiative (Luke iii. 16; Matt. i. 7; Matt. iii. 11), and of which the sacramental rite, the Baptism of John, was appointed by Christ to remain as the sign and figure; and still more, perhaps, my belief respecting the Mystery of the Eucharist, (concerning which I hold the same opinions as Bucer,[2] Peter Martyr, and presumably Cranmer himself)—these convictions and this belief will, I doubt not, be deemed by the Orthodox *de more Grotii*, who improve the *letter* of Arminius with the *spirit* of Socinus, sufficient data to bring me in guilty of irrational and Superstitious Mysticism. But I abide by a maxim, which I learnt at an early period of my theological studies, from Benedict Spinoza:—Where the alternative lies between the Absurd and the Incomprehensible, no wise man can be at a loss which of the two to prefer. To be

---

[1] Dedication to Taylor's 'Holy Dying,' p. 295, Bohn's Standard Library edition.—ED.

[2] Appendix to Strype's 'Life of Cranmer.'—ED.

called irrational, is a trifle; to *be* so, and in matters of religion, is far otherwise: and whether the irrationality consists in men's believing (that is, in having persuaded themselves that they believe) *against* reason, or *without* reason, I have been early instructed to consider it as a sad and serious evil, pregnant with mischiefs, political and moral. And by none of my numerous instructors so impressively, as by that great and shining light of our Church in the æra of our intellectual splendour, Bishop Jeremy Taylor: from one of whose works, and that of especial authority for the safety as well as for the importance of the principle, inasmuch as it was written expressly *ad populum*, I will now, both for its own intrinsic worth, and to relieve the attention, wearied, perhaps, by the length and argumentative character of the preceding *discussion*, interpose the following Aphorism.[1]

APHORISM XX.

JEREMY TAYLOR.

Whatever is against right reason, that no faith can oblige us to believe. For though reason is not the positive and affirmative measure of our faith, and our faith ought to be larger than our [*speculative*] reason, and *take* something into her heart, that reason can never take into her eye; yet in all our creed there can be nothing *against* reason. If reason justly contradicts an article, it is not "of the household of Faith." In this there is no difficulty, but that in practice we take care that we do not call *that* reason, which is not so (*see* p. 122). For although reason is a right judge,[2] yet it ought not to pass sentence in an inquiry of faith, until all the information be brought in; all that is

---

[1] Slightly altered from the 'Worthy Communicant,' chap. iii. sect. v.; p. 523, vol. xv. of Heber's edition of Jeremy Taylor's works.—ED.

[2] Which it could not be, in respect of spiritual truths and objects super-sensuous, if it were the same with, and merely another name for "the faculty judging according to sense"—that is, the Understanding, or (as Taylor most often calls it in distinction from Reason) *Discourse* (*discursus seu facultas discursiva vel discursoria*). The Reason, so instructed and so actuated as Taylor requires in the sentences immediately following, is what I have called the Spirit. [See also note near the end of Aphorism VIII.—ED.]

within, and all that is without, all that is above, and all that is below; all that concerns it in experience, and all that concerns it in act: whatsoever is of pertinent observation and whatsoever is revealed. For else reason may argue very well and yet conclude falsely. It may conclude well in logic, and yet infer a false proposition in theology (p. 115). But when our judge is fully and truly informed in all that whence she is to make her judgment, we may safely follow her whithersoever she invites us.

APHORISM XXI.

JEREMY TAYLOR.

He that speaks against his own reason, speaks against his own conscience: and therefore it is certain, no man serves God with a good conscience, who serves him against his reason.

APHORISM XXII.

JEREMY TAYLOR.

By the eye of reason through the telescope of faith, that is, Revelation, we may see what without this telescope we could never have known to exist. But as one that shuts the eye hard, and with violence curls the eye-lid, forces a fantastic fire from the crystalline humour, and espies a light that never shines, and sees thousands of little fires that never burn; so is he that blinds the eye of reason, and pretends to see by an eye of faith. He makes little images of notions, and some atoms dance before him; but he is not guided by the light, nor instructed by the proposition, but sees like a man in his sleep. IN NO CASE CAN TRUE REASON AND A RIGHT FAITH OPPOSE EACH OTHER.

NOTE PREFATORY

TO

APHORISM XXIII.—Less on my own account, than in the hope of fore-arming my youthful friends, I add one other

transcript from Bishop Taylor, as from a writer to whose
name no taint or suspicion of Calvinistic or schismatical
tenets can attach, and for the purpose of softening the
offence which, I cannot but foresee, will be taken at the
positions asserted in paragraph the first of Aphorism VII.,
and the documental proofs of the same in the next pages;
and this by a formidable party composed of men ostensibly
of the most dissimilar creeds, *regular* Church-divines, voted
orthodox by a great majority of suffrages, and the so-called
Free-thinking Christians, and Unitarian divines. It is the
former class alone that I wish to conciliate: so far at least
as it may be done by removing the aggravation of *novelty*
from the offensive article. And surely the simple re-asser-
tion of one of "the two great things," which Bishop Taylor
could assert as a fact,—which, he took for granted, that
no Christian would think of controverting,—should at
least be controverted without bitterness by his successors
in the Church. That which was perfectly safe and orthodox in 1657, in the judgment of a devoted Royalist and
Episcopalian, ought to be at most but a venial heterodoxy
in 1825. For the rest, I am prepared to hear in answer—
what has already been so often, and with such theatrical
effect dropped, as an *extinguisher*, on my arguments—the
famous concluding period of one of the chapters in Paley's
Moral and Political Philosophy, declared by Dr. Parr to
be the *finest* prose passage in English literature.[1] Be it
so. I bow to so great an authority. But if the learned
Doctor would impose it on me as the *truest* as well as the
finest, or expect me to admire the logic equally with the
rhetoric—ἀφίσταμαι—I start off! As I have been *un-
English* enough to find in Pope's tomb-epigram on Sir
Isaac Newton nothing better than a gross and wrongful
falsehood, conveyed in an enormous and irreverent hyperbole; so with regard to this passage in question, free as it
is from all faults of taste, I have yet the hardihood to confess, that in the sense in which the words *discover* and
prove, are here used and intended, I am not convinced of
the truth of the principle, (that he alone discovers who
proves), and I question the correctness of the particular

---

[1] Coleridge quotes this passage in his Conclusion.—ED.

case, brought as instance and confirmation. I *doubt* the validity of the assertion as a *general* rule; and I *deny* it, as applied to matters of *faith*, to the verities of religion, in the belief of which there must always be somewhat of moral election, "an act of the *Will* in it as well as of the Understanding, as much *love* in it as discursive power. True Christian Faith must have in it something of in-evi-dence, something that must be made up by duty and by obedience."[1] But most readily do I admit, and most fer-vently do I contend, that the miracles worked by Christ, both as miracles and as fulfilments of prophecy, both as signs and as wonders, made plain discovery, and gave un-questionable proof, of his divine character and authority; that they were to the whole Jewish nation true and appro-priate evidences, that HE was indeed come who had pro-mised and declared to their forefathers, *Behold your God will come with vengeance, even God with a recompense. He will come and save you.*[2] I receive them as proofs, there-fore, of the truth of every word, which he taught who was himself THE WORD: and as sure evidences of the final victory over death and of the life to come, in that they were manifestations of HIM, who said: *I am the resurrection and the Life!*

The obvious inference from the passage in question, if not its express import, is: *Miracula experimenta crucis esse, quibus solis probandum erat, homines non, pecudum instar, omnino perituros esse.* Now this doctrine I hold to be altogether alien from the *spirit*, and without authority in the *letter*, of Scripture. I can recall nothing in the history ᷤof human belief, that should induce me, I find nothing in my own moral being that enables me, to understand it. I can, however, perfectly well understand, the readiness of *those* divines in *hoc Paleii dictum ore pleno jurare, qui nihil aliud in toto Evangelio invenire posse profitentur.* The most unqualified admiration of this superlative passage I find perfectly in character for those, who while Socinianism and Ultra-Socinianism are spreading like the roots of an elm, on and just below the surface, through the whole land, and *here and there* at least have even dipped under the garden-

---

[1] J. Taylor's ' Worthy Communicant.'—H. N. C.
[2] Isaiah xxxiv. compared with Matt. x. 34, and Luke xii. 49.—H. N. C.

fence of the Church, and blunted the edge of the labourer's
spade in the gayest *parterres* of our Baal-hamon, who,—
while heresies, to which the framers and compilers of our
Liturgy, Homilies, and Articles would have refused the
very name of Christianity, meet their eyes on the list of
religious denominations for every city and large town
throughout the kingdom—can yet congratulate themselves
with Dr. Paley, in his book on the Evidences, that *the rent
has not reached the foundation*[1]—that is, that the corruption
of man's will; that the responsibility of man in any sense
in which it is not equally predicable of dogs and horses;
that the divinity of our Lord, and even his pre-existence;
that sin, and redemption through the merits of Christ;
and grace; and the especial aids of the Spirit; and
the efficacy of prayer; and the subsistency of the Holy
Ghost; may all be extruded without breach or rent in the
essentials of Christian Faith;—that a man may deny and
renounce them all, and remain a *fundamental* Christian,
notwithstanding. But there are many who cannot keep
up with Latitudinarians of such a stride; and I trust that
the majority of serious believers are in this predicament.
Now for all these it would seem more in character to be of
Bishop Taylor's opinion, that the belief in question is *pre-
supposed* in a convert to the Truth in Christ—but at all
events not to circulate in the great whispering gallery of
the religious public suspicions and hard thoughts of those
who, like myself, are of this opinion; who do not dare
decry the religious instincts of humanity as a baseless
dream; who hold, that to excavate the ground under the
faith of all mankind, is a very questionable method of
building up our faith, as Christians; who fear, that instead
of adding to, they should detract from, the honour of the
Incarnate Word by disparaging the light of the Word,
that was in the beginning, and which lighteth *every* man;
and who, under these convictions, can tranquilly leave it to
be disputed, in some new Dialogues in the shades, between
the fathers of the Unitarian Church on the one side, and
Maimonides, Moses Mendelssohn, and Lessing on the other,
whether the famous passage in Paley does or does not

[1] Conclusion, Part III. ch. 8.—H. N. C.

contain the three dialectic flaws, *petitio principii*, *argumentum in circulo*, and *argumentum contra rem a premisso rem ipsam includente.*

Yes! fervently do I contend, that to satisfy the understanding, that there is a future state, was not the *specific* Object of the Christian Dispensation; and that neither the belief of a future state, nor the *rationality* of this belief, is the *exclusive* attribute of the Christian religion. An *essential*, a *fundamental*, article of *all* religion it is, and therefore of the Christian; but otherwise than as in connexion with the salvation of mankind from the *terrors* of that state, among the essential articles *peculiar* to the Gospel Creed (those, for instance, by which it is *contra*-distinguished from the creed of a religious Jew) I do not place it. And before sentence is passed against me, as heterodox, on this ground, let not my judges forget, who it was that assured us, that if a man did not believe in a state of retribution after death, previously and on other grounds, *neither would he believe, though a man should be raised from the dead.*

Again, I am questioned as to my *proofs* of a future state by men who are so far, and *only* so far, professed believers, that they admit a God, and the existence of a Law from God: I give them: and the questioners turn from me with a scoff or incredulous smile. Now should others of a less scanty Creed infer the weakness of the reasons assigned by me from their failure in convincing *these* men; may I not remind them, Who it was, to whom a similar question was proposed by men of the same class? But at all events it will be enough for my own support to remember it; and to know that HE held such questioners, who could not find a sufficing proof of this great all-concerning verity in the words, *The God of Abraham, the God of Isaac, and the God of Jacob* unworthy of any other answer—men not to be satisfied by *any* proof—by any such proofs, at least, as are compatible with the ends and purposes of all religious conviction; by any proofs, that would not destroy the faith they were intended to confirm, and reverse the whole character and quality of its effects and influences. But if, notwithstanding all here offered in defence of my opinion, I must still be adjudged heterodox and in error,—what can I say, but that *malo cum Platone errare*, and take refuge behind the ample shield of BISHOP JEREMY TAYLOR.

APHORISM XXIII.

Jeremy Taylor.

In order to his own glory, and for the manifestation of his goodness, and that the accidents of this world might not overmuch trouble those good men who suffered evil things, God was pleased to do TWO GREAT THINGS. The one was: that he sent his Son into the world to take upon him our nature, that every man might submit to a necessity, from which God's own Son was not exempt, when it behoved even *Christ to suffer*, and so to enter into glory. The other great thing was: that God did *not only by Revelation* and the Sermons of the Prophets *to his Church*, but even to ALL MANKIND *competently* teach, and *effectively* persuade, that the soul of man does not die; that though things were ill here, yet to the good who usually feel most of the evils of this life, they should end in honour and advantages. And therefore Cicero had reason on his side to conclude, that there is a time and place after this life, wherein the wicked shall be punished, and the virtuous rewarded; when he considered that Orpheus and Socrates, and many others, just men and benefactors of mankind, were either slain or oppressed to death by evil men. *And all these received not the promise.* But when virtue made men poor; and free speaking of brave truths made the wise to lose their liberty; when an excellent life hastened an opprobrious death, and the obeying Reason and our Conscience lost us our lives, or at least all the means and conditions of enjoying them: it was but time to look about for *another* state of things, where justice should rule, and virtue find her own portion. And therefore men cast out every line, and turned every stone, and tried every argument: *and sometimes proved it well, and when they did not, yet they believed strongly;* and THEY WERE SURE OF THE THING, WHEN THEY WERE NOT SURE OF THE ARGUMENT.[1]

[1] Sermon at the Funeral of Sir George Dalston.—H. N. C.

COMMENT.

A fact may be truly stated, and yet the Cause or Reason assigned for it mistaken; or inadequate; or *pars pro toto* —one only or few of many that might or should have been adduced. The preceding Aphorism is an instance in point. The phenomenon here brought forward by the Bishop, as the ground and occasion of men's belief of a future state —viz. the frequent, not to say ordinary, disproportion between moral worth and worldly prosperity—must, indeed, at all times and in all countries of the civilized world have led the observant and reflecting few, the men of meditative habits and strong feelings of natural equity, to a nicer consideration of the current belief, whether instinctive or traditional. By forcing the Soul in upon herself, this enigma of saint and sage, from Job, David and Solomon to Claudian and Boetius,—this perplexing disparity of success and desert, has, I doubt not, with such men been the occasion of a steadier and more distinct consciousness of a *something* in man different *in kind*, and which not merely distinguishes but contra-distinguishes, him from brute animals—at the same time that it has brought into closer view an enigma of yet harder solution—the fact, I mean, of a *contradiction* in the human being, of which no traces are observable elsewhere, in animated or inanimate nature. A struggle of jarring impulses; a mysterious diversity between the injunctions of the mind and the elections of the will; and (last not least) the utter incommensurateness and the unsatisfying qualities of the things around us, that yet are the only objects which our senses discover, or our appetites require us to pursue :—hence for the finer and more contemplative spirits the ever-strengthening suspicion, that the two phenomena must in some way or other stand in close connexion with each other, and that the Riddle of Fortune and Circumstance is but a form or effluence of the Riddle of Man :—and hence again, the persuasion, that the solution of both problems is to be sought for—hence the presentiment, that this solution will be found—in the *contra*-distinctive constituent of humanity, in the *something* of human nature which is exclusively human ;—and—as the objects discoverable by the senses, as all the bodies and substances that we can touch, measure, and weigh, are either mere totals, the unity of which results from the parts, and is of course only apparent; or substances, the unity of action of which is owing to the nature or arrangement of the partible bodies which they actuate or set in motion, (steam for instance, in a steam-engine); as on the one hand the conditions and known or conceivable properties of all the objects which perish and utterly *cease* to be, together with all the properties which we ourselves have in common with these perishable things, differ *in kind* from the acts and properties peculiar to our humanity, so that the former cannot even be conceived, cannot without a contradiction in terms be predicated, of the proper and immediate subject of the latter—(for who would not smile at an ounce of Truth, or a square foot of Honour?)—and as, on the other hand, whatever things in visible nature *have* the character of Permanence, and endure amid continual flux unchanged like a rainbow in a fast-flying shower, (for example, Beauty, Order, Harmony, Finality, Law,) are all akin to the *peculia* of humanity, are all *congenera* of Mind and Will, without which indeed they would not only exist in vain, as pictures for moles, but actually not *exist* at all;—hence, finally, the conclusion, that the soul of man, as the subject of Mind and Will, must likewise possess a principle of permanence, and be destined to endure. And were these grounds lighter than they are, yet as a small weight will make a scale descend, where there is nothing in the opposite scale, or *painted* weights, which have only an illusive relief or prominence; so in the scale of immortality slight reasons are in effect weighty, and sufficient to determine the judgment, there being no counter-weight, no reasons against them, and no facts in proof of the contrary, that would not prove equally well the cessation of the eye on the removal or diffraction of the eye-glass, and the dissolution or incapacity of the musician on the fracture of his instrument or its strings.

But though I agree with Taylor so far, as not to doubt that the misallotment of worldly goods and fortunes was one principal occasion, exciting well-disposed and spiritually-awakened natures by reflections and reasonings, such as I have here supposed, to mature the presentiment of immor-

tality into full consciousness, into a principle of action and
a well-spring of strength and consolation; I cannot concede
to this circumstance any thing like the importance and
extent of efficacy which he in this passage attributes to it.
I am persuaded, that as the belief of all mankind, of all[1]
tribes, and nations, and languages, in all ages, and in all
states of social union, it must be referred to far deeper
grounds, common to man as man; and that its fibres are to
be traced to the *tap-root* of humanity. I have long entertained, and do not hesitate to avow, the conviction, that
the argument, from Universality of belief, urged by Barrow
and others in proof of the first article of the Creed, is neither
in point of *fact*—for two very different objects may be
intended, and two, or more, diverse and even contradictory
conceptions may be expressed, by the same *name*—nor in
legitimacy of conclusion as strong and unexceptionable, as
the argument from the same ground for the continuance of
our personal being after death. The bull-calf *butts* with
smooth and unarmed brow. Throughout animated nature,
of each characteristic organ and faculty there exists a pre-
assurance, an instinctive and practical anticipation; and no
pre-assurance common to a whole species does in any
instance prove delusive.[2] All other prophecies of nature
have their exact fulfilment—in every other *ingrafted word*
of promise, nature is found true to her word; and is it in

[1] I say, *all:* for the accounts of one or two travelling French *philosophers*, professed atheists and partizans of infidelity, respecting one or
two African hordes, Caffres, and poor outlawed Boschmen, hunted out
of their humanity, ought not to be regarded as exceptions. And as to
Hearne's assertion respecting the non-existence and rejection of the
belief among the Copper-Indians, it is not only hazarded on very weak
and insufficient grounds, but he himself, in another part of his work,
unconsciously supplies data, from whence the contrary may safely be
concluded. Hearne, perhaps, put down his friend Motannabbi's *Fort*-
philosophy for the opinion of his tribe; and from his high appreciation
of the moral character of this murderous gymnosophist, it might, I fear,
be inferred, that Hearne himself was not the very person one would, of
all others, have chosen for the purpose of instituting the inquiry.

[2] See Baron Field's Letters from New South Wales. The poor
natives, the lowest in the scale of humanity, evince no symptom of any
religion, or the belief of any superior power as the maker of the world;
but yet have no doubt that the spirits of their ancestors survive in the
form of porpoises, and mindful of their descendants with imperishable
affection, drive the whales ashore for them to feast on.

her noblest creature, that she tells her first lie?—(The reader will, of course, understand, that I am here speaking in the assumed character of a mere naturalist, to whom no light of revelation had been vouchsafed; one, who

——————with gentle heart
Had worshipp'd Nature in the hill and valley,
Not knowing what he loved, but loved it all!)

Whether, however, the introductory part of the Bishop's argument is to be received with more or less qualification, the *fact* itself, as stated in the concluding sentence of the Aphorism, remains unaffected, and is beyond exception true.

If other argument and yet higher authority were required, I might refer to St. Paul's Epistle to the Romans, and to the Epistle to the Hebrews, which whether written by Paul or, as Luther conjectured, by Apollos, is out of all doubt the work of an Apostolic man filled with the Holy Spirit, and composed while the Temple and the glories of the Temple worship were yet in existence. Several of the Jewish and still Judaizing converts had begun to vacillate in their faith, and to *stumble at the stumbling-stone* of the contrast between the pomp and splendour of the old Law and the simplicity and humility of the Christian Church. To break this sensual charm, to unfascinate these bedazzled brethren, the writer to the Hebrews institutes a comparison between the two religions, and demonstrates the superior spiritual grandeur, the greater intrinsic worth and dignity of the religion of Christ. On the other hand, at Rome where the Jews formed a numerous, powerful, and privileged class (many of them, too, by their proselyting zeal and frequent disputations with the priests and philosophers trained and exercised polemics) the recently-founded Christian Church was, it appears, in greater danger from the reasonings of the Jewish doctors and even of its own Judaizing members, respecting the *use* of the new revelation. Thus the object of the Epistle to the Hebrews was to prove the *superiority* of the Christian Religion; the object of the Epistle to the Romans to prove its *necessity*. Now there was one argument extremely well calculated to stagger a faith newly transplanted and still lose at its roots, and which, if allowed, seemed to preclude the *possibility* of the

Christian religion, as an especial and immediate revelation from God—on the high grounds, at least, on which the Apostle of the Gentiles placed it, and with the exclusive rights and *superseding* character, which *he* claimed for it. "You admit" (said they) "the divine origin and authority of the Law given to Moses, proclaimed with thunders and lightnings and the voice of the Most High heard by all the people from Mount Sinai, and introduced, enforced, and perpetuated by a series of the most stupendous miracles. Our religion then was given by God: and can God give a perishable imperfect religion? If not perishable, how can it have a successor? If perfect, how can it need to be superseded?—The entire argument is indeed comprised in the latter attribute of our Law. We know, from an authority which you yourselves acknowledge for divine, that our religion is perfect. *He is the Rock, and his Work is perfect.* (*Deuter.* xxxii. 4.) If then the religion revealed by God himself to our forefathers is *perfect*, what need have we of another?"—This objection, both from its importance and from its extreme plausibility, for the persons at least, to whom it was addressed, required an answer in both Epistles. And accordingly, the answer is included in the one (that to the Hebrews) and it is the especial purpose and main subject of the other. And how does the Apostle answer it? Suppose—and the case is not impossible [1]—a man of sense, who had studied the evidences of Priestley and Paley with Warburton's Divine Legation, but who should be a perfect stranger to the Writings of St. Paul: and that I put *this*

---

[1] The case here supposed actually occurred in my own experience in the person of a Spanish refugee, of English parents, but from his tenth year resident in Spain, and bred in a family of wealthy, but ignorant and bigoted, Roman Catholics. In mature manhood he returned to England, disgusted with the conduct of the priests and monks, which had indeed for some years produced on his mind its so common effect among the better-informed natives of the South of Europe—a tendency to Deism. The results, however, of the infidel system in France, with his opportunities of observing the effects of irreligion on the French officers in Spain, on the one hand; and the undeniable moral and intellectual superiority of Protestant Britain on the other; had not been lost on him: and here he began to think for himself and resolved to *study* the subject. He had gone through Bishop Warburton's Divine Legation, and Paley's Evidences; but had never read the New Testament consecutively, and the Epistles not at all.

question to him:—"What do *you* think, will St. Paul's answer be?" "Nothing," he would reply, "can be more obvious. It is in vain, the Apostle will urge, that you bring your notions of probability and inferences from the arbitrary interpretation of a word in an absolute rather than a relative sense, to invalidate a known *fact*. It is a *fact*, that your Religion is (in *your* sense of the word) *not* perfect: for it is deficient in one of the two essential constituents of all true religion, the belief of a future state on solid and sufficient grounds. Had the doctrine indeed been revealed, the stupendous miracles, which you most truly affirm to have accompanied and attested the first promulgation of your religion, would have supplied the requisite proof. But the doctrine was not revealed; and your belief of a future state rests on no solid grounds. You believe it (as far as you believe it, and as many of you as profess this belief) without revelation, and without the only proper and sufficient evidence of its truth. Your religion, therefore, though of divine Origin is, (if taken in disjunction from the new revelation, which I am commissioned to proclaim) but a *religio dimidiata;* and the main purpose, the proper character, and the paramount object of Christ's mission and miracles, is to supply the missing half by a clear discovery of a future state;—and (since "he alone discovers who proves") by proving the truth of the doctrine, now for the first time declared with the requisite authority, by the requisite, appropriate, and alone satisfactory *evidences*."

But *is* this the Apostle's answer to the Jewish oppugners, and the Judaizing false brethren, of the Church of Christ? —It is *not* the answer, it does not resemble the answer returned by the Apostle. It is neither parallel nor corradial with the line of argument in either of the two Epistles, or with any one line; but it is a *chord* that traverses them all, and only touches where it cuts across. In the Epistle to the Hebrews the directly contrary position is repeatedly *asserted:* and in the Epistle to the Romans it is every where *supposed*. The death to which the Law sentenced all sinners (and which even the Gentiles without the *revealed* Law had announced to them by their consciences, *the judgment of God having been made known even to them* must be the same death, from which they were saved by the faith of the Son of God;

or the Apostle's reasoning would be senseless, his antithesis a mere equivoque, a play on a word, *quod idem sonat, aliud vult*. Christ *redeemed mankind from the curse of the Law:* and we all know, that it was not from temporal death, or the penalties and afflictions of the present life, that believers have been redeemed. The Law, of which the inspired sage of Tarsus is speaking, from which no man can plead excuse; the Law miraculously delivered in thunders from Mount Sinai, which was inscribed on tables of stone for the *Jews,* and written in the hearts of *all* men (*Rom.* ii. 15.)—the Law *holy and spiritual!* what was the great point, of which this Law, in its own name, offered no solution? the mystery, which it left behind the veil, or in the cloudy tabernacle of types and figurative sacrifices? Whether there was a judgment to come, and souls to suffer the dread sentence? Or was it not far rather—what are the means of escape; where may grace be found, and redemption? St. Paul says, the latter. The Law brings condemnation : but the conscience-sentenced transgressor's question, " What shall I do to be saved ? Who will intercede for me ? " she dismisses as beyond the jurisdiction of her court, and takes no cognizance thereof, save in prophetic murmurs or mute out-shadowings of mystic ordinances and sacrificial types.— Not, therefore, *that* there is a Life to come, and a future state ; but *what* each individual Soul may hope for itself therein ; and on what grounds ; and that this state has been rendered an object of aspiration and fervent desire, and a source of thanksgiving and exceeding great joy ; and by whom, and through whom, and for whom, and by what means and under what conditions—*these* are the *peculiar* and *distinguishing* fundamentals of the Christian Faith ! These are the revealed Lights and obtained Privileges of the Christian Dispensation ! Not alone the knowledge of the boon, but the precious inestimable Boon itself, is the *Grace and Truth that came by Jesus Christ !* I believe Moses, I believe Paul ; but I believe *in* Christ.

APHORISM.

ON BAPTISM.

LEIGHTON.

In those days came John the Baptist, preaching.—It will suffice for our present purpose, if by these[1] words we direct the attention to the origin, or at least first Scriptural record, of BAPTISM, and to the combinement of PREACHING therewith; their aspect each to the other, and their concurrence to one excellent end : the Word unfolding the Sacrament, and the Sacrament sealing the Word; the Word as a Light, informing and clearing the sense of the Seal; and this again, as a Seal, confirming and ratifying the truth of the Word; as you see some significant seals, or engraven signets, have a word about them expressing their sense.

But truly the word is a light and the sacraments have in them of the same light illuminating them. This *sacrament* of Baptism, the ancients do particularly express by *light*. Yet are they both nothing but darkness to us, till the same light shine in our hearts; for till then we are nothing but darkness ourselves, and therefore the most luminous things are so to us. Noonday is as midnight to a blind man. And we see these ordinances, the word and the sacrament, without profit or comfort for the most part, because we have not of that Divine Light within us. And we have it not, because we ask it not.

---

[1] By certain Biblical philologists of the Teutonic school (men distinguished by learning, but still more characteristically by hardihood in conjecture, and who suppose the Gospels to have undergone several successive *revisions and enlargements* by, or under the authority of, the sacred historians) these words are contended to have been, in the first delivery, the common commencement of all the Gospels κατὰ σάρκα (that is, *according to the flesh*), in distinction from St. John's or the Gospel κατὰ πνεῦμα (that is, *according to the Spirit*).

COMMENT;

Or an Aid to Reflection in the forming of a sound Judgment respecting the purport and purpose of the Baptismal Rite, and a just appreciation of its value and importance.

A born and bred Baptist, and paternally descended from the old orthodox Non-conformists, and both in his own and in his father's right a very dear friend of mine, had married a member of the National Church. In consequence of an anxious wish expressed by his lady for the baptism of their first child, he solicited me to put him in possession of my Views respecting this controversy; though principally as to the degree of importance which I attached to it. For as to the point itself, his natural prepossession in favour of the persuasion in which he was born, had been confirmed by a conscientious examination of the arguments on both sides. As the Comment on the preceding Aphorism, or rather as an expansion of its subject matter, I will give the substance of the conversation: and amply shall I have been remunerated, should it be read with the interest and satisfaction with which it was heard. More particularly, should any of my readers find themselves under the same or similar circumstances.

Our discussion is rendered shorter and more easy by our perfect agreement in certain preliminary points. We both disclaim alike every attempt to explain any thing *into* Scripture, and every attempt to explain any thing *out of* Scripture. Or if we regard either with a livelier aversion, it is the latter, as being the more fashionable and prevalent. I mean the practice of both high and low *Grotian* Divines to *explain away* positive assertions of Scripture on the pretext, that the *literal sense* is not agreeable to reason, that is, THEIR *particular* reason. And inasmuch as (in the only right sense of the word), there is no such thing as a *particular* reason, they must, and in fact they *do*, mean, that the literal sense is not accordant to their *understanding*, that is, to the *notions* which *their* understandings have been taught and accustomed to form in *their* school of philosophy. Thus a Platonist who should become a Christian, would at once, even in texts susceptible of a different interpretation, recognize, because he would expect to find, several doctrines which the disciple of the Epicurean or mechanic school will not receive on the most positive declarations of the Divine Word. And as we agree in the opinion, that the *Minimi-fidian* party [1] err grievously in the latter point, so I must concede to you, that too many Pædo-baptists (*assertors of Infant Baptism*) have erred, though less grossly, in the former. I have, I confess, no eye for these smoke-like wreaths of inference, this ever widening spiral *ergo* from the narrow aperture of perhaps a single text; or rather an interpretation forced into it by construing an idiomatic phrase in an artless narrative with the same absoluteness, as if it had formed part of a mathematical problem. I start back from these inverted Pyramids, where the apex is the base. If I should inform any one that I had called at a friend's house, but had found nobody at home, the family having all gone to the play; and if he on the strength of this information, should take occasion to asperse my friend's wife for unmotherly conduct in taking an infant, six months old, to a crowded theatre; would you allow him to press on the words "*nobody*" and "*all*" the family, in justification of the slander? Would you not tell him, that the words were to be interpreted by the nature of the subject, the purpose of the speaker, and their ordinary acceptation; and that he must, or might have known, that infants of that age would not be admitted into the theatre? Exactly so, with regard to the words, *he and all his household.* Had Baptism of infants at that early period of the Gospel been a known practice, or had this been previously demonstrated,—then indeed the argument, that in all probability there were one or more infants or young children in so large a family, would be no otherwise objectionable than as being superfluous, and a sort of anticlimax in logic. But if the words are cited as the proof, it would be a clear *petitio principii*, though there had been nothing else against it. But when we turn back to the Scriptures preceding the narrative, and find

---

[1] See Comment to Aphorism VIII., par. 3.—ED.

repentance and belief demanded as the terms and indispensable conditions of Baptism—*then* the case above imagined applies in its full force. Equally vain is the pretended analogy from Circumcision, which was no Sacrament at all ; but the means and mark of national distinction. In the first instance it was, doubtless, a privilege or mark of superior rank conferred on the descendants of Abraham. In the Patriarchal times this rite was confined (the first governments being Theocracies) to the priesthood, who were set apart to that office from their birth. At a later period this token of the *premier class* was extended to Kings. And thus, when it was re-ordained by Moses for the whole Jewish nation, it was at the same time said—Ye are *all* Priests and Kings; ye are a consecrated People. In addition to this, or rather in aid of this, Circumcision was intended to distinguish the Jews by some indelible sign : and it was no less necessary, that Jewish children should be recognizable as Jews, than Jewish adults—not to mention the greater safety of the rite in infancy. Nor was it ever pretended that any Grace was conferred with it, or that the rite was significant of any inward or spiritual operation. In short, an unprejudiced and competent reader need only peruse the first thirty-three paragraphs of the eighteenth section of Taylor's Liberty of Prophesying ; and then compare with these the remainder of the Section added by him after the Restoration : those, namely, in which he *attempts* to overthrow his own arguments. I had almost said, *affects :* for such is the feebleness, and so palpable the sophistry of his answers, that I find it difficult to imagine, that Taylor himself could have been satisfied with them. The only plausible arguments apply with equal force to Baptist and Pædo-baptist ; and would prove, if they proved any thing, that both were wrong, and the Quakers only in the right.

Now, in the first place, it is obvious, that nothing conclusive can be drawn from the silence of the New Testament respecting a practice, which, if we suppose it already in use, must yet, from the character of the first converts, have been of comparatively rare occurrence ; and which from the predominant, and more concerning, objects and functions of the Apostolic writers (1 *Corinth.* i. 17.) was

not likely to have been mentioned otherwise than inciden-
tally, and very probably therefore might not have occurred
to them to mention at all. But, secondly, admitting that
the practice was introduced at a later period than that in
which the Acts of the Apostles and the Epistles were composed : I should yet be fully satisfied, that the Church
exercised herein a sound[1] discretion. On either supposition, therefore, it is never without regret that I see a
divine of our Church attempting to erect forts on a position
so evidently commanded by the strong-hold of his antagonists. I dread the use which the Socinians may make of
their example, and the Papists of their failure. Let me
not, however, deceive you. (*The reader understands, that I
suppose myself conversing with a Baptist.*) I am of opinion,
that the divines on your side are chargeable with a far
more grievous mistake, that of giving a carnal and *Judaizing*
interpretation to the various Gospel texts in which the
terms, *baptism* and *baptize*, occur, contrary to the express
and earnest admonitions of the Apostle Paul. And this I
say, without in the least retracting my former concession,
that the texts appealed to, as commanding or authorizing
Infant Baptism, are all without exception made to bear a
sense neither contained nor deducible : and likewise that
(historically considered) there exists no sufficient *positive*
evidence, that the Baptism of infants was instituted by the
Apostles in the practice of the Apostolic age.[2]

---

[1] That every the least *permissible* form and ordinance, which at
different times it might be expedient for the Church to enact, are pre-
enacted in the New Testament ; and that whatever is not to be found
there, ought to be allowed *no where*—this has been *asserted*. But that it
has been *proved*, or that the tenet is not to be placed among the *revul-
sionary* results of the Scripture-slighting Will-worship of the Romish
Church ; it will be more sincere to say, I disbelieve, than that I doubt.
It was chiefly, if not exclusively, in reference to the extravagances built
on this tenet, that the great Selden ventured to declare, that the words,
Scrutamini Scripturas, had set the world in an uproar.

Extremes *appear* to generate each other ; but if we look steadily,
there will most often be found some common error, that produces both
as its positive and negative poles. Thus superstitions go *by pairs*, like
the two Hungarian sisters, always quarrelling and *inveterately averse,*
but yet joined at the trunk.

[2] More than this I do not consider as necessary for the argument.
And as to Robinson's assertions in his History of Baptism, that infant

Lastly, we both coincide in the full conviction, that it is neither the outward ceremony of Baptism, under any form or circumstances, nor any other ceremony, but such a faith in Christ as tends to produce a conformity to his holy doctrines and example in heart and life, and which faith is itself a declared mean and condition of our partaking of his spiritual body, and of being *clothed upon* with his righteousness,—that properly makes us Christians, and can alone be enjoined as an Article of Faith necessary to Salvation, so that the denial thereof may be denounced as a damnable heresy. In the strictest sense of essential, this alone is the essential in Christianity, that the same spirit should be growing in us which was in the fulness of all perfection in Christ Jesus. Whatever else is named essential is such because, and only as far as, it is instrumental to this, or evidently implied herein. If the Baptists hold the *visible rite* to be indispensable to salvation, with what terror must they not regard every disease that befalls their children between youth and infancy ! But if they are saved by the faith of the parent, then the outward rite is not essential to salvation, otherwise than as the omission should arise from a spirit of disobedience : and in this case it is the cause, not the effect, the wilful and unbaptized heart, not the unbaptizing hand, that perils it. And surely it looks very like an *inconsistency* to admit the vicarious faith of the parents and the therein implied promise, that the child shall be Christianly bred up, and as much as in them lies prepared for the communion of saints—to admit this, as safe and sufficient in their own instance, and yet to denounce the same belief and practice as hazardous and

Baptism did not commence till the time of Cyprian, who condemning it as a general practice, allowed it in particular cases. by a dispensation of charity ; and that it did not actually become the ordinary rule of the Church, till Augustine in the fever of his Anti-Pelagian dispute had introduced the Calvinistic interpretation of Original Sin, and the dire state of Infants dying unbaptized—I am so far from acceding to them, that I reject the whole statement as rash, and not only unwarranted by the authorities he cites, but unanswerably confuted by Baxter, Wall, and many other learned Pædo-baptists before and since the publication of his work. I confine myself to the assertion—not that Infant Baptism was *not ;* but—that there exist no sufficient proofs that it *was* the practice of the Apostolic age.

unavailing in the Church—the same, I say, essentially, and only differing from their own by the presence of two or three Christian friends as additional securities, and by the promise being expressed!

But you, my filial friend! have studied Christ under a better teacher—the Spirit of Adoption, even the spirit that was in Paul, and which still speaks to us out of his writings. You remember and admire the saying of an old divine, that a ceremony duly instituted was a Chain of Gold round the Neck of Faith; but if in the wish to make it co-essential and consubstantial, you draw it closer and closer, it may strangle the Faith it was meant to deck and designate. You are not so unretentive a scholar as to have forgotten the *pateris et auro* of your Virgil: or if you were, you are not so inconsistent a reasoner, as to translate the Hebraism, spirit and fire in one place by spiritual fire, and yet to refuse to translate water and spirit by spiritual water in another place: or if, as I myself think, the different position marks a different sense, yet that the former must be *ejusdem generis* with the latter—the Water of Repentance, reformation in *conduct;* and the Spirit that which purifies the inmost *principle* of action, as fire purges the metal substantially and not cleansing the surface only!

But in this instance, it will be said, the ceremony, the outward and visible sign, is a Scripture ordinance. I will not reply, that the Romish priest says the same of the anointing of the sick with oil and the imposition of hands. No, my answer is: that this is a very sufficient reason for the continued observance of a ceremonial rite so derived and sanctioned, even though its own beauty, simplicity, and natural significancy had pleaded less strongly in its behalf. But it is no reason why the Church should forget, that the perpetuation of a thing does not alter the nature of the thing, and that a ceremony to be perpetuated is to be perpetuated as a *ceremony.* It is no reason why, knowing and experiencing even in the majority of her own members the proneness of the human mind to [1] superstition,

---

[1] Let me be permitted to repeat and apply the *note* in a former page. Superstition may be defined as *superstantium* (*cujusmodi sunt ceremoniæ et signa externa quæ, nisi in significando nihili sunt et ʃæne nihil*) *sub*stantiatio.

the Church might not rightfully and piously adopt the measures best calculated to check this tendency, and to correct the abuse, to which it had led in any particular rite. But of superstitious notions respecting the baptismal ceremony, and of abuse resulting, the instances were flagrant and notorious. Such, for instance, was the frequent deferring of the baptismal rite to a late period of life, and even to the death-bed, in the belief that the mystic water would cleanse the baptized person from all sin and (if he died immediately after the performance of the ceremony) send him pure and spotless into the other world.

Nor is this all. The preventive remedy applied by the Church is legitimated as well as additionally recommended by the following consideration. Where a ceremony answered and was intended to answer several purposes, which purposes at its first institution were blended in respect of *the time*, but which afterwards, by change of circumstances (as when, for instance, a large and ever-increasing proportion of the members of the Church, or those who at least bore the Christian name, were of Christian parents), were necessarily dis-united—*then* either the Church has no power or authority delegated to her (which is shifting the ground of controversy)—or she must be authorized to choose and determine, to which of the several purposes the ceremony should be attached.—Now one of the purposes of Baptism was—the making it *publicly manifest*, first, what individuals were to be regarded by the *world* (*Phil.* ii. 15.) as belonging to the visible communion of Christians : inasmuch as by their demeanour and apparent condition, the general estimation of *the city set on a hill and not to be hid* (*Matth.* v. 14.) could not but be affected—the city that even *in the midst of a crooked and perverse nation* was bound not only to give no cause, but by all innocent means to prevent every innocent occasion, of *rebuke*. Secondly, to mark out, for the Church itself, those that were entitled to that *especial* dearness, that watchful and disciplinary love and lovingkindness, which *over and above* the affections and duties of philanthropy and universal charity, Christ himself had enjoined, and with an emphasis and in a form significant of its great and especial importance,—*A New Commandment I*

give unto you, that ye love one another. By a charity wide
as sunshine, and comprehending the whole human race, the
body of Christians was to be placed in contrast with the
proverbial misanthropy and bigotry of the Jewish Church
and people : while yet they were to be distinguished and
known to all men, by the peculiar love and affection displayed by them towards the members of their own community ; thus exhibiting the intensity of sectarian attachment, yet by the no less notorious and exemplary practice
of the duties of universal benevolence, secured from the
charge so commonly brought against it, of being narrow
and exclusive. " How *kind* these Christians are to the poor
and afflicted, without distinction of religion or country ;
but how they *love each other !* "

Now combine with this the consideration before urged—
the duty, I mean, and necessity of checking the superstitious abuse of the baptismal rite : and I then ask, with
confidence, in what way could the Church have exercised a
sound discretion more wisely, piously, or effectively, than
by fixing, from among the several ends and purposes of
Baptism, the outward ceremony to the purposes here
mentioned ? How could the great body of Christians be
more plainly instructed as to the true nature of all outward
ordinances ? What can be conceived better calculated
to prevent the ceremony from being regarded as other and
more than a ceremony, if not the administration of the
same on an *object*, (yea, a dear and precious *object*) of
spiritual duties, though the *conscious* subject of spiritual
operations and graces only by anticipation and in hope ;—
a subject unconscious as a flower of the dew falling on it,
or the early rain, and thus emblematic of the myriads who
(as in our Indian empire, and henceforward, I trust, in
Africa) are temporally and even morally benefited by the
outward existence of Christianity, though as yet ignorant
of its saving truth ! And yet, on the other hand, what
more reverential than the application of this, the common
initiatory rite of the East sanctioned and appropriated by
Christ—its application, I say, to the very subjects, whom
he himself commanded to be *brought* to him—the children
in arms, respecting whom *Jesus was much displeased with
his disciples, who had rebuked those that brought them !* What

more expressive of the true character of that originant yet
generic stain, from which the Son of God, by his mysterious
incarnation and agony and death and resurrection, and by
the Baptism of the Spirit, came to cleanse the children of
Adam, than the exhibition of the outward element to
infants free from and incapable of *crime*, in whom the
evil principle was present only as *potential* being, and
whose outward semblance represented the kingdom of
Heaven ?   And can it—to a man, who would hold himself
deserving of *anathema maranatha* (1 *Cor.* xvi. 22.) if he
did not *love the Lord Jesus*—can it be nothing to such a
man, that the introduction and commendation of a new
inmate, a new spiritual ward, to the assembled brethren in
Christ (—and this, as I have shown above, was *one* purpose
of the baptismal ceremony) does in the baptism of an
infant recall our Lord's own presentation in the Temple on
the eighth day after his birth ?   Add to all these considerations the known fact of the frequent exposure and the
general light regard of infants, at the time when Infant
Baptism is by the Baptists supposed to have been first
ruled by the Catholic Church, not overlooking the humane
and charitable motives, that influenced Cyprian's decision
in its favour.   And then make present to your imagination, and meditatively contemplate the still continuing
tendency, the profitable, the *beautiful* effects, of this ordinance *now* and for so many centuries back, on the great
mass of the population throughout Christendom—the
softening, elevating exercise of faith and the conquest
over the senses, while in the form of a helpless crying babe
the presence, and the unutterable worth and value, of an
immortal being made capable of everlasting bliss are
solemnly proclaimed and carried home to the mind and
heart of the hearers and beholders !   Nor will you forget
the probable influence on the future education of the child,
the opportunity of instructing and impressing the friends,
relatives, and parents in their best and most docile mood.
These are, indeed, the *mollia tempora fandi.*

It is true, that by an unforeseen accident, and through the
propensity of all zealots to caricature partial truth into
total falsehood—it is too true, that a tree the very contrary
in quality of that shown to Moses (*Exod.* xv. 25.) was

afterwards *cast into the sweet waters from this fountain*, and made them like *the waters of Marah*, too bitter to be drunk. I allude to the Pelagian controversy, the perversion of the article of Original Sin by Augustine, and the frightful conclusions which this *durus pater infantum* drew from the article thus perverted. It is not, however, to the predecessors of this African, whoever they were that authorized Pædo-baptism, and at whatever period it first became general—it is not to the Church at the time being, that these consequences are justly imputable. She had done her best to preclude every superstition, by allowing in urgent cases any and every adult, man and woman, to administer the ceremonial part, the outward rite, of baptism: but reserving to the highest functionary of the Church (even to the exclusion of the co-presbyters) the more proper and spiritual purpose, namely, the declaration of repentance and belief, the free Choice of Christ, as his Lord, and the open profession of the Christian title by an individual in his own name and by his own deliberate act. *This* office of religion, the essentially moral and spiritual nature of which could not be mistaken, this most *solemn* office the Bishop alone was to perform.

Thus—as soon as the *purposes* of the ceremonial rite were by change of circumstances divided, that is, took place at different periods of the believer's life—to the *outward* purposes, where the effect was to be produced on the consciousness of others, the Church continued to affix the *outward rite;* while to the substantial and spiritual purpose, where the effect was to be produced on the individual's own mind, she gave its beseeming dignity by an ordinance not figurative, but standing in the direct cause and relation of *means* to the *end.*

In fine, there are two great purposes to be answered, each having its own subordinate purposes, and desirable consequences. The Church answers both, the Baptists one only. If, nevertheless, you would still prefer the union of the Baptismal rite with the Confirmation, and that the Presentation of Infants to the assembled Church had formed a separate institution, avowedly prospective—I answer: first, that such for a long time and to a late period was my own judgment. But even then it seemed

to me a point, as to which an indifference would be less inconsistent in a lover of truth, than a zeal to separation in
a professed lover of peace. And secondly, I would revert
to the history of the Reformation, and the calamitous
accident of the Peasants' War: when the poor ignorant
multitude, driven frantic by the intolerable oppressions of
their feudal lords, rehearsed all the outrages that were
acted in our own times by the Parisian populace headed by
Danton, Marat, and Robespierre; and on the same out-
rageous principles, and in assertion of the same RIGHTS OF
BRUTES to the subversion of all the DUTIES OF MEN. In our
times, most fortunately for the interest of religion and
morality, or of their prudential substitutes at least, the
name of Jacobin was every where associated with that of
Atheist and Infidel. Or rather, Jacobinism and Infidelity
were the two heads of the Revolutionary Geryon—connatural misgrowths of the same monster-trunk. In the
German Convulsion, on the contrary, by a mere but most
unfortunate *accident*, the same code of *Caliban* juris-
prudence, the same sensual and murderous excesses, were
connected with the name of Anabaptist. The abolition of
magistracy, community of goods, the right of plunder,
polygamy, and whatever else was fanatical were comprised in the word, Anabaptism. It is not to be imagined,
that the Fathers of the Reformation could, without
a miraculous influence, have taken up the question of
Infant Baptism with the requisite calmness and freedom
of spirit. It is not to be wished, that they should have
entered on the discussion. Nay, I will go farther. Unless
the abolition of Infant Baptism can be shown to be involved in some fundamental article of faith, unless the
practice could be proved fatal or imminently perilous to
salvation, the Reformers would not have been justified in
exposing the yet tender and struggling cause of Pro-
testantism to such certain and violent prejudices as this
innovation would have excited. Nothing less than the
whole substance and efficacy of the Gospel faith was the
prize, which they had wrestled for and won; but won
from enemies still in the field, and on the watch to re-
take, at all costs, the sacred treasure, and consign it
once again to darkness and oblivion. If there be a *time*

for all things, this was not the time for an innovation, that would and must have been followed by the triumph of the enemies of Scriptural Christianity, and the alienation of the governments, that had espoused and protected it.

Remember, I say this on the supposition of the question's not being what you do not pretend it to be, an essential of the Faith, by which we are saved. But should it likewise be conceded, that it is a *disputable* point—and that in point of fact it is and has been disputed by divines, whom no pious Christian of any denomination will deny to have been faithful and eminent servants of Christ; should it, I say, be likewise conceded that the question of Infant Baptism is a point, on which two Christians, who perhaps differ on this point only, may differ without giving just ground for impeaching the piety or competence of either—in this case I am obliged to infer, that the person who *at any time* can regard this difference as *singly* warranting a separation from a religious Community, must think of schism under another point of view, than that in which I have been taught to contemplate it by St. Paul in his Epistles to the Corinthians.

Let me add a few words on a diversity of doctrine closely connected with this : the opinions of Doctors Mant and D'Oyly as opposed to those of the (so called) Evangelical clergy. "The Church of England" (says Wall) [1] "does not

---

[1] Conference between Two Men that had Doubts about Infant Baptism. By W. Wall, Author of the History of Infant Baptism, and Vicar of Shoreham in Kent. A very sensible little tract, and written in an excellent spirit : but it failed, I confess, in satisfying my mind as to the existence of any decisive proofs or documents of Infant Baptism having been an Apostolic usage, or specially intended in any part of the New Testament : though deducible *generally* from many passages, and in perfect accordance with the *spirit* of the whole.

A mighty wrestler in the cause of Spiritual Religion and *Gospel* morality, in whom more than in any other contemporary I seem to see the spirit of Luther revived, expressed to me his doubts whether we have a right to deny that an infant is capable of a spiritual influence. To such a man I could not feel justified in returning an answer *ex tempore*, or without having first submitted my convictions to a fresh revisal. I owe him, however, a deliberate answer ; and take this opportunity of discharging the debt.

The objection supposes and assumes the very point which is denied, or

require assent and consent" to either opinion " in order to
lay communion." But I will suppose the person a *minister :*
but minister of a Church which has expressly disclaimed
all pretence to infallibility; a Church which in the construction of its Liturgy and Articles is known to have
worded certain passages for the purpose of rendering them
subscribable by both A and Z—that is, the opposite
parties as to the points in controversy. I suppose this
person's convictions those of Z, and that out of five passages
there are three, the more natural and obvious sense of
which is in his favour; and two of which, though not
absolutely *precluding* a different sense, yet the more probable
interpretation is in favour of A, that is, of those who do

at least disputed—namely, that Infant Baptism is specially injoined in the
Scriptures. If an express passage to this purport *had* existed in the New
Testament—the other passages, which evidently imply a spiritual operation
under the condition of a preceding spiritual act on the part of the person
baptized, remaining as now—*then* indeed, as the only way of removing
the apparent contradiction, it *might* be allowable to call on the Anti-
pædobaptist to prove the negative—namely, that an infant a week old is
not a subject capable or susceptible of spiritual agency. And, *vice
versa*, should it be made known to us, that infants are not without
reflection and self-consciousness—*then*, doubtless, we should be entitled
to infer that they were capable of a spiritual operation, and consequently
of that which is signified in the baptismal rite administered to adults.
But what does this prove for those, who (as D D. Mant and D'Oyly)
not only cannot show, but who do not themselves profess to believe, the
self-consciousness of a new-born babe, but who rest the defence of Infant
Baptism on the *assertion*, that God was pleased to affix the performance
of this rite to his offer of Salvation, as the indispensable, though
arbitrary, condition of the infant's salvability ?—As Kings in former
ages, when they conferred lands in perpetuity, would sometimes, as the
condition of the tenure, exact from the beneficiary a hawk, or some
trifling ceremony, as the putting on or off of their sandals, or whatever
else royal caprice or the whim of the moment might suggest. But *you*,
honoured Irving, are as little disposed, as myself, to favour *such*
doctrine !

> Friend, pure of heart and fervent ! we have learnt
> A different lore ! We may not thus profane
> The Idea and Name of Him whose absolute Will
> *Is* Reason—Truth Supreme !—Essential Order ! [1]

---

[1] For a further opinion upon Edward Irving see note at pp. 153-4 of
the 1839 edition of Coleridge's ' Church and State.'—Ed.

not consider the Baptism of an Infant as *prospective*, but
hold it to be an *opus operans et in præsenti*.   Then I say,
that if such a person regards these two sentences or single
passages as obliging or warranting him to abandon the
flock entrusted to his charge, and either to join such, as
are the avowed Enemies of the Church on the double
ground of its particular Constitution and of its being an
Establishment, or to set up a separate Church for himself
—I cannot avoid the conclusion, that either his conscience
is morbidly sensitive in one speck to the exhaustion of the
sensibility in a far larger portion; or that he must have
discovered some mode, beyond the reach of my conjectural
powers, of interpreting the Scriptures enumerated in the
following excerpt from the popular tract before cited, in
which the writer expresses an opinion, to which I assent
with my whole heart: namely,

"That all Christians in the world that hold the same
fundamentals ought to make one Church, though differing
in lesser opinions; and that the sin, the mischief, and
danger to the souls of men, that divide into those many
sects and parties among us, does (for the most of them)
consist not so much in the opinions themselves, as in their
dividing and separating for them.   And in support of this
tenet, I will refer you to some plain places of Scripture,
which if you please now to peruse, I will be silent the
while.   See what our Saviour himself says, *John* x. 16.
John xvii. 11.   And what the primitive Christians practised,
Acts ii. 46, and iv. 32.   And what St. Paul says, 1 *Cor.* i.
10, 11, 12, and 2, 3, 4; also the whole 12th chapter: *Eph.*
ii. 18, &c. to the end.   Where the Jewish and Gentile
Christians are showed to be *one body, one household, one
temple fitly framed together*: and yet these were of different
opinions in several matters.—Likewise chap. iii. 6, iv.
1—13. *Phil.* ii. 1, 2, where he uses the most solemn adjura-
tions to this purpose.   But I would more especially recommend to you the reading of *Gal.* v. 20, 21. *Phil.* iii. 15,
16, the 14th chapter to the *Romans*, and part of the 15th,
to verse 7, and also *Rom.* xv. 17.

"Are not these passages plain, full, and earnest?   Do
you find any of the controverted points to be determined
by Scripture in words nigh so plain or pathetic?"

Marginal Note written (in 1816) by the Author in his own copy of Wall's work.

This and the two following pages are excellent. If I addressed the ministers recently seceded, I would first prove from Scripture and Reason the justness of their doctrines concerning Baptism and Conversion. 2. I would show, that even in respect of the Prayer-book, Homilies, &c. of the Church of England, taken as a whole, their opponents were comparatively as ill off as themselves, if not worse. 3. That the few mistakes or inconvenient phrases of the Baptismal Service did not impose on the conscience the necessity of resigning the pastoral office. 4. That even if they did, this would by no means justify schism from Lay-membership : or else there could be no schism except from an immaculate and infallible Church. Now, as our Articles have declared that no Church is or ever was such, it would follow that there is no such sin as that of Schism—that is, that St. Paul wrote falsely or idly. 5. That the escape through the channel of Dissent is from the frying-pan to the fire—or, to use a less worn and vulgar simile, the escape of a leech from a glass-jar of water into the naked and open air. But never, never, would I in one breath allow my Church to be fallible, and in the next contend for her absolute freedom from all error—never confine inspiration and perfect truth to the Scriptures, and then scold for the perfect truth of each and every word in the Prayer-book. Enough for me, if in my heart of hearts, free from all fear of man and all lust of preferment, I believe (as I do) the Church of England to be the *most* Apostolic Church; that its doctrines and ceremonies contain nothing dangerous to Righteousness or Salvation ; and that the imperfections in its Liturgy are spots indeed, but spots on the sun, which impede neither its light nor its heat, so as to prevent the good seed from growing in a good soil and producing fruits of Redemption.[1]

*** The author had written and intended to insert a similar exposition on the Eucharist. But as the leading view has been given in the Comment on Redemption, its length induces him to defer it, together with the Articles on Faith and the philosophy of Prayer, to a small supplementary volume.[2]

---

[1] Here the editor of the 1843 edition was able to give two pages of additional matter by the author, tending, as Coleridge said, to the "clearing up" of "the chapter on Baptism," and the proving "the substantial accordance of my scheme with that of our Church." The addition is from Coleridge's MS. Note-books, and bears date May 8, 1828.—ED.

[2] This note appeared in the early editions only. The "supplementary volume" was never published, though the "Essay on Faith," at p. 425, v. 4, of Coleridge's "Remains" (1838), and "Notes on the Book of Common Prayer" (p. 5, v. 3, the same), may be the parts here mentioned as written to appear in it. We republish these two fragments at the end of the present volume, pp. 341 and 350.—ED.

CONCLUSION.

I AM not so ignorant of the temper and tendency of the age in which I live, as either to be unprepared for the *sort* of remarks which the literal interpretation of the Evangelist will call forth, or to attempt an answer to them. Visionary ravings, obsolete whimsies, transcendental trash, and the like, I leave to pass at the price current among those who are willing to receive abusive phrases as substitutes for argument. Should any suborner of anonymous criticism have engaged some literary bravo or buffoon beforehand, to vilify this work, as in former instances, I would give a friendly hint to the operative critic that he may compile an excellent article for the occasion, and with very little trouble, out of Warburton's tract on Grace and the Spirit, and the Preface to the same. There is, however, one objection which will so often be heard from men, whose talents and reputed moderation must give a weight to their words, that I owe it both to my own character and to the interests of my readers, not to leave it unnoticed. The charge will probably be worded in this way :—There is nothing new in all this ! (*as if novelty were any merit in questions of Revealed Religion !*) It is *Mysticism*, all taken out of William Law, after he had lost his senses, poor man ! in brooding over the visions of a delirious German cobbler, Jacob Behmen.

Of poor Jacob Behmen I have delivered my sentiments at large in another work. Those who have condescended to look into his writings must know, that his characteristic errors are ; first, the mistaking the accidents and pecu-liarities of his own over-wrought mind for realities and modes of thinking common to all minds : and secondly, the confusion of nature, that is, the active powers com-municated to matter, with God the Creator. And if the same persons have done more than merely looked into the present volume, they must have seen, that to eradicate, and, if possible, to preclude both the one and the other stands prominent among its avowed objects.[1]

Of William Law's works I am acquainted with the " Serious Call; " and besides this I remember to have read a small tract on Prayer, if I mistake not, as I easily may, it being at least six-and-twenty years [2] since I saw it. He may in this or in other tracts have quoted the same passages from the fourth Gospel as I have done. But surely this affords no presumption that my conclusions are the same with his ; still less, that they are drawn from the same premisses : and least of all, that they were adopted from his writings. Whether Law has used the phrase, assimilation by faith, I know not ; but I know that I should expose myself to a just charge of an idle parade of my reading, if I recapitulated the tenth part of the authors, ancient, and modern, Romish and Reformed, from Law to Clemens Alexandrinus and Irenæus, in whose works the same phrase occurs in the same sense. And after all, on such a subject how worse than childish is the whole dispute!

Is the fourth Gospel authentic ? ˅ And is the interpretation I have given, true or false ? These are the only questions which a wise man would put, or a Christian be anxious to answer. I not only believe it to be the true sense of the texts ; but I assert that it is the only true, rational, and even *tolerable* sense. And this position alone I conceive myself interested in defending. I have studied with an open and fearless spirit the attempts of sundry learned critics of the Continent, to invalidate the authenticity of this Gospel, before and since Eichhorn's Vindication. The result has been a clearer assurance and (as far as this was possible) a yet deeper conviction of the genuineness of *all* the writings, which the Church has attributed to this Apostle. That those, who have formed an opposite conclusion, should object to the use of expressions which they had ranked among the most obvious marks of spuriousness, follows as a matter of course. But that men, who with a clear and cloudless assent receive the sixth

---

[1] See Preliminary to Aphorisms on Spiritual Religion, &c.—Ed.
[2] So in first edition, 1825.—Ed.

chapter of this Gospel as a faithful, nay, *inspired* record of
an actual discourse, should take offence at the repetition of
words which the Redeemer himself, in the perfect fore-
knowledge that they would confirm the disbelieving,
alienate the unsteadfast, and transcend the present capacity
even of his own Elect, had chosen as the *most* appropriate ;
and which, after the most decisive proofs, that they *were*
misinterpreted by the greater number of his hearers, and
not understood by any, he nevertheless repeated with
stronger emphasis and *without comment* as the *only* appropriate symbols of the great truth he was declaring, and to
realize which ἐγένετο σὰρξ ;[1]—that in their own discourses
these men should hang back from all express reference to
these words, as if they were afraid or ashamed of them,
though the earliest recorded ceremonies and liturgical
forms of the primitive Church are absolutely inexplicable,
except in connexion with this discourse, and with the
mysterious and *spiritual,* not allegorical and merely ethical,
import of the same ; and though this import is solemnly
and in the most unequivocal terms asserted and taught by
their own Church, even in her Catechism, or compendium
of doctrines necessary for all her members ;—*this* I may,
perhaps, *understand ;* but *this* I am not able to vindicate or
excuse.

There is, however, one opprobrious phrase which it may
be profitable for my younger readers that I should explain,
namely, Mysticism. And for this purpose I will quote a
sentence or two from a Dialogue which, had my prescribed
limits permitted, I should have attached to the present
work ; but which with an Essay on the Church, as instituted by Christ, and as an establishment of the State, and a
series of letters on the right and the superstitious use and

---

[1] Of which our *he was made flesh,* is an inadequate translation.—The
Church of England in this as in other doctrinal points, has preserved the
golden mean between the superstitious reverence of the Romanists, and
the avowed contempt of the Sectarians, for the writings of the Fathers,
and the authority and unimpeached traditions of the Church during the
first three or four centuries. And how, consistently with this honour-
able characteristic of our Church, a minister of the same could, on the
Sacramentary scheme now in fashion, return even a plausible answer
to Arnauld's great work on Transubstantiation (not without reason the
boast of the Romish Church), exceeds my powers of conjecture.

estimation of the Bible, will appear in a small volume by themselves, should the reception given to the present volume encourage or permit the publication.[1]

MYSTICS AND MYSTICISM.

Antinöus.—" What do you call Mysticism ? And do you use the word in a good or a bad sense ? "

Nöus.—" In the latter only; as far, at least, as we are now concerned with it. When a man refers to *inward feelings* and *experiences,* of which mankind at large are not conscious, as evidences of the truth of any opinion—such a man I call a Mystic : and the grounding of any theory or belief on accidents and anomalies of individual sensations or fancies, and the use of peculiar terms invented, or perverted from their ordinary significations, for the purpose of expressing these *idiosyncrasies* and pretended facts of interior consciousness, I name Mysticism. Where the error consists simply in the Mystic's attaching to these anomalies of his individual temperament the character of *reality,* and in receiving them as permanent truths, having a subsistence in the Divine Mind, though revealed to himself alone; but entertains this persuasion without demanding or expecting the same faith in his neighbours—I should regard it as a species of enthusiasm, always indeed to be deprecated, but yet capable of co-existing with many excellent qualities both of head and heart. But when the Mystic by ambition or still meaner passions, or (as sometimes is the case) by an uneasy and self-doubting state of mind which seeks confirmation in outward sympathy, is led to impose his faith, as a duty, on mankind generally : and when with such views he asserts that the same experiences would be vouchsafed, the same truths revealed, to *every man* but for his secret wickedness and unholy will —such a Mystic is a Fanatic, and in certain states of the public mind a dangerous member of society. And most

---

[1] These were the afterwards published ' On the Church and State, according to the Idea of Each,' 1830, and ' Confessions of an Inquiring Spirit,' 1840. The latter we republish in the present volume; see p. 285.—ED.

so in those ages and countries in which Fanatics of elder standing are allowed to persecute the fresh competitor. For under these predicaments, Mysticism, though originating in the singularities of an individual nature, and therefore essentially anomalous, is nevertheless highly *contagious*. It is apt to collect a swarm and cluster *circum fana*, around the new *fane :* and therefore merits the name of Fanaticism, or as the Germans say, *Schwärmerey*, that is, *swarm-making*."

We will return to the harmless species—the enthusiastic Mystics ;—a species that may again be subdivided into two ranks. And it will not be other than germane to the subject, if I endeavour to describe them in a sort of allegory, or parable. Let us imagine a poor pilgrim benighted in a wilderness or desert, and pursuing his way in the starless dark with a lantern in his hand. Chance or his happy genius leads him to an Oasis or natural Garden, such as in the creations of my youthful fancy I supposed Enos [1] the Child of Cain to have found. And here, hungry

[1] Will the reader forgive me if I attempt at once to illustrate and relieve the subject by annexing the first stanza of the poem composed in the same year in which I wrote the Ancient Mariner and the first book of Christabel ?

> " Encinctur'd with a twine of leaves,
> That leafy twine his only dress !
> A lovely boy was plucking fruits
> In a moonlight wilderness.*
> The moon was bright, the air was free,
> And fruits and flowers together grew
> On many a shrub and many a tree :
> And all put on a gentle hue,
> Hanging in the shadowy air
> Like a picture rich and rare.
> It was a climate where, they say,
> The night is more belov'd than day.
> But who that beauteous boy beguil'd,
> That beauteous boy to linger here ?
> Alone, by night, a little child,
> In place so silent and so wild—
> Has he no friend, no loving mother near ? "
>
> WANDERINGS OF CAIN.

---

* " By moonlight, in a wilderness."—' Poetical Works,' edit. 1863.—ED.

and thirsty, the way-wearied man rests at a fountain; and the taper of his lantern throws its light on an over-shadowing tree, a boss of snow-white blossoms, through which the green and growing fruits peeped, and the ripe golden fruitage glowed. Deep, vivid, and faithful are the impressions, which the lovely Imagery comprised within the scanty circle of light, makes and leaves on his memory! But scarcely has he eaten of the fruits and drunk of the fountain, ere scared by the roar and howl from the desart he hurries forward: and as he passes with hasty steps through grove and glade, shadows and imperfect behold-ings and vivid fragments of things distinctly seen blend with the past and present shapings of his brain. Fancy modifies sight. His dreams transfer their forms to real objects; and these lend a substance and an *outness* to his dreams. Apparitions greet him; and when at a distance from this enchanted land, and on a different track, the dawn of day discloses to him a caravan, a troop of his fellow-men, his memory, which is itself half fancy, is interpolated afresh by every attempt to recall, connect, and *piece out* his recollections. His narration is received as a madman's tale. He shrinks from the rude laugh and contemptuous sneer, and retires into himself. Yet the craving for sympathy, strong in proportion to the intensity of his convictions, impels him to unbosom himself to abstract auditors; and the poor Quietist becomes a Pen-man, and, all too poorly stocked for the writer's trade, he borrows his phrases and figures from the only writings to which he has had access, the sacred books of his religion. And thus I shadow out the enthusiast Mystic of the first sort; at the head of which stands the illuminated Teutonic theosopher and shoemaker, honest Jacob Behmen, born near Gorlitz, in Upper Lusatia, in the 17th of our Elizabeth's reign, and who died in the 22nd of her suc-cessor's.

To delineate a Mystic of the second and higher order, we need only endow our pilgrim with equal gifts of nature, but these developed and displayed by all the aids and arts of education and favourable fortune. *He* is on his way to the Mecca of his ancestral and national faith, with a well-guarded and numerous procession of merchants and fellow-

pilgrims, on the established track. At the close of day
the caravan has halted: the full moon rises on the desert:
and he strays forth alone, out of sight but to no unsafe
distance; and chance leads *him* too, to the same oasis or
Islet of Verdure on the Sea of Sand. He wanders at
leisure in its maze of beauty and sweetness, and thrids his
way through the odorous and flowering thickets into open
spots of greenery, and discovers statues and memorial
characters, grottos, and refreshing caves. But the moon-
shine, the imaginative poesy of nature, spreads its soft
shadowy charm over all, conceals distances, and magnifies
heights, and modifies relations: and fills up vacuities with
its own whiteness, counterfeiting substance; and where
the dense shadows lie, makes solidity imitate hollowness;
and gives to all objects a tender visionary hue and softening. Interpret the moonlight and the shadows as the
peculiar genius and sensibility of the individual's own
spirit: and here you have the other sort: a Mystic, an
Enthusiast of a nobler breed—a Fenelon. But the resi-
dentiary, or the frequent visitor of the favoured spot, who
has scanned its beauties by steady day-light, and mastered
its true proportions and lineaments, he will discover that
both pilgrims have indeed been there. *He* will know, that
the delightful dream, which the latter tells, is a dream of
truth; and that even in the bewildered tale of the former
there is truth mingled with the dream.

But the Source, the Spring-head, of the Charges which
I anticipate, lies deep. Materialism, conscious and avowed
Materialism, is in ill repute: and a confessed Materialist
therefore a rare character. But if the faith be ascertained
by the fruits: if the predominant, though most often un-
suspected, persuasion is to be learnt from the influences,
under which the thoughts and affections of the man move
and take their direction; I must reverse the position.
ONLY NOT ALL ARE MATERIALISTS. Except a few individuals,
and those for the most part of a single sect: every one,
who calls himself a Christian, holds himself to have a soul
as well as a body. He distinguishes mind from matter,
the *subject* of his consciousness from the *objects* of the same.
The former is his mind: and he says, it is immaterial.
But though *subject* and *substance* are words of kindred

roots, nay, little less than equivalent terms, yet nevertheless it is exclusively to sensible *objects*, to bodies, to modifications of matter, that he habitually attaches the attributes of reality, of substance. Real and tangible, substantial and material, are synonyms for him. He never indeed asks himself, what he means by Mind? But if he did, and tasked himself to return an honest answer—as to what, at least, he had hitherto meant by it—he would find, that he had described it by negatives, as the opposite of bodies, for example, as a somewhat opposed to solidity, to visibility, and the like, as if you could abstract the capacity of a vessel, and conceive of it as a somewhat by itself, and then give to the emptiness the properties of containing, holding, being entered, and so forth. In short, though the proposition would perhaps be angrily denied in words, yet *in fact* he thinks of his *mind*, as a *property*, or *accident* of a something else, that he calls a *soul* or *spirit*: though the very same difficulties must recur, the moment he should attempt to establish the difference. For either this soul or spirit is nothing but a thinner body, a finer mass of matter: or the attribute of self-subsistency vanishes from the soul on the same grounds, on which it is refused to the mind.

I am persuaded, however, that the dogmatism of the Corpuscular School, though it still exerts an influence on men's notions and phrases, has received a mortal blow from the increasingly *dynamic* spirit of the physical sciences now highest in public estimation. And it may safely be predicted that the results will extend beyond the intention of those, who are gradually effecting this revolution. It is not chemistry alone that will be indebted to the genius of Davy, Oersted, and their compeers: and not as the founder of physiology and philosophic anatomy alone, will mankind love and revere the name of John Hunter. These men have not only *taught*, they have compelled us to admit, that the immediate objects of our *senses*, or rather the grounds of the visibility and tangibility of all objects of sense, bear the same *relation* and similar proportion to the *intelligible* object—that is, to the object which we actually *mean* when we say, "It is such or such a thing," or "I have seen this or that,"—as the paper, ink, and differently combined straight and curved lines of an edition of Homer bear to what we understand by the words Iliad and Odyssey. Nay, nothing would be more easy than so to construct the paper, ink, painted capitals, and the like, of a printed disquisition on the eye, or the muscles and cellular texture (the flesh) of the human body, as to bring together every one of the sensible and ponderable *stuffs* or elements, that are *sensuously* perceived in the eye itself, or in the flesh itself. Carbon and nitrogen, oxygen and hydrogen, sulphur, phosphorus, and one or two metals and metallic bases, constitute the whole. It cannot be these, therefore, that we mean by an *eye*, by our *body*. But perhaps it may be a particular *combination* of these? But here comes a question: In this term do you or do you not include the *principle*, the *operating cause*, of the combination? If *not*, then detach this eye from the body. Look steadily at it—as it might lie on the marble slab of a dissecting room. Say it were the eye of a murderer, a Bellingham: or the eye of a murdered patriot, a Sidney!—Behold it, handle it, with its various accompaniments or constituent parts, of tendon, ligament, membrane, blood-vessel, gland, humours; its nerves of sense, of sensation, and of motion. Alas! all these names like that of the organ itself, are so many Anachronisms, figures of speech to express that which has been: as when the Guide points with his finger to a heap of stones, and tells the traveller, "That is Babylon, or Persepolis."—Is this cold jelly *the light of the body?* Is this the *Micranthropos* in the marvellous microcosm? Is this what you *mean* when you well define the eye as the telescope and the mirror of the soul, the seat and agent of an almost magical power?

Pursue the same inquisition with every other part of the body, whether integral or simply ingredient; and let a Berzelius or a Hatchett be your interpreter, and demonstrate to you what it is that in each actually meets your senses. And when you have heard the scanty catalogue, ask yourself if *these* are indeed the living *flesh*, the *blood* of life? Or not far rather—I speak of what, as a man of common sense, you really *do*, not what, as a philosopher, you *ought* to believe—is it not, I say, far rather the distinct and individualized agency that by the given combinations utters and bespeaks its presence? Justly and with

strictest propriety of language may I say, *speaks*. It is to
the coarseness of our senses, or rather to the defect and
limitation of our percipient faculty, that the *visible* object
appears the same even for a moment.   The characters,
which I am now shaping on this paper, abide.   Not only
the forms remain the same, but the particles of the colour-
ing stuff are fixed, and, for an indefinite period at least,
remain the same.   But the particles that constitute the
size, the visibility of an organic structure[1] are in perpetual
flux.   They are to the combining and constitutive power
as the pulses of air to the voice of a discourser; or of
one who sings a roundelay.   The same words may be
repeated ; but in each second of time the articulated air
hath passed away, and each act of articulation appropriates
and gives momentary form to a new and other portion.   As
the column of blue smoke from a cottage chimney in the
breathless summer noon, or the steadfast-seeming cloud on
the edge-point of a hill in the driving air-current, which
momently condensed and recomposed is the common phantom of a thousand successors ;—such is the flesh, which
our *bodily* eyes transmit to us ; which our palates taste ;
which our hands touch.

But perhaps the material particles possess this combining power by inherent reciprocal attractions, repulsions,
and elective affinities ; and are themselves the joint artists
of their own combinations ?   I will not reply, though well
I might, that this would be to solve one problem by
another, and merely to shift the mystery.   It will be sufficient to remind the thoughtful querist, that ever herein
consists the essential difference, the contra-distinction, of
an organ from a machine ; that not only the characteristic
shape is evolved from the invisible central power, but the
material mass itself is acquired by assimilation.   The germinal power of the plant transmutes the fixed air and the
elementary base of water into grass or leaves ; and on
these the organific principle in the ox or the elephant
exercises an alchemy still more stupendous.   As the unseen
agency weaves its magic eddies, the foliage becomes
indifferently the bone and its marrow, the pulpy brain, or

[1] See p. 40.—ED.

the solid ivory. That what you see *is* blood, *is* flesh, is itself the work, or shall I say, the translucence, of the invisible Energy, which soon surrenders or abandons them to inferior powers (for there is no pause nor chasm in the activities of Nature), which repeat a similar metamorphosis according to *their* kind;—these are not fancies, conjectures, or even hypotheses, but *facts;* to deny which is impossible, not to reflect on which is ignominious. And we need only reflect on them with a calm and silent spirit to learn the utter emptiness and unmeaningness of the vaunted Mechanico-corpuscular Philosophy, with both its twins, Materialism on the one hand, and Idealism, rightlier named *Subjective Idolism*, on the other: the one obtruding on us a World of Spectres and Apparitions ; the other a mazy Dream !

Let the Mechanic or Corpuscular Scheme, which in its absoluteness and strict consistency was first introduced by Des Cartes, be judged by the results. By its fruits shall it be known.

In order to submit the various phenomena of moving bodies to geometrical construction, we are under the necessity of abstracting from corporeal substance all its *positive* properties, and obliged to consider bodies as differing from equal portions of space [1] only by figure and

---

[1] Such is the conception of body in Des Cartes' own system, *body* is every where confounded with *matter*, and might in the Cartesian sense be defined, Space or Extension, with the attribute of Visibility. As Des Cartes at the same time zealously asserted the existence of intelligential beings, the reality and independent Self-subsidence of the soul, Berkeleyanism or Spinosism was the immediate and necessary consequence. Assume a *plurality* of self-subsisting souls, and we have Berkeleyanism ; assume one only (*unam et unicam substantiam*), and you have Spinosism, that is, the assertion of one infinite self-subsistent, with the two attributes of thinking and appearing. *Cogitatio infinita sine centro, et omniformis apparitio.* How far the Newtonian *vis inertiæ* (interpreted any otherwise than as an arbitrary term = x y z, to represent the unknown but necessary supplement or integration of the Cartesian notion of body) has patched up the flaw, I leave for more competent judges to decide. But should any one of my Readers feel an interest in the speculative principles of Natural Philosophy, and should be master of the German language, I warmly recommend for his perusal the earliest known publication of the great founder of the Critical Philosophy (written in the twenty-second year of his age!), on the then eager controversy between the Leibnitzian

mobility. And as a *fiction of science*, it would be difficult
to overvalue this invention. It possesses the same merits
in relation to Geometry that the atomic theory has in
relation to algebraic calculus. But in contempt of common
sense, and in direct opposition to the express declarations
of the inspired historian (*Genesis i.*) and to the tone and
spirit of the Scriptures throughout, Des Cartes propounded it as *truth of fact*: and instead of a World *created*
and filled with productive forces by the Almighty *Fiat*,
left a lifeless Machine whirled about by the dust of its
own Grinding: as if Death could come from the living
Fountain of Life; Nothingness and Phantom from
the Plenitude of Reality! the Absoluteness of Creative
Will!

Holy! Holy! Holy! let me be deemed mad by all men,
if such be thy ordinance: but, O! from *such* madness save
and preserve me, my God!

When, however, after a short interval, the genius of
Kepler, expanded and organized in the soul of Newton, and
there (if I may hazard so bold an expression) refining
itself into an almost celestial clearness, had expelled the
Cartesian *vortices*;[1] then the necessity of an active power,

and the French and English Mathematicians, respecting the living
forces—*Gedanken von der wahren Schätzung der lebendigen Kräfte:*
1747—in which Kant demonstrates the *right reasoning* to be with the
latter; but the Truth of *Fact*, the evidence of *Experience*, with the
former; and gives the explanation, namely: Body, or Corporeal
Nature, is something else and more than geometrical extension, even
with the addition of a *vis inertiæ*. And Leibnitz, with the Bernouillis,
erred in the attempt to demonstrate geometrically a problem not susceptible of geometrical construction.—The tract, with the succeeding
Himmels-system, may with propriety be placed, after the *Principia* of
Newton, among the striking instances of early Genius; and as the
first product of the Dynamic Philosophy in the Physical Sciences,
from the time, at least, of Giordano Bruno, whom the idolaters burnt
for an Atheist, at Rome, in the year 1600. See the Friend,' pp. 151-
55. [Or pp. 69, 70, Bohn's edition.—ED.]

[1] For Newton's own doubtfully suggested ether, or *most* subtle
fluid, as the ground and immediate Agent in the phenomena of universal
gravitation, was either not adopted or soon abandoned by his disciples;
not only as introducing, against his own canons of right reasoning,
an *ens imaginarium* into physical science, a suf*fiction* in the place of a
legitimate sup*position;* but because the substance (assuming it to exist)
must itself form part of the problem, it was meant to solve. Meantime
Leibnitz's pre-established harmony, which originated in Spinosa, found

of positive forces present in the material universe, forced itself on the conviction. For as a Law without a Lawgiver is a mere abstraction ; so a *Law* without an Agent to realize it, a *Constitution* without an abiding Executive, is, in fact, not a Law but *an Idea*. In the profound emblem of the great tragic poet, it is the powerless Prometheus fixed on a barren Rock. And what was the result ? How was this necessity provided for ? God himself—my hand trembles as I write ! Rather, then, let me employ the word, which the religious feeling, in its perplexity suggested as the substitute—the *Deity itself* was declared to be the real agent, the actual gravitating power ! The law and the law-giver were identified. God (says Dr. Priestley) not only does, but *is* every thing. *Jupiter est quodcunque vides*. And thus a system, which commenced by excluding all life and immanent activity from the visible universe and evacuating the natural world of all nature, ended by substituting the Deity, and reducing the Creator to a mere anima mundi : a scheme that has no advantage over Spinosism but its inconsistency, which does indeed make it suit a certain Order of intellects, who, like the *pleuronectœ* (or flat fish) in ichthyology which have both eyes on the same side, never see but half of a subject at one time, and forgetting the one before they get to the other are sure not to detect any inconsistency between them.

And what has been the consequence ? An increasing unwillingness to contemplate the Supreme Being in his *personal* attributes : and thence a distaste to all the peculiar doctrines of the Christian Faith, the Trinity, the Incarnation of the Son of God, and Redemption. The young and ardent, ever too apt to mistake the inward triumph in the detection of error for a positive love of truth, are among the first and most frequent victims to this epidemic *fastidium*. Alas ! even the sincerest seekers after light are not safe from the contagion. Some have I known, constitutionally religious—I speak feelingly ; for I

no acceptance ; and, lastly, the notion of a corpuscular substance, with properties *put* into it, like a pincushion hidden by the pins, could pass with the unthinking only for any thing more than a confession of, ignorance, or technical terms expressing a hiatus of scientific insight.

speak of that which for a brief period was my own state—
who under this unhealthful influence have been so estranged
from the heavenly *Father*, the *Living* God, as even to
shrink from the personal pronouns as applied to the Deity.
But many do I know, and yearly meet with, in whom a
false and sickly *taste* co-operates with the prevailing
fashion : many, who find the God of Abraham, Isaac, and
Jacob, far too *real*, too substantial; who feel it more in
harmony with their indefinite sensations

> To worship Nature in the hill and valley,
> Not knowing what they love :—

and (to use the language, but not the sense or purpose of
the great poet of our age) would fain substitute for the
Jehovah of their Bible

> A sense sublime
> Of something far more deeply interfused,
> Whose dwelling is the light of setting suns,
> And the round ocean and the living air ;
> A motion and a spirit, that impels
> All thinking things, all objects of all thought,
> And rolls through all things !
>
> WORDSWORTH.

And this from having been educated to understand the
Divine Omnipresence in any sense rather than the alone
safe and legitimate one, the presence of all things to God !
Be, it, however, that the number of such men is *comparatively* small ! And be it (as in fact it often *is*) but a
brief stage, a transitional state, in the process of intellectual
Growth ! Yet among a numerous and increasing class of
the higher and middle ranks, there is an inward withdrawing from the Life and Personal Being of God, a turning of
the thoughts exclusively to the so-called physical attributes,
to the Omnipresence in the counterfeit form of ubiquity, to
the Immensity, the Infinity, the Immutability ;—the attributes of space with a notion of Power as their *substratum*,
a FATE, in short, not a Moral Creator and Governor ! Let
intelligence be imagined, and wherein does the conception
of God differ essentially from that of Gravitation (conceived
as the cause of Gravity) in the understanding of those, who
represent the Deity not only as a necessary but as a
necessitated Being ; those, for whom justice is but a scheme

of general laws; and holiness, and the divine hatred of sin, yea and sin itself, are words without meaning or accommodations to a rude and barbarous race? Hence, I more than fear, the prevailing taste for books of Natural Theology, Physico-Theology, Demonstrations of God from Nature, Evidences of Christianity, and the like. *Evidences* of Christianity! I am weary of the word. Make a man feel the *want* of it; rouse him, if you can, to the self-knowledge of his *need* of it; and you may safely trust it to its own Evidence,—remembering only the express declaration of Christ himself: *No man cometh to me, unless the Father leadeth him.* Whatever more is desirable—I speak now with reference to Christians generally, and not to professed students of theology—may, in my judgment, be far more safely and profitably taught, without controversy or the supposition of infidel antagonists, in the form of Ecclesiastical history.

The last fruit of the mechanico-corpuscular philosophy, say rather of the mode and direction of feeling and thinking produced by it on the educated class of society; or that result, which as more immediately connected with my present theme I have reserved for the last—is the habit of attaching all our conceptions and feelings, and of applying all the words and phrases expressing reality, to the objects of the senses: more accurately speaking, to the images and sensations by which their presence is made known to us. Now I do not hesitate to assert, that it was one of the great purposes of Christianity, and included in the process of our Redemption, to rouse and emancipate the soul from this debasing slavery to the outward senses, to awaken the mind to the true *criteria* of reality, namely, Permanence, Power, Will manifested in Act, and Truth operating as Life. *My words*, said Christ, *are spirit:* and they (that is, the spiritual powers expressed by them) *are truth;* that is, *very* Being. For this end our Lord, who came from heaven to *take captivity captive*, chose the words and names, that designate the familiar yet most important objects of sense, the nearest and most concerning things and incidents of corporeal nature:—Water, Flesh, Blood, Birth, Bread! But he used them in senses, that could not without absurdity be supposed to respect the mere *phœnomena*, water, flesh, and the like, in senses that by no possibility could apply to the colour, figure, specific mode of touch or taste produced on ourselves, and by which we are made aware of the presence of the things, and *understand* them— *res, quæ sub apparitionibus istis statuendæ sunt.* And this awful recalling of the drowsed soul from the dreams and phantom world of sensuality to *actual* reality,—how has it been evaded! These words, that were Spirit! these Mysteries, which even the Apostles must wait for the Paraclete, in order to comprehend,—these spiritual things which can only be *spiritually* discerned,—were mere metaphors, figures of speech, oriental hyperboles! "All this means *only* Morality!" Ah! how far nearer to the truth would these men have been, had they said that Morality means all this!

The effect, however, has been most injurious to the best interests of our Universities, to our incomparably constituted Church, and even to our national character. The few who have read my two Lay Sermons are no strangers to my opinions on this head; and in my Treatise on the Church and Churches, I shall, if Providence vouchsafe, submit them to the Public, with their grounds and historic evidences in a more systematic form.

I have, I am aware, in this present work furnished occasion for a charge of having expressed myself with slight and irreverence of celebrated Names, especially of the late Dr. Paley. O, if I were fond and ambitious of literary honour, of public applause, how well content should I be to excite but one third of the admiration which, in my inmost being, I feel for the head and heart of Paley! And how gladly would I surrender all hope of contemporary praise, could I even approach to the incomparable grace, propriety, and persuasive facility of his writings! But on this very account I believe myself bound in conscience to throw the whole force of my intellect in the way of this triumphal car, on which the tutelary genius of modern Idolatry is borne, even at the risk of being crushed under the wheels! I have at this moment before my eyes the eighteenth of his Posthumous Discourses : the amount of which is briefly this,—that all the words and passages in the New Testament which express and contain the *peculiar* doctrines of

T

Christianity, the paramount objects of the Christian Revelation, all those which speak so strongly of the value, benefit, and efficacy, of the death of Christ, assuredly mean *something*; but *what* they mean, nobody, it seems can tell! But doubtless we shall discover it, and be convinced that there is a substantial sense belonging to these words—in a future state! Is there an enigma, or an absurdity, in the Koran or the Vedas which might not be defended on the same pretence? A similar impression, I confess, was left on my mind by Dr. Magee's statement or exposition (*ad normam Grotianam*) of the doctrine of Redemption; and deeply did it disappoint the high expectations, sadly did it chill the fervid sympathy, which his introductory chapter, his manly and masterly disquisition on the sacrificial rites of Paganism, had raised in my mind.

And yet I cannot read the pages of Paley, here referred to, aloud, without the liveliest sense, how plausible and popular they will sound to the great majority of readers. Thousands of sober, and in their way pious, Christians, will echo the words, together with Magee's kindred interpretation of the death of Christ, and adopt the doctrine for their *Make-faith;* and why? It is feeble. And whatever is feeble is always plausible: for it favours mental indolence. It is feeble: and feebleness, in the disguise of confessing and condescending strength, is always popular. It flatters the reader by removing the apprehended distance between him and the superior author; and it flatters him still more by enabling him to transfer to himself, and to appropriate, this superiority; and thus to make his very weakness the mark and evidence of his strength. Ay, quoth the *rational* Christian—or with a sighing, self-soothing sound between an Ay and an Ah!—*I* am content to think, with the great Dr. Paley, and the learned Archbishop of Dublin——

Man of Sense! Dr. Paley *was* a great man, and Dr. Magee *is* a learned and exemplary prelate; but YOU do not *think* at all!

With regard to the convictions avowed and enforced in my own Work, I will continue my address to the man of sense in the words of an old philosopher:—Tu vero crassis auribus et obstinato corde respuis quæ forsitan vere perhibeantur. Minus hercule calles, pravissimis opinionibus *ea putari mendacia, quæ vel auditu nova, vel visu rudia, vel certe supra captum cogitationis (extemporaneæ tuæ) ardua videantur:* quæ si paulo accuratius exploraris, non modo compertu evidentia, sed etiam factu facilia, senties.[1]

In compliance with the suggestion of a judicious friend, the celebrated conclusion of the fourth Book of Paley's Moral and Political Philosophy, referred to in p. 230 of this volume, is here transprinted for the convenience of the reader :—

" Had Jesus Christ delivered no other declaration than the following—' The hour is coming, in the which all that are in the grave shall hear his voice, and shall come forth : they that have done good, unto the resurrection of life, and they that have done evil unto the resurrection of damnation : '—he had pronounced a message of inestimable importance, and well worthy of that splendid apparatus of prophecy and miracles with which his mission was introduced and attested : a message in which the wisest of mankind would rejoice to find an answer to their doubts, and rest to their inquiries.—It is idle to say, that a future state had been discovered already :—it had been discovered as the Copernican system was ;—it was one guess among many. He alone discovers, who proves ; and no man can prove this point, but the teacher who testifies by miracles that his doctrine comes from God."

Pædianus says of Virgil,—*Usque adeo expers invidiæ, ut siquid erudite dictum inspiceret alterius, non minus gauderet ac si suum esset.* My own heart assures me, that this is less than the truth : that Virgil would have read a beautiful passage in the work of another with a higher and purer delight than in a work of his own, because free from the apprehension of his judgment being warped by self-love, and without that repressive modesty akin to shame, which in a delicate mind holds in check a man's own secret thoughts

[1] *Apul. Metam.* 1.—H. N. C.

and feelings, when they respect himself. The cordial admiration with which I peruse the preceding passage, as *a master-piece of composition,* would, could I convey it, serve as a measure of the vital importance I attach to the convictions which impelled me to animadvert on the same passage as *doctrine.*

APPENDIX A.

A SYNOPTICAL SUMMARY OF THE SCHEME OF THE ARGUMENT TO PROVE THE DIVERSITY IN KIND [1] OF THE REASON AND THE UNDERSTANDING. SEE P. 143.

The Position to be proved is the *difference in kind* of the Understanding from the Reason.

The Axiom, on which the Proof rests, is : Subjects, which require essentially different General Definitions, differ *in kind* and not merely *in degree*. For difference *in degree* forms the ground of *specific* definitions, but not of *generic* or general.

Now Reason is considered either in relation to the Will and Moral Being, when it is termed the [2] Practical Reason = A: or relatively, to the intellective and Sciential Faculties, when it is termed Theoretic or Speculative Reason = *a*. In order therefore to be compared with the Reason ; the Understanding must in like manner be distinguished into the Understanding as a Principle of *Action*, in which relation I call it the Adaptive Power, or the faculty of selecting and adapting Means and Medial of proximate ends = B : and the Understanding, as a mode and faculty of thought, when it is called Reflection = *b*.

---

[1] This summary did not appear in the first edition.—ED.

[2] N. B. The Practical Reason alone *is* Reason in the full and substantive sense. It is reason in its own sphere of *perfect freedom ;* as the source of *IDEAS*, which Ideas, in their conversion to the responsible Will, become Ultimate Ends. On the other hand, Theoretic Reason, as the ground of the Universal and Absolute in all logical *conclusion* is rather the *Light* of Reason in the *Understanding*, and known to be such by its contrast with the contingency and particularity which characterize all the proper and indigenous growths of the Understanding.

Accordingly, I give the General Definitions of these four :
that is, I describe each severally by its *essential characters :*
and I find, that the definition of A differs *toto genere* from
that of B, and the definition of *a* from that of *b.*

Now subjects that require essentially different definitions
do themselves differ in kind.   But Understanding and
Reason require essentially different definitions.   Therefore
Understanding and Reason differ in kind.

APPENDIX B.

ON INSTINCT:

By Professor J. H. Green.

[This is the discourse an early report of which was the
foundation of Coleridge's remarks upon instinct, &c., which
appear at pp. 160 - 164.   It was first added as an
Appendix to the " Aids to Reflection," in the edition of
1843; being extracted from an Appendix to Professor
Green's " Vital Dynamics," [1] 1840, where it appears at pp.
88-96.   It was then given without the Professor's introductory words, which we now add.—Ed.]

The following remarks on the import of instinct are those
to which Coleridge refers in the " Aids to Reflection " (p.
177, last edition [2]) as in accordance with his view of the
understanding, differing in degree from instinct, and in
kind from reason; and whatever merit they possess must
have been derived from his instructive conversation.   They
are here inserted in the hope that they may interest the
reader in connexion both with the passages of the preceding

[1] ' Vital Dynamics : The Hunterian Oration before the Royal College
of Surgeons in London, 14th February, 1840; by Joseph Henry Green,
F.R.S., Late Professor of Anatomy to the College : Professor of
Anatomy to the Royal Academy : One of the Surgeons to St. Thomas's
Hospital.'   8vo.   William Pickering, 1840.—Ed.

[2] This must have been the 4th edition, 1839, the latest corrected by
the author, and that which supplies our text in the main.   Coleridge's
reference is at pp. 166-170 of the present edition.—Ed.

discourse, and with the writings of Coleridge on this important subject.

What is Instinct ? As I am not quite of Bonnet's opinion "that philosophers will in vain torment themselves to define instinct, until they have spent some time in the head of the animal without actually being that animal," I shall endeavour to explain the use of the term. I shall not think it necessary to controvert the opinions which have been offered on this subject, whether the ancient doctrine of Descartes, who supposed that animals were mere machines; or the modern one of Lamarck, who attributes instincts to habits impressed upon the organs of animals, by the constant efflux of the nervous fluid to these organs, to which it has been determined in their efforts to perform certain actions, to which their necessities have given birth. And it will be here premature to offer any refutation of the opinions of those who contend for the identity of this faculty with reason, and maintain that all the actions of animals are the result of invention and experience ; —an opinion maintained with considerable plausibility by Dr. Darwin.

Perhaps the most ready and certain mode of coming to a conclusion in this intricate enquiry will be by the apparently circuitous route of determining first, what we do not mean by the word. Now we certainly do not mean, in the use of the term, any act of the vital power in the production or maintenance of an organ : nobody thinks of saying that the teeth grow by instinct, or that when the muscles are increased in vigour and size in consequence of exercise, it is from such a cause or principle. Neither do we attribute instinct to the direct functions of the organs in providing for the continuance and sustentation of the whole co-organized body. No one talks· of the liver secreting bile, or of the heart acting for the propulsion of the blood, by instinct. Some, indeed, have maintained that breathing, even voiding the excrement and urine, are instinctive operations; but surely these, as well as the former, are automatic, or at least are the necessary result of the organization of the parts in and by which the actions are produced. These instances seem to be, if I may so say, below instinct. But again, we do not attribute

instinct to any actions preceded by a will conscious of its
whole purpose, calculating its effects, and predetermining
its consequences, nor to any exercise of the intellectual
powers, of which the whole scope, aim, and end are intellectual.   In other terms, no man, who values his words,
will talk of the instinct of a Howard, or of the instinctive
operations of a Newton or Leibnitz, in those sublime efforts,
which ennoble and cast a lustre, not less on the individuals
than on the whole human race.

To what kind or mode of action shall we then look for
the legitimate application of the term ?   In answer to this
query, we may, I think, without fear of the consequences,
put the following cases as exemplifying and justifying the
use of the term Instinct in an appropriate sense.   First :
when there appears an action, not included either in the
mere functions of life, acting within the sphere of its own
organismus ; nor yet an action attributable to the intelligent
will or reason ; yet, at the same time, not referable to any
particular organ,—we then declare the presence of an
Instinct.   We might illustrate this in the instance of a
bull-calf butting before he has horns, in which the action
can have no reference to its internal economy, to the
presence of a particular organ, or to an intelligent will.
Secondly, likewise (if it be not indeed included in the
first), we attribute Instinct where the organ is present ; if
only the act is equally anterior to all possible experience on
the part of the individual agent, as for instance, when the
beaver employs its tail for the construction of its dwelling ;
the tailor-bird its bill for the formation of its pensile
habitation ; the spider its spinning organ for fabricating
its artfully woven nets, or the viper its poison fang for its
defence.   And lastly, generally, where there is an act of the
whole body as one animal, not referable to a will conscious of
its purpose, nor to its mechanism, nor to a habit derived from
experience, nor previous frequent use.   Here with most
satisfaction, and without doubt of the propriety of the
word, we declare an Instinct ; as examples of which, we
may adduce the migratory habits of birds ; the social
instincts of the bees, the construction of their habitations,
composed of cells formed with geometrical precision,
adapted in capacity to different orders of the society, and

forming storehouses for containing a supply of provisions;
—not to mention similar instances in wasps, ants, termites;
and the endless contrivances for protecting the future
progeny.

But if it be admitted that we have rightly stated the
application of the term, what, we may ask, is contained in
the examples adduced, or what inferences are we to make
as to the nature of Instinct itself, as a source and principle
of action? We shall, perhaps, best aid ourselves in the
enquiry by an example, and let us take a very familiar one
of a caterpillar taking its food. The caterpillar seeks at
once the plant which furnishes the appropriate aliment, and
this even as soon as it creeps from the ovum; and the food
being taken into the stomach, the nutritious part is
separated from the innutritious, and is disposed of for the
support of the animal. The question then is, what is
contained in this instance of instinct? In the first place
what does the vital power in the stomach do, if we
generalize the account of the process, or express it in its
most general terms? Manifestly it selects and applies
appropriate means to an immediate end, prescribed by the
constitution;—first, of the particular organ, and then of
the whole body or organismus. This we have admitted is
not instinct. But what does the caterpillar do? Does it
not also select and apply appropriate means to an immediate
end, prescribed by its particular organization and constitution? But there is something more; it does this according to circumstances;—and this we call Instinct. But
may there not be still something more involved? What
shall we say of Hüber's humble-bees? A dozen of these
were put under a bell glass along with a comb of about ten
silken cocoons, so unequal in height as not to be capable of
standing steadily. To remedy this, two or three of the
humble-bees got upon the comb, stretched themselves over
its edge, and with their heads downwards, fixed their fore-
feet on the table on which the comb stood, and so with
their hindfeet kept the comb from falling. When these
were weary others took their places. In this constrained
and painful posture, fresh bees relieving their comrades at
intervals, and each working in its turn, did these affectionate little insects support the comb for nearly three days;

at the end of which time they had prepared sufficient wax
to build pillars with it. And what is still further curious,
the first pillars having got displaced, the bees had again
recourse to the same manœuvre. What then is involved in
this case ? Evidently the same selection and appropriation
of means to an immediate end as before; but observe !
according to varying circumstances.

And here we are puzzled ;—for this becomes Understanding. At least no naturalist, however predetermined to
contrast and oppose Instinct to Understanding, but ends
at last in facts in which he himself can make out no
difference. But are we hence to conclude that the instinct
is the same, and identical with the human understanding ?
Certainly not ;—though the difference is not in the essential
of the definition, but in an addition to, or modification of,
that which is essentially the same in both. In such cases,
namely, as that which we have last adduced, in which
instinct assumes the semblance of understanding, the act
indicative of instinct is not clearly prescribed by the
constitution or laws of the animal's peculiar organization,
but arises out of the constitution and previous circumstances of the animal, and those habits, wants, and that
predetermined sphere of action and operation which belong
to the race, and beyond the limits of which it does not
pass. If this be the case, I may venture to assert that I
have determined an appropriate sense for instinct :—
—namely, that it is a Power of selecting and applying
appropriate means to an immediate end, according to
circumstances, and the changes of circumstances, these
being variable and varying; but yet so as to be referable
to the general habits, arising out of the constitution and
previous circumstances of the animal considered not as an
individual, but as a race.

We may here, perhaps, most fitly explain the error of
those who contend for the identity of Reason and Instinct,
and believe that the actions of animals are the result of invention and experience. They have, no doubt, been deceived,
in their investigation of Instinct, by an efficient cause simu-
lating a final cause ; and the defect in their reasoning has
arisen in consequence of observing in the instinctive operations of animals the adaptation of means to a relative

end, from the assumption of a deliberate purpose. To this freedom or choice in action and purpose, instinct, in any appropriate sense of the word, cannot apply, and to justify and explain its introduction, we must have recourse to other and higher faculties than any manifested in the operations of instinct. It is evident, namely, in turning our attention to the distinguishing character of human actions, that there is, as in the inferior animals, a selection and appropriation of means to ends—but it is (not only according to circumstances, not only according to varying circumstances, but it is) according to varying Purposes. But this is an attribute of the intelligent will, and no longer even mere understanding.

And here let me observe that the difficulty and delicacy of this investigation are greatly increased by our not considering the understanding (even our own) in itself, and as it would be were it not accompanied with, and modified by, the co-operation of the will, the moral feeling, and that faculty, perhaps best distinguished by the name of Reason, of determining that which is universal and necessary, of fixing laws and principles whether speculative or practical, and of contemplating a final purpose or end. This intelligent will,—having a self-conscious purpose, under the guidance and light of the reason, by which its acts are made to bear as a whole upon some end in and for itself, and to which the understanding is subservient as an organ or the faculty of selecting and appropriating the means— seems best to account for that progressiveness of the human race, which so evidently marks an insurmountable distinction and impassable barrier between man and the inferior animals ; but which would be inexplicable were there no other difference than in the degree of their intellectual faculties.

Man doubtless has his instincts, even in common with the inferior animals, and many of these are the germs of some of the best feelings of his nature. What, amongst many, might I present as a better illustration, or more beautiful instance, than the *storgè* or maternal instinct ? But man's instincts are elevated and ennobled by the moral ends and purposes of his being. He is not destined to be the slave of blind impulses, a vessel purposeless,

unmeant.   He is constituted by his moral and intelligent
will, to be the first freed being, the master-work and the
end of nature; but this freedom and high office can only
co-exist with fealty and devotion to the service of truth
and virtue.   And though we may even be permitted to
use the term Instinct, in order to designate those high
impulses, which in the minority of man's rational being,
shape his acts unconsciously to ultimate ends, and which in
constituting the very character and impress of the humanity
reveal the guidance of Providence; yet the convenience of
the phrase, and the want of any other distinctive appellation for an influence *de supra*, working unconsciously in and
on the whole human race, should not induce us to forget
that the term instinct is only strictly applicable to the
Adaptive Power, as the faculty, even in its highest proper
form, of selecting and adapting appropriate means to proximate ends according to varying circumstances,—a faculty
which however, only differs from human understanding in
consequence of the latter being enlightened·by reason,—
and that the principles which actuate man as ultimate ends,
and are designed for his conscious possession and guidance,
are best and most properly named Ideas.